The politics of airport expansion in the United Kingdom

Manchester University Press

Issues in Environmental Politics

series editors Mikael Skou Andersen and Duncan Liefferink

At the start of the twenty-first century, the environment has come to stay as a central concern of global politics. This series takes key problems for environmental policy and examines the politics behind their cause and possible resolution. Accessible and eloquent, the books make available for a non-specialist readership some of the best research and most provocative thinking on humanity's relationship with the planet.

The politics of airport expansion in the United Kingdom

Hegemony, policy and the rhetoric of 'sustainable aviation'

Steven Griggs and David Howarth

Manchester University Press

Manchester and New York

distributed in the United States exclusively by Palgrave Macmillan

Published by Manchester University Press
Oxford Road, Manchester M13 9NR, UK
and Room 400, 175 Fifth Avenue, New York, NY 10010, USA
www.manchesteruniversitypress.co.uk

Distributed in the United States exclusively by
Palgrave Macmillan, 175 Fifth Avenue, New York,
NY 10010, USA

Distributed in Canada exclusively by
UBC Press, University of British Columbia, 2029 West Mall,
Vancouver, BC, Canada V6T 1Z2

British Library Cataloguing-in-Publication Data
A catalogue record for this book is available from the British Library

Library of Congress Cataloging-in-Publication Data applied for

ISBN 978 0 7190 7613 8 *hardback*

First published 2013

Typeset in Sabon by R. J. Footring Ltd, Derby
Printed in Great Britain by CPI Antony Rowe Ltd, Chippenham, Wiltshire

Contents

Boxes

Preface and acknowledgements

This book has taken a long time to complete. In part, this reflects the fact that our object of investigation – the ongoing debates in the UK to problematise, frame and reframe a policy of 'sustainable aviation' – has constantly mutated. In fact, as we show in our final chapter, it is still a hotly contested issue. It is also because our interest in aviation and airports policy stretches back to our initial efforts to critically explain the emergence and impact of local opposition and protest to the building of a second runway at Manchester airport in the mid-1990s. Following a phrase employed in a *Times* leader, we explored the dynamics of the so-called 'Vegans and Volvos' alliance, which brought together local residents, direct action protesters and environmental social movements in a novel coalition. This coalition echoed the strategies and tactics of successful campaigns against road-building projects in the 1980s and 1990s, and thus extended the focus of environmental movements in the transport field. For our part, we endeavoured to analyse the way in which the practices of campaigners and local residents began to reshape the evolution of aviation policy in the UK more generally, even though their particular campaign proved unsuccessful. As protest against airport expansions developed, we continued our analysis of the different logics of collective action exhibited by various forms of citizen protest in the campaigns against the proposed expansion of Heathrow and of Stansted during the 1990s, and then into the first decade of the new century.

But following the announcement by the New Labour government that it intended to formulate a new long-term strategy for aviation, we also began to focus on the lengthy and widespread public consultations leading up to the publication of the air transport white paper in 2003, and the logics of aviation policy more generally. Our various articles and essays on these topics not only charted and analysed these events and processes, but they also provided a vital context for helping us to understand and explain the evolution of aviation and airports policy in the UK over the last fifteen or twenty years.

Of course, the political import of aviation and airports in the UK (and elsewhere) stretches further back than this. Ever since the 1950s, various local communities, environmental activists and groups have viewed the construction and expansion of airports with suspicion and even hostility. The different proposals to build a third London airport in the 1960s and 1970s, and the intense political struggles they evinced, which culminated in the opening of the new terminal at Stansted airport in 1991, have been the subject of great public and academic interest. The battles that arose from subsequent proposals to expand Heathrow, Stansted and other regional airports, which we examine in depth in this book, have stimulated similar public interest and protest. Struggles over the building and expansion of airports have surfaced in all major industrial societies in recent times. Battles over Roissy-Charles de Gaulle, Nantes, Frankfurt, Narita and Schiphol, to name but a few, have shaped our understanding of the UK context, though our study has restricted its comparative focus to UK airports only.

Our concern with airports policy and the aviation industry in the UK since the 1950s is reflected in multiple problematisations, which we set out in chapter 2 of this book. Yet our overarching framing of the problem concerns the dynamic interplay between policy-making practices, on the one hand, and the political and policy coalitions which strive to shape the policy agenda and various outcomes, on the other. This is reflected in one of our key problematisations, which focuses on the seemingly intractable tension between aviation as a driver of economic growth, and the need to protect the social and natural environment from the deleterious impact of noise and aviation emissions. Indeed, although this problematisation has become dominant only during the last decade, like Marx's (1973: 106–7) conceptualisation of the role of 'one specific kind of production which predominates over the rest' in any particular society, it provides 'a general illumination which bathes all the other colours and modifies their particularity'.

Equally, our concern with these various issues draws upon our interest in developing a distinctive poststructuralist approach to policy-making, especially with respect to questions about problem formulation, the framing and reframing of key societal issues, and the logic of policy change and inertia. Poststructuralist policy analysis, which we set out in the first chapter, provides the theoretical approach with which we seek to problematise and analyse the events and processes we describe in the book. Recent years have brought many new voices into the study of government, politics and policy analysis. More traditional, descriptive approaches, which focused on in-depth case studies of particular institutions or policy domains, have been challenged by more scientific paradigms, which have stressed the role of law-like explanations, or the importance of causal mechanisms, both of which ought to yield testable predictions. Interpretivists have rejected these more scientific approaches in the name of critical theory, more ethnographically orientated research strategies, or various forms of discourse analysis. The universalism of the scientific model has thus been questioned by more particularistic and singular analyses of governance and policy-making practices.

Our approach seeks to steer a course between the search for law-like explanations and the production of purely particularistic interpretations which self-consciously reject all general theoretical concepts and logics. 'Theory-informed empirical research' is one way of describing our approach, though this label can cover many different methods and logics of explanation. We accept this description, as long as it does not mean the subsumption of particular processes and events under general laws or overweening causal mechanisms, which cannot be shaped or 'distorted' in their application, and as long as it recognises the key role of constructing problematisations of particular phenomena and processes. Logics, practices and regimes are thus employed in this study, and not laws, causal mechanisms or contextualised interpretations.

Of course, the proof of the pudding is in the eating. Only our specific interpretations and explanations of the problems we explore, using the approach we elaborate, can vindicate our methods, strategies and concepts. In developing this perspective, our ideas and approach have been shaped by their public testing in various forums and seminars. These include a Research Seminar Series sponsored by the Economic and Social Research Council (ESRC), 'Discourse Theory Network in Methodological Innovation', which was convened by David Howarth, Aletta Norval and Ewen Speed from April 2008 until March 2010. The seminar series gave us the chance to present the basic elements of our theoretical approach, as well as various substantive arguments pertaining to aviation, many of which eventually found their way into the book.

We have also been fortunate enough to present different parts of this book in numerous conferences, seminars, workshops and departmental seminars over the last ten or so years, as well as at the Essex Summer School in Discourse Analysis, where we set out our approach and its application to the case of UK aviation. In particular, we presented four of the main empirical chapters of the book at the annual Interpretivist Policy Analysis (IPA) conferences at Kassel (2009), Grenoble (2010), Cardiff (2011) and Tilburg (2012). Our approach to rhetoric, policy analysis and sustainable aviation was delivered at the annual Political Studies Association conference in Manchester in April 2009. We also had the opportunity to present our analysis of political economy and discourse theory to a conference at Cardiff University in May 2009. The revised version of this paper became the third chapter of the book, which we read to Departmental Seminars at De Montfort and Nottingham Universities in the autumn of 2009. The material comprising chapter 7 was presented to the Social Science Seminar Series at the School of Environmental Sciences at the University of East Anglia in May 2012. Many of the reflections that inform this book can be traced back to earlier discussions, beginning in January 2008, when we participated in a workshop organised by the Green Alliance, which was attended by Lord Anthony Giddens, Dr Paul Hilder and Steven Hale. They took shape and benefited from our many interactions with Eva Sørensen and Jacob Torfing, and their colleagues, during our visits over the years to the Centre for Democratic Network Governance at the University of Roskilde. During one such visit, we set out our initial thoughts on the mediatisation of airport struggles to participants at an international doctoral workshop in media, communication and journalism kindly organised in 2009 by Signe Jørgensen. We advanced these ideas, as well as our approach to 'policy as practice' more generally, with doctoral students at King Charles University in Prague in February 2011, where we were welcomed by Martin Nekola and Anna Durnova.

We thank all those who have commented upon and criticised aspects of the papers, as well as offering helpful advice and information. In particular, we would like to thank those who hosted, and participated in, the panels, workshops and seminars which we attended, as well as all those who have engaged with our work over the course of this project. They include Heidrun Åm, Steffen Böhm,

Terrell Carver, Tony Colman, Jonathan Davies, Michael Farrelly, Alan Finalyson, Frank Fischer, Bent Flyvbjerg, Richard Freeman, Herbert Gottweis, Maarten Hajer, Stephen Jeffares, Bob Jessop, Todd Landman, Vivien Lowndes, Martin Marcussen, Navdeep Mathur, Hugh Miller, Graham Parkhurst, Matthew Paterson, Jernej Pikalo, Donatella della Porta, Lawrence Pratchett, Jules Pretty, Dieter Rucht, Sanford Schram, Helen Sullivan, Ngai-Ling Sum, John Turnpenny, Henk Wagenaar, Graham Walker, Hugh Ward, Albert Weale, Mark Wenman, Hugh Willmott and Dvora Yanow. A special mention must go to Brian Jacobs and Geoff Dudley, with whom we took the first steps in this project many years ago.

We would also like to thank our co-convenor, Lucy Budd, and all the participants in an ESRC-sponsored seminar series entitled 'The Prospects for Sustainable Aviation: Negotiating and Mediating Between Competing Perspectives' (reference number ES/I003029/1) for their presentations and interventions. The seminar series, which began in January 2010 and concluded in September 2012, provided us with an invaluable set of perspectives and reflections from fellow academics working on the different dimensions of aviation policy and politics, and from the key stakeholders who have been participating in the ongoing debate about the UK aviation industry and its perceived infrastructure requirements. Although we are unable to list all the valuable contributions made throughout this series, we would like to express our gratitude to Pete Adey, Kevin Anderson, Jonathan Beaverstock, John Bowen, Christian Bröer, Tom Budd, James Connelly, Lisa Davison, Andrew Goetz, Charlotte Halpern, Mark Harvey, Stephen Ison, Ute Knippenberger, Lauren Roffey, Chris Rootes, Callum Thomas and John Urry. In particular, we would like to thank those outside the world of academia who have freely given their time to support our research and the seminar series: Carole Barbone (Stop Stansted Expansion), Rachel Burbridge (Eurocontrol), Dan Edwards (Civil Aviation Authority), Nic Ferriday (Aviation Environment Federation), Roger Gardner (SIGMA), Jeff Gazzard (Manchester Airport Environment Network, AirportWatch and GreenSkies), Robbie Gillett (Plane Stupid), Anita Goldsmith (Greenpeace), Tony Greaves (Campaign Against Second Runway – Manchester Airport Joint Action Group), Stephen Hammond (National Air Traffic Services), Stephen Hardwick (British Airports Authority), Cait Hewitt (Aviation Environment Federation), Barry Humphreys (British Air Transport Association), Joe Irvin

(Freedom to Fly), Andy Jefferson (Sustainable Aviation), Tim Johnson (Aviation Environment Federation), Jean Leston (World Wide Fund For Nature – UK), Steve Mayner (2M), Jamie McCrae (Campaign Against Second Runway – Manchester Airport Joint Action Group), Jeremy Pine (Uttlesford District Council), Oscar Reyes (Transnational Institute), Neil Robinson (East Midlands airport), Brian Ross (Stop Stansted Expansion), John Stewart (HACAN ClearSkies and Airport-Watch), Graham Stringer MP (Blackley and Broughton), Andrew Taylor (Uttlesford District Council) and John Twigg (Manchester airport). Over the course of the study many have given up their time to respond to our interview questions – some more than once. We expect that they will recognise their comments and reflections in the book, but in the interests of anonymity we have made sure that no quotations are directly attributable to any one of them.

We are also happy to acknowledge a number of intellectual and personal debts of gratitude in composing the substance of the book. We would like to thank the production team at Manchester University Press for their professional support and steely patience in getting this book into print. In particular, we are extremely thankful to Ralph Footring for his great care in copy-editing our manuscript and flexibility in the production of the book. We are also grateful to the anonymous readers for their helpful comments on the book proposal and the final manuscript. The book draws upon ideas developed by members of the Essex School of Discourse Analysis, as well as previous theoretical research about the relationship between discourse, power and critical policy analysis. Ernesto Laclau and Chantal Mouffe have inspired us to continue and develop their innovative approach to political analysis, which they have elaborated since the mid-1970s. We would also like to thank Jason Glynos for his thoughts on our project, and for his role in developing the 'logics approach', which we seek to employ and develop in this book. Jane Bennett and William Connolly have helped us to explore the connection between different forces engaged in struggle and to link the social and natural worlds in a more nuanced way. A final word of thanks must be given to those participants of the Doctoral Seminar in Ideology and Discourse Analysis in the Department of Government at the University of Essex, who read, discussed and commented upon various parts of the manuscript.

We would also like to thank Aletta Norval and Geoff Dudley for reading the final manuscript and making important and useful suggestions. In short, our manuscript has benefited immensely from these public and private commentaries, though it goes without saying that the arguments we put forward have undergone substantial empirical and theoretical modification, and that the final product reflects our considered views on the problems we have constructed and explored.

Finally, our most important and deepest debt is to the members of our respective families – Madeline, Martha, and Ruth; Aletta and James – who have supported this project through thick and thin, and who have had to put up with the usual heartache and frustration, the regular and interminable phone calls between the authors, as well as the odd moments of joy and happiness, which have accompanied the writing of this book.

Abbreviations

AEF	Aviation Environment Federation
AOA	Airport Operators Association
ASLEF	Associated Society of Locomotive Engineers and Firemen
ATWP	air transport white paper (2003)
BA	British Airways
BAA	British Airports Authority
BATA	British Air Transport Association
BBC	British Broadcasting Corporation
BCal	British Caledonian Airways
BCC	British Chambers of Commerce
BEA	British European Airlines
BOAC	British Overseas Airways Corporation
CAA	Civil Aviation Authority
CBI	Confederation of British Industry
CC	Competition Commission
CCC	Committee on Climate Change
CO_2	carbon dioxide
CPRE	Campaign to Protect Rural England (from 2003; previously Council for the Protection of Rural England)
DEFRA	Department for Environment, Food and Rural Affairs
DETR	Department of the Environment, Transport and the Regions
DfT	Department for Transport
DTI	Department of Trade and Industry
DTLR	Department for Transport, Local Government and the Regions
EAC	(House of Commons) Environmental Audit Committee

ETS	emissions trading scheme
EU	European Union
FoE	Friends of the Earth
GACC	Gatwick Area Conservation Campaign
GATCOM	Gatwick Airport Consultative Committee
GDP	gross domestic product
GMB	General, Municipal, Boilermakers and Allied Trade Union
HACAN	Heathrow Association for the Control of Aircraft Noise (to 1999; thereafter HACAN ClearSkies)
IATA	International Air Transport Association
IPCC	Intergovernmental Panel on Climate Change
KLM	Koninklijke Luchtvaart Maatschappij (Royal Dutch Airlines)
MP	Member of Parliament
NATS	National Air Traffic Services
NEF	New Economics Foundation
NO_2	nitrogen dioxide
NoTRAG	No Third Runway Action Group Heathrow Airport
OEF	Oxford Economic Forecasting
PASC	Public Administration Select Committee
PCS	Public and Commercial Services Union
PSDH	Project for the Sustainable Development of Heathrow
RAeS	Royal Aeronautical Society
RAF	Royal Air Force
RCEP	Royal Commission on Environmental Pollution
RMT	National Union of Rail, Maritime and Transport Workers
RUCATSE	Runway Capacity to Serve the South-East (of England)
SASIG	Strategic Aviation Special Interest Group (of the Local Government Association)
SDC	Sustainable Development Commission
SEU	Social Exclusion Unit
SSE	Stop Stansted Expansion
T2000	Transport 2000
TSSA	Transport Salaried Staffs' Association
UK	United Kingdom
US	United States

If you were asked to take a Martian to visit a single place that captures all the themes running through the modern world – from our faith in technology to our destruction of nature, from our interconnectedness to our romanticising of travel – then you would almost certainly have to head to an airport. Airports, in all their turmoil, interest and beauty, are the imaginative centres of our civilisation.

Alain de Botton, *A Week at the Airport: A Heathrow Diary* (Profile Books, 2009)

Introduction

The increase of air traffic presents great problems, which must be solved if Britain is to maintain the *outstanding place in civil aviation* which she has already won in the face of *keen international competition*. In the years to come the air will be hardly less essential to our well-being than the sea. To no small extent, the future of this country in world trade and as a great power will depend on our holding and indeed advancing our place in this form of transport. (*London's Airports White Paper*, Cmd 8902; Ministry of Civil Aviation, 1953: 3; our emphasis)

Aviation is a great British success story, and one of the major strengths of the UK economy, both now and for the future. (DfT, 2002b: 12)

Aviation is one of the fastest-growing contributors to world-wide emissions. Unchecked it will grow to a substantial proportion of global emissions, making a climate-safe future difficult or impossible – and undermining reductions achieved by other sectors. (AirportWatch, 2009a: 1)

Ever since the Wright brothers' first historic flight in 1903, modern aviation has been a source of immense excitement, social promise and political controversy. From its humble beginnings in the US at the start of the twentieth century, powered flight has mutated into one of the key symbols of power and progress in the global world order. Vital to what sociologists like Manuel Castells (1996), Anthony Giddens (1991), David Harvey (1989) and John Urry (2000) have labelled the compression of space and time in late modernity, and essential to the acceleration of world trade, global travel and international tourism, the aviation industry has often been presented as synonymous with mobility, economic growth and the generation of jobs.[1] Although the geographical and social distribution of air travel still remains highly uneven, it has rapidly become an accepted and embedded social practice for many citizens across the world.[2] Business travellers, tourists, commuters, students and migrants criss-cross the sky each day in the pursuit of profit, holidays, novel experiences, educational achievement and new places to live and work. Global sporting events (like the FIFA World Cup and the Olympic Games), music and cultural festivals, international conferences and religious pilgrimages bring together millions of people from around the world, and air travel is often the preferred (and sometimes the only) mode of transportation. Not unlike the horrific attacks on the Twin Towers in 2001, the eruption of the Icelandic volcano Eyjafjallajökull in April and May 2010 vividly demonstrated our growing dependency on aviation, as the ensuing ash clouds caused mass disruption to travel and global trade patterns (Budd *et al.*, 2011).

These trends and events are reflected in the widespread coverage of air travel, airlines and airports in newspapers and television news programmes, as well as numerous representations in popular culture. Novels, television drama series (like *Mile High* and *Pan Am*) and sundry Hollywood movies glamorise and satirise the world of international airlines and airports. Fly-on-the-wall documentaries such as *Airline*, *Airport*, *Luton Airport*, *Nothing to Declare* and *Stansted*, and even mockumentaries like *Come Fly With Me*, have captured the popular imagination with their everyday portrayals of passengers and staff working at the UK's largest airports. In no small measure, their success is due to the fact that experiences of air travel have become relatively commonplace for large numbers of people in advanced industrial societies.

Yet the growth of air travel and the aviation industry has also brought widespread disruption to local residents and citizens, in the form of noise and air pollution, and the destruction of homes, historical buildings, villages and communities, as well as negative impacts on the natural environment. Airports are expensive forms of infrastructure, which require housing, roads and often rail access; they also bring with them particular forms of commercial activity, such as retailing and service industries. They use large tracts of land, often curtailing neighbourhood construction and development, and (in some eyes) regional economic growth. Airports also serve as nodes in wider transportation networks and systems. Many different agencies and governmental authorities at the local, national and international levels have their responsibilities directly affected by decisions to expand an airport or to restrict its operation, or to build a new one. Traditionally, development projects have been carried out by a single agency with a narrow mandate; other agencies have then assisted in the realisation of specific goals. But airport issues are never limited to a single policy or organisational sector, and thus require the interaction and coordination of disparate agencies and parties in various policy sub-systems. The resultant complexity exacerbates the potential for political conflict and planning paralysis (Feldman and Milch, 1982: 113).

The targets of citizens' protests against airport development have usually been levels of compensation for falling property prices (often taking the form of traditional bargaining between airport authorities and residents), noise and air pollution, as well as environmental damage, and proposed developments have sometimes led to violent antagonisms between popular movements and states (see for example Apter, 1987; Apter and Sawa, 1984; Feldman and Milch, 1982; Nelkin and Pollak, 1977). Troubled politicians, policy-makers and citizens have agonised about the location and growth of airports, as well as other prerequisites of modern aviation, such as road and rail infrastructure. Important policy questions have also been asked about the availability and price of aviation fuel, the development of new aviation technology and the effectiveness of various anti-nuisance mechanisms, such as runway alternation and noise corridors. More recently, since the early 2000s, air travel has been closely linked to the problems of climate change and peak oil, whose combined effects threaten not only the future of the aviation industry, but the continued existence of our planet in its current form.[3]

The enormous expansion of aviation in the UK since the Second World War has provoked a series of disparate claims regarding the desirability, feasibility, location, size, expansion, impact, regulation and character of airports, as well as the other practices and infrastructures associated with the industry. At certain times, particular demands focused on specific airports were combined with demands to halt the proposed building or expansion of airports in different places, and sometimes demands were linked with other issues, such as the economy or the environment. Nonetheless, the practice of incremental planning and policy-making, which was undergirded by a strategy of 'predict and provide', has resulted in an accelerating logic of aviation expansion, most of which has been concentrated in the major London airports in the south-east of England. Until 2003 there were persistent demands for a national plan for the growth and location of airports and other components of the aviation industry that would set out a clear and coherent set of objectives, alongside the appropriate means to achieve such ends.

Of course, there were significant differences between those who favoured greater expansion and those who wanted the tighter management of demand; there were also differences about the precise location and character of expansion. But there was a belief that a rational airports strategy at the national level could be brokered among diverse stakeholders and interests. Indeed, the New Labour government led by Tony Blair promised to realise this goal by initiating and overseeing a major consultation process in the first years of the new millennium. This was followed by the publication of a comprehensive white paper in 2003. That white paper promised a 'balanced approach' which would inform a policy of 'sustainable aviation', though it involved giving the go-ahead for a massive programme of airport expansion across the UK (DfT, 2003a).

Yet no sooner had the plans for national expansion been hatched and made public than the government and the aviation industry were confronted by an even more pressing series of questions and demands. Local residents, environmental campaigners and scientific experts began to raise questions about the connections between the growth of individual airports and the expansion of the aviation industry as a whole. Crucially, they also posed tricky questions about the linkage between the expansion of the aviation industry, both within the UK and at the global level, and the problem of climate change. In fact, the entire meaning of the aviation industry, as well as its effects on residents, communities, the environment and the biosphere, began to be queried in different quarters. At the start of the second decade of this century, the aviation industry, government and affected stakeholders found themselves trapped in a stalemate about the prospects for sustainable aviation. The 'jet set' practices of air travel and the promises of increasing mobility have been progressively resignified as the 'looming problem in the sky' (Tyndall Centre, 2005a: 47).

The naming and framing of policy problems

This book stands at the intersection of three related concerns. The first and most substantive focus of the book, which we name and frame in this section, arises from the paradoxes and contradictions surrounding various attempts by UK governments to formulate and implement a workable aviation policy, especially with respect to the expansion of airport capacity in the south-east of England. Of particular importance in this regard is the tension between, on the one hand, the role of airports and aviation as drivers of economic growth and prosperity and, on the other hand, their considerable and growing negative impacts on the natural and social environment. At the same time, while many citizens express concerns about the environmental impact of air travel, they still continue to fly in ever-increasing numbers.

More precisely, then, our book explores the way in which the airports issue in the UK has been transformed from a difficult, though ultimately tractable, policy problem into a 'wicked' or 'messy' policy controversy, and it explores the various po litical and rhetorical strategies that have emerged to resolve it. We also enquire into the way in which those groups and coalitions which appeared to lose the battle over the future direction of airports policy in 2003 have been able to stall and possibly reverse the proposals by the pro-expansion lobby to expand Heathrow, Gatwick and Stansted airports, following the formation of the Conservative–Liberal Democrat coalition government in May 2010. This problematisation poses ancillary questions about: the character of the regime of aviation expansion in the post-war period; the voicing of competing demands to address the imperatives of economic growth and environmental protection; the way in which the rhetoric of scientific discourse and expert knowledge affects policy-making; the role of government in mediating and directing aviation policy; and the future trajectories of the UK aviation industry.

In keeping with our theoretical approach, our explanation of these issues seeks to integrate numerous factors and conditions, so that, in Marx's pregnant phrase, it comprises 'a rich totality of many determinations and relations' (Marx, 1973: 100). In our view, the formation of the coalition government in May 2010, which was in turn preceded by a shift in the ideological orientation and policy of the Conservative Party under the leadership of David Cameron, coupled with the effective campaigning strategies of opposition groups and social movements, constitute the significant variables in accounting for this policy reversal. Yet we also contend – and this is one of our central claims – that if there had not been a wider reframing or cultural resignification of aviation as an 'emblematic issue' of climate change, then there would not have been such concerted opposition to the Labour Party's 2003 proposals, and the Conservative–Liberal

Democrat coalition would not have decided to place a moratorium on the building of new runways soon after coming to office in May 2010.

In short, by constructing a genealogical narrative of the various aspects of the aviation problem in the UK context since the Second World War, we seek to explore the discursive conditions and practices that made possible the naming and reframing of this pressing issue. We endeavour to critically explain the shift from a context in which the growth of aviation was perceived to be an unquestioned good, in which the key contentions concerned the location and extent of growth – questions about the means to achieve an accepted set of policy ends – to a situation in which both the ends and the means of aviation have begun to be problematised and questioned. Whether or not this results in a major shift in transport policy remains to be seen, and this question is addressed at the end of the book.

Wicked problems

This brief statement of our substantive focus brings us to our second and third sets of concerns, namely the construction and possible resolution of so-called wicked problems in the policy process, and the theoretical assumptions, concepts and logics with which to explore them. Problem definition and the practices of problem setting, not to mention their attempted resolution, have preoccupied much policy analysis in recent years.[4] Constructivist policy researchers have queried the traditional concern with 'problem closure', that is, the prior specification of a series of socially acceptable solutions for clearly defined policy problems (Hajer, 1995: 22). Going back to the early 1970s, Rittel and Webber (1973) defined 'wicked' as opposed to 'tame' policy problems, which in their view had a number of distinguishing characteristics. They stressed, for example, that there can be 'no definitive formulation of a wicked problem', for such problems are inherently uncertain and invariably contested. They also argued that wicked problems have 'no stopping rule', so that whether or not such a problem has been resolved is as open to dispute as its definition. Admitting 'no immediate and no ultimate test of a solution', the attempted resolution of these problems creates 'waves of consequences over an extended – virtually an unbounded – period of time'. In other words, wicked issues are 'essentially unique' dilemmas, which are often the symptoms of other problems, and are beset with competing formulations, contrasting evidence bases and complex interdependencies (Rittel and Webber, 1973: 161–7; Hulme, 2009: 333–5).

More recent discussions have focused on the emergence of 'messy' problems in the policy process, which generate persistent and divisive conflicts about how best to tackle them and often require 'clumsy' solutions (Ney, 2009: 7; Verweij and Thompson, 2006). For example, in a series of illuminating case studies presented in their book *Frame Reflection*, Donald Schön and Martin Rein explore how certain social and political problems can often give rise to 'intractable policy controversies' (Schön and Rein, 1994; see also Rein and Schön, 1996). Disputes of this sort, they argue, often arise in debates about rising crime, poverty, economic recession or environmental destruction, and 'are immune to resolution by appeal to the facts', so that 'disputes about such issues tend to be intractable, enduring, and seldom finally resolved' (Schön and Rein, 1994: 4).

In seeking to analyse and resolve these sorts of problems, Rein and Schön develop a distinctive approach to policy analysis which privileges the role of policy discourses, frames and frame conflicts, as well as the role of metaphors, narratives and images, which key actors use to hold frames together. Such representational forms provide the repertoires for social actors to construct their worlds and engage in conflict, while policy discourse is understood as 'verbal exchange or dialogue, about policy issues' (Schön and Rein, 1994: 31). Frames, by contrast, are 'underlying structures of belief, perception, and appreciation' (Schön and Rein, 1994: 23). More fully, a frame:

> is a way of selecting, organizing, interpreting, and making sense of a complex reality to provide guideposts for knowing, analysing, persuading, and acting. A frame is a perspective from which an amorphous, ill-defined, problematic situation can be made sense of and acted on. (Rein and Schön, 1993: 146)

According to Schön and Rein, there is no way to falsify a frame and so policy controversies are not often resolved by simply examining the facts or by reasoned argument. As the parties in the dispute are not frame neutral, there is no objective yardstick with which to judge frames. Indeed, as rival forces can perceive and make sense of social reality only through a frame, 'the very task of making sense of complex, information-rich situations requires an operation of selectivity and organization, which is what "framing" means' (Schön and Rein, 1994: 30). Hence, in a policy controversy, each party (re-)presents their own story, and these often conflicting narratives portray very distinct perceptions of reality. The stories name and fix features that

have been selected from reality in frames, which are constructed for
a particular situation, and which constitute the actor's view of social
reality. The process of naming and framing thus defines the problem
out of an essentially imprecise reality. In short, then, through naming
and framing the function of problem-setting is executed, and thus
the 'normative leap' towards the construction of policy (re)solutions
occurs (Schön and Rein, 1994).

This in part leads to the intractable character of certain policy
problems. While the public manifestation of policy conflict can often
take the form of reasonable disagreements about facts and scientific
evidence, such conflict is more often than not rooted in incompatible
values, where the latter shape the judgements and decisions of those
involved in the construction and resolution of messy problems. In
Rein and Schön's words, policy controversies

> cannot be understood in terms of the familiar separation of questions
> of value from questions of fact, for the participants construct the prob-
> lems of their problematic policy situations through frames in which
> facts, values, theories and interests are integrated. Given the multiple
> social realities created by conflicting frames, the participants disagree
> both with one another and also about the nature of their disagree-
> ments. (Rein and Schön, 1993: 145)

There are, in other words, 'situations in which no available choice is
a good one, because we are involved in a conflict of *ends* which are
incommensurable' (Schön, 1993: 150).

As we have intimated, our framing of the politics of aviation in
the UK context focuses on the emergence and constitution of aviation
as a 'messy' or 'wicked' policy problem. We also explore the various
ways in which British governments and officials, as well as sections
of the aviation industry, have sought to resolve this problem. But
though frame analysis provides a useful set of tools, we draw more
upon poststructuralist discourse theory to problematise and analyse
our object of study. We thus supplement Rein and Schön's initial intuitions about problem setting, frame conflict and the role of metaphors
and narratives with concepts and logics drawn from poststructuralist
discourse theory, which leads us to rearticulate the distinction between
policy discourse and policy practice.[5] Our concern is thus to critically
explain the discursive conditions that made possible the recontextu-
alisation and transformation of airports and aviation, as well as the
obstacles that have rendered the problem intractable, and that continue to do so.

The discursive articulation of aviation as a wicked policy problem

Our decision to supplement existing accounts of framing and reframing with developments in discourse analysis and critical policy studies highlights the third main contribution of our study: the endeavour to operationalise and apply poststructuralist discourse theory to particular empirical problems and cases. Recent years have brought a host of discursive approaches to the study of society and politics, not to mention variations of discourse analysis in the related fields of linguistics, anthropology, literary studies and the human sciences more generally (see Glynos *et al.*, 2009; Howarth, 2000, 2013). By using the logics and concepts of discourse theory, especially the role of rhetoric, heresthetic, hegemony and fantasy, this study seeks to demonstrate the added value of employing poststructuralist discourse theory in the concrete empirical research of policy problems.

Of course, we are not alone in this enterprise, as others have similarly sought to articulate discursive accounts of the process. Of particular importance in this regard is Maarten Hajer's *The Politics of Environmental Discourse* (1995), which builds upon the work of Foucault and others to elaborate a discursive account of policy change. Focused on the emergence of ecological modernisation discourse in Britain and the Netherlands during the 1980s and 1990s, Hajer's argumentative approach to discourse analysis, with its innovative concepts of discourse coalitions, storylines, discursive affinities and closures, goes some way in accounting for the production of 'discursive hegemony', in which 'actors try to secure support for their definition of reality' (Hajer, 1995: 59). We have also profited from the way in which policy theorists have elaborated discursive and interpretive approaches to policy analysis, which stress the role of deliberation, metaphor and rhetoric.[6]

Yet our particular understanding of discourse, with its distinctive concepts of hegemony, rhetoric, heresthetic and fantasy, which are connected together by what we call the logics of critical explanation, adds a distinctive twist to these accounts of policy change. To begin with, in seeking to operationalise the category of hegemony for policy analysis, we distinguish between the policy, the institutional and the societal/cultural aspects of hegemony, which enables us to explain and evaluate crucial shifts in aviation policy, as well as the obstacles and impediments to change. We also focus on the articulation of rival arguments and narratives by competing forces, as well as the figures and tropes through which they are expressed, and the subjective modalities and forms of enunciation that make them possible.

But our focus on rhetoric is not restricted to the form and content of its expression, for we are also concerned with what rational choice theorists call the art of strategic manipulation – or heresthetic – which in Riker's words involves 'structuring the world so you can win' (Riker, 1996: x). As we argue in the book, a crucial part of turning a losing coalition into a winning one revolves around the way in which key actors can render certain societal dimensions visible or invisible, thus making possible the construction of demands and political frontiers. How these demands are then linked together or broken asunder is also critical to the production of winning alliances and campaigns, and this is where we link our account of hegemony to discourse, rhetoric and heresthetic.

Finally, we are not just preoccupied with the creation of equivalential linkages between different demands to produce more universal projects, but we are also interested in the way in which certain signifiers and discourses provide points of subjective identification to which social actors remain attached. It is here that the affective dimension of our approach comes to the fore, which we explore via the concepts of fantasy, myth, identity and ideology. We are also interested in the way in which interests and identities interact, and how novel ideas emerge and are taken up in the policy process. These various theoretical elements are introduced at various points in our text, in conjunction with particular problems and questions.

But what is our study of airport policy a case of, and what kind of case is it? How was it selected and analysed? Contrary to much discussion about case studies, their scientific status, and research methodology more generally, these are easy questions to ask, but more difficult ones to address. On the one hand, the book can be seen as an exemplary case study of the complex layers of processes and practices that produced a wicked or messy policy problem, as well as the efforts by government and other actors to resolve the controversy in a democratic fashion. But at the same time the study also consists of a series of connected case studies of particular events and processes, each of which shapes the case as a whole. Hence it contains particular case studies of different campaigns against aviation expansion at different airports, as well as analyses of the logic and formation of various discourse coalitions during and after the national consultative exercise between 2000 and 2003. We also present a detailed investigation of the

Heathrow case, which is uniquely important in the UK context, and at the same time is paradigmatic of the problem surrounding aviation in our late-modern world.[7]

Arguments and structure of the book

In summary, therefore, our critical explanation of the policy changes in the sphere of aviation delineates the various logics and practices that led to the cultural resignification of aviation in the UK, and the effects of this reframing on the policy positions and decisions of successive governments. Developing a poststructuralist approach to policy analysis, and set against a contradictory regime of aviation expansion, we explore the construction of rival discourse coalitions in the period of the consultation process for the 2003 white paper, and following the decision by the New Labour government to give the go-ahead for airport expansion. We focus in particular on the discursive and rhetorical strategies that were articulated, informed and employed by key actors and forces, as well as the various attempts to deal or manage the problem by the government. Our conclusion explores the current impasse surrounding aviation policy in the UK.

Our efforts to address these various problematisations are reflected in the main arguments and structure of the book. Yet in order to explore these problems and questions, we need first to say something about the theoretical resources we draw upon in this study. In chapter 1, therefore, we set out our theoretical approach in a way that respects both the contextualised self-interpretations of the actors involved, while bringing into play a series of connected theoretical concepts and logics that can enable us to elaborate a critical *explanans*, which can render our *explanandum* more intelligible. As these theoretical resources rely heavily on our understanding of poststructuralist discourse theory, we explicate the latter's ontological assumptions, rebutting those critics who have queried its basic commitments. It thus provides us with the opportunity to elaborate the theoretical framework that we use to address the problematisations analysed in the book. (We suggest that readers more interested in the pudding than in the recipe go straight to chapter 2, and then consult the theoretical chapter when and if necessary.)

In chapter 2 we set out our detailed problematisation of the UK aviation industry and its attendant practices and infrastructure requirements. Not only do we say a little more about the concept of problematisation, where we build *inter alia* on the work of Michel Foucault, but we endeavour to connect this idea to the particular issues and dilemmas thrown up in the policy domain. We then define and outline the five main problematisations that we explore in the book: the institution and installation of the regime of aviation expansion during the Second World War; the struggle over the expansion or regulation of aviation at the start of the new century; the subsequent reframing of aviation; the governmental and industry responses to the resignification of aviation; and the current policy stalemate.

Chapter 3 shows how the myths surrounding the UK's military and commercial aviation were consolidated into what we might call a collective social imaginary that conferred on aviation its sacrosanct position. In turn, this then fuelled and sustained the post-war logic of aviation expansion. When coupled with the articulation of various fantasmatic narratives, which gripped both powerful interests and the wider public, as well as the skilful employment of various political logics by successive political leaders, the post-war period saw the emergence and sedimentation of a powerful logic of aviation expansion. Our chapter thus demonstrates the continuities and path dependencies of the post-war regime, and its materialisation in key organisations and state apparatuses, such as the Ministry of Civil Aviation, Ministry of Transport (MoT) and the Department for Transport (DfT), as well as the Department for Trade and the Department of the Environment.

But the logic of aviation expansion was not without its broader contradictions and challenges, not least in the form of demands for additional capacity, particularly in the south-east of England, which competed against emerging demands for environmental protection, as well as the embedded demands of local residents for less airport noise and air pollution. Faced with the piecemeal incrementalism of successive governments, rival groups came to coalesce around the demand for government leadership and the formulation of a long-term aviation strategy. Taking office in 1997, with no white paper on aviation since 1985, New Labour responded to these pressures by embarking upon a national consultation, which was designed to engineer a broad dialogue and consensus over the future of aviation, ahead of announcing its own long-term strategic plan for airport capacity. Yet this new space also created the opportunity for the putting together of new discourse coalitions that sought to shape public policy in their own images. Chapter 4 thus explores the emergence and formation of Freedom to Fly and AirportWatch, which sought respectively to advance and curtail the aviation industry. It also analyses their strategies and impact on the UK aviation industry.

Although the publication of the 2003 white paper promised to resolve the great debate about the trajectory of UK aviation, the proposed resolution called for a massive expansion of airport infrastructure across the country. It thus made clear the government's conception of sustainable aviation, which many regarded as completely unsustainable. In our analysis of the white paper in chapter 5 we endeavour to characterise the discourse and rhetoric of the government's proposals. Here we focus initially on the genre and framing of the air transport white paper, before providing the concrete detail of the government's proposals for a viable policy of sustainable aviation. We thus concentrate on the way in which the government constructed the character and future trajectory of aviation in the UK, while mentioning the increasing environmental impacts of air travel. The problem of sustainable aviation, we suggest, was represented as one of achieving a 'balanced strategy', and the white paper elaborated a series of political strategies and tactics designed to realise this goal and negate opposition to its proposals for expansion.

No sooner had those calling for growth won the day when the problematisation of airports and aviation took a surprising turn. The immediate aftermath of the 2003 white paper brought forth concerted efforts by local residents, environmental campaigners and scientific experts, as well as some concerned politicians, to resignify the role of airports and aviation in a radical way. Connecting the proposed expansion of the airports to the national and global expansion of aviation, and linking this articulation to the problem of climate change, enabled opponents of airport expansions at Heathrow, Stansted and elsewhere to change the meaning and import of aviation, thus laying the basis for political and policy change. Chapter 6 explores the discursive processes and practices that enabled the reframing of aviation in the first decade of the new century, and pays particular attention to the role of the repeated interventions of scientists and experts in reshaping the policy discourse of aviation. It also details the way in which the UK government and the aviation industry have attempted to counter these evolving protests and arguments.

The struggles over the location, character, growth, impact and use of Heathrow airport have always been at the centre of the debate about aviation in the UK. As we show in chapter 3, Heathrow was earmarked during the Second World War to be the main commercial airport in the UK and it has retained this dominant position as the UK's leading international hub airport ever since. In many senses, its unique position exemplifies the problems of aviation, especially the contradictions between demands for economic growth, on the one hand, and the defence and protection of local communities and the environment, on the other. Chapter 7 explores the struggles over the proposals to build a third runway at Heathrow, focusing in part on the decision by the Labour government of Gordon Brown in January 2009 to support its expansion in the dying days of its thirteen-year hold on power, as well as the strategies and tactics of campaigners who were ultimately able to overturn that decision.

At the start of the second decade of the twenty-first century aviation finds itself at a crossroads. Is the future of aviation in the UK (and across the world) best captured by the image of an aerotropolis, in which it 'will not just be a powerful engine for local economic development, but also a whole new international forum for ideas and innovation, offering a place for travellers to exchange knowledge, shop, eat, sleep, be entertained and conduct business' (Kasarda and Lindsay, 2011)? Or might it become the new tobacco industry, in which it is relegated to a marginal and largely outmoded form of transport in a world marked by peak oil and rampant climate change? But perhaps both scenarios are too extreme and unrealistic, and should be replaced by more moderate and compromising positions that lie between these two poles? If the latter, what form do they take and how can they be critically evaluated? Our concluding chapter explores these emergent discourses about the future of aviation, while also drawing out the overall conclusions and prescriptions of the study.

The main text was completed in mid-2012. But since then there have been important developments in UK aviation policy, which have confirmed the difficulties of reaching a successful and legitimate policy solution. Constructing a durable policy settlement in aviation continues to be a precarious undertaking, replete with unexpected twists and turns. Yet one thing remains clear: it will certainly be marked by persistent challenges from supporters of the aviation industry as well as opponents of airport expansion. Much depends on the political ambitions of government, coupled with its capacity to define a clear policy line with which it can lead and educate the public. Our Epilogue, written in February 2013, explores how the Conservative–Liberal Democrat coalition, which entered office in May 2010 with a strong commitment to a moratorium on airport expansion in the south-east of England, has endeavoured to manage the growing clamour for expansion at UK airports. From the spring of 2012 onwards, the coalition government faced a backlash from supporters of aviation expansion. In September 2012, it established an independent airport commission – the Davies Commission – which was due to report in 2015. We examine the political pressures on the coalition, while explaining the emergence of a policy impasse at the beginning of 2013 and reflect upon the implications of the deadlock for the government and campaigners opposed to expansion.

Notes

1 Aviation is an integral element of what Sheller and Urry (2006) have proposed as a new 'mobilities paradigm' for social sciences.

2 In her study of the phenomenology of air passengers, Budd (2011) concludes that air travel has changed our understandings of mobility, as well as our perceptions of time, speed, distance and space.

3 See Gilbert and Perl (2010), Gössling and Upham (2009), Kasarda and Lindsay (2011: 329–58), McManners (2012), Mitchell (2011), Pulford (2008). 'Peak oil' is generally understood as that moment in time when the maximum extraction of petroleum has been reached, at which point the rate of global oil production begins its terminal decline, though there is some dispute about its precise measurement. New technologies, rising prices and new modes of extraction (particularly of shale oil) have led many to question whether peak oil will be a reality in the near future. See George Monbiot in the *Guardian*, 2 July 2012.

4 See Baumgartner and Jones (1993), Dery (2000), Hoppe (2010), Kingdon (1984), Ney (2009), Rochefort and Cobb (1994), Stone (2001).

5 In developing their arguments, Schön and Rein distinguish between a discourse of policy debate, in which 'policy stories', and the frames they articulate, fulfil 'the rhetorical functions of persuasion, justification, and symbolic display', and a discourse of policy practice, in which 'policy stories' constitute in part the array of laws, regulations, policy instruments and behaviours that constitute 'what policies actually mean in action' (Schön and Rein, 1994: 32). While useful as an analytical device, our approach (which we set out in chapter 1) rejects an ontological separation between the symbolic and the practical.

6 See Bevir and Rhodes (2003), Fischer (1995, 2000, 2003, 2009), Gottweis (2003, 2006), Torfing (1998, 1999), Torgerson (1999), Wagenaar (2011), Yanow (1996, 2000).

7 For a discussion of different types of case study, which is broadly compatible with our approach, see Flyvbjerg (2001). For applications of this approach to different empirical cases, see Flyvbjerg *et al.* (2012).

1

Discourse, rhetoric and logics

The notion common to all the work that I have done since *Madness and Civilization* is that of problematization, though it must be said that I never isolated this notion sufficiently. But one always finds what is essential after the event; the most general things are those that appear last. It is the ransom and reward for all work in which *theoretical questions are elaborated on the basis of a particular empirical field....* Problematization doesn't mean representation of a pre-existing object, nor the creation by discourse of an object that doesn't exist. It is the totality of discursive and non-discursive practices that introduces something into the play of the true and false and constitutes it as an object for thought (whether in the form of moral reflection, scientific knowledge, political analysis, etc.). (Foucault, 1988: 257; our emphasis)

We gain very little once identities are conceived as complexly articulated collective wills, by referring to them through simple designations such as classes, ethnic groups, and so on, which are at best names for transient points of stabilisation. The really important task is to understand the logics of their constitution and dissolution, as well as the formal determination of the spaces in which they interrelate. (Laclau, 2000: 33)

A number of contemporary innovators in the field of policy studies draw sustenance from the 'discursive turn' in the human and social sciences, as well as the ideas of poststructuralism that often accompany this trend. The turn to discourse has focused our attention on the need for understanding, interpretation and critical evaluation in social and political analysis, rather than the search for law-like or causal explanations. Discourse analysts and interpretivists of various hues thus privilege the political construction of meanings and identities in and through the policy process, and they question the sharp separation between questions of fact and questions of value. In pursuing these ideals, they have developed notions like narratives, storylines, framing, discourse coalitions, interpretation, rhetoric and argumentation to critically explain the initiation, formulation, implementation and evaluation of public policies in various contexts and settings.

Yet the injection of poststructuralist ideas and techniques into the field of policy studies has been diverse and complex, so that discursive policy analysis assumes various shapes and sizes. It includes those who wish to break radically from positivist perspectives (Fischer, 2003), as well as those who seek mainly to supplement positivist viewpoints by treating discourses as particular systems of belief or conceptual frameworks for apprehending the world (Dryzek, 1997: 8; Weale, 1992). In this chapter, we demonstrate how one particular type of discursive policy analysis, poststructuralist policy analysis, when articulated with elements of critical discourse analysis and rhetorical political analysis, can contribute important tools and concepts for the conduct of critical policy studies. Our approach goes beyond a minimal and cognitive conception of discourse, in which discourse is reduced to simply another variable that can be subjected to empirical testing, and which often gives rise to what we might term 'discourse-lite' forms of explanation and interpretation (Torfing, 2005: 25). Rather, we employ a 'thicker' conception of discourse theory in which discourse does not just consist of an abstract cognitive system of beliefs and words, but is a constitutive dimension of social relations. It does not merely describe or make known a pre-existing or underlying reality, but serves partly to bring that reality into being for subjects (Gottweis, 2003: 251).

In expounding our approach, we begin by setting out the ontological assumptions of poststructuralist discourse theory, showing how its categories and logics can help us to analyse the politics of policy change as a hegemonic struggle, while also foregrounding the rhetorical and affective dimension of policy-making. Using the category of discourse, we thus develop a poststructuralist reading of the Gramscian concepts of hegemony and power, and we outline our understanding of the connections between discourse and rhetoric. We then employ the Lacanian logic of fantasy to focus our attention on the enjoyment subjects procure from their identifications with certain policy practices, signifiers and figures. Finally, we turn to questions of methodology and the techniques of discursive policy analysis. Those who employ a 'thicker', more constitutive conception of discourse have often faced charges of failing to critically reflect upon questions of method and research strategy, and of not properly attending to the normative implications of policy-making (Critchley, 2004; Torfing, 2005; Townshend, 2003). In response to such claims, we outline the steps of what we term 'the logics of critical explanation', focusing our attention on problematisation, social, political and fantasmatic logics, and articulation, judgement and critique (Glynos and Howarth, 2007). We start by discussing how poststructuralist policy analysis helps us to reconceptualise the study of public policy.

Poststructuralist policy analysis: questions of ontology

Poststructuralist policy analysis includes various approaches that share a series of family resemblances with one another (for further discussion, see Howarth, 2013; Howarth and Griggs, 2012). Alongside other types of interpretive policy analysis, it focuses on the role of meanings in shaping human actions and social institutions in the policy-making process. Yet it is equally (if not more) concerned with the ways in which meanings are created and contested by rival political forces in particular policy settings, and how these settings are related to wider social systems and power relations. The approach thus assumes that even the most sedimented practices, objects and categories of policy-making are ambiguous and radically contingent entities, whose meaning can be articulated in various ways by differently located social actors (see Miller, 2002, 2012; Miller and Fox, 2007). Poststructuralist policy analysts also explore the way in which subjects are formed and act in the policy-making process, as well as the wider structures of social relations within which they operate.

In this perspective, then, natural, physical and cultural phenomena acquire their meaning in specific discourses; in our jargon they are 'discursively constructed'. Objects and things in this approach certainly 'exist' independently of any particular discourse, but their meaning and significance – and how they are engaged with by social actors – depends on their position within particular symbolic frameworks. Poststructuralist policy analysis thus rejects essentialist accounts of policy-making which assume that objects, human subjects or social formations have underlying and fixed essences (evident, for example, in the economic determinism and class reductionism of explanations of social and political change in Marxism, and in some versions of critical realism). By contrast, it assumes that 'social, political, or natural phenomena and ... their meanings', which are inextricably intertwined, are 'constantly moving, changing and shifting in various directions' (Gottweis, 2003: 249).

Against this background, we conceptualise policy programmes such as new public management, social inclusion or sustainable development, as well as institutions like administrative systems or governance networks, as more or less sedimented systems of discourse (cf. March and Olsen, 1989; Torfing *et al.*, 2012). As Ernesto Laclau and Chantal Mouffe insist, 'a discursive structure is not a merely "cognitive" or "contemplative" entity; it is an articulatory practice which constitutes and organises social relations' (Laclau and Mouffe, 1985: 96). Discourses in our perspective are thus partially fixed systems of rules, norms, resources, practices and subjectivities, which are constituted politically by the construction of social antagonisms and the creation of political frontiers. They are finite and contingent constructions, whose production involves the exercise of power, as well certain forms of exclusion. This means that every discursive structure is uneven and hierarchical (Howarth, 2009: 313). Bearing this in mind, we shall say a little more about our conception of discourse, before turning to its broad implications for policy analysis.

Our understanding of discourse rests on three moves. First, we extend the scope of discourse theory beyond the analysis of 'texts and talk in contexts' so as to include social actions and political practices. All objects and social practices are discursive, in that their meaning and position depend upon their articulation within socially constructed systems of rules and differences (Howarth and Stavrakakis, 2000: 3; Laclau and Mouffe, 1985). For example, the discourse of air transport policy is not exhausted by the talk or language of policy guidance, ministerial speeches or white papers. It also includes a diverse array of actions and practices, such as forecasting, noise measurement, planning rules and public inquiries, as well as airport regulations, air traffic management and even package holidays. In other words, language, actions and objects are intertwined in what we call 'discourse'.

Secondly, by grounding our understanding of discourse in the work of Saussure (1983) and in structural linguistics more generally, we understand discourses as relational and differential configurations of elements that comprise agents (or subjects), words and actions. These elements are individuated and rendered intelligible within the context of a particular practice, in which each element acquires its meaning only in relation to the others (Howarth, 2009: 311–12). What we term aviation policy discourse thus establishes systems of relations between different objects and practices, including airports, airlines, noise contours, flight paths, landing patterns and so forth. It provides subject positions or roles with which actors can identify, whether these are the 'business flyer', the 'leisure passenger', 'air traffic controllers', or the 'national carrier', 'British Airports Authority' and so on. At the same time, the meaning and significance of such practices is acquired only within a particular historical context. For example, 'jet-set' appeals to the luxury of flying were possible only in the particular conjuncture of the 1930s; they lacked credibility in the era of mass aviation consumption, which emerged in the 1980s and 1990s with the advent of low-cost carriers. To borrow from the work of Rein and Schön (1993: 153), discourse thereby installs a particular kind of coherence by bringing 'things named' into a 'composite whole'. But, in so doing, the identities of elements are modified. This is evident, for instance, in the transformation of the understandings of 'aviation' and 'sustainable development' when they are articulated into the discourse of 'sustainable aviation'.

Finally, drawing on poststructuralists like Jacques Derrida (1978, 1982), Michel Foucault (1972, 1981, 1984a) and Jacques Lacan (2006), we stress the radical contingency and structural undecidability of discursive structures (Howarth, 2009: 312). This arises because we assume that all systems of meaning are, in a fundamental sense, incomplete. By saying that discourses are incomplete, we do not mean that they are simply missing something, as when we say that we have not ticked all the boxes on a bureaucratic form. Incompletion in our view highlights an absence or negativity that structurally prevents the completion of a discourse, thereby indicating its limits. Discourses are thus incomplete systems of meaningful practice, because they are predicated on the exclusion of certain elements. Yet these excluded elements are required for the very identity of the discourse. Aviation policy in the UK in the aftermath of the Second World War came to rest in part on how discourses of expansion constructed antagonisms or drew political boundaries with US competitors, thereby institutionalising demands for aviation expansion and excluding alternative practices and possibilities.

Put differently, this means that any identity or order is marked by what Henry Staten (1984) and Ernesto Laclau (2005: 69–71) call a 'constitutive outside'. This absence or negativity prevents the full constitution of a discursive structure, so that every structure is thus dislocated. Yet this 'out-of-joint-ness' is evident only in particular dislocations or events that show their incompletion, while the construction of social antagonisms signifies the limits of any discourse or social order, that is, its contestation by competing political forces. Discourses are thus contingent and historical constructions, which are always vulnerable to those political forces that are excluded in their production, as well as the dislocatory effects of events beyond their control (Howarth, 2000: 109).

In short, then, discourse is in one respect a kind of social practice that links together and modifies heterogeneous elements in changing historical formations (Laclau and Mouffe, 1985: 96). The outcomes of such practices are discursive formations, in which the linkages between the elements of these systems are relational and differential. Discursive formations are finite, uneven and incomplete.[1] Both as a practice and as an incomplete system of related moments, discourse also presupposes a world of contingent elements – linguistic and non-linguistic, social and natural – that can be linked together in various ways. Elements are best conceived as 'floating signifiers', which can in certain circumstances be articulated by rival political projects seeking to fix their meaning and import, whereas moments are those elements that are firmly positioned in a particular discourse. Nodal points are those privileged points of signification within a discourse that partially fix the meaning of practices and institutional configurations, while empty signifiers provide the symbolic means to represent these essentially incomplete orders. The function of the latter is to incarnate the 'absent fullness' of an essentially incomplete discursive system. Put differently, floating signifiers are ideological elements that are not securely fixed in a particular discourse and can thus be constructed in diverse ways, whereas empty signifiers are points of fixation that can hold together multiple and even contradictory demands in a precarious unity (Laclau, 1990, 1995). This perspective is consistent with a minimal realism that acknowledges the existence of the objects and processes that we think about, although our practices of reflection are never external to the life-worlds into which we are thrown. Indeed, it is only within such symbolic orders that we encounter such objects.

What does this mean for the study of public policy? In the first instance, it suggests that one of the primary tasks of policy analysis is to explain critically why and how a particular policy has been formulated, accepted and implemented, rather than others. It thus privileges the general concern with policy change or policy reversal, on the one hand, and policy inertia and policy sedimentation, on the other. This focus gives rise to a particular set of questions for the policy analyst. What are the conditions for particular policy discourses to become dominant or hegemonic? How do we account for the reproduction and transformation of such hegemonic policy orders and practices? How do we explain the 'grip' of certain policy discourses? And how are such dominant orders contested?

In addressing such questions, poststructuralist policy analysis, in our view, must situate the practices of policy-making in relation to wider social and political contexts. Policy analyses and evaluations have thus to be conducted in relation to broader societal tendencies and changes (see Fischer, 1995, 2000). Yet because policy-making emerges and operates in different social contexts, its analysis must be located at the intersection of processes operating at multiple spatial scales, be they the micro-processes of an organisation or the more macro-processes of national government (Bridge and McManus, 2000: 13). Policy is also shaped by the overall balances of political forces in society and the changing configurations of hegemony therein. In addition, these political practices are intimately related to other socio-economic processes, such as the contradictions and dynamics of the local, national and global political economy, as well as other social practices and cultural representations.

In equal fashion, an effective policy analysis must, in our view, have a critical and normative commitment. Policy analysts should seek to deconstruct 'taken for granted' regimes of policy practices and objects, while exposing their particular exclusionary logics and proposing alternative counter-logics. This means that our particular understanding of policy-making privileges the role of power and political processes, characterising policies as the contingent outcomes of political struggles between competing discourses. 'Politics' here is understood as the contestation and institution of social relations and practices, and it discloses the contingent character of any practice or institution by showing the role of power and exclusion in its formation (Laclau, 1990). Every discursive structure, as we argue above, will be uneven, heterogeneous and hierarchical.

Yet what are the implications of this primacy of politics for our understanding of policy-making? Why do particular policies become sedimented? How are they overthrown? By radicalising the insights of the Marxist theorist Antonio Gramsci (1971), and by drawing on the work of Laclau and Mouffe (1985, 1987), we argue that policy discourses are stabilised and challenged by multiple hegemonic operations, whose general structure consists of the logics of equivalence and difference. This means that the concept of hegemony is central to the perspective we put forward here, as policy change or policy inertia will be the outcome of hegemonic struggles (Howarth, 2009). We need, therefore, to say a few words about our distinctively poststructuralist conception of hegemony.

A poststructuralist conception of hegemony

Laclau, Mouffe and other proponents of poststructuralist discourse analysis have combined Gramsci's path-breaking reflections on hegemony with more recent developments in critical theory (such as structural Marxism, Foucauldian genealogy and Lacanian psychoanalysis) to engage in a wider deconstruction of the Marxist tradition (Howarth and Stavrakakis, 2000; Laclau and Mouffe, 1985; Norval, 1994, 1996; Torfing, 1998, 1999). Working within this perspective, we delineate two aspects of hegemony that are vital in developing a viable approach to critical policy analysis.[2] On the one hand, hegemony is a type of rule or governance which captures the way in which a regime, practice or policy holds sway over a set of subjects by a particular entwining of consent, compliance and coercion. On the other hand, hegemony is a practice of politics that involves the linking together of disparate demands to forge hegemonic projects or 'discourse coalitions' (Hajer, 1995) which can contest a particular form of rule, practice or policy (Howarth, 2009: 317). In practice, of course, these aspects are intimately related. Hegemony as a form of rule presupposes various practices of transformism, negotiation, compromise and bargaining, while the struggle to develop counter-hegemonic movements presupposes certain forms of rule which the movements challenge and seek to transform. Yet on analytical if not ontological grounds, it is possible to separate these two aspects.

Before elucidating these aspects in more detail, two important conceptual issues are worth clarifying. In the first place, in our analysis, we use the concepts of discourse coalition and hegemonic project more or less synonymously, although we acknowledge that they arise from different intellectual traditions. Maarten Hajer's notion of a discourse coalition emerges from his reading of Foucault, as well as his critical engagement with other policy perspectives, such as Paul Sabatier's advocacy coalition framework (Sabatier, 1988, 1991), whereas the idea of a hegemonic project is derived from the work of Antonio Gramsci, and then developed by Stuart Hall (1988), Bob Jessop (1982, 2002a, 2002b), Ernesto Laclau and Chantal Mouffe (1985), and others. But it is pertinent to note that Hajer has also engaged with the latter corpus of work in his analysis of urban politics (Hajer, 1989). Both approaches stress the linking together of different actors and groups in the context of an identifiable set of practices. However, while Hajer understands the 'glue' of discourse coalitions to be the sharing of a particular set of story lines, we draw upon work on the construction of hegemonic practices to examine the ways in which actors and groups identify with empty signifiers over a particular period of time. As we argue below, we thus seek to take Hajer's approach in a more poststructuralist direction by emphasising the concept of hegemony and its conditions for achieving dominance, while seeking to articulate a different understanding of the connection between identity and interests (Griggs and Howarth, 2002).

The second conceptual issue pertains to the concept of demand, which is manifestly important in this conception of hegemony and thus for our empirical analysis. Following Laclau's discussion of this notion in *On Populist Reason* (2005), a *social demand* is intimately connected to a subject's experience of contingency, which is usually engendered by the occurrence of a dislocatory event and the way a particular subject responds to it. One immediate reaction to a dislocatory event might be to constitute the experience of contingency as a *grievance*. In other words, the matter might be constructed as an issue affecting a group or community, whose response can then be articulated as a *request* in the public domain. If the relevant public authority can process the request in a satisfactory way, then the matter is likely to end there. But the failure of the relevant authority to respond adequately to a request, at least from the perspective of the aggrieved subject, can lead to its hardening into a demand (Laclau, 2005: 73–4). Indeed, if this demand publicly challenges the norm of a practice or regime, which is usually manifested in terms of a particular public policy, then it takes on a political character. In short, then, a demand is political to the extent that it publicly contests the norms of a particular practice or policy regime in the name of a principle or ideal (Glynos and Howarth, 2007: 115–16).

1. Hegemony as a political form or regime

We shall now explore each dimension of hegemony in turn, using our empirical case of aviation policy in the UK to illustrate and develop our theoretical arguments. Hegemony as a form of rule speaks in general to the way in which subjects accept and conform to a particular regime, practice or policy, even though they may have previously resisted or opposed it. In this guise, the concept enables us to characterise different forms of concrete governance, shedding light on how different policy regimes are stabilised and reproduced through diverse practices of transformism, negotiation, compromise and bargaining (Howarth, 2009: 318–20). More fully, two opposed ideal types of hegemony as a form of rule can be specified, each of which comprises different blends of force and consent. What we might term a situation of 'organic hegemony' represents a type of rule in which subjects actively consent to a particular practice or regime, so that the role of force or domination recedes into the background. At the opposite pole of the continuum, we find a situation of 'inorganic hegemony', which designates a practice or regime where subjects at best comply with, or even actively resist, such forms, so that relations of force, coercion and compulsion are necessary to secure an order.

As we argue in chapter 3 of this book, for example, sharp political struggles during the Second World War and its immediate aftermath resulted in the emergence of a new regime of aviation expansion, which was consolidated and sustained during the post-war consensus, and then gathered momentum during the 1980s and 1990s, when successive governments pursued an agenda of liberalisation, deregulation and privatisation. But accompanying the installation of this hegemonic policy regime, especially since the start of the new century, aviation has increasingly been associated with collective environmental costs, notably rising carbon emissions and climate change, noise and air pollution, and widespread disruption for those living in the communities near airports, all of which have spurred the emergence of counter-hegemonic discourse coalitions (Griggs and Howarth, 2012).

Opposition to the hegemonic regime of airport expansion was continuously countered by governments, officials and the aviation industry via a series of strategies. Such strategies included: different forms of consultation, though local communities felt they had little or no say over final decisions; short-term concessions that imposed limits on noise or runway use at airports; as well as a set of procedural mechanisms, notably official hearings and public inquiries, which framed decisions not in terms of their environmental impact but as narrow technocratic planning decisions. But the inorganic character of this hegemonic regime of expansion was often manifested when such mechanisms failed to gain consent or compliance for plans for expansion and local campaigners turned to direct action and protest to challenge proposals for expansion. For example, at Manchester airport, in the late 1990s, local residents rejected the outcome of the public inquiry and joined forces with direct action environmentalists to combat the second runway (Griggs and Howarth, 2002). Later on, the inability of government to generate consent and compliance was further demonstrated during the campaign against the third runway at London Heathrow airport. Following further government announcements of expansion in 2006, John Stewart, the leader of the anti-expansion local resident group HACAN ClearSkies, proclaimed that 'there will be the mother of all battles if the Government tries to expand Heathrow … the Government doesn't seem to realise the forces lining up against it…. We've stopped speaking to the Department for Transport. We've started speaking to Earth First!' (*Observer*, 1 January 2006).

Different dimensions and modalities of the concept of hegemony as a type of rule can thus be unfolded. But it is important to stress that in whatever ways we employ this term to characterise different forms of concrete governance, the rhetorical dimension of a hegemonic relation retains a similar form: a particular set of demands and values comes to function in a universal way, thus representing a concrete 'totality' or order that exceeds them (Laclau, 2005: 72). In this model, each demand is split between a universal and a particular dimension. For example, in the case of airport expansion in the UK, we can say that the universal dimension is evident in the demand for growth, so that individual airlines might demand an expansion of the aviation industry (the universal dimension) but lobby for such expansion in different locations such as London Heathrow, Manchester or Birmingham airports (the particular dimension). The hegemonic relation rests upon one of the demands – in this instance the desire for growth – coming to play a universal function, thus representing and giving sense to the entire chain of demands.

Expressed in rhetorical terms, this relation is best captured by the figure of synecdoche, whereby a part represents the whole. The relation between part and whole thus furnishes an important means to conceptualise the hegemonic relation, though a thorough empirical analysis will also require an account of the identifications and attachments through which subjects are gripped by such regimes and practices. In turn, this involves a passage through the categories of fantasy and ideology (which we mention below), as well as the operation of hegemony as a political practice, which involves the interplay between metonymy and metaphor.

2. Hegemony as a political practice

Having briefly explicated the concept hegemony as a form or type of rule, we shall now consider it as a kind of political practice, which involves the making and breaking of political coalitions. This second aspect of hegemony highlights the linking together of different demands and identities in efforts to challenge and even replace a given practice or social order. Here, hegemony is a type of political relation or practice that involves the drawing of equivalences between disparate elements via the construction of political frontiers that divide social fields into opposed camps (Howarth, 2009: 318). In this way, as we have argued, the identities that compose an equivalential chain are modified by the practice. For example, as we show in chapter 4, local campaigns to oppose particular airport expansions before and after the 2003 white paper were linked together into a broader coalition against airport expansion *per se*. These demands were in turn connected to a wider series of adjacent social demands for environmental protection and corporate regulation by finding points of equivalence among diverse struggles. Local residents campaigning against New Labour proposals for a third runway at London Heathrow thus drew equivalences between their demands against expansion at the airport and the demands of direct action environmentalists calling for measures to counter climate change, principally in the form of reductions in carbon emissions. In this case, the very identities of local struggles were modified or overdetermined to reflect their more universal character, while the content of the new demand was given by a more general opposition to government's overall national policy of airport expansion, and/or to its environmental consequences (Griggs and Howarth, 2004, 2008, 2012).

In rhetorical terms, the second aspect of hegemony foregrounds the metonymical dimension of political practices. As a rhetorical strategy, metonymy captures the movement from one thing to another thing which is adjacent or alongside it. The 'Crown', for example, is used as a substitute for 'the Queen'. If metaphor links by means of similarity, metonymy connects by contiguity (Culler, 1997: 71). Here we use the trope of metonymy to symbolise the way in which a particular group or movement located in a particular sphere begins to take responsibility for tasks and activities in adjacent or contiguous spheres of social relations, thus seeking to hegemonise such demands. In recent times, for example, climate change activists have begun to take-up demands about airport expansion, whereas anti-airport expansion groups have begun to include demands about the environment and climate change in their campaigns.

Yet this focus does not preclude the metaphorical dimension. On the contrary, the role of metaphor is essential, because if a group is to successfully hegemonise the demands and identity of others it must create analogical relations – forms of resemblance – between such demands, while articulating empty signifiers that can partially fix or condense such demands into a more universal (if ultimately precarious) unity. Here again, one particular difference will begin to assume a more universal function, with empty signifiers acting as a means of representation, which enables the articulation of internal differences, while simultaneously showing the limits of a group's identity and its dependence on an opposition to other groups (see Howarth, 1997, 2000; Laclau, 1996, 2005). This second aspect of hegemony shares important features with Laclau's recent theory of populism, which focuses on the construction of equivalential linkages between dispersed social and political demands. Populist forms of politics in this approach require the production of specific means of representation, such as 'floating' and 'empty' signifiers, which can serve as points of subjective identification (Laclau, 2005; Laclau and Mouffe, 1985). Consider the struggle against apartheid in South Africa during the 1980s. In this context, the slogan 'UDF Unites, Apartheid Divides', which was articulated by the United Democratic Front (UDF), functioned to hold together a diverse set of social demands – demands for equal political representation, better wages, improved education and decent public services – that were put forward by a number of different social actors in various spaces during the crisis (Howarth, 2005).

In this conception, populism is not a specific ideological *content* – a set of rhetorical appeals calling for an end to 'illegal immigration', or a right-wing politician in the UK demanding that Britain 'withdraw from the EU' – nor is it a certain *type* of movement, political party or leader, who is against the system for example, though this is not to argue that rhetoric is not an important element of populist discourse. On the contrary, as we note below, rhetoric is constitutive of *all* political practice, including populist appeals and logics. Instead, populist discourses speak directly to the political *dimension* of social relations. In other words, if the political refers to the contestation and institution of specific sets of social relations, then the logic of populism captures the practices through which society is divided into opposed camps in the endless struggle for hegemony (Glynos and Howarth, 2007; Laclau and Mouffe, 1985). A populist politics thus involves the construction of a collective agency or project – 'the people', 'the nation' or 'the community' – through the drawing of a political frontier between a 'we' and a 'they' – the underdog against the establishment for example – within a social formation; and the latter presupposes a set of antagonisms and the availability of indeterminate ideological elements (or floating signifiers) whose meanings and import can be partially fixed in a particular ideological formation through articulatory practices (see Griggs and Howarth, 2008).

If we revisit our empirical case, we can see that those agents who have sought to garner support for aviation expansion (especially since the 1990s) have endeavoured to link together more and more demands, not only for growth at particular airports but also for jobs across manufacturing and high-technology sectors, cheap leisure flights, increased mobility and the protection of the tourist industry. As more and more demands have been added to the chain of equivalences, so the universal signifier – 'expand the aviation industry in the UK' – has been emptied of content, thus becoming a 'tendentially empty signifier' to use Laclau's term (Laclau, 1996: 47). In the case of the 2003 public consultation surrounding the future of airport expansion in the UK, it was the name of the pro-growth coalition – Freedom to Fly – that came to signify the universal need for growth, thus functioning as an empty signifier to unify the coalition around something that was perceived to be lacking, or at least under threat from those protesting against expansion (Howarth and Griggs, 2006).

Hegemony and policy analysis

The concept of hegemony has been employed in various forms of policy analysis. One impressive account is developed in Maarten Hajer's investigation of ecological modernisation discourse in the Netherlands and the UK during the 1980s and 1990s. Hajer stresses the plurality of discourses at work in the world at any particular time,

while also highlighting the plurality of discourses that are appealed
to in the realm of environmental policy (Hajer, 1995: 45–6). He then
draws on Foucault's theory of discourse to elaborate a programme
of argumentative discourse analysis, in which 'coherence is not an
essential feature of a discourse' but is directly correlated to the level
of institutionalisation of the practices of that discourse (Hajer, 1995:
44). The discourse of law, for example, is highly institutionalised
through repetition, the norm of precedent, jurisprudence and so on,
and is thus highly coherent and structured (Hajer, 1995: 45). In short,
the degree to which policy discourses are coherent depends on their
institutional environment and the history of their implementation
and sedimentation.

The role of these discourses in shaping the actions of individuals
is described in terms of Giddens' structuration theory, in which the
structure is both 'enabling and constraining' (Hajer, 1995: 48); the
subjects of a discursive structure are thus both limited in their actions
by the structure and at the same time create the structure through
their actions (Giddens, 1979, 1984). Given this, individuals have the
capacity for strategic action by creating 'catchphrases', or appropri-
ating the tropes of different discourses, thus changing the structure,
as well as the particular subject positions they inhabit within it, as
best they can, through the actions available to them (Hajer, 1995:
50). For Hajer, this arises from the Foucauldian contention that discursive change occurs or fails to occur through the cumulative results
of a number of contestations at the micro-level (Hajer, 1995: 47).
Hajer also draws on social psychologists like Rom Harré and Michael
Billig to argue that 'storylines' draw together different discursive
strands to 'give meaning to specific physical or social phenomena'
and to 'suggest unity in the bewildering variety of separate discursive
components of a problem' (Hajer, 1995: 56). This produces his argumentative approach to policy analysis, where politics is conceived in
terms of 'a struggle for discursive hegemony in which actors try to
secure support for their definition of reality' (Hajer, 1995: 58–9).

Hajer's work is helpful in suggesting that one of the conditions
for the hegemonic success of a discourse is the degree to which it
is institutionalised and sedimented within organisational practices.
More fully, in assessing the dominance of any given discourse, he
distinguishes between discourse structuration and discourse institutionalisation. The former occurs when significant numbers of
individuals use a discourse to conceptualise and constitute the world,

whereas the latter takes place when the discourse 'solidifies' into particular institutional arrangements and organisational practices that frame policy processes. He thus proposes a two-step procedure for measuring the influence of a discourse: if many people use it to make the world intelligible (discourse structuration) and if it solidifies into institutions and organisational practices (discourse institutionalisation), then it is possible to claim that a particular discourse is dominant (Hajer, 2005: 303–5).

But Hajer's insight needs to be developed further. In fact, it is possible to delineate three levels of hegemony in the policy domain: policy hegemony; institutional hegemony; and societal or cultural hegemony. What is more, these three levels do not necessarily overlap. For one thing, policy hegemony may be achieved in a particular subsystem without the concomitant realisation of institutional or societal hegemony. At the same time, policy change does not translate automatically into a shift in the organisation of a state apparatus, or in the underlying beliefs, norms and values of the wider public.

In this sense, the conditions for hegemonic success in the policy realm are threefold: a change in legislation or laws; the transformation of those institutions that are charged with implementing new rules and regulations, or at least the winning of sufficient compliance among powerful actors within those institutions (which usually involves some form of organisational transfiguration); and the winning of consent and compliance among wider sectors of society. The winning of hegemony in the policy arena is thus a complex process, which involves political victories, wider institutional innovation and even broader cultural transfigurations. These are the yardsticks through which we can measure the winning of hegemony in the policy domain. But of course it is important to note that hegemony does not require *complete* active or passive consent, or indeed full compliance. It requires the winning of consent and compliance in a number of key institutions and 'sites' of a particular social formation, coupled at times with the coercion of resistant forces and recalcitrant elements (Hall, 1988: 7).

The achievement of hegemony in a policy domain, or with respect to a particular practice or regime of practices, is connected to our understanding of myth, social imaginary and fantasy, and thus the role of dislocations and crises, which make their construction and existence possible.[3] Myths in our approach are not irrational, negative or primitive modes of apprehending the world, but new forms of thinking and belief, which emerge in response to the dislocation of social relations and practices. The elaboration of a myth speaks to a situation of crisis by providing a pure form of fullness: the representational means to move beyond a crisis by envisaging a new practice or regime. Ideas about a 'promised land' or a 'New Jerusalem' are instances of myth in this sense: they emerge in response to particular demands and grievances, which are in turn made possible by experiences of dislocation and disruption, by providing new principles of reading, seeing and interpretation (Laclau, 1990: 60).

Myths can thus function as 'surfaces of inscription' on which various dislocations and demands can be written, though this surface is always incomplete. But this means that the fluid and indeterminate nature of these mythical surfaces of inscription serve as the condition of possibility for the constitution of broader 'collective social imaginaries'. This idea is predicated on the unstable relationship between any surface of inscription and the various demands and identities that are inscribed upon it. At this intersection, either the surface is hegemonised (captured) by what it represents, so that the surface is eliminated in favour of literality, or the opposite occurs, and the moment of fullness predominates and the surface becomes a space of representation upon which any number of social demands and any possible dislocations can be inscribed. If the latter occurs, myths are transformed into collective social imaginaries, which can serve as a discursive horizon for an entire social formation (Laclau, 1990: 63–7).

The emergence of myths and the construction of collective social imaginaries thus correspond to our understanding of the production and realisation of hegemony. In an important sense, the successful construction of a social imaginary signals the achievement of hegemony in a policy domain or social order, because it strongly shapes the accepted and taken-for-granted way of doing things. Moreover, the degree to which a new myth and social imaginary conceals its radical contingency by propagating a pure form of fullness – which in turn requires the scapegoating and othering of difference, and thus intimates the possibility of horrific consequences if the myth or imaginary is threatened or disrupted – determines whether or not a new imaginary displays the features of a fantasmatic narrative. In our view, then, the more a new imaginary covers over its own contingency, the more it takes the form of a fantasmatic narrative. Hegemonies built on fantasmatic narratives and identifications are thus inattentive to the contingency, fragility and plurality of things, and are prone to the elaboration of radically utopian or dystopian images of the future.

Discourse and rhetoric

Our discussion of hegemony has highlighted the rhetorical dimension of discourse theory at the ontological level. In our view, rhetorical categories are embedded in the ontological presuppositions of post-structuralist discourse theory. This is because our version of discourse theory arises from a conception of language that questions the founding role of natural reference, in which language is separated from reality, and words are seen to denote objects in the world, coupled with the impossibility of any ultimate literality or fixity of meaning, which means that social relations are conceded an irreducibly symbolic status (Howarth, 2000; Laclau and Mouffe, 1985). For example, discourse theorists emphasise the pivotal role of catachresis – the 'transfer of terms from one place to another', which is 'employed when no proper word exists' (Parker, 1990: 60) – in order to highlight the historicity of meaning and the contingency of objectivity. If, following Cicero and Friedrich Nietzsche, there is no necessary correspondence between words and things, and if our language is somehow lacking in the face of a world with more things than the words we have to name them, then there is a constitutive role for the moment of naming, and that naming is always vulnerable to further rhetorical displacement and redescription (Laclau, 2005: 71–2). But this emphasis on catachresis stems in turn from the centrality of rhetorical categories in the way we understand the social world. There are many sources of this centrality. For example, Jacques Derrida's emphasis on discourse – 'the moment when language invaded the universal problematic' – stresses an irreducible 'play of differences' in the constitution of meaning, while his reworking of the concept of metaphor emphasises the way in which all objectivity involves at its root a catachretic impulse when that which is absent – the thing-in-itself – is made present by the operation of language (Derrida, 1978).[4]

Rhetoric, in this view, is not a cloak or disguise that functions to conceal basic interests and identities, but is partly involved in constituting those identities and interests. Indeed, one could go so far as to say that discourse theory is essentially a tropological approach to social and political theory, in that social relations are constructed in the interstices between literality and figuration, fixity and unfixity, necessity and contingency (see Laclau, 2000: 73–9). But while these ontological assumptions are essential for the conceptual underpinnings of discourse theory, they are useful only when employed in the concrete analysis of empirical events and processes. An ontical analysis of particular case studies is thus an essential supplement to the ontological dimensions of discourse theory. What is more, we must explore the way in which rhetorical categories and figures are integral to the construction of particular practices and regimes.

Now, rather belatedly, there have been efforts more recently to employ rhetorical analysis in political science and public policy. Interpretivists, social constructionists and various schools of discourse analysis have embraced rhetorical analysis, though with different emphases. Bevir and Rhodes (2003) develop an explicitly interpretivist perspective that centres on individual agents whose malleable beliefs are situated in incomplete discursive traditions. But, though their approach makes room for the role of rhetorical analysis, it is conceded only an instrumental value, which enables actors to articulate and advance their interests and preferences (Glynos and Howarth, 2007: 75). In other words, not unlike Riker's (1986, 1996) rationalist perspective, they lay too much emphasis on the strategic dimension of rhetoric.

Other policy theorists, such as Maarten Hajer (2009), Christopher Hood (1998) and Dvora Yanow (1996), have incorporated the role of storylines and metaphors to account for the formation of discourse coalitions, and for the justification, legitimation and implementation of policy decisions. In this respect, their work extends Donald Schön's (1993) concept of 'generative metaphors', which are defined as often implicit or even unconscious figures or tropes that structure the way in which policy problems are seen and tackled. For example, images and talk of 'urban decay', which connect poor housing and neighbourhood infrastructure to the idea of 'tooth decay', evoke certain associations about a phenomenon that makes possible the characterisation of a problem while at the same time prescribing solutions for its remedy, which are rooted in the idea of human well-being. Finally, theorists Norman Fairclough, Ruth Wodak and Lilie Chouliaraki also focus on the analysis of rhetoric in developing their project of critical discourse analysis (Chouliaraki and Fairclough, 1999; Fairclough, 2001; Fairclough and Wodak, 1997). But, though they contribute important resources to political analysis by highlighting relevant tropes and logics, their primary concern is to expose the false consciousness and fallacies that conceal more basic interests and desires.

In seeking to go beyond the instrumental conceptions of rational choice and certain versions of interpretivism, while not restricting the role of rhetoric to an analysis of figures like metaphor, Alan Finlayson elaborates a more constitutive conception of rhetoric, which he calls rhetorical political analysis. Starting with a distinctive agonistic conception of politics, which is understood as 'the "arena" within which we see expressed the irreducible and contested plurality of public life, the ineradicable contestation of differing world-views', rhetorical political analysis focuses on the role of argumentative practices and persuasion in the inevitable disputes over political decisions and courses of action that are the very stuff of democratic politics (Finlayson, 2007: 552). An important strength of Finalyson's proposal is that he provides a series of analytical strategies for investigating different kinds of argumentative practice in different contexts of political life. For example, he draws attention to: various 'rhetorical situations' that provide the rules within which arguments take place; the form and content of arguments, that is, the type of argument and the substantive subject under dispute; the various problematisations and framings of issues; the various genres of rhetoric, especially deliberative political rhetoric; the role of narratives and commonplaces in the structuring of arguments; and finally the three basic forms of appeal in rhetorical strategies, that is, logos, ethos and pathos (see Gottweis, 2006).

Critical for our explanation of the changing politics and policy of airport expansion is the making and breaking of projects or discourse coalitions. Framed in terms of hegemonic practices, as we have already noted, the immediate focus in this regard is to explore the intersecting logics of equivalence and difference, to characterise and explain the coupling or decoupling of heterogeneous social demands. But this also involves important rhetorical and strategic elements. As we intimate above, William Riker, one of the founders of contemporary rational choice theory, has supplemented formal rational choice explanations of decision-making with an emphasis on the role of rhetoric in the forging and disruption of political coalitions (Riker, 1986, 1996). In a telling phrase, Riker coined the term 'heresthetic' to capture the 'art of political manipulation' by which politicians use a variety of strategic devices to bring about favourable outcomes (Riker, 1986).[5] These devices include: practices of determining who are to be the relevant sets of agents in a particular situation; inventing new actions and political practices that circumvent existing ones; framing and reframing the evaluation of outcomes by others so that actors can improve their prospects of achieving goals; and altering the perceptions and character of individual preferences by various rhetorical operations and interventions (Riker, 1996; Shepsle, 2003: 309–10).[6]

But of equal importance in this regard is the construction of new discourses that can win over subjects to a particular project or coalition while disorganising and marginalising opposing coalitions. One way of doing this involves the practice of rhetorical or paradiastolic redescription (for example Rorty, 1989; Skinner, 2002). In the contemporary context, this trope has been most developed by Quentin Skinner, for whom the practice of rhetorical redescription consists

> of replacing a given evaluative description with a rival term that serves to picture the action no less plausibly, but serves at the same time to place it in a contrasting moral light. You seek to persuade your audience to accept your new description, and thereby to adopt a new attitude towards the action concerned. (Skinner, 2002: 183, cited in Howarth, 2005: 343)

Skinner illustrates his point by reinterpreting a famous passage in Nietzsche's opening essay of *The Genealogy of Morality*, in which the German philosopher asks the reader to 'have a little look down into the secret of how *ideals are fabricated* on this earth?' (Nietzsche, 1994: 27–8). Intervening in the European tradition of thinking, Nietzsche's aim in this aphorism is to demonstrate how 'the slave morality of the Christians succeeded in overturning the moral world of antiquity by rhetorically redescribing a number of vices as their neighbouring virtues' (Skinner, 1999: 70). In Nietzsche's incomparable words,

> impotence which doesn't retaliate is being turned into 'goodness'; timid baseness is being turned into 'humility'; submission to people one hates is being turned into 'obedience' (actually towards someone who, they say, orders this submission – they call him God). The inoffensiveness of the weakling, the very cowardice with which he is richly endowed, his standing-by-the-door, his inevitable position of having to wait, are all given good names such as 'patience', which is also called *the* virtue; not-being-able-to-take-revenge is called not-wanting-to-take-revenge, it might even be forgiveness ('for *they* know not what they do – but we know what *they* are doing!'). They are also talking about 'loving your enemy' – and sweating while they do it. (Nietzsche, 1994: 27–8)

In short, according to Nietzsche, 'This workshop where *ideals are fabricated* – it seems to me just to stink of lies' (Nietzsche, 1994: 28). Even more telling, as Skinner puts it, Nietzsche's own rhetoric makes visible a highly successful practice of paradiastole, in which classical vices were renamed and redescribed as Christian virtues. Indeed, for Skinner (and for us) this practice is a key logic through which one discourse can displace and replace another. As Skinner suggests, it is not the conceptual content of events, practices or actions which, through their descriptions, determine the invoked name (see Glynos and Howarth, 2007). Instead, the conceptual change is the outcome of debates over how to characterise or name something:

> The more we succeed in persuading people that a given evaluative term applies in circumstances in which they may never have thought of applying it, the more broadly and inclusively we shall persuade them to employ the given term in the appraisal of social and political life. (Skinner, 2002: 186, cited in Glynos and Howarth, 2007: 187)

The logic of rhetorical redescription thus goes hand in hand with the practice of structuring the terrain of argumentation so that certain demands and interests are organised in and out of the policy-making process.

To adapt Elmer Schattschneider's marvellous phrase, all forms of argumentation exude a partiality in favour of exploiting certain kinds of conflict and suppressing others, because argumentation and rhetoric are, in his words, 'the mobilization of bias': some issues and arguments are organised into politics while others are organised out (Schattschneider, 1960: 71). For example, if opponents of aviation expansion were to accept that the current struggles over airport expansion were about the achievement of sustainable aviation, they would immediately rule out more radical demands and claims. This logic of rhetorical redescription and the structuring of various terrains of argumentation finds echoes in what Peter Bachrach and Morton Baratz famously called the 'power of non-decisionmaking', that is, the decision not to decide, by immunising core issues from debate and contestation through, for example, agenda-setting (Bachrach and Baratz, 1962, 1963, 1970).

Overall, the current theoretical discussions about rhetoric in political analysis and policy research, either implicitly or explicitly, ask us to choose between a strategic or constitutive conception of rhetoric, or between a focus on particular rhetorical devices or the role of arguments, or between a more descriptive or critical orientation. But for poststructuralist discourse theorists these oppositions are not so stark. In political discourse theory, with our distinction between the ontological and the ontical, we can focus both on the constitutive character of rhetoric (and language more generally) in our understanding of social relations, and on the instrumental use of particular figures (such as metaphors, which are condensed in particular signifiers, phrases and images) in constructing coalitions and hegemonic projects; we can also focus on particular tropes and the role of arguments in practices of decision-making and persuasion; and we can seek both to understand and to criticise arguments in relation to broader discourses and ideologies. For example, metaphor helps us to develop a grammar of concepts for the understanding of practices and regimes, as well as the particular devices that can hold divergent demands and interests together in precarious fixations.

The affective dimension of policy practices

Hegemony is thus a form of rule and a quintessential type of political practice, and we have stressed the importance of rhetoric in our approach. However, we have yet to say something about why and how particular policies 'stick'. How and why are subjects gripped by the particular devices or signifiers in which public policies are formulated and communicated? Or, conversely, how and why are subjects not held fast by such discourses? We address these questions by turning to the affective dimension of policy change and by considering the related notion of 'lack' and the unconscious and affective investments of subjects in certain rhetorical devices, signifiers and images. It is here that the Lacanian logic of fantasy, which has been developed by theorists such as Slavoj Žižek, can focus our attention on the enjoyment subjects procure from their identifications with certain signifiers and figures (Glynos, 2001, 2008a, 2008b; Lacan, 2006; Žižek, 1989, 1997).

It is important to stress that fantasy is not an ideological illusion or a form of false consciousness that comes between a subject and social reality. On the contrary, in the Lacanian approach, fantasies partly organise an individual's perceptions of reality and structure their understanding of social relations and orders by covering over their radical contingency. Social relations thus appear to subjects as natural and sedimented (Glynos and Howarth, 2007: 117–20). Indeed, one of the indicators of the 'success' of a fantasy is its very invisibility: the fact that it supports social reality without our being conscious of it. On the other hand, the visibility of fantasmatic figures and devices – their disclosure and appearance as fantasies – means that they cease to function properly in this regard. Of course, there are different ways to break with or come to terms with social fantasies and their grip, ranging from their repression to their traversal.

The logic of fantasy thus operates to bring a form of ideological closure to the radical contingency of social relations, and to naturalise the different relations of domination within which a subject is enmeshed. It does this through a fantasmatic narrative or discourse, which promises a fullness-to-come once a named or implied obstacle is overcome – the beatific dimension of fantasy – or that predicts disaster if the obstacle cannot be surmounted, which might be termed the horrific dimension of fantasy, though in any particular instance the two work hand in hand (Stavrakakis, 1999: 108–9; 2007). The beatific side, as Žižek puts it, has 'a stabilizing dimension' on policy regimes, while the horrific aspect possesses 'a destabilizing dimension', where the other is presented as a threatening or irritating force that must be rooted out or destroyed (Žižek, 1998: 192). On the whole, then, fantasmatic logics capture the various ways in which subjects organise their enjoyment by binding themselves to particular objects and representations so as 'to resolve some fundamental antagonism' (Žižek, 1997: 11).

In fact, we can see such fantasmatic appeals in operation in the post-war development of UK aviation policy. Throughout the post-war institution of the regime of aviation expansion, the threat of foreign competition, in particular from the United States, operated as something akin to a horrific fantasy for UK policy-makers and manufacturers. If actualised, this fantasy carried the threat of destroying UK aviation and its drive to secure global markets in the post-war period. At the same time, politicians and policy-makers repeatedly articulated beatific appeals to aviation; the growth of civil and military aircraft manufacturing, the development of more sophisticated and safer technologies, the very experience of flying and the 'jet-set', as well as the promise of mass tourism, were intimately connected with a discourse of modernisation and progress, which was an essential ingredient in countering the perception of the UK's inexorable economic decline. More recently, in the run-up to the 2003 public consultation over the future of aviation, the Labour government and supporters of expansion sought (but ultimately failed) to rhetorically redefine the question of airport expansion in terms of sustainable aviation, articulating a beatific fantasy in which aviation expansion and environmental sustainability could be linked in a harmonious and mutually reinforcing fashion.

The role of subjective desire and attachment thus adds further elements to the conceptual grammar of poststructuralist policy analysis by providing the means to explore the way in which identities are stabilised and given direction, as well as the moments when such identifications begin to lose their adhesion or fail to resonate at all. But this ontological focus must still be articulated in particular empirical contexts; in other words, the basic categories and logics of the approach have to inform our concrete analysis of particular practices, thus modifying or adding to our existing interpretations of policy change or stability. In short, they must be employed at the ontical level of investigation (Mulhall, 1996: 4). Yet this raises methodological questions about the operationalisation of psychoanalytical categories and logics. How do we study discourses? How do we describe, explain, criticise and evaluate? Here we turn to the logics of critical explanation.

Conducting critical policy studies: logics of critical explanation

Building on the work of Glynos and Howarth (2007, 2008a), and what they have termed the 'logics of critical explanation', our response to the questions posed at the end of the last section can be elaborated in five linked steps: problematisation; retroduction; logics; articulation; and critique. In this section, we describe each step and show how they are interconnected.

1. Problematisation

First, following Foucault, our approach begins with the task of problematising a particular practice, policy or regime. This task requires an engagement both with the field of academic questions pertaining to one's object of analysis, as well as with the social and political issues that confront the analyst in a specific historical conjuncture (Foucault, 1984a). In the case of UK aviation policy, as we shall show in the next chapter, there is no single 'problem', but rather a series of ongoing problematisations, which vary according to the interpretations of different stakeholders. Moreover, each problematisation exhibits different dimensions of aviation, be it the political economy of aviation and international competition, the limits of democratic stakeholder engagement in decision-making or the management of international regulation and environmental risk.

On a more theoretical level, the practice of problematisation in the domain of 'politics' concerns 'a movement of critical analysis in which one tries to see how the different solutions to a problem have been constructed; but also how these different solutions result from a specific form of problematisation' (Foucault, 1997: 118–19). In his later writings, Foucault employs this approach in his accounts of governmentality, neoliberalism and the hermeneutics of the self. For example, as Foucault presciently noted in the *Birth of Biopolitics*, the architects of neoliberal discourse called for a novel series of governmental technologies and rationalities that problematised the role of government and the state in fostering economic growth and efficiency, and in preserving the fragile freedom of the market economy by targeting and acting upon its conditions of existence. This was pursued by defending the precarious rules of the market order from unwelcome state interventions, which would inevitably distort the logic of free competition, often through the mobilisation of fascist and totalitarian others, and by cultivating, regulating and disciplining the identities and subjectivities that were required for its operation (Foucault, 2008).

The technique of problematisation yields a potentially distinctive form of critical policy analysis, as it effectively synthesises his previously elaborated archaeological and genealogical methods of discourse analysis (Foucault, 1985: 11–12). Put in more programmatic terms, the practice of problematisation begins with a pressing and unsettling series of issues in the present – no matter how vague or indeterminate they may initially be – which then elicit thought and critical engagement (Foucault, 1977). These perplexing phenomena thus constitute the necessary starting point for any creative engagement and intervention (for example Foucault, 1977: 23). But writing a 'history of the present' does not involve a presentist or teleological conception of history, in which the historian understands the past in terms of the present, or sees in the past the origins of the present. Instead, it begins with the problematisation of an issue confronting the historian in society, and then seeks to examine its contingent historical and political emergence. The genealogist or critic thus seeks to uncover the 'lowly origins' and 'play of dominations' that produced the phenomenon, while also showing possibilities excluded by the dominant logics of historical development. By producing alternative narratives, the genealogist thus discloses new possibilities – alternative ideals perhaps – foreclosed by existing interpretations.

The construction of genealogical narratives performs a number of explanatory and critical functions in our approach. On the one hand, they are important in challenging sharp, and thus misleading, continuities and discontinuities among events and phenomena, often favoured by essentialist or teleological approaches, by stressing the contingencies, reiterations and complexities of dispersed events. In Foucault's words,

> Genealogy does not resemble the evolution of a species and does not map the destiny of a people. On the contrary, to follow the complex course of descent is to maintain passing events in their proper dispersion; it is to identify the accidents, the minute deviations – or conversely the complete reversals – the errors, the false appraisals and the faulty calculations that give birth to those things that continue to exist and have value for us. (Foucault, 1984a: 81)

On the other hand, the careful elaboration of a genealogical narrative focuses on key moments of arising, when various possibilities for action and identification become visible, clashes between opposed forces occur and certain decisions are taken. Just 'as it is wrong to search for descent in an uninterrupted continuity', argues Foucault, so 'we should avoid thinking of emergence as the final term of a historical development.... These developments may appear as a culmination, but they are merely the current episode in a series of subjugations' (Foucault, 1984a: 83).

In this approach, then, an object of study is never simply given or self-evident. It is always constructed by the analyst in a series of relaying movements with the problematisations that arise out of the phenomena investigated. This means that a range of disparate empirical facts, events and trends have to be constituted as a problem, and the problem has to be located at the appropriate level of abstraction and complexity. The problem then has to be addressed and perhaps resolved – or at times 'dissolved' – by a careful genealogical disentangling, which exposes the various historical threads and trajectories that constitute the problems and identities we confront in the present; and the latter emerge only via the various struggles and political clashes between forces in critical conjunctures over time (Foucault, 1984a). Indeed, this genealogical accounting of a problem and its ensuing identity lays bare excluded possibilities that can, in turn, form the basis for alternative problematisations and projects.

The notion of problematisation in Foucault's writings has often been associated with abstract philosophical discussions and topics – problems about 'being', 'truth', 'sexuality' or 'subjectivity', for example – though even here he insists that the analysis of questions of a 'general import' must be analysed 'in their *historically unique form*' (Foucault, 1984b: 49; our emphasis). In our case, however, problems have to be articulated at the much more concrete level of policy analysis. But here we are assisted by the fact that the strategy of problematisation has been adopted by a number of poststructuralists and critical theorists in the fields of history, as well as social and political analysis (see Campbell 1998; Flynn, 2005; Glynos and Howarth, 2007: 167–71; Rose, 1999). Nikolas Rose, for example, has drawn inspiration from Foucault to indicate how the 'problem of government' is framed by a certain understanding of freedom as the absence of coercion or domination (Rose, 1999: 11).

Also drawing on Foucault, as well as poststructuralist discourse analysis and feminist theory, Carol Bacchi begins with the idea that problems are not given, but are social constructions. She thus challenges the view that governments simply react to pre-existing problems by arguing that they are active in creating or producing various problems. In advancing her arguments, Bacchi does not claim that the issues or experiences to which a policy refers are not real, but rather that 'calling these conditions "problems" or "social problems" fixes them in ways that need to be interrogated' (Bacchi, 2010: 4; see also Bacchi, 2009). By focusing on problematisations within specific policy texts and programmes, rather than problems that are assumed to exist, she explores their role in practices of governing and policy-making (Bacchi, 2009). Bacchi focuses her attention on the way in which specific public proposals contain a particular representation of a problem, before interrogating the latter's conditions of possibility and then developing alternatives. We are also interested in the way problems are constituted within governmental frameworks and programmes. But we seek to extend the notion of problematisation in and beyond the policy field to include those political practices and processes that lead to the production or transformation of policies and proposals, as well as the ongoing societal struggles to shape and modify their implementation and reformulation of policies. Finally, while we acknowledge the importance of government in constructing problems, we also insist that societal problematisations are vital in shaping and changing public problems. Policies and the way they shape the terms of political debate are thus themselves produced through problemat-isations articulated by a wide range of social actors.

The concept of problematisation can thus be applied to a range of philosophical and non-philosophical topics. Yet at this high level of methodological abstraction, it is a multidimensional technique that needs further fleshing out if it is to be helpful for the analy-sis of politics and public policy. At least two aspects need further specification. In the first place, like many other policy issues, prob-lematisations occur in different social sites and at varying spatial scales.[7] Problems of aviation are constituted locally, nationally and globally; they span social, political, economic and cultural dimen-sions of analysis. The structural focus of this analysis maps onto the archaeological component of Foucault's method of problematisation. Issues and paradoxes have thus to be constructed by furnishing the rules, assumptions and conditions that gave rise to them. In addition to these spatial and structural questions, practices of problematisation also occur in different historical conjunctures. This focus on critical moments foregrounds the temporal dimension of problematisation, thus highlighting the genealogical element of Foucault's approach, and it highlights the narrative quality of his critical explanations.

The method of problematisation thus incorporates the spatial and temporal dimensions, while stressing the notions of descent and emer-gence as opposed to the search for origins and essence. Its aim is to produce genealogical narratives of pressing issues that confront us in the present by problematising misleading narratives, which are in turn premised on particular ways of constituting and seeing the problem, and by elaborating alternative stories that highlight the contingency and undecidability of historical trajectories. But though it is analytic-ally useful to separate out the spatial and temporal dimensions of problematisation, while exploring events in their proper perspective, it is still important to stress that any actual object of investigation is always overdetermined.

Drawing on Foucault, then, we begin with the practice of problem-atisation, which for us is one of the most difficult and yet vital tasks in critical policy analysis. Yet Foucault's approach has been criticised for its alleged explanatory and normative deficits (for example Habermas, 1987; Taylor, 1985b, 1985c, 1989). There are some commentators who doubt whether Foucault's talk of problematisation adds any further substance to his methods of analysis, or whether it is little more than a retrospective formalisation of his Nietzschean-inspired genealogical

approach to the study of history and society. Other critics have questioned the explanatory and critical adequacy of problematisation.
Does the practice of problematisation lead to a kind of descriptivism
that does not and cannot explain social phenomena in causal terms?
Does it entail a kind of 'crypto-normativism' (to use Habermas's
expression) that criticises and evaluates various objects of study
without an articulated ground or foundation for their study? Like
other poststructuralist perspectives, Foucault's work stands charged
of a vicious 'performative self-contradiction' that engages in the practice of critique and explanation without furnishing the grounds for
that criticism (see for example Habermas, 1987). Alternatively, he is
accused of engaging in a purely 'negative critique' that does not – and
cannot – propose alternative normative ideals and values with which
to confront the relations of power and domination he analyses.

The validity of these allegations is disputed, but we cannot enter
into the vigorous debates they have spawned here. (Without offering
reasons in this text, we believe that they miss their mark by some
distance.) Nonetheless, our strategy is to proceed *as if* they were
true, for the next steps of our method seek explicitly to bring out the
explanatory and critical aspects of the logics approach. As against the
allegation that Foucault and other interpretivists simply tell stories
without explaining the phenomena they investigate, we argue that the
appropriate *form of explanation* in critical policy analysis is retroductive, and not purely inductive or deductive.

2. Retroduction

This brings us to the second step of the logics approach. Borrowing
from Charles Sanders Peirce's idea of retroductive reasoning, it furnishes the resources to develop an appropriate *form* of explanation
in policy analysis (Peirce, 1957). As Derek Sayer puts it, the task of
retroduction 'amounts to ... observing a fact and then professing to
say what ... it was that gave rise to the fact' (Sayer, 1983: 116). In brief,
then, a *retroductive form of explanation* in the social sciences consists
in the positing of a hypothesis or proto-explanation, which insofar as
it renders a problematised phenomenon intelligible, can then be said
to account for it.

More fully, the explanatory task begins with a paradox or a wondrous phenomenon. In our empirical case, one such phenomenon was
the failure of the New Labour government to implement its desire to
expand the UK's airport capacity in the aftermath of the 2003 white

paper. A further paradox that we explore in the book arises from the sharpening contradiction between aviation as a necessary driver of economic growth, on the one hand, and its depiction as an integral cause of climate change, on the other.

Anomalies or paradoxes like these must then be constructed as a tractable *explanandum*, for which an appropriate *explanans* can be advanced. A wondrous phenomenon is thus rendered more intelligible if and only if a putative explanans were to hold (Hanson, 1961; Peirce, 1957). In our case, for example, we advance the hypothesis that it was the ability of campaigners and protesters to draw equivalences between airport expansions, the aviation industry and climate change, thus bringing about a resignification of these phenomena, which can (partially) explain the change we are investigating. Critical explanation thus proceeds by seeking to render a problematised phenomenon more intelligible. It involves the production of a hypothesis that is tested through a to-and-fro movement with the available empirical data until we are persuaded that the putative explanans clears away the confusion and properly fits the phenomenon under consideration.

But while a commitment to retroduction problematises the dominant causal model, and the inductive and deductive modes of reasoning upon which it depends, it still leaves a number of possible candidates – or particular combinations of candidates – that can provide a retroductive mode of critical explanation. These include approaches that emphasise the ideas and self-interpretations of social actors, as well as those that stress the role of causal mechanisms in overcoming the problems with the law-like model of explanation (Glynos and Howarth, 2008b: 7).

3. Logics

Building on the arguments developed by Glynos and Howarth (2007) in *Logics of Critical Explanation*, we argue that the content of any putative explanans should be couched principally in terms of logics, rather than laws, causal mechanisms or cultural interpretations. This, then, is the third component of the logics approach. The logic of a discourse captures the rules that govern a practice, policy or policy regime, as well as the conditions that make such rules possible and impossible.

Three types of logic are singled out in the approach. Social logics enable one to characterise social practices in different contexts. They are thus multiple and contextual: there are as many logics as there are situations that an investigator explores. They may capture economic, social, cultural and political processes: a particular logic of competition or commodification, for example, or a specific logic of bureaucratisation in a particular social context. For instance, 'enforced ethnic and racial separation for political domination and economic exploitation' is a stylised way of characterising the logic of apartheid discourse in South Africa (see for example Norval, 1996).

But while the discernment of social logics relies to some extent on the self-interpretations of actors involved in the practice, social logics are not sufficient to explain and evaluate practices. We thus supplement the recourse to social logics by introducing political and fantasmatic logics (Glynos and Howarth, 2007, 2008a, 2008b). Political logics enable analysts to explain and potentially criticise the emergence and formation of a social practice or regime. Of particular importance in this regard are the logics of equivalence and difference. The former enable the research to grasp the way in which political frontiers are constructed via the linking together of social demands and identities, while the latter capture the way in which demands are negated, disarticulated, mediated and negotiated by various institutions. Politics is thus understood as the contestation and institution of social relations and practices, and it discloses the contingent character of any practice or institution by showing the role of power and exclusion in its formation. As such, political logics can help us to show other possibilities of social organisation when the 'ignoble origins' of rules and norms are reactivated, contested and instituted. Put like this, it is no coincidence that the concept of political logics is intimately related to Foucault's method of genealogy, which enabled Foucault to chart the complex lines of descent and emergence in the formation of an identity or a rule, and to disclose alternative paths and possibilities.

Fantasmatic logics provide the means to explain and potentially criticise the way subjects are gripped by discourses. Fantasy is intimately connected to the category of ideology, which is here understood as the logic of concealing the contingency of social relations and naturalising the relations of domination in discourses or meaningful practices. An important focus in this regard is on the production of certain fantasmatic narratives, which structure the way different social subjects are attached to certain signifiers, and on the different types of 'enjoyment' subjects procure in identifying with discourses and believing the things they do. The identification of fantasmatic logics thus enables us to disclose a particular way in which subjects identify and are gripped by a discourse or set of practices. That is, they allow us to detect the particular narratives that provide ideological closure for the subject, thereby masking over the contingency of social relations and naturalising the relations of domination in discourses or meaningful practices such that they appear to subjects as natural and 'given'.

4. Articulation

Any prospective explanans will inevitably comprise a plurality of logics, as well as other causal mechanisms, descriptions and empirical conditions, which have to be linked together in order to render a problematic phenomenon intelligible. Here we stress the method of articulation – the fourth element of the approach – which involves the practice of linking together different concepts and empirical raw materials to produce an explanatory complex of many relations and determinations. This logic is articulatory in that it seeks to gather together and modify the identity of each of the elements that is combined to form a specific explanans of a practice or regime (see Marx, 1973: 100). For example, in her study of health care practices, Annemarie Mol identifies different logics of treating diabetes, where she seeks to pinpoint what is 'local', 'fragile' and yet pertinently coherent in their articulation (Mol, 2008: 8–9). In identifying these logics, she alludes to the practice of articulation, in which she acknowledges that she has not exhausted the range of potential logics in her study, preferring to leave out much of the 'noise in order to distill a "pure" form out of mixed events' (Mol, 2008: 10).

A question that often arises with respect to our approach concerns the identification of relevant rhetorical figures or theoretical concepts that constitute an explanatory chain. How do we know what counts in reality as an empty signifier, or a relevant metaphor or metonym? As against subsumptive logics, which are invariably built upon a spurious logic of scientific operationalisation that sets out the necessary and sufficient conditions for 'applying' a concept to an object, we favour an approach based on intuition, theoretical expertise and the method of articulation. This means that researchers have to immerse themselves in a given discursive field consisting of texts, documents, interviews and social practices, before drawing on their theoretical expertise to make particular judgements as to whether something counts as an x: is x a metaphor, logic of equivalence or an empty signifier? They then have to decide upon its overall import for the problem investigated.

Such theoretical expertise is acquired by learning and using the specific language games which form the grammar of the researcher's theoretical approach. And if, indeed, a practice or signifier does count as an instance of an *x*, an integral part of this logic of judgement consists in deciding what the precise relevance and importance of the *x* is in constructing a narrative that explains a phenomenon, or dissolves a particular paradox. These elements – intuitions, theoretical expertise, judgements and so forth – form part of what we call the method of articulation. This method consists of a practice of explanation that links specific theoretical and empirical elements together (*explanans*), in order to account for a singular, problematised phenomenon (*explanandum*). In this picture, the ultimate 'proof of the pudding' consists in the production of narratives explaining problematised phenomena, which in turn depends partly on the relevant community of critical scholars.

A final issue in this regard concerns the fact that we characterise certain signifiers or practices in different ways in different contexts. In our study, for example, the notion of sustainable aviation has multiple functions and meanings. This variation reflects, in part, its different usages in the multiple historical contexts and practices in which it appears. But it is also because, in our judgement (and thus in our characterisations), the term operates in various ways with differential effects. For example, the Labour government struggled to turn the idea of sustainable aviation into an empty signifier or generative metaphor that would hold various demands and storylines together, thus concealing any tensions within its proposed discourse. But its opponents, by contrast, sought to destabilise this project and struggled to turn the term into what we have called a floating signifier. If the latter were to be successful, which in our view it was, then the meaning of sustainable aviation would become more indeterminate and thus an object of fierce political contestation. At other times, we use the notion of sustainable aviation to characterise New Labour's overall discourse on aviation. But, again, it is the specific context and our empirical narrative (built on our judgements) that serves as the ultimate criterion to evaluate the plausibility and consistency of our claims. In short, then, we have applied various theoretical concepts to the ostensibly same phenomenon or words, although it is through these characterisations that we have sought to discern different rhetorical operations and political practices.

5. Critique

Finally, each of these logics, when articulated together to form an explanatory complex, enables the critic to render visible the contingent character of a practice, policy or institution by showing the role of power, exclusion and closure in its formation and reproduction. As Foucault made explicit in his later writings, exhibiting the contingency of a practice or identity provides a vital inroad into its critique and evaluation. His genealogical studies were carried out in part to 'separate out, from the contingency that has made us what we are, the possibility of no longer being, doing, or thinking what we are, do, or think' (Foucault, 1984b: 46).

Constructed around different responses to radical contingency, social, political and fantasmatic logics endeavour to formalise these intuitions and tactics. The practice of critique is predicated on the centrality of political and fantasmatic logics, for their discernment enables us to highlight the contingency and undecidability of particular social relations and structures. The political dimension is evident in those conjunctures when social relations are formed and challenged by the exercise of power, and where exclusions and foreclosures occur. They thus indicate the moments of the potential reactivation of previously taken political decisions and institutionalisations, thus making possible various forms of resistance against systems of domination. The ideological dimension is evident in those fantasmatic narratives that function to conceal contingency and naturalise relations of domination.

In contrast to the role of ideology and political domination, we propose a conception of ethics that starts from an acknowledgement of the radical contingency and fragility of things, while affirming the contestability of our political decisions and social practices. As we argue in our concluding thoughts, where in the light of our empirical analysis we address the possibility of a reasonable policy of sustainable aviation in the UK, this ethical counterweight to the ideological dimension of social relations and the naturalisation of domination is a form of critique that affirms a particular role for government. But it also seeks to articulate and endorse alternative normative proposals, which we do in chapter 7.

Questions of data

In advancing our arguments, we draw upon the tools and techniques of documentary analysis and semi-structured interviews, concentrating systematically on the 'official public discourses' of the opposed forces engaged in the struggle over airport expansion in the UK. Part of our focus is on the heterogeneous set of policy documents – white papers, government legislation, policy papers and guidance – which crystallised successive government thinking on the issue. Here we focus on policies as texts or written representations, whose inscription presupposes certain codes, styles of argumentation, presentational modes and forms of language (Ball, 1994: 16–21). Such texts are, of course, produced by an array of actors, who seek to impose a measure of control or authority over the meaning and import of the policy documents. Policies are in this sense an assemblage of 'becomings', whose significance and implication are an object of ongoing political contestation. But they are also consumed in particular ways by diverse subjects, who seek equally to interpret and reiterate them in certain ways, thus shaping their meaning in the process. As we have intimated, our analysis employs the tools of rhetorical and literary theory, Foucaultian problematisation and Lacanian psychoanalysis, to investigate the key figures and tropes that feature in policy texts, as well as the ways in which problems and objects are constructed, and certain narratives appear and function.

But it is important to stress that we do not confine ourselves to the narrow study of policy as 'text', for we also employ a broader notion of textuality that includes a wide range of signifying practices (Derrida, 1981). Put differently, we also focus on policy as discourse, thus extending our approach to include the way in which linguistic and non-linguistic structures (which are intertwined) condition and constrain possible ways of thinking, speaking and acting (Ball, 1994: 21–4). Here the focus is less on individual actors and their intentions and strategies, and more on the discursive systems within which they are positioned. Such discourses, which in our view are the product of articulatory practices, enable the construction of particular objects, concepts, subjects and styles of thinking, though they also exclude other elements, which cannot be spoken about or acted upon. As we have noted, our intention in this regard is to seek to excavate the rules of discourse by discerning the ensemble of social, political and fantasmatic logics which are articulated together in any particular discursive formation. Finally, we are interested in the political forces and agencies that shape these rules and logics, which we analyse through our poststructuralist conception of hegemony.

We also focus on a carefully selected set of media statements made by key agents and groups; interviews given by elite actors; articles and reports that appeared in major national newspapers; and a series of in-depth semi-structured interviews that were conducted with important social actors. We also analyse the practices and political struggles of the consultation processes which took place between December 2000 and December 2003, and then during the attempts to implement the plans for expansion in 2008 and 2009. Informing these practices of data collection and analysis is an interpretive approach to the identification and study of different communities of meaning. This means that alongside our observation and characterisation of the discursive practices of the different forces involved, we examine the linguistic and non-linguistic practices of the actors involved by seeking to discern their different logics; their construction of equivalential relations between disparate demands; and the role of metaphors and empty signifiers in their articulation of specific discourses (see for example Howarth, 2004; Yanow, 2000).

More specifically, the archive of documents constructed for this study includes all official reports released by the Department for Transport from the opening of consultation by the New Labour government in 2000 until the coalition government's release of its draft aviation policy framework in 2012. The assembled corpus comprised different genres of documents, from scoping documents, consultation documents and ministerial speeches through to white papers, aviation policy reports and departmental responses to parliamentary select committees. It was supplemented by three further systematic documentary reviews. First, we surveyed environmental policy reports and white papers from other government ministries (notably the Treasury, the Department for Environment, Food and Rural Affairs, the Department of Energy and Climate Change, the Department of Trade and Industry and their changing affiliations over time). We identified, in particular, documents that made reference to aviation policy and transport policy. Secondly, we examined aviation reports from a range of public bodies, including, for example, the Sustainable Development Commission, the Committee on Climate Change and the Civil Aviation Authority, as well as parliamentary bodies and political parties, namely the Environmental Audit Committee and the Conservative Party policy review under David

Cameron. Finally, archival research through the online search engine of the National Archives was undertaken to bring together minutes of Cabinet discussions, draft white papers and official reports at decisive moments of post-war airport expansion, which we supplemented with the official reports of government inspectors at public inquiries into expansion at Heathrow, Gatwick and Stansted from the 1970s to the 1990s.

In addition, we assembled a corpus of policy reports, position statements, briefings and press releases from local resident groups, anti-aviation expansion lobbies and environmental pressure groups, scientific and expert bodies, as well as think-tanks, representatives of the aviation industry, trade unions, chambers of commerce, and air-port owners and their trade associations. In so doing, we undertook over the course of the study searches of the online organisational and press archives of Stop Stansted Expansion, AirportWatch and HACAN ClearSkies, bringing together responses to public consulta-tions and public inquiries, position statements and press releases. This was supported by further reviews of the webpage archives and content of groups such as Plane Stupid, the Aviation Environment Federation, the British Airports Authority and the British Air Trans-port Association. We also systematically analysed the web-based online organisational archives of Freedom to Fly, Flying Matters and the Sustainable Aviation initiative. These surveys were supplemented by the analysis of airport expansion articles in the national press, specifically during consultation periods for the 2003 white paper and the third runway at Heathrow. This included online searches of the following newspapers: *Guardian, Financial Times, Independent, Observer, Daily Mail, Telegraph, Sun* and *London Evening Standard*.

Our use of semi-structured interviews has generated one particular 'space' for dialogue with primary stakeholders. We first made contact with stakeholders during the consultation for the 2003 white paper, and our engagement with them continued throughout the consulta-tion, as well as the campaign against the third runway at Heathrow. During our ongoing investigation of the case we also endeavoured to send draft reports and papers to stakeholders for their comment and discussion, and have used these exchanges to modify our inter-pretations. (In fact, our overall interaction with relevant actors and groups goes back to our analyses of the ways in which various groups and coalitions sought to prevent the expansion of Manchester airport during the mid-1990s – see Griggs and Howarth, 2002, 2004.) This

longitudinal engagement, especially evident in our in-depth interviews, has offered the opportunity for us (and the stakeholders) to
engage in practices of critical reflection; to 'test' our emerging interpretations of the case; and to assess ongoing strategies and tactics.

Conclusion

We have thus outlined our main ontological presuppositions, concepts
and logics with which we analyse our research problems, articulating them within our discursive approach to policy analysis. What is
more, these elements are connected together by Foucault's method
of problematisation to provide an overall logic of analysis. It will be
recalled that Foucault's later writing integrates his archaeological – or
synchronic – concern with the rules that structure discursive practices, and which serve as the means to include and exclude certain
statements, with a genealogical – or diachronic – focus that explores
the historical genesis of various identities and objects by analysing
their emergence, descent and political constitution. His approach thus
consists of four connected elements. He begins with what he calls a
'history of the present', in which an enquiring subject is confronted
by a pressing theoretical or practical issue, which calls for thinking
and critical intervention. This issue then has to be registered and
constructed as a problem by focusing on the rules that constitute the
perplexing issue or phenomenon as an object of investigation. Thirdly,
efforts are directed at explaining the emergence and formation of
the object by tracing out its descent from dispersed elements and by
exploring moments of political contestation during which certain
alternatives are excluded or deferred. Finally, this approach contains
a critical dimension, in that excluded alternatives – both actual and
imagined – are considered and interjected into the object of study, so
that alternative resolutions of the problem can be articulated.

As is evident in this book, we supplement Foucault's approach by
formalising some of the concepts that remain implicit in the elaboration of his method, as well as the particular genealogies he elaborates,
and by locating them in what we have called the logics of critical
explanation. Critical policy studies, we suggest, should thus offer
retroductive explanations, couched in terms of social, political and
fantasmatic logics that are articulated together in a particular set of
circumstances to render a problematic phenomenon intelligible. The
practice of critique itself is predicated on the central role of political

and fantasmatic logics in conducting policy enquiry. It is their discernment that enables us to highlight the contingency and undecidability of particular social relations and structures, and to move beyond 'negative critique' to the generation of positive alternatives for social and political organisation. In the next chapter, we shall delineate the multiple problematisations of aviation and airports in the UK.

Notes

1   We are tempted to say that discursive formations share important family resemblances with Foucault's concept of a *dispositif*, or what others would call an assemblage, but the making good of these claims would require much reflection and greater conceptualisation.
2   This section builds upon and develops ideas set out in Howarth (2000, 2009).
3   The concepts of myth, social imaginary and fantasy are introduced and elaborated upon in Howarth (2013).
4   One of the most arresting contributions in this regard is Nietzsche's reflections on metaphor (Nietzsche, 2006: 114–23). These points are spelled out in Howarth and Griggs (2006).
5   Iain McLean (2001) has used the work of Riker and his understanding of heresthetics to explain key 'turning points' in British political history.
6   Ish-Shalom has sought to supplement the work of Riker with the concept of rhetorical capital, which refers to the 'aggregative persuasive resources inherent in entities' (Ish-Shalom, 2008: 281). Such rhetorical capital rests in part on how the persuasive forces of entities forge sets of relations with other internal and external elements (Ish-Shalom, 2008: 283).
7   Typically, for example, problems in aviation often arise at particular airports and the surrounding 'airport communities'. But they may also be posed in a particular region of a country, especially those areas where demand for aviation expansion is greater, or where there is a dearth of airport capacity. At the same time, questions about aviation and airports are frequently posed at the national level, either in the form of public policies or in terms of party politics. Increasingly, of course, issues about the aviation industry also arise at the supra-national level, whether this involves regulation at various inter-state levels, or endeavours to institute or change global agreements and regimes.

2
Problematising 'sustainable aviation' in the UK

We are calling for a cap [on global aviation emissions] that would *not* require people to fly less than today, but would constrain aviation emissions growth going forward.... Such a cap together with deep emissions cuts in other sectors would limit the risk of dangerous climate change and the very damaging consequences for people here and in other countries that this would have. (David Kennedy, chief executive officer of the Committee on Climate Change, *Guardian*, 9 September 2009; our emphasis)

The cuts that will be required elsewhere, in other areas of the economy that many people would judge to be at least as important as aviation will have to be far more serious than we have formerly anticipated.... The question for the Government remains, as it did with their approval of the new airport facilities at Heathrow, why are they prepared to treat aviation so differently from every other sector of the economy? (Hugh Raven, commissioner of the UK's Sustainable Development Commission, *Today*, BBC Radio 4, 9 September 2009)

Many listeners to the BBC's *Today* programme on 9 September 2009 would have been struck by the words of Hugh Raven, the commissioner of the UK's Sustainable Development Commission (SDC), which was then the government's independent watchdog on sustainable development.[1] He was asked to comment on a letter from the government's official climate advisers, the Committee on Climate Change (CCC), to the Energy and Climate Change Secretary, Ed Miliband, and the Transport Secretary, Lord Adonis, in the run-up to the United Nations Copenhagen climate talks in December 2009. The letter warned that the UK may have to cut emissions of greenhouse gases by 90 per cent in all other sectors of the economy by 2050 in order for the aviation sector to restrict its emissions to 2005 levels and thus to continue to grow. The proposal called for even bigger cuts than the 80 per cent drop on 1990 levels already planned for households and industry in the UK.[2]

Commenting on the letter, Raven raised questions about why the CCC had accepted that UK aviation should be allowed to expand in the way it had, and why it should continue to do so.[3] He argued that the CCC's statement 'starkly reveals' the 'assumptions' made in government circles about the growth of aviation. 'For the first time', he said, 'we can clearly see the thinking in government about the *sacrosanct nature* of aviation' (our emphasis). He went on to claim that even the 'rather lax regime' proposed by the CCC of pegging back aviation emissions to 2005 levels was 'not compatible' with the UK government's policy of expanding Heathrow airport. Indeed, the additional facilities proposed in the plans for a third runway made the CCC's predictions 'unfeasible'. In short, Raven strongly queried why the UK aviation industry should be 'treated differently' from other sectors of the UK economy, such as energy, transport and food production. Why should aviation, he asked, continue to enjoy a 'disproportionate share' of carbon emissions up to 2050?

Responding to these charges, later on the *Today* programme, David Kennedy, the chief executive officer of the CCC, denied that aviation and air travel were 'sacrosanct' and acknowledged that aviation was a 'real problem', in that it could contribute 20 per cent of global emissions by 2050 if not properly regulated. Yet, looking at the issue from 'an economic perspective' in which, in his words, 'we don't get into the politics of these things', he still insisted that the global aviation industry could meet the stringent targets of reducing its emissions to 2005 levels. Discussing options for the future, he argued that it was 'not all about constraining demand growth', but should involve the development of 'more efficient planes' and a greater use of biofuels, which 'will be able to be used in planes going forward'. He accepted that we may need to think about 'constraining demand growth', but this did not mean 'cutting demand', nor stopping people 'going on holiday abroad'. The 'grandstanding' of environmental protest was contrasted with a pragmatic and realistic stance.[4]

Also interviewed on the programme, and in a not dissimilar vein to Kennedy, the former Labour minister Brian Wilson, who was at the time the chair of the pro-aviation industry coalition Flying Matters,[5] argued that the CCC's proposals were 'hugely challenging' and 'difficult to achieve' for the aviation industry, though the industry would strive to meet them through the mechanisms stipulated in the letter, that is, through emissions trading and technological improvements. Taken in the round, however, he claimed that the challenge posed by aviation was not about 'artificial and unrealistic constraints, which would inevitably hit lower income people hardest'. 'Short term measures', such as increased taxes to manage demand, designed to make it much more difficult for people to fly, were, he said, 'not feasible politically', nor were they 'useful in the environmental sense'. Instead, according to Wilson, 'the field in which Britain can lead the world and make a huge contribution is through technology', that is, the improvement of aircraft performance, which will affect all countries. He thus dismissed the 'silly demands' and 'sloganising' of 'so-called environmental movements', whose proposals to curb global aviation would impede world trade, thus damaging third world producers and leaving them in poverty.

Other voices did not concur with these judgements. For example, the Greenpeace climate change campaigner Vicky Wyatt was notably less sanguine about the problem of aviation emissions: 'We already fly more than any other nation on Earth and other industries such as the power sector would have to reduce their emissions even further to create room for the aviation sector to grow even more. Electricity consumers could end up footing the bill.' In her view, 'Any government of whatever stripe, were they to follow the committee's advice, would find it almost impossible to build a third runway at Heathrow.... The only way to make the deep cuts in aviation emissions that we need is to stop building new runways, like the one at Heathrow'.[6] Her words were echoed by the main opposition parties. In the run-up to the 2010 general election, both the Tories and the Liberal Democrats pledged themselves against the building of a third runway at Heathrow and against the further expansion of Stansted. Of course, this is not to forget the local protesters and more radical environmental protesters who threatened and executed direct action in their campaigns to stop the planned expansions at Heathrow, Stansted and elsewhere. Indeed, in no small measure the increased politicisation of aviation has been partly a result of their campaigns and protests to protect local communities from airport expansions and to demonstrate the impact of the aviation industry on climate change. The efforts of groups like HACAN ClearSkies, Stop Stansted Expansion, Plane Stupid and so on have placed aviation squarely on the political agenda.

This typical exchange of views, often expressed in this kind of rhetoric, crystallises one of the many paradoxes and contradictions surrounding the regime of aviation expansion in the UK since 2000. The 'sacrosanct nature' of aviation, coupled with its insatiable demand for transport infrastructure, is pitted against the problem of carbon emissions and the industry's contribution to climate change. Sustainable development is contrasted with an unmanaged and unplanned regime of aviation expansion in the UK. The horrors of climate change are set against the bleak prospects of economic decline. Key oppositions like these raise a central question about the politics of sustainable aviation in the UK. Why and how has the UK aviation industry assumed a 'sacrosanct' position among politicians and expert opinion? Or, at least, why is it often perceived as 'sacrosanct'? In this chapter we develop our multiple and evolving problematisations of UK aviation. But we begin with an analysis of the centrality of aviation to modern lifestyles and its development in the UK.

The rise and rise of modern aviation

Like many facets of modern life, the aviation industry is a mixed blessing. For a large number of people in advanced industrial societies, and a growing number in developing countries, air travel is a harbinger of progress, modernisation and economic development. Flying, with its attendant practices and infrastructural requirements – airports, rail and road networks, hotels, carparks, air traffic control, and so forth – constitutes a key component of the accelerating pace of late capitalist societies, bringing into being the 'multiple world of aeromobilities' that splice together our daily lives in an age of globalisation and air travel (Cwerner, 2009: 3). Aviation and airports have captured the popular imagination, conjuring up visions of cheap, safe travel, rapid business transactions in an increasingly globalised world, an essential means for face-to-face contacts between dispersed families and friends, and promises of exotic holiday destinations. Air travel, as we suggest above, has entered into social norms and daily practices, with flying transforming our understandings, for example, of appropriate birthday celebrations or weekend breaks, while at the same time shifting our patterns of food consumption through the rapid rise of international air freight traffic (Randles and Mander, 2009). In the eyes of many experts and commentators, unlike other parts of the transport sector, aviation thus occupies an exceptional position as 'no other mode of transportation enables such rapid movement of people and goods across countries and continents' (Barrett and Waitz, 2010: 15).

In many discussions of contemporary aviation, it is now customary to encounter lists of stylised facts that highlight the expansion of the airline industry, airports and their related infrastructures on a global scale. These lists frequently appear in the pages of glossy airline or airport publications, on the websites of airline companies and their business associations, as well as in policy documents, government white papers, academic studies, popular books and newspaper articles. Yet they are still striking, perhaps even startling. Taken together, the travel and tourism industry constitutes one of the largest economic sectors in the world, estimated to be worth, both directly and indirectly, some $5,991 billion, or 9.1 per cent of world gross domestic product (GDP) and 8.8 per cent of world employment in 2011.[7] The airline industry generated revenues of approximately $547 billion in 2010, with an estimated global economic impact in 2007 of $3,557 billion or 7.5 per cent of world GDP. It generates some 32 million jobs globally, employing directly around 5.5 million people (4.7 million in airlines and airports and 782,000 in civil aerospace) (IATA, 2011a, 2011b). In 2010, the industry carried 2.4 billion passengers on 23,000 aircraft operated by 1,715 airlines from 3,750 airports across the globe.[8] This equates to some half a million or more people in the air at any one moment across the globe, an average which is predicted to rise to approximately one million by 2014 (Bowen, 2010: 2). Such growth is far from restricted to established markets and aviation hubs (although there is a huge disparity in rates of flying across the globe – see Cwerner, 2009). On the contrary, the growth of new markets is even more impressive. Of the 800 million new passengers predicted for 2014, it is expected that 360 million (45 per cent) will travel on Asia Pacific routes, with 214 million accounted for by China alone. Indeed, China, followed closely by the United Arab Emirates, Vietnam, Malaysia and Sri Lanka, are forecast to be the fastest-growing markets for international passenger traffic from 2011 to 2014 (IATA press release no. 8, 14 February 2011).

Business and leisure travel has expanded at a rapid rate, with flying becoming the dominant mode of transportation in both transcontinental and intercontinental travel. On some short-haul routes, low-cost airlines have even begun to compete against road and rail transport (Bowen, 2010: 2–3). The advent of low-cost airlines has triggered the rapid development of 'leisure passengers', while putting pressure on the valuable market for carriers of first-class and business-class travel. The latter still represents some 10 per cent of all passengers, though more business travellers are switching to economy fares (Graham, 2010: xvii–xviii; see also Beaverstock *et al.*, 2010; Derudder *et al.*, 2011), while some businesses are turning to hiring their own private jets for executive travel (Budd and Graham, 2009).

Yet even this does not exhaust the inexorable growth of global aviation, as it omits the role of air freight and military aviation. For example, in 2009, 26 million tonnes of cargo was also transported by plane, and this was predicted to rise by 8.2 per cent a year between 2009 and 2014 (IATA press release no. 8, 14 February 2011). In fact, a 2004 study calculated that air cargo made up some 40 per cent of world trade by value, although less than 1 per cent by weight (Kasarda *et al.*, 2004; cited in Bowen, 2010: 3).

The growth of air freight has followed what Gilbert and Perl (2010: 53–8) characterise as a 'revolution' in the industry in the 1980s. This began with the development by Federal Express in the 1980s of hub-and-spoke networks specifically for air cargo flights, which, through integration with local transport networks, enabled the creation of overnight 'door-to-door' delivery, first in North America and then across the globe. International express freight grew at more than twice the rate of all air cargo traffic in the first decade of the twenty-first century, averaging 12.9 per cent annual growth (AirportWatch, 2009b: 5). What is more, alongside the inexorable expansion of commercial aviation, there has also been a steady and considerable growth of military aviation. In important respects, commercial and military aviation have always been joined at the hip. Major spurs to techno-logical innovation were brought about by the needs of war machines, while many commercial airports began their lives as military runways. The aerospace industry remains a critical part of aviation in general. Although it is the case that (in the US context) the commercial aircraft fleet currently uses approximately seven times the fuel consumed by military aviation (navy and air force only), the growth of military aviation and its needs are still noteworthy (Waitz *et al.*, 2005).

Aviation thus spans the divisions we usually make in the study of political economy between transportation, distribution, exchange, consumption and production. Not only is it a vital cog in the func-tioning of modern transport systems and in various types of exchange, but it is equally bound up with practices of individual and collective consumption, as well as processes of production. For example, in addition to supporting multimodal transportation and commercial networks, airports are often vast emporia of retailing and leisure activities, as well as spaces for face-to-face business interactions. Equally, the manufacture of airliners connects aviation intimately to the growing global aerospace industry, as well as the production of military aircraft and their attendant facilities.

Indeed, in a widely publicised book, John Kasarda and Greg Lindsay posited a necessary link between the logics of globalisation and the logic of aviation expansion, which they argue is manifesting itself in the form of the 'aerotropolis' (Kasarda and Lindsay, 2011). The latter is a city that is deliberately built around an airport, with concentric rings of air transport-dependent businesses, homes and shopping malls, all criss-crossed by 'aerolanes' and 'aerotrains', highways and trains. They are cities designed to service the needs of companies, which need to be close to global air hubs to keep up with competitors; they are urban spaces that are more connected to Chinese factories or Kenyan flower growers than to a neighbouring town. Aerotropoli thus operate in a globalised world dictated by competition between complex supply chains, rather than individual companies alone. In the authors' words, the aerotropolis:

> represents the logic of globalization made flesh in the form of cities. Whether we consider it to be good or simply inevitable the global village holds these truths to be self-evident: that customers on the far side of the world may matter more than those next door; that costs must continually be wrung from every piece of business in a market-share war of all against all; that the pace of business, and of life, will always move faster and cover more ground; and that we must pledge our allegiance if we want to our iPhones, Amazon orders, fatty tuna, Lipitor and Valentine's Day roses at our doors tomorrow morning. If the airport is the mechanism making all of these things possible … then everything else – our factories, offices, homes, schools – will be built accordingly. The aerotropolis … will be a new kind of city, one native to our era of instant gratification – call it the Instant Age. (Kasarda and Lindsay, 2011: 6)

The statistics and scenarios are impressive and thought-provoking. But, as we suggest above, perhaps they do not convey the extent to which aviation has become a deeply embedded social practice, exhibiting its own logics and imperatives. In a world of growing (albeit unequal and uneven) material affluence, greater mobility, more intensive patterns of immigration and emigration, the rapid development and diffusion of aircraft technologies, increasing globalisation, and so forth, the desire of people to meet face to face with their families, friends and acquaintances, or to study and learn in different cities, countries and even continents, has grown considerably, and it is likely to grow even further. Business trips by air, often to conferences and conventions, have for many people become routine. The logics of aviation expansion and aeromobilities have become sedimented in many, if not all, countries of the globe (Urry, 2009).

UK aviation

The global trends and trajectories described above are strongly reflected in the UK context. The number of passengers flying to, from or between UK airports almost quadrupled between 1980 and 2010 (from 58 to 211 million, even allowing for its decline from its peak of some 240 million passengers in 2007 before the global economic recession) (DfT, 2011a: 1; House of Commons Library, 2011a: 15). Approximately 10 per cent of passengers at UK terminals arrived or departed on domestic flights, while 90 per cent flew on international flights (House of Commons Library, 2011a: 15). Of these international passenger movements, 71 per cent were to or from European destinations, with Spain (an important holiday destination for British tourists) accounting for 17 per cent of all international passenger movements in 2010 (DfT, 2011a: 3). Reflecting the growth in passenger numbers travelling on holidays or to visit family and friends, business trips by UK residents accounted for only 13 per cent of all UK visits abroad in 2008 (a fall from 15 per cent or 2.7 million visits in 1980) (DfT, 2009: 94; see also Faulconbridge and Beaverstock, 2008).

In fact, the numbers of passengers passing through British airports have increased approximately 100-fold since 1950, with forecasts predicting continued expansion to 480 million passengers flying from or arriving at UK airports by 2030 (House of Commons Library, 2011a: 4). In addition, air freight more than doubled in the UK in the 1990s, increasing from 580,000 tonnes in 1970 to 2.2 million tonnes in 2002 (AirportWatch, 2009b: 5), with some 2.3 million tonnes of freight handled at UK airports in 2010 (House of Commons Library, 2011a: 4; DfT, 2011a: 1). The aviation industry has an 'economic footprint' of around £26 billion, with an economic output of £9 billion, directly employing approximately 120,000 people (DfT, 2012: 13).

Estimates suggest that the aviation industry accounts for 1.1 per cent of the UK's GDP (OEF, 2006: 5; House of Commons Library, 2011a: 4) or 0.7 per cent of GVA (gross value added) of the UK economy (Oxera, 2009: i).[9] Furthermore, as a 2005 parliamentary report on the UK aerospace industry made clear, 'the UK aerospace industry (UKAI) remains one of the most successful sectors of UK manufacturing' (House of Commons Trade and Industry Committee, 2005: 3). It has an annual turnover of approximately £23 billion and directly employs 100,000 workers (DfT, 2012: 14).

Throughout the post-war period of expansion, successive British governments, like most governments in advanced industrial societies, accepted two connected beliefs about aviation. The first belief was that it was difficult, if not impossible, for a national government to intervene in an intrinsically global and internationalised aviation industry. The second was that, because aviation was, by definition, good for the economy, any national interference, say by the UK government, would simply result in UK business in general, not to mention the aviation industry in particular, losing its competitive advantage to other states (Whitelegg, 2003: 236). In the UK context, this was manifest in a 'predict and provide' model of policy-making which problematised the issues primarily as the provision of sufficient infrastructure and capacity for the continued expansion of aviation *and*, from the 1970s and 1980s, the escalating marketisation, deregulation and liberalisation of air transport. Such marketisation contributed to the increasing fragmentation of the governance of UK aviation, bringing new actors into the policy arena, not least the privatised British Airways (BA) and British Airports Authority (BAA) (Caves and Gosling, 1997; Humphreys *et al.*, 2007). Route entry barriers were lowered on domestic and international routes and new low-cost scheduled airlines such as Ryanair and easyJet entered the market (Calder, 2006; Humphreys, 2003: 24). By 2010, easyJet carried more passengers than BA (some 42 million to 30 million respectively), although BA flew twice as many passenger kilometres (105 billion as opposed to 49 billion) (DfT, 2011a: 4).

New terminals were opened at Stansted and Manchester and a second runway was given the go-ahead at Manchester. A proposal for a fifth terminal at Heathrow was put forward in 1992, which led to a public inquiry – the longest in UK history – and the new terminal was eventually opened in 2008 (Griggs and Howarth, 2012). Heathrow remained in 2010 the UK's busiest airport, handling 31 per cent of UK terminal passengers and 63 per cent of all freight tonnes. It was the fourth largest passenger airport in the world, behind Atlanta, Beijing and Chicago, handling the largest number of international terminal passengers in the world (61 million in 2010). It is striking that London airports continued to account in 2010 for 60 per cent of all terminal passengers in the UK, although terminal passengers at regional airports increased by 32 per cent from 2000 to 2010 (DfT, 2011a: 2).

Against this background, successive UK governments and business elites have trumpeted the aviation industry and the expansion of airports as one of the few success stories in the embattled field of modern transport policy. Indeed, for many, following the expansion of aviation after the First and Second World Wars, airports 'became symbols of progressive thinking and utopian planning' (Gordon, 2008: 13). The white paper *The Future of Air Transport* (DfT, 2003a), the strategic plan for the development of air transport in the UK, came down at the end of 2003 firmly on the side of promoting expansion to meet projected demand for air travel, with environmental concerns relegated to a relatively subsidiary role. Although plans were rejected for any new airports, extra runways were proposed for Stansted, Edinburgh and Birmingham, with another runway likely at either Heathrow or Gatwick. Expansion plans were also approved for runway extensions at a large number of regional airports, as well as for new terminals at Manchester, Glasgow and Cardiff (Dudley, 2004).

On 15 January 2009, the Secretary of State for Transport, Geoff Hoon, announced to Parliament the long-awaited policy decision on the future development of Heathrow airport. The decision to give the green light to the building of a third runway brought to an end a policy cycle that had begun back in 2001, when the government opened the consultation for the 2003 white paper. The go-ahead to expand Heathrow had been preceded by the government's confirmation of its plans to increase capacity at Stansted.[10] The proposed developments, whose estimated costs were between £6.8 and £7.6 billion, would have enabled the number of flights at Heathrow to grow to more than 700,000 per annum (from 473,000), although there was to be an initial limit of 605,000 flights (*Financial Times*, 16 January 2009). Passenger numbers at the airport were expected to rise from 67 million a year to about 120 million per year by 2030. Carbon emissions were predicted to rise to 23.6 million tonnes by 2030, from 17.1 million tonnes. It was also estimated that up to 700 homes in the nearby village of Sipson would have had to be destroyed to make way for the new transport infrastructure, but the government claimed that the expansion of Heathrow would create up to 8,000 jobs by 2030 and provide up to 60,000 new jobs in the construction phase.[11]

Yet these economic figures, as well as the legality and morality of the decision to expand Heathrow, were sharply contested by those opposed to the decision. Following the entry into office of the Conservative–Liberal Democrat coalition in May 2010, New Labour's plans for expansion at Heathrow and Stansted were reversed, as the new government imposed a moratorium on new runways in the southeast. This policy reversal, arguably the most significant victory for the environmental movement since the abandonment of the road-building programme in the 1990s, brought to the fore the changing fortunes of the aviation industry in recent years. Indeed, its expansion was never without contestation. While passenger numbers continued to expand and successive governments invested in new airports and infrastructure throughout the second half of the twentieth century, air transport was nonetheless indicted by local communities surrounding airports, or those who had the misfortune to live beneath the ever-expanding array of flight paths, for causing unacceptable levels of air and noise pollution, the destruction of local communities, the disruption of settled practices and ways of life, as well as the stimulation of unsustainable and destructive forms of economic development. More recently, however, as we suggest above, the economic benefits of aviation have been further challenged, while its future development has been increasingly brought into question, not least by the new politics of climate change and new alliances of local residents and environmental protesters, the onset of peak oil and global recession. As one leading cultural critic puts it, the airport

> is at once a place, a system, a cultural artefact, that brings us face-to-face with the advantages as well as the frustrations of modernity. The sprawling hybrid nature of the subject challenges easy assumptions. Its history has been a recurrent cycle of anticipation and disappointment, success and failure, innovation and obsolescence. (Gordon, 2008: 5)

Encountering turbulence

The enormous expansion of aviation across the globe since the Second World War provoked a series of disparate and sometimes combined concerns about the desirability, feasibility, location, size, expansion, impact, regulation and character of airports, as well as the other practices and infrastructures associated with the industry (for a discussion of emerging campaigns in the late 1960s and early 1970s against airport expansion see, for example, Apter and Sawa, 1984; Feldman and Milch, 1982; Pepper, 1980). In the UK context, the logic of aviation expansion has been accompanied by local and national protests, the formation of discourse coalitions that brought together local and national opponents of aviation expansion, as well as policy vacillations and policy reversals. For example, a national campaign group called AirportWatch was formed in 2002 in an effort to shape both local decisions to build or extend airports and national policies. The new alliance could draw upon the resources of long-established local resident groups against expansion, many of which had conducted prolonged campaigns against the third London airport in the late 1960s and early 1970s (Bromhead, 1973; Hall, 1982; Kirby, 1982; McKie, 1973; Perman, 1973). Indeed, while groups like HACAN ClearSkies experienced many defeats in the public inquiries into the proposed expansion at Heathrow, and while the anti-growth coalition appeared to lose the battle with the publication of the 2003 white paper, which came out in favour of national airport expansion, the subsequent resignification of aviation led to the abandonment of these proposals by the Conservative–Liberal Democrat coalition.

Even more telling is the way that aviation is increasingly associated with collective environmental costs and climate change (Gössling and Upham, 2009). For critics, aviation is deeply enmeshed in what philosophers like Charles Taylor (1985a: 247; 1985b: 47–9) have labelled the 'civilization of work and productivity', and what William Connolly (2008) has called the 'paradox of consumption'. Aviation currently accounts for 2–3 per cent of global emissions of carbon dioxide, but this figure is predicted to rise to 15–20 per cent by 2050 if the industry is left unchecked. If no action is taken, emissions from aviation could account in the UK for 35 per cent of the country's total allowable emissions by 2050 (CCC, 2009a).

At the same time, the reliance of the aviation industry on increasing amounts of oil runs up against the problem of peak oil. Richard Gilbert and Anthony Perl (2010) have sketched out one such scenario, where they envisage a world in which ever-rising oil prices have cut domestic flying by 40 per cent by 2025. In this particular picture of the future, the number of major airports will drop from around 400 to 50, and rather than multiple flights an hour between major hubs, only a few super-jets each carrying around 800 passengers will connect large cities on a daily basis. The rest of a large industrial nation's transport network (like that of the US) will switch over to trains, trolley buses and other vehicles, which are able to plug into a solar- and wind-powered grid (Gilbert and Perl, 2010: 223–81). Much of the required communication, as well as economic transactions, will rely upon new forms of technological interaction (Kasarda and Lindsay, 2011: 333).

The problem of peak oil is often linked to the problem of peak travel, which in the industrial world may be close at hand (Millard-Ball and Schipper, 2011). Some commentators have alleged that after 50 years of rapid increase, the number of miles travelled per person per year in advanced countries has begun to decrease or even reverse. Car travel per person seems to have peaked at about 4,000 miles per year in Japan, around 7,000 miles in Europe and about 9,000 miles in Australia and Canada. The US, at around 13,000 miles per person, may be seeing a sustained fall. Although in part this decline is most likely the result of rising fuel prices and economic stagnation, there is growing evidence of a saturation in the need for car travel. Similar trends are also evident for public transport and domestic air travel, as well as freight transport (Goodall, 2011a, 2011b, 2012; but see Jackson, 2011). In fact, the affective pull of aviation encounters increasing challenges as passengers experience more congestion at international airports, lengthy security checks and its association (especially in the media) with terrorist attacks and the spread of disease, as seen in the reactions to the spread of severe acute respiratory syndrome (SARS) in 2003.

The aviation industry is also bound up with the vicissitudes of the global economy, as well as the national economies that comprise it. As expected, the aviation industry has tended to grow rapidly in periods of economic growth, but it is especially vulnerable to economic down-turn, when plans for airport and airline expansions are often shelved because of a slow-down in global trade and passenger demand. As is well documented, the recent global financial crisis resulted in record numbers of bankruptcies and mergers, as well as the restructuring of the airline industry (Franke and Florian, 2011). (Periods of intense competition have also stimulated the formation of passenger airline alliances, such as Star Alliance, SkyTeam and Oneworld, which are often justified in terms of cost reductions and a range of traveller benefits, but which are also associated with higher prices and fewer destinations.) Again, as might be expected, the airline industry is es-pecially vulnerable to rising oil prices. For example, the stagflationary conditions in the US, sparked by the financial crisis in 2008, forced

American carriers to abandon free baggage, free tickets, food, flight attendants and even themselves (via mergers) in increasingly desperate efforts to offset an 80 per cent increase in the price of jet fuel (Kasarda and Lindsay, 2011: 331). And in the UK, passenger numbers dipped for the first time in seventeen years in 2008, with 4.6 million fewer passengers travelling through UK airports.[12] At the same time, UK air freight, having been relatively stable since 2000, also declined following the global recession in 2008 (AirportWatch, 2009b: 15–16).

In short, therefore, where once the aviation industry and its insatiable need for more and better airports were seen as symbolic gateways to freedom, modernity and economic development – and for many they still are – today they are associated with environmental degradation, the disruption of local communities, congestion, security checks and delays (see B. Graham, 2008). As John Bowen puts it, air transport in the twenty-first century is at once 'troubled but triumphant' (Bowen, 2010: 1). It is characterised by new coalitions and shifting patterns of participation, with new actors articulating competing policy frames. Uncertainty abounds about the extent to which the aviation industry contributes to climate change, especially at high altitude, while a chain of interdependencies ties aviation to business, employment and our daily lives.

In our terms, the aviation industry and its desire for airport capacity have become the site of a wicked policy problem, which is riven with multiple policy paradoxes. For example, while the global economic recession challenges the very vitality of the industry, it also lowers its growing carbon emissions, addressing in part its contribution to global warming. While the supporters and lobbies of the aviation industry confidently predict future expansion and demand more transport infrastructure, those who foresee the dangers or opportunities of peak oil predict the collapse of the industry in the near future. Aviation taxes could be used to manage demand, thus limiting (in theory) carbon emissions. But they might also undermine the competitive advantage of national carriers in the global economy. These divergent beliefs and interests, which have proved so difficult to balance and reconcile, have culminated in what we name the current impasse in UK aviation policy.

Evolving problematisations of UK aviation

Our brief consideration of the paradoxes facing the UK aviation industry shows that the task of 'problematising the problematisations' is complicated. For one thing, there is no single or obvious 'problem' that has emerged to be described and analysed. Instead, there are a range of ongoing problematisations by multiple agents of different facets of the aviation industry. The 'problem' of aviation is constituted and thus understood differently by the UK government, airlines, airport operators and passengers, not to mention environmental protestors, conservationists, citizens and the local communities affected or threatened by airport expansions. The 'solutions' they articulate and propose are thus relative to these problematisations and their underlying assumptions; they are similarly diverse and often opposed. What is more, such subjectivities and constituencies are themselves complex and differentiated entities. For example, there are different sorts of airlines, with differing goals and capacities, which construct the problem in various and often competing ways. The same is true for airports, local communities and national political actors.

At the same time, the 'problem' emerges, as discussed in chapter 1, in different social contexts and at the intersection of processes operating at *multiple* spatial scales (Bridge and McManus, 2000: 13). For local communities the problem of airports is often constructed in terms of their impacts on the quality of life and their contributions to the local and regional economies. These impacts in turn evoke various forms of political representation and protest. At the national level, the issue is problematised in terms of policy-making and policy implementation: the various pressures and demands placed on legislatures and ministries to take decisions about the overall framework and trajectory of transport policy, and its connection to other policy sectors and issues, such as the economy and the environment. But these policy-making practices are equally related to the overall political dynamics of national spaces. Policy-making and implementation are shaped by the overall balances of political forces in society and the changing configurations of hegemony therein. And finally these political practices are intimately related to other socio-economic processes, such as the contradictions and dynamics of the local, national and global political economy, as well as other social practices and cultural representations.

But this means that the question of airports is also dispersed and arrayed along various *dimensions* of analysis. As we have suggested, these include: the political economy of aviation; questions about planning, public policy and administration in the national political sphere; the role of campaigning, protest and direct action as they operate on the terrain of civil society, which in turn shapes attitudes, preferences and policy; and the environmental impacts and questions raised by aviation. Each dimension contains a further range of issues and questions. For example, the political economy of aviation in the UK concerns questions about: the net contribution of aviation to the British economy; the changing ownership patterns of the airports and airlines; the relationship between the airlines and the airport operators; the external costs of aviation for the environment and the wider community; the growth, questioning and break-up of monopolies; and so on. And each of these questions is related to the overall logics of capitalist accumulation and different forms of political regulation in particular states and political economies.

In our perspective, we connect the construction of problems to the articulation of social and political demands, which are in turn set against the contradictions of particular practices or regimes. Of course, the construction of demands is not automatic, for they arise out of the *failures* and *dislocations* of social practices, which 'appear' only when normal ways of 'going on' are interrupted. In sum, demands are constituted out of the frustrations and grievances that arise from the making visible of the ontological 'negativity' that inhabits all social relations. But equally, while demands are rooted in these disrupted practices, they can also be linked together to form wider identities and political projects that can challenge existing relations in the name of something new. They can, of course, be *disarticulated* by the operation of other political logics.

In turn, the intersection of such practices and processes, and the dislocations they may engender, can constitute the raw materials for the construction of other problems in different social contexts, or at different institutional levels of a particular social system. Importantly for us, the role of government (or the state) in contemporary societies has in modern times become a privileged site for constructing and dealing with such problems, which emerge out of a variety of competing social demands and claims. But before seeking to tackle these problems in various ways, governments first need to 'know' the character of the problems. For example, a government may construct the crisis of aviation as a problem about reaching the correct balance between the need for more airport capacity, on the one hand, and the need to mitigate environmental impacts and effects on local communities, on the other, and then propose a policy of sustainable aviation, before then employing various practices and techniques to deal with it in the attempt to restore an effective equilibrium.

Seen against this backdrop, our evolving study of UK aviation and airports has led to the construction of a series of different problems, which in turn arise from various problematisations of the phenomenon in changing social sites at distinct spatial scales. Each of these problematisations has been shaped by concerns in the present. Our dominant framing and problematisation of the paradox of aviation focuses on the tensions and contradictions that arise from the resignification of aviation as a wicked policy problem and the current stalemate in aviation policy. Yet this overall framing of the issues needs itself to be unpacked. At least five interconnected spatial and temporal problematisations can be discerned for the period under consideration.

1. Instituting the regime of commercial aviation expansion

The first major problematisation of commercial aviation arose during the Second World War, as British ministers, officials and business leaders sought to capitalise on the UK's ostensibly advantageous position in the field of aviation, where the latter was seen against the threat of US (and to a lesser degree European) competition. A series of key questions occupied the minds of the principal decision-makers in this critical conjuncture. How could the fledgling UK aviation industry build on its perceived technological and geo-political advantages so that it could successfully compete with the emergent US superpower? What plans and policy instruments were necessary to achieve this goal? How could the UK negotiate favourable international agreements and regimes that would support its nascent industry in the face of actual and potential international competition?

Our problematisation of these problematisations focuses on the way the initial decisions and public policies that were undertaken in this period made possible a seemingly inexorable logic of aviation expansion in the post-war period. How did the aviation industry manage to achieve a 'sacrosanct' position for British politicians and decision-makers during this period? What were the political, social and ideological conditions that gave succour to the aviation industry? Put in our theoretical language, what were the myths, collective imaginaries and fantasies that underpinned the expansion of aviation and its attendant requirements? What political strategies and tactics were elaborated in this period to deal with the threats and challenges to the aviation industry? In short, how can we critically explain the emergence, formation and reproduction of the aviation regime in the post-war period?

2. Dealing with competing demands for national expansion and demand management

The practice of incremental planning and policy-making that was undergirded by a strategy of 'predict and provide' in the post-war period resulted in an accelerating logic of aviation expansion, concentrated in the major London airports in the south-east of England. There were persistent demands for a national plan for the growth and location of airports and other components of the aviation industry that would set out a clear and coherent set of objectives, alongside the appropriate means to achieve such ends. Of course, there were significant differences between those who favoured greater expansion and those who favoured the tighter management of demand; there were also fierce debates about where to locate new airports or where best to expand existing ones. But there was a belief that a rational airports strategy at the national level could be brokered among diverse stakeholders and interests. Indeed, as the century wore on, and no national plan was forthcoming, those favouring more expansion began to charge governments with 'dithering' and 'piecemeal development'. Various administrations were accused of failing to take the lead with respect to the adequate provision of airport capacity (Caves and Gosling, 1997: 320). Traditional planning procedures such as the public inquiry system came under attack for constituting 'the main obstacle to the addition of airport capacity because it is adversarial and the loser loses all' (Caves and Gosling 1997: 315). While others advocated a proper system of compensation for those who suffer costs, as this would ease and speed the process of expansion (Egan, 1990), more extremist criticisms of the government condemned the biased outcomes of public inquires (Wynne, 2010).

The election of New Labour in 1997 promised to resolve these issues decisively. The problem for the incoming government was to formulate and implement a legitimate policy of sustainable growth in the aviation industry by balancing the competing demands being expressed at the time. The new government initiated a large-scale public consultation in its second term between 2000 and 2003. This process culminated in the publication of the 2003 white paper – *The Future of Air Transport* – which called for the massive expansion of airport infrastructure across the country. In exploring these issues, our second problematisation examines the dislocatory effects of aviation expansion on local residents and communities, as well as the various ways in which these disruptions were translated into grievances and demands. Our questions focus on the character and dynamics of competing discourse coalitions that emerged during the consultation process, as well as the conditions that made them both possible and vulnerable. We also explore the way in which the government sought to manage the competing demands and to legitimise its decisions.

3. Resignifying aviation

As we suggest above, while the 2003 white paper clearly came out in favour of airport expansion, no sooner had those calling for growth won the day than the aviation industry was confronted by an even more pressing series of questions and demands. Local residents, environmental campaigners and scientific experts began to raise questions about the connections between the growth of individual airports and the expansion of aviation in the UK as a whole, and across the globe. Significantly, they also exposed the linkage between expansion of the aviation industry (within the UK and globally) and the problem of climate change. In fact, the sedimented meanings of the aviation industry and its impacts on residents and the environment began to be queried. New anti-aviation direct action organisations such as Plane Stupid emerged, supporting new tactics and more direct forms of protest, such as those evident in the Camp for Climate Action at Heathrow. Such radical protesters began to construct the problem of airports as a symptom of the contradictory development of neoliberal global capitalism. And their solution to the problem of aviation involved a thorough-going transformation of the underlying capitalist system and the regulatory infrastructure that enables its reproduction.

Our problematisation of this third issue thus focuses on the ways groups and communities endeavoured to reframe the meaning of airports and aviation in a radically new way. We seek to critically explain the way in which different agents sought to connect the proposed expansion of individual airports to the national and global expansion of aviation, while linking this articulation to the problem of global climate change, thus laying the basis for political and policy change. More precisely, we concentrate on the construction of equivalential connections between disparate demands, as well as the role of scientific evidence in challenging the government's case for airport expansion.

4. Governmentality and other logics of difference

The increasingly vocal and more generalised campaign to change the meaning of aviation among elites and in the popular imaginary put the government and the industry on the defensive. On the one hand, the problem of aviation now focused on the task of implementing the proposals that had been elaborated in the 2003 white paper, while finding the appropriate ways to counter the mounting challenge to these policies and plans. On the other hand, the various opponents of expansion sought to consolidate their advances, while translating their campaign into more concrete policy outcomes. Our problematis-ation thus focuses on the ways in which the government and industry have sought to negate the growing challenge, while articulating the means to address the policy problem that was now emerging. How could those who favoured expansion counter the growing pressures to change the overall direction of aviation policy? What strategies and tactics were elaborated and followed in an effort to offset the growing political and ideological challenge?

Here we focus on the rhetorical devices, ideological practices and governmental rationalities through which the Labour government sought to deal with the problems brought about by the reframing of aviation. More particularly, we examine the various strategies and tactics, which in our view comprise a logic of difference, through which the government sought to negate opposition and then im-plement its plans. Included in the latter are its own endeavours at ideological reframing; the role of government as an honest broker; the logic of incentivisation; the diverse tactics and practices associ-ated with what some have termed 'the conduct of carbon conduct' (Paterson and Stripple, 2010); and the role of emissions trading as a solution to the environmental impacts of aviation. But we also seek to expose the limits and divisions of the various rationalities that were devised and employed by the government in dealing with what had now evolved into a wicked policy problem.

5. *The current impasse*
The dramatic resignification of aviation in the period following the publication of the 2003 white paper, the failed attempts by the proponents of aviation to translate the aims of the proposals into con-crete outcomes and the entry into office of the Conservative–Liberal Democrat coalition government in May 2010 seemed to resolve the issue. For example, in the scoping document *Developing a Sustainable Framework for UK Aviation*, published in March 2011, officials at the Department for Transport declared that while 'some elements' of the previous administration's *The Future of Air Transport* white

paper 'might still be relevant, many of its provisions are no longer fit for purpose' (DfT, 2011b: 9). Going further, in his foreword to the document, Philip Hammond, the new Transport Secretary, argued that the 2003 white paper was 'fundamentally out of date, because it fails to give sufficient weight to the challenge of climate change' (DfT, 2011b: 4).

But the subsequent moratorium on the building of new airports in the south-east of England has posed a new set of problems, which dominates our contemporary understandings of aviation. In fact, the scoping document concluded with no less than forty questions that needed to be addressed in the next white paper, which was promised for 2013. Whether the government can stand its ground in the face of future demands for airport expansion, and whether it can articulate an alternative transport strategy that can mitigate the effects of aviation while promoting economic growth, remain moot points. The aviation industry, for its part, remains unhappy about the 'current stalemate', which it sees as damaging UK aviation, as well as the prospects for sustained economic growth. These sentiments are reflected by Barry Humphreys, who was the chair of the British Air Transport Association (BATA). Commenting on the challenges ahead following his appointment in April 2009, he argued that

> by any measure, these are challenging times for the air transport industry. Never has there been a greater need for the united voice of UK airlines to be heard by government and regulators. BATA has a key role to play in ensuring that the industry can prosper again and continue to service the travelling public in the way that it has done for many years. We should not forget that the UK airline industry has been a success story of which the country should be proud.[13]

More generally, supporters of the coalition government's moratorium on airport expansion in the south-east, as well as those who would like to go further in reducing the negative impacts of the aviation industry, face the challenge of sustaining their campaigns, as well as their public support, if and when economic growth returns to the UK.

Our problematisation of the current impasse or stalemate, as various interested parties have named it, focuses on the way in which the apparent 'losers' of the 2003 white paper became 'winners' after the formation of the Conservative–Liberal coalition government in May 2010. Our analysis focuses on the role of government and the major political parties, as well as the key groups and movements in shaping the policy agenda. We also explore the cultural and political resignification of aviation and the environment as our crucial explanatory variable. Finally, we evaluate the emergent discourses on the future of UK aviation and the way these discourses are being employed by their proponents to frame UK aviation and its policy requirements. We delineate two major discourses, each of which presents a different diagnosis and resolution of the aviation problem, and then seek to evaluate each perspective, with a view to elaborating our preferred solutions and conclusions.

Conclusion

The rest of the book analyses each of these problematisations and seeks to provide solutions to the various sets of questions they raise. We start by setting out the 'ignoble origins' of the regime of aviation and airport expansion, which was established during and after the Second World War. Not only is this characterisation of the changing logics of airport expansion important in its own right, for we emphasise the myths, fantasies and path dependencies that accompanied its installation, but it also sets the scene for our analysis of the demands about airports that gathered momentum in the late 1990s under the New Labour government.

Notes

1 The Sustainable Development Commission closed on 31 March 2011 following the decision of the Conservative–Liberal Democrat coalition government, elected in May 2010, to reduce the number of government-sponsored non-department public bodies in what was deemed to be a 'bonfire of the quangos'.
2 The CCC also stated that global aviation emissions should be capped at the Copenhagen climate talks. The Committee was asked by government to advise on what should be done about emissions from aviation. We discuss this report further in chapter 7.
3 To listen to the interviews on the *Today* programme, see http://news.bbc.co.uk/today/hi/today/newsid_8245000/8245460.stm (accessed 27 December 2012).
4 In Kennedy's view, one long-haul leisure flight per family every three years would be acceptable; three long-haul flights per year per family, as we all become richer, would not be sustainable.

5 Flying Matters disbanded in April 2011 after the departure of four of its members (British Airways, the British Airports Authority, the Manchester Airport Group and Virgin Atlantic). See *Travel Weekly*, www.travelweekly.co.uk/Articles/2011/04/11/36805/airline-industry-lobby-group-grounded-from-april.html (accessed 9 November 2011).

6 Greenpeace press release, 9 September 2009, www.endseurope.com/docs/90909a.doc (accessed 25 April 2012).

7 Figures from the World Travel and Tourism Council, www.wttc.org/research/economic-impact-research/regional-reports/world (accessed 18 November 2011).

8 Figures from ATAG (Air Transport Action Group), Facts and Figures, www.atag.org/facts-and-figures.html (accessed 18 November 2011).

9 As we shall discuss below, the economic impact of aviation is highly contested, especially the findings of the assessments of Oxford Economic Forecasting (OEF).

10 *Hansard*, House of Commons Debates, 15 January 2009, vol. 486, col. 360. The decision was accompanied by plans to build new roads and rail links to connect the runway and new terminal to the other five and to London. There were also proposals to make more use of motorway hard shoulders to shorten travel times for motorists and buses going to and from the new terminal. Promises to build a new high-speed train link connecting Heathrow and Birmingham (but not Manchester or Leeds) and the development of electric cars completed the government's plans to improve the UK's transport infrastructure.

11 *Hansard*, House of Commons Debates, 15 January 2009, vol. 486, col. 358.

12 Figures from the website of the Civil Aviation Authority (CAA), www.caa.co.uk/application.aspx?catid=14&pagetype=65&appid=7&newstype=n&mode=detail&nid=1726 (accessed 18 November 2011).

13 BATA press release, 24 April 2009, www.bata.uk.com/Web/Documents/media/Pressreleases/New%20BATA%20Chairman%20240409.pdf (accessed 23 April 2012).

3
The post-war regime of aviation expansion

During the next few years, the UK has an opportunity, which may not recur, of developing aircraft manufacture as one of our main export industries. On whether we grasp this opportunity and so establish firmly an industry of the utmost strategic and economic importance, our future as a great nation may depend. (Duncan Sandys, UK Minister of Supply, 1952, cited in Lyth, 2003: 90)

Almost every airport policy decision in the last 40 years has been controversial. Wherever there is an airport, or the potential for an airport in this crowded island, there are people who object to its development, understandably so, and their views are of the utmost importance. But the aviation industry plays a vital role in transporting people and supports a large number of jobs of all sorts. Any responsible Government must take account of the interests of all these people. Airlines and airports exist only to serve the needs of the travelling public. Air travel is no longer for the privileged few; it is our objective to bring it within the reach of more and more people. Every Government has had to face these dilemmas and attempt to reconcile these conflicting interests. It is not an easy task. (Nicholas Ridley, Secretary of State for Transport, *Hansard*, House of Commons Debates, 30 January 1985, vol. 72, col. 291)

The more they went on, the more I realised how the aviation industry has had successive governments twisted around its little finger. The assumption seems to be that airports will carry on growing indefinitely, however unbearable life becomes for those under the flight paths. (Chris Mullin, UK minister responsible for aviation, Department of the Environment, Transport and the Regions, 1999–2001; Mullin, 2010: 77)

New Labour entered the 1997 general election campaign with a manifesto commitment to 'put concern for the *environment* at the heart
of policy-making'. If elected, the then opposition pledged to tackle
climate change and ozone depletion, promising to pursue a new
internationalism in the European Union (EU) and deliver a 20 per
cent reduction in the UK's carbon emissions by 2010. Yet it gave little
or no policy salience to the impact of air travel on climate change.
The two sentences of its manifesto devoted to aviation simply stated
that its 'guiding objectives' in the domain of air transport were to be
'fair competition, safety and environmental standards', before adding
that it 'want[ed] all British carriers to be able to compete fairly in the
interests of consumers'.[1] Its transport policy priorities lay elsewhere,
namely the reversal of the Conservative road-building programme;
following widespread protest against that programme, its reversal
had become the public benchmark of New Labour's environmental
credentials and its claims for a sustainable transport policy (Dudley
and Richardson, 2000; Paterson, 2007).

On taking office, however, New Labour immediately encountered
an array of contradictory demands and grievances in aviation, as
pro-growth coalitions clashed with local residents and environmental
protesters at Manchester airport and London Heathrow. At Heathrow, local resident groups, local councils and environmental lobbies
were soon to be embroiled in the third year of a public inquiry,
fighting proposals to construct a fifth terminal at the international
hub airport, which had secured broad support from airlines, business, finance capital and trade unions.[2] At Manchester, environmental
protesters were making their final preparations to resist forced evic-
tions from their camp in the Bollin Valley on the site of a proposed
second runway as Tony Blair, the new Labour Prime Minister, entered
Downing Street. The protest had achieved national media prominence
in the spring of 1997, as self-styled 'eco-warriors', importing the
tactics of the anti-roads movement into the field of air transport
policy, dug tunnels and built tree camps on the proposed site for
the new runway. In fact, the struggle at Manchester, the first anti-
airport expansion protest to bring together local residents and direct
action environmentalists, ushered in a new dynamic of environmental
protest in air travel – the so-called 'Vegans and Volvos' alliance –
which opposed the regional growth coalition that favoured expansion
(Griggs *et al.*, 1998; Griggs and Howarth, 2000, 2002). These tensions
and policy contradictions had also emerged in the international arena,

as concerns over climate change rose up the international agenda, and the EU moved to complete its liberalisation of the 'single market' for civil aviation in European skies (Dobson, 1995, 2007).

How the New Labour government would deal with these demands raised significant political challenges, both for the maintenance of its support across its various political constituencies and for the continued legitimacy of its espoused commitment to a sustainable transport policy. In this chapter, we explore how the shifting set of demands in aviation policy interacted with the contradictory regime of aviation policy, where the latter had provided the conditions for the rapid expansion of air travel during the second half of the twentieth century. We thus seek to construct a genealogical narrative of post-war British aviation by delineating the social, political and fantasmatic logics that worked together to forge and prolong the contradictory regime of aviation expansion. We demonstrate that the 'ignoble origins' of aviation expansion can be traced back to political struggles and decisions that occurred at the end of the Second World War. We argue that once these decisions had become embedded in government institutions and practices, the logic of expansion acquired a certain path dependency and so gathered a seemingly unstoppable momentum. In particular, we focus on the way in which certain myths and fantasmatic narratives prevented and displaced the construction of antagonisms to expansion. Aviation expansion resonated with the all-important myths of post-war Britain, and successive governments had recourse to what we call a series of fantasmatic narratives, which articulated both the 'beatific' benefits of aviation expansion for the British economy, as well as the 'horrific' threats of overcapacity at British airports on economic and social well-being and the 'threat' of competition from the US in the aftermath of the Second World War. These myths and fantasmatic narratives were pivotal in sustaining successive governments' investments in civil aviation.

The chapter proceeds by analysing the predominance of Heathrow as the 'jewel in the crown' of UK aviation. Questions about capacity overload at UK airports, which were underpinned by a well rehearsed logic of 'predict and provide', became the scourge of post-war governments, and so emerged as the dominant policy 'problem' confronting politicians and officials. At the same time, the maintenance of Heathrow's competitiveness resonated with the preoccupations of government ministers and chimed with the interests of national airlines, the development of the aerospace industry and the economic well-being of the nation. With this in mind, we then turn to the privatisation, deregulation and liberalisation of air transport in the 1990s. Here we examine how these new policies not only brought into question the dominance of Heathrow by generating growth in international flights at regional airports, but brought new, low-cost carriers into the aviation market, thus triggering further demands for expansion, as well as challenges to the established practices of traditional airlines.

Of course, aviation expansion throughout the second half of the twentieth century was not without its broader contradictions and challenges. Having set out the UK government's, and the aviation industry's, preoccupations with capacity issues in the south-east of England, especially expansion at Heathrow and London, we next investigate the campaigns of local residents against airport noise and air pollution. Here we analyse how the incorporation of emerging environmental demands offered the opportunity to develop more universal, rather than just particularistic, campaigns against airport expansion. But importantly, we also demonstrate that, despite the twists and turns of air transport policy, aviation gelled with the all-important myths of post-war Britain. Once lodged in the fabric of the British state, as well as the nation's psyche, the logic of aviation expansion had acquired a path dependence which was proving difficult, if not impossible, to dislodge.

London Heathrow: the 'jewel in the crown'

That there was an inexorable expansion of air travel following the end of the Second World War is one of the established 'facts' of aviation policy. At the beginning of the 1950s, terminal passenger numbers in UK airports stood at 2.8 million. By 1960, that figure had risen to 10.1 million, only to continue climbing to 31.6 million in 1970, 57.8 million in 1980 and 102.4 million in 1990, before reaching almost 146 million in 1997, the year New Labour entered office (House of Commons Library, 2011a: 15). This rise in passenger numbers was periodically punctured by moments of crisis and the highly public collapse of carriers, notably in the early 1970s, early 1980s and early 1990s, when economic recessions temporarily threatened demand for air travel. Yet these crises were little more than short-term deflations in the growth of passenger numbers when set against the long-term expansion of air travel in the second half of the twentieth century. In fact, aviation analysts worked to a 'rule of thumb' that demand for air travel would rise (or fall) at around twice the rate of any change in the UK's economy measured in terms of gross domestic product (GDP). From the mid-1970s until the early 2000s, this 'rule of thumb' projection was relatively accurate, if a little on the cautious side. The long-term growth of air traffic was just below 6 per cent a year or approximately two-and-a-half times the rate of growth of the UK's GDP (CAA, 2008: 14). In the 1990s, much of this growth came as a result of the liberalisation of air travel in the EU, coupled with the entry of 'no frills' carriers into the UK aviation market and the growth of regional airports (CAA, 1998, 2005).

Significantly for the character and intensity of the grievances and demands facing New Labour, much of this rapid growth of air transport had taken place at airports in the south-east of England, and nowhere more so than at London Heathrow. Heathrow had been enshrined towards the end of the Second World War as the UK's future international hub airport, with a 1945 command paper on British air services from the Ministry of Civil Aviation asserting that its development would ensure the 'highest standards required for trans-oceanic aircraft' (cited in House of Commons Library, 2009: 8). Indeed, it was to become home to the national carriers, British Overseas Airways Corporation (BOAC) and British European Airlines (BEA), which dominated available slots at the growing airport, such that the interests of the national carrier were to go hand in hand with the defence of the position of Heathrow as a competitive international hub airport. As late as 1994, British Airways (BA), the now privatised descendant of BOAC and BEA, still accounted for nearly 45 per cent of all movements at Heathrow, benefiting significantly from the competitive advantage that came from the volume of international travel that went through the airport (Lyth, 1998: 64).

Heathrow formally opened to passengers on 31 May 1946, operating initially with a 'tent village' in place of terminals (House of Commons Library, 2011b: 2). The actual development of the airport had begun in June 1944, though the construction was incomplete when the airport was transferred to the Ministry of Civil Aviation at the beginning of 1946. The first use of the airport was for a civil flight, which took place for publicity purposes, when a British South American Airways Lancastrian aircraft took off on a long-distance proving flight to South America (Sherwood, 2009: 74–7). By the end of its first year of operation, however, the airport served eighteen destinations and had 60,000 passengers and 2,400 tons of cargo passing through its doors (House of Commons Library, 2011b: 2). A million passengers per year passed through Heathrow for the first time in 1953 and two years later it opened its first terminal, the Europa Building (now Terminal Two). Such expansion continued, with the Oceanic Terminal opening to long-haul flights in 1961 (renamed Terminal Three in 1968), to be followed by the opening of a new short-haul terminal in 1968 (now Terminal One), the expansion of Terminal Three in 1978 and the opening of Terminal Four in 1986. Access to the airport from central London was improved, first by the extension of the Piccadilly underground line out to Heathrow in 1977, and then by the opening of the direct train line from Paddington in 1998, not forgetting the improved road access through the opening of the M4 Heathrow spur (House of Commons Library, 2009, 2011b).

By the early 1950s, however, ministers were already raising concerns about the crowded airspace over London and potential capacity constraints at London's international hub and the need to develop Gatwick (Cabinet Office, 1952). Gatwick was designated as the second London airport in a 1953 white paper, when it was identified as an 'overspill' for congested Heathrow (Hall, 1982: 20). It subsequently closed for redevelopment and reopened in 1958 as the 'new' Gatwick airport, with an extended runway and new terminal building. Yet it failed to mount any significant challenge to the dominance of Heathrow, not least because, despite incentives at the time, foreign airlines resisted using Gatwick as a base for scheduled international flights (Conservative Political Centre, 1973: 11). By 1965, passenger numbers at Heathrow had risen to 10.5 million (an increase of over 4 million in the previous four years), with air traffic movements (take-offs and landings) at the airport reaching over 192,000 a year. At Gatwick, however, passenger numbers remained at 1.4 million (an increase of 0.6 million in the previous four years), with air traffic movements of 28,600 a year (Cabinet Office, 1967). Some ten years later, in 1976, Heathrow was still dominant, handling 23.2 million passengers out of some 31 million passengers travelling through London airports – almost three times more than Gatwick and the other London airports (Stansted and Luton) put together. It is striking that over half of the 43.6 million passengers using UK airports in 1976 passed through Heathrow (Cabinet Office, 1978).

The dominance of Heathrow was due in part to its operation as an international hub, with an increasing proportion of its passengers using the airport to transfer between routes and to connect to different destinations. By 1991, over one in four passengers using the airport were transfer passengers, with the practice of 'interlining' (particularly Europe–North America, and Europe–Asia/Oceania) increasing by over 33 per cent between 1987 and 1991 (CAA, 1993: xi, 14). In fact, over 200 destinations were served by Heathrow in 1994. Significantly, as recently as 2006, the Treasury was to point out that this proportion of transfer passengers was 'the highest proportion of interlining passengers (25%) of any airport in the world'.[3]

The development of regional airports (meaning in practice airports outside London) remained limited, despite repeated declarations by governments that their development should counterbalance the dominance of the south-east and London Heathrow (Department of Trade, 1976a). Typically, in Cabinet discussions of the 1967 white paper on a third London airport, airports outside London were characterised as 'generally under-utilised and uneconomic' (Cabinet Office, 1967). Yet policy commitments to expand regional airports remained somewhat half-hearted. In 1978, in his note accompanying the presentation of a draft airports white paper to Cabinet, the Secretary of State for Trade, despite recognising government support for the development of regional airports, ultimately concluded that 'because the overwhelming proportion of passengers live in the South East, the white paper rejects suggestions that measures should be introduced to force these passengers to use airports in the regions' (Cabinet Office, 1978: 2). Indeed, despite government support, a 1985 white paper concluded that there remained 'much spare capacity at the regional airports, particularly runway capacity' (Department of Transport, 1985: 30).

Regional airports did expand on the back of independent airlines, private charter flights and the growing market for low-cost foreign holidays (Department of Transport, 1985: 27, 29). By 1984, regional airports handled approximately a third of all UK air passengers, over 60 per cent of all domestic air traffic and roughly half of all passengers on international charter services. But this traffic was concentrated at just a few airports outside London, notably Manchester, Glasgow, Aberdeen and Birmingham (which by the mid-1980s together handled 70 per cent of all passengers carried on international scheduled flights from regional airports); and they still accounted for less than 7 per cent of passengers on international scheduled flights, with international scheduled services from regional airports limited 'almost entirely to Europe and the Near East' (Department of Transport, 1985: 27).

Against this background, airports policy in the post-war period was repeatedly conceptualised as a problem of south-east development and ultimately that of London Heathrow and its international competitiveness. The geographical location of Heathrow, particularly its closeness to urban communities and its prevailing weather conditions, constrained its development. The Wilson Committee on the Problem of Noise from surface transport, industry, aircraft and other sources reported in 1963 that noise levels for many people living near Heathrow were 'more than they can be reasonably expected to tolerate' (cited in Edwards Committee, 1969: 228). Indeed, the Committee concluded that 'Heathrow has proved to have been established in a much too densely populated area, and no good solution to the noise problem is possible' (cited in House of Commons Library, 2009: 9). Successive governments were thus ultimately faced with resolving the conundrum of expanding Heathrow, as it was argued that this would provide the greatest economic gains, albeit in the process generating the greatest environmental costs. Such considerations persistently dogged government, so much so that in 1996 members of the Transport Select Committee reported that the Department of Transport

> told us that it had ruled out the options of full parallel runways at Heathrow and Gatwick because 'the environmental objections to both those options were so enormous as to make them unrealistic.... At Heathrow ... it would have involved destruction of 3,300 houses.... Ministers took the view that that would be so environmentally damaging as not to be sensible to proceed'. (Cited in House of Commons Library, 2009: 13)

In fact, capacity concerns at Heathrow drove much of the policy debate surrounding the development of a third London airport in the 1960s and early 1970s. By the early 1950s, Gatwick, as we noted above, had been designated as London's second airport. There followed over two decades of reversals, evasions and protests over the development of a third London airport, which were to end in 1974 with the reversal of plans to construct a new airport at Maplin Sands (or Foulness) in Essex (Hall, 1982). The abandonment of a third London airport stoked demands for expansion at Heathrow and in the south-east. Indeed, the 1975 London airport strategy consultation document put forward the prospect of a fifth terminal at Heathrow, a second terminal at Gatwick, as well as expanding capacity at Stansted up to 16 million passengers a year and developing Luton (Department of Trade, 1975). However, the 1978 airports policy white paper concluded that development at Heathrow should not go beyond a fourth terminal, arguing that the airport 'occupied a restricted site' which could not 'handle satisfactorily' 50 million passengers a year (cited in House of Commons Library, 2009: 12).

In December 1979, the Conservative government eventually agreed to the construction of a fourth terminal at Heathrow and finally designated Stansted as the third London airport (a decision that had initially been taken in the 1950s and which had put an end to plans to develop a new international airport or recommence work at Maplin). Outlining his government's policy to the House of Commons, John Nott, Secretary of State for Trade, offered support for a new terminal building at Stansted, while declaring that the Conservative government would look favourably upon expansion at regional airports, particularly East Midlands, Birmingham and Manchester airports.[4] Following subsequent public inquiries into airport capacity, which were led by Graham Eyre QC, and which recommended further development at Stansted (Eyre *et al.*, 1985), the government approved plans in June 1985 to expand the capacity of the airport to accommodate up to 15 million passengers a year, although it imposed an initial cap of 7–8 million passengers.[5] Thereafter, the Thatcher government repeatedly skirted around the issue of a fifth terminal and the construction of a third runway at Heathrow. The Runway Capacity to Serve the South-East (RUCATSE) report, which was compiled by a working group in the Department of Transport, and which published its recommendations in 1993, supported the need for additional runway capacity in the region, but the working group concluded that there should be no third runway at Heathrow. In its words, while 'Heathrow would afford the greatest benefits to the air transport industry and passengers', it would 'also give rise to the greatest scale of disbenefits in terms of noise impact on people, land use and property demolition' (cited in House of Commons Library, 2009: 13). Addressing the House of Commons in February 1995, the then Conservative Secretary of State for Transport endorsed the RUCATSE findings, announcing that he was 'clear that BAA [British Airports Authority] should not consider the options … for a third runway at Heathrow' (cited in House of Commons Library, 2009: 13). Notwithstanding this pronouncement, BAA, the owner of Heathrow, announced its proposals to build Terminal Five at the airport in May 1992, with the Conservative government opening a public inquiry into the planned expansion, having stated in 1979 that Heathrow should be limited to four terminals.

In broad brush strokes, this was the contradictory policy legacy inherited by the incoming New Labour government in 1997. In the main, it flowed inexorably from the decision to enshrine Heathrow as the preferred choice for expansion at the end of the Second World War. In opposition, the Labour transport spokesperson, Michael Meacher, had agreed with the Conservative endorsement of the RUCATSE report. Yet he had also recognised the challenging policy implications of the management of rising passenger demand in the south-east, pointing out that 'if the number of passengers in the South-East keeps on going up by 7 per cent each year as it has in the past two years, it will be unsustainable' (*Independent*, 3 February 1995). The pressures of rising passenger demand were to become more intense as the liberalisation of route controls in the EU accelerated the development of civil air transport, adding capacity pressures at Heathrow (see below). The upshot was that Heathrow's continued international competitive advantage was put into question, especially as its global and domestic competitors expanded their infrastructure capacity. (Schiphol announced major investment plans in 1988, opening a fifth runway in 2003, while Frankfurt increased its capacity to three runways in 1984 and announced plans for a fourth in 1998.)

In fact, following the EU liberalisation of air transport in the 1990s, London's predominance in international traffic was increasingly challenged as regional airports expanded the number of international destinations they served, albeit primarily on short-haul routes. Passenger numbers at Manchester rose by 34 per cent from 1993 to 1998, with the airport opening a second terminal in 1993 and gaining approval for the construction of a second runway in 1997. At Birmingham, the number of terminal passengers rose by 64 per cent in the same period, with the airport opening a second terminal in 1991.[6] International traffic at regional airports, which was one-quarter of that of London in 1980, rose to one-third in 1990, and continued to rise to approximately half by 2004 (CAA, 2005: 5). International scheduled destinations increased from fifteen at Manchester airport in 1990 to sixty in 2004, while Birmingham saw an increase from thirteen to thirty-six. Over the same period, international scheduled flights at the two airports rose by more than two and a half times (CAA, 2005: 10).

Such pressures served to fuel demands for expansion at Heathrow by key sectors of the aviation industry. Equally important, however, was the increased competition to Heathrow from other London airports, notably Stansted. The opening of a new terminal at Stansted in

1991 was followed by a 156 per cent increase in the number of terminal passengers between 1993 and 1998. During the same period, passenger numbers increased by 123 per cent at Luton, which had opened a new terminal building somewhat earlier, in 1985, and 45 per cent at Gatwick, which opened its new North Terminal in 1988 and new international departure lounges in 1994. London City airport, which opened in 1987, was serving some 1.4 million passengers by 1998.[7]

Yet the growth at other London and regional airports should not detract from the continued rise of passenger numbers at Heathrow, which rose by 27 per cent from 1993 to 1998 – approximately 13 million additional passengers. Heathrow remained by far the leading international hub in the UK, with twice as many passengers as Gatwick and almost ten times as many as Stansted in 1998.[8] Access to Heathrow continued to remain a competitive advantage for regional airports and their transfer passengers (CAA, 2005: 101), as well as an advantage for international carriers. In the late 1990s, Peter Lyth threw doubt on the attraction of Stansted for international carriers:

> its lack of appeal to the flag-carriers and BA in particular, despite the opening of an attractive new terminal in 1991, has dimmed its prospects somewhat; it remains to be seen if the regional and holiday carriers which use it at present will be joined by larger international airlines as Heathrow's congestion worsens. (Lyth, 1998: 65)

Nonetheless, despite these various developments, and conflicting interpretations, with the expansion of other London airports and regional hubs such as Manchester and Birmingham, Heathrow's dominance of the UK aviation market was arguably on the wane when New Labour arrived in office, with its market share falling from 41.7 per cent of all UK terminal passengers in 1990 to 38 per cent in 1998 (and to 31.6 per cent by 2003).[9]

Overall, therefore, the exponential expansion of aviation in post-war Britain was more or less continuous. But it is clear that expansion centred on the south-east of England, or more specifically London, and London Heathrow, the UK's designated international hub airport and home of the national carrier, BA. When New Labour arrived in office, the predominance of Heathrow as an international hub was under increasing threat as passenger numbers at the likes of Gatwick, Stansted, Manchester and Birmingham grew, as did numbers of routes at its international competitors. Growth at the international hub had generated persistent capacity questions which repeatedly left governments of both the left and right facing the decision either to suffer the environmental and political costs of expansion at Heathrow and other London airports or to opt for a new third London airport. So much so that the decision whether – and where – to construct a third London airport was to rumble on through the 1960s and 1970s and into the 1980s, despite the decision to abandon it in the face of strident opposition to the construction of a new international airport at Maplin in 1974 (Hall, 1982: 38–50).

The logics of predict and provide

Such expansionist developments and concerns over capacity were partly driven by a powerful set of social logics, which are commonly characterised in the domain of transport policy as the logics of 'predict and provide', which were instituted and sedimented during the post-war period (Dudley and Richardson, 2000). In short-hand, the discourse of 'predict and provide' constructed the policy 'problem' facing government in civil aviation as one of ensuring the provision of sufficient airport infrastructure – principally runways and terminals – to meet rising passenger demand and to protect the interests of the national carrier. This dominant problematisation was still prevalent in the 1980s, with the 1985 airports policy white paper, the last white paper in aviation before New Labour entered office, clearly prioritising the view that airports policy should 'foster a strong and competitive British airline industry by *providing enough airport capacity where it is needed*' (Department of Transport, 1985: 5; our emphasis). And while there might have been moves towards marketisation, the over-riding 'problem' facing government was still deemed to be that of providing adequate airport infrastructure to meet growing demand.

   This particular problematisation of airports policy privileged the development of specific technologies of government and modes of argumentation. It elevated the art of forecasting into one of the primary technologies of government, such that technocratic arguments over projections of rising passenger numbers punctuated policy deliberations; indeed, the contestation of such projections provided the necessary, but often insufficient, means of entry into policy debates for external stakeholders and local resident groups – see for example Hall's (1982: 21) discussion of the methods of forecasting passenger demand for a third London airport in the 1960s and 1970s. Equally, it favoured particularistic arguments and decisions about the development needs of individual airports, as well as about the merits of one site over another. Writing in the early 1970s, David Perman bemoaned the fact that 'airlines, local authorities, airport users, business, travel agents, workers and environmentalists [are] in the position of having to fight each battle as it arises without relevance [*sic*] to the battle being fought in the neighbouring airport area' (Perman, 1973: 32). White papers in the post-war period were thus structured around discussions of rising passenger numbers and predictions of growth across individual airports or regions. Constructing credible forecasts of passenger demand became the privileged means for government to legitimise decisions on expansion, albeit an increasingly contested form of legitimacy, as the saga of the third London airport and quality-of-life challenges to expansion in the 1960s and 1970s showed.

In fact, airport policy was often played out 'in the future', as rival stakeholders produced competing projections of rising demands on airports for ten- or twenty-year periods, often with recourse to the horrific fantasy of 'capacity overload', which became a regular trope of government. For example, as early as July 1952, in Cabinet discussions various concerns about the capacity of existing airport infrastructure to meet demand led to calls for the development of Gatwick as a response to the forecast of a further doubling of flights in the London area by 1960 (Cabinet Office, 1952). In a similar fashion, over twenty-five years later, the Secretary of State for Trade echoed in Cabinet concerns over the limits of existing airport capacity by informing ministers in his presentation of the 1978 airports policy white paper that 'there is, therefore, a risk that demand will exceed planned capacity at the end of the 1980s if traffic grows at the highest forecast rate' (Cabinet Office, 1978: 2). Indeed, at a Cabinet meeting in August 1979, the Secretary of State for Trade noted that overcrowding at Heathrow was 'acute' and he went on to argue that it was imperative for the government to deny permission for new airlines to use the international hub, while accepting that certain services would have to be transferred to Gatwick (Cabinet Office, 1979: 2).

Governments of various hues came to acknowledge the vagaries of forecasting, even in their own white papers. By the 1985 white paper, which was put forward by the Thatcher government, the practice of forecasting was in many ways on the wane, only to be replaced in government circles by the role of market mechanisms, which emerged as the favoured policy instrument to coordinate infrastructure growth and patterns of rising demand. Indeed, the social logics of 'predict and provide' were to come under increasing challenge, as concerns about the environment and climate change made their way onto the policy agenda. As the protests over the location of the proposed third London airport demonstrated, the regime of expansion was marked by the vicissitudes of political protest, the changing balances of political forces in local communities and the country at large, as well as the policy reversals of successive governments. But before we turn to such opposition, we have already intimated that, in the 1990s, the logic of expansion was to gather momentum, as the Thatcher government, aided and abetted by the EU, embarked upon a wave of privatisation, deregulation and liberalisation in air transport. This increasing liberalisation of the European skies stimulated another set of demands, which New Labour also had to address once in office.

Privatisation, deregulation and liberalisation of the European skies

Aviation expansion in the three decades following the Second World War was primarily directed by the state through the nationalisation of leading airlines, the public ownership of major airports and the public provision of other transport infrastructure. The 1944 Chicago Convention, the foundation of the post-war international regime in air travel, came to rest upon the sovereignty of the nation-state, the negotiation of bilateral air service agreements between governments and the dominance of national 'flag carriers' (Hanlon, 2000). Bilateral agreements enshrined the rights of national governments to grant scheduled international air services access to national airspace, designating carriers and regulating traffic rights, tariffs and capacity and safety regulations on specific routes. It was not that uncommon for airlines to pool revenues on particular routes, while governments often deferred to the International Air Transport Association (IATA), the association of international airline companies, to fix tariffs on certain routes. Such agreements protected the monopolies of national carriers, particularly in Europe, where the national airline came to symbolise the power and status of the nation (see Dienel and Lyth, 1998: 1–3; Doganis, 1973; Doganis, 2006: 27–31; Wheatcroft, 1964).

In the UK, the Attlee government, which was elected in 1945, moved quickly to create two national carriers; BOAC was designated to provide long-haul flights and BEA to offer short-haul and domestic flights. BOAC had formed in 1939 as a state-owned carrier through the nationalisation of Imperial Airways and British Airways

Limited. In 1946, BEA was created out of a division of BOAC and the subsequent nationalisation of independent British scheduled airlines (Lyth, 1995).[10] These moves were initially replicated in the domain of airport ownership, when the Attlee government announced plans to take airports into public ownership, although many airports were already under state control as a result of the war (McKie, 1973: 41–2). And yet, as early as 1947, the government, which was increasingly pre-occupied with budgetary deficits and funding investments in post-war construction, backtracked on its plans to purchase a total of forty-four airports and bring them into public ownership (Perman, 1973: 29).

Instead, in the words of Colin Buchanan, who was a leading transport planner and member of the Roskill Commission into the location of a third London airport, airports policy from the 1950s is better described as a 'Have-a-Go' policy, whereby 'virtually any organisation, council or individual who thought himself capable of operating an airport could now do so' (Perman, 1973: 30). Many local authorities did establish their own airports, while other airports returned from military to local authority control after the Second World War. For example, in 1950 Manchester airport passed into local authority hands, while Birmingham airport returned to local authority control some ten years later. Major airports thus remained outside government jurisdiction, which, 'in practical terms, and above all in planning terms ... hardly made sense' (McKie, 1973: 53). In a note of dissent against the policy recommendations of the Roskill Commission, Buchanan added to his criticisms of airport policy, suggesting that 'civil aviation was for some years a more or less parentless child handed around from one ministry to another' (Roskill report, 'Note of Dissent', cited in McKie, 1973: 57).

Grievances like those voiced by Buchanan crystallised into repeated demands for a national airport plan, particularly at the end of the 1960s, when the incrementalism and poor governance of airport policy since the end of the war came under increasing public scrutiny (Fordham, 1970: 307; McKie, 1973; Perman, 1973). Notably, in 1967 the aviation policy expert Rigas Doganis complained in his Fabian Society pamphlet *A National Airport Plan* that 'in 1945 the Labour government promised order. Today there is chaos' (cited in Perman, 1973: 30). BAA had been established in 1965 to manage the three state-owned airports in London – Heathrow, Gatwick and Stansted – as well as Prestwick in Scotland. It was subsequently to take responsibility for the management of Glasgow, Edinburgh and

Aberdeen in 1971 and acquired Southampton in 1990 (House of Commons Transport Select Committee, 2008: 5). Such moves towards a partial rationalisation of airport governance were replicated in the creation of the Civil Aviation Authority (CAA). Its emergence followed the criticisms made by the Edwards Committee on the future of civil aviation about the fragmented governance of the airports (Edwards Committee, 1969: 223), as well as its claim that 'the whole air transport operation needs to be approached as an integrated system' (Edwards Committee, 1969: 250). The CAA began operating in 1972 as a single regulatory body for aviation, thus replacing the Air Transport Licensing Board, parts of the Board of Trade and the Air Regulation Board (House of Commons Library, 2011c: 2–3).

But the monopoly of the national carriers was barely loosened until the expansion of the market for package tours in the 1960s, when private airlines began to pose 'for the first time ... a threat to the confident ascendancy of BEA and BOAC' (Corbett, 1965: 144; see also Lyth, 1995: 81). One such independent operator was the charter company Laker Airlines, which was established in 1966 by the British entrepreneur Freddie Laker, and which was one of the forerunners of the 'no-frills' carriers that emerged in the 1990s. Laker gained a licence in October 1972 to operate low-fare scheduled services out of Stansted to New York. In its 1969 report, the Edwards Committee had proposed the introduction of a 'second force' airline to compete against BEA and BOAC on selected routes. The acceptance of this recommendation resulted in the opening up of certain long-haul BOAC routes to competition from the leading independent carrier, British Caledonian (BCal), with BCal starting services out of Gatwick to New York and Los Angeles in April 1973.

These limited experiments in 'double designation' were brought to an abrupt end by the fall in passenger numbers on cross-Atlantic routes, largely caused by the 1973 oil crisis. BCal stopped its flights to New York and Los Angeles in November 1974. In July 1975, the then Secretary of State for Trade, Peter Shore, responded to falling passenger numbers by ending competition between British airlines on long-haul scheduled flights (Department of Trade, 1976b: 2). Laker Airlines' Skytrain experiment, which promised low-cost 'walk on' scheduled services to New York, with no advanced ticket reservation, was thus brought to an end, when government revoked its operating licence (Sampson, 1984: 185–204). This decision was motivated by protectionism towards the recently created national carrier, BA, which was formed in 1974 from the merger of BOAC and BEA. In a command paper on future aviation policy, Shore estimated that 'BA would incur losses of about £6 million a year if the Laker Skytrain and one corresponding US service were to be operated' (Department of Trade, 1976b: 4–5). Moving away from competition on routes, Shore carved up the world into complementary, but not competitive, 'spheres of interest' between national flag carriers and selected independent airlines, thereby paving the way in principle 'for much closer co-operation between BA and BCal' (Department of Trade, 1976b: 4).

Challenges to state-regulated air transport markets continued, however, often taking inspiration from developments in the US. Under the Carter presidency, American air transport underwent a process of deregulation, which brought about the development of low-cost carriers, notably the market leader in the US, Southwest Airlines. In the UK, Laker won an appeal against the revocation of his operating licence in 1977, just as the UK and the US completed the renegotiation of the 1946 Bermuda bilateral air services agreement. Bermuda II came into operation with Laker designated as the second UK 'flag carrier' between London and New York, operating this time out of Gatwick (Sampson, 1984: 189). This was because BCal had permanently suspended its cross-Atlantic services from Gatwick in its 'spheres of interest' collaboration with BA. SkyTrain offered flights to the US for approximately two-thirds of the cost of BA flights. It was Laker, for Hudson and Pettifer (1979: 196), who thus 'virtually single-handed … broke up the established IATA-supported Atlantic fare structure'.

But it was only under the Thatcher governments of the 1980s that the interventionist and regulatory role of the state in supporting and advancing UK aviation finally gave way to the primacy of the market and private enterprise, as 'go-for-growth' expansionist plans came on the back of the liberalisation, deregulation and global commercialisation of the aviation industry (see Caves and Gosling, 1997; Glaister *et al.*, 2006: 20–7; A. Graham, 2008a: 10–67; A. Graham, 2008b: 103–5). In 1981, Sir John King (later to become Lord King and to be dubbed Thatcher's 'favourite businessman') was appointed chairman of BA and he was handed the task of preparing the national carrier for privatisation. After extensive restructuring and rebranding, and with tremendous media fanfare, the company was floated on the London Stock Exchange in February 1987; the initial share offering was eleven times oversubscribed. In the same year, the government privatised BAA, now known as 'BAA Limited', and six other airports

(Starkie, 2004: 390–4). Both privatisations were heralded as major success stories in breaking with the restrictions of nationalisation and state regulation by injecting healthy competition and by stimulating consumption. Following privatisation, BAA expanded the proportion of its terminal space allocated to retailing activities and promoted the development of its retail business. Terminal areas came to provide more shops and restaurants, and passengers were routed through these retailing spaces to maximise their exposure to retail opportunities (A. Graham, 2008a, 2008b). Rising passenger spending at terminals increasingly contributed to the income of airports and provided a means for airports to cross-subsidise landing fees to attract carriers (Humphreys *et al.*, 2007). This strategy was particularly significant for expanding regional airports in the 1990s, which, in the words of a CAA study, now pursued

> a more commercially focused approach, seeking to maximise non-aviation revenues in order to price their landing fees competitively and improve their facilities, attract services to their airport and realise the full potential of their business and the regional economy. (CAA, 2005: 101)

Within the EU, the Thatcher government also led demands for the liberalisation of aviation, introducing the first liberal air services agreement in the EU with the Benelux countries in 1985. The UK government subsequently used its 1986 presidency of the Council of Ministers to move towards the adoption in 1987 of the first liberalisation package of the European skies (House of Commons Library, 2010: 4). That package was then followed by the adoption of further measures in July 1990 and June 1992, all of which progressively undermined state-controlled aviation markets and the privileging of bilateral agreements (Kassim and Stevens, 2009). It is notable that the special status for national flag carriers, in route licensing, or protection from competition, was no longer permitted, while restrictions on low fares were dismissed and carriers were attributed rights to fly between and within member states of the EU. Indeed, it was in April 1997, one month before New Labour came to office, that UK carriers gained the so-called 'cabotage' right to fly internal routes within another member state.

The lowering of route barriers on domestic and international routes within the EU triggered the entry of more low-cost scheduled airlines into the market, which were now able to compete against the newly privatised national carrier, BA (Humphreys, 2003: 24). Thus easyJet, established in 1995, began flying from Luton to Edinburgh and Glasgow, while Ryanair flew out of Stansted to Prestwick from 1996. Established in 1990, Ryanair under Michael O'Leary imitated the 'no frills' budget strategy of Southwest Airlines by negotiating discounts with airports on landing and departing fees in exchange for the promise of delivering passengers to the commercial centres that were now airport terminals (Creaton, 2005: 100). In 1994, following the first round of European liberalisation, some fifty-seven new airlines were established, although thirty-seven were out of business within two years (Creaton, 2005: 115). BA responded by creating its own 'no frills' subsidiary, Go, in 1998 (which was bought by easyJet in 2002) (CAA, 2005: 62–8).

In summary, under the guise of continuity and persistent expansion, particularly at Heathrow and in the south-east of England more generally, it is possible to discern a new set of logics, regulations and policy instruments, as the state-driven expansion of the postwar regime gave way to market-led expansion from the late 1970s onwards. But what demands did this place on New Labour? In many ways, New Labour entered office in the midst of a revolution in air transport, which was accelerating passenger demand, not least within the category of what became known as 'leisure travellers', while also putting pressure on airport capacity, the market superiority of flag carriers, as well as traditional relations between government and the industry. In the first place, it was becoming evident that the entry of low-cost carriers was the main driver behind the growth of regional airports and Stansted (which was the base for much of Ryanair's operations). Secondly, low-cost carriers increased competition on short-haul flights, which led to falling fares on the routes where they operated and shifts in the pattern of business flying – a key component of the business model of traditional carriers (CAA, 1998; 2005). Thirdly, the logic of liberalisation amplified pressures on slot allocation at international airports. For example, CAA's 1998 assessment of the first five years of liberalisation found that the share of national carriers on international routes had fallen by 10 per cent compared with 1992, and that airport congestion had worsened at the EU's busiest airports, notably Heathrow and Gatwick (cited in House of Commons Library, 2010: 13–14). This exponential expansion was not without its contradictions, and it provoked protests and increasing demands to place constraints on the expansion of air transport. As we noted at the beginning of this chapter, New Labour entered office at the back end of the protest against the second runway at Manchester airport, and it also faced a highly contentious decision over whether to go ahead with the construction of a fifth terminal at Heathrow. It is to such protests against expansion that we now turn.

Contradictions, protests and demands

All policy regimes are marked by dislocatory experiences, which can then be constructed as grievances, demands, coalitions and counter-hegemonic projects. The installation and sedimentation of the contradictory regime of aviation in post-war Britain was no exception to this rule. For one thing, the inexorable logic of aviation expansion was the source of widespread dislocation, which destabilised local communities, urban and rural, large and small, often leading to the construction of political grievances, protests and social demands. Until the 1990s, most of the grievances and demands associated with aviation centred on the problems of noise, air pollution, disruption and compensation. These quality-of-life issues were then decisively supplemented in the 1990s by environmental questions and the issue of climate change (Griggs and Howarth, 2007a).

Struggles against rising levels of noise pollution at airports took hold in the 1960s. The introduction of turbo-jet engines on passenger aircraft flying across the south-east of England triggered the formation of national lobbies against aircraft noise, which brought together the Noise Abatement Society, the British Association for the Control of Aircraft Noise, the United Kingdom Federation Against Aircraft Nuisance and the Local Authorities Aircraft Noise Council (Perman, 1973: 26). HACAN, the Heathrow Association for the Control of Aircraft Noise, the local resident anti-Heathrow expansion group, has its own origins in the decision of Kew residents in December 1966 to take action against the noise pollution caused by the changing flight patterns of planes over south London (Griggs and Howarth, 2004). The deleterious effects of noise pollution remained an enduring cause of concern for those opposed to airport expansion. Over time, it was associated with various hazards, including for example the disturbance of sleep patterns and reduced educational achievement, as aircraft noise impaired the ability of children who lived below flight paths to concentrate and study optimally. At the public inquiry into the fourth terminal at Heathrow in the late 1970s, the government inspector frequently invoked the continued campaigns of local residents against noise pollution, thus recognising the frustrations of local residents who 'feel strongly that they are deprived of the right to bring a grievance about aircraft noise before a court of law' (Glidewell, 1979: 22). Some twenty years later, in December 1998, environmental and local authority groups launched yet another anti-aircraft noise campaign, arguing that

> for too long aircraft noise has brought misery to hundreds of thousands of people. Yet new laws to protect communities near airports have been shelved again and again … it is the time for the Government to update the law and give people living near airports some peace and quiet.[11]

The emerging struggles against airport expansion came to the boil at the end of the 1960s over the proposed location of a new third London airport, which was designed to resolve the perceived capacity problems at Heathrow. The struggles at various sites – Stansted, Cublington, Aylesbury, Nuthampstead and Foulness – are well documented (Buchanan, 1981; Cook, 1967; Hall, 1982; McKie 1973; Perman, 1973). They are etched in the psyche of many campaigners and are still celebrated as moments when 'ordinary people rose up in revolt against the tyranny of technology' (Desmond Fennell, chair of Wing Airport Resistance Association, cited in Perman, 1973: 165). These local conservation campaigns, which articulated appeals for the protection of rural areas, agricultural land and traditional ways of life, punctuated the politics of airport expansion during the late 1960s and early 1970s, as each government policy reversal over the location of the third London airport fuelled new grievances and campaigns. Such campaigns only subsided when, with falling demand for air travel following the economic recession of the early 1970s, the minority Labour government under the premiership of Harold Wilson withdrew plans to build a third London airport, thus putting an end to the early planning and construction work at Maplin in Essex – the estuary site which the government had settled upon after high-profile public opposition to expansion at both Stansted and Cublington.

Indeed, the significance of these policy equivocations in response to local resident protest campaigns is exemplified in the story of London's third airport, which Peter Hall (1982) has characterised as one of the UK's 'great planning disasters'. In 1961, a report from the House of Commons Estimates Committee advocated further studies into the suitability of Stansted to become the third London airport. Subsequently, in June 1963, an Interdepartmental Committee selected Stansted as the site of the third London airport. This decision was rejected following a public inquiry, in which the inspector declared the case for Stansted was not convincing; a further review was called for. The report of the inspector, which was made public in 1967, was countered by a 1967 white paper, which, despite the report of the inspector, confirmed Stansted as the third London airport.

But in 1968, following concerted opposition from local residents to the development of Stansted, the government established the Roskill Commission, which was led by a high court judge, to make its own independent recommendations as to the optimal site for the third airport. After three years, its investigation came out in favour of Cublington in Buckinghamshire, although one member of the Commission, the famous transport planner Colin Buchanan, wrote a widely cited 'Note of Dissent', which challenged the decision and the cost–benefit analysis that informed it. He argued in favour of an estuary airport at Maplin to minimise environmental impacts (Buchanan, 1971; Roskill Commission, 1971; see also Morris, 1997: 97). Amidst public opposition and vigorous lobbying, the Heath government rejected Cublington, plumping instead for the building of an international airport at Maplin Sands (or Foulness). No sooner had work begun on the site than it was abandoned in 1974 by the Wilson government. Subsequently, Stansted was confirmed again as the third London airport by the Thatcher government in 1979 – a decision that had been set out by civil servants in 1953, as intimated by Anthony Greenwood, Housing and Local Government Minister in a parliamentary debate on the 1967 airports white paper:

> It is quite clear, looking back, that at least from 1953 onwards the assumption was consistently made that Stansted would be the third London Airport. That assumption helped to determine the routing of air traffic, including military traffic … and also helped to determine the distribution of military airfields and other installations. (Anthony Greenwood, Housing and Local Government Minister, cited in McKie, 1973: 55)

Throughout the saga of the third London airport, as well as the early campaigns against airport expansion (which were often associated with this proposal), local residents tended to voice an array of different grievances about noise control, the local quality of life and the protection of rural areas. Such campaigns are best characterised as 'environmental conservation campaigns' (Byrne, 1997: 129), which sought in a particularistic fashion to prevent airport expansion at specific sites, be it Stansted, Cublington or Heathrow, rather than to advance broader campaigns against airport expansion at all sites across the UK. Reporting in the later 1960s, the Edwards Committee deliberately shied away from any direct discussion of specific airport sites, because it was wary of attracting the attention of local campaigners, whom it characterised as 'local patriots' (Edwards Committee, 1969: 220). In addition, as recognised by the director of research for the Roskill Commission, campaigns tended to privilege conservationist issues or questions about the community's quality of life, and were thus concerned with mitigating local noise and air pollution, as well as protecting local housing and communities (Thompson, 1972: 23). Conservationist demands of this sort were couched in the discourse of environmentalism, with one editorial in *The Times* in April 1971 describing the decision to cite a third London airport at Maplin as the defeat of the engineers by the environmentalists (cited in Sharman, 1971: 137).

While these campaigns were significant in protecting local communities and raising awareness about the negative impacts of aviation on local environments, they did not to any significant degree express demands to control environmental pollution from aviation beyond specific airport communities; nor did they endeavour to integrate aviation issues into broader policy agendas or alternative projects for social and political change (Griggs and Howarth, 2007a). Typically, for example, at the public inquiry into the construction of Terminal Five at Heathrow, Dermot Cox, the then chair of HACAN, clearly stated in his closing statement that 'HACAN is a single-issue group and aircraft noise is the reason why we are present at this Inquiry' (HACAN, 1999: 28).

Yet alternative, more universal demands for social and political change were soon to be percolating in international policy arenas and national commissions, as governments responded to the emerging environmental policy agenda and demands for sustainable development.[12] At the 1992 Earth Summit in Rio, the UK government signed up to the United Nations Framework Convention on Climate Change, which committed it to reduce carbon dioxide emissions to 1990 levels by 2000. In national terms, this translated into a flurry of white papers and official declarations. These included the 1990 white paper *This*

Common Inheritance, as well as four white papers in January 1994 on sustainable development, climate change, biodiversity and sustainable forestry (for a discussion of these international developments and national transport policy, see Dudley and Richardson, 2000: 155, 179–85). In the EU, the European Commission's Fifth Environmental Action Programme, which was signed by member states in February 1993, articulated the discourse of sustainable mobility within the field of transport policy. Pursuing this focus on sustainability and transport, the UK Round Table on Sustainable Development released its own policy paper entitled *Defining a Sustainable Transport Sector* in 1996.

Scientific and expert inquiries into aviation emissions and their impact on climate change had surfaced in the late 1960s and early 1970s, when plans were announced to develop supersonic aircraft, thus provoking concerns about the emissions of nitrogen oxides in the stratosphere (Lee, 2009: 27–8). The Royal Commission on Environmental Pollution (RCEP) in a 1971 report had drawn public attention to the noise and environmental problems associated with supersonic flight (five years before Concorde, the supersonic Anglo-French airliner, came into service). Although plans for supersonic fleets did not materialise in practice, the early to mid-1990s saw repeated scientific publications on aviation and its impact on climate change (Lee, 2009: 28). Advocating the need for sustainable development, while also expressing concerns about aviation emissions within the UK, the RCEP in its 1994 report *Transport and the Environment* reproduced appeals to make the 'organising metaphor' of sustainable mobility the new frame for national transport policy.

More fully, the RCEP report recognised the long-term impact of aviation on global warming and the atmosphere, and it warned of the 'irreversible damage to the Earth's atmosphere from the growth of air transport, or at least serious damage of a long-term nature' (paragraph 5.33, cited in RCEP, 2002: 3). It also endorsed the management of demand for air transport by adopting the rhetoric of 'polluter pays'. This was reflected in its calls for the environmental costs of air travel to be made aware to passengers, so as to dampen down growing passenger demand, and for an end to the 'anomaly that airlines do not pay tax on fuel'. It is noteworthy that the RCEP recommended that air travel be discouraged for domestic and near-European journeys, where rail could offer a competitive alternative (recommendation 109).[13] In so doing, it questioned the very assumptions of 'predict and provide' policies in aviation, which, it suggested, produced self-fulfilling prophecies of growing demand and passenger numbers. The RCEP went on to condemn expansionist aviation policies as incompatible with sustainable development:

> an unquestioning attitude towards future growth in air travel, and an acceptance that the projected demand for additional facilities and services must be met, are incompatible with the aim of sustainable development. (1994: paras 5.33)[14]

At the public inquiry into the fifth terminal at Heathrow, the government inspector, Roy Vandermeer, claimed to have been informed by ministers and officials in the departments responsible for aviation that 'the intention has always been that a balance must be struck between economic need for new capacity and the environmental impacts it might have', with the government accepting 'that greater weight would now be attached to environmental considerations' (Vandermeer, 2001a: 17). Opponents of expansion, such as Hillington Council, Friends of the Earth (FoE) and a consortium of ten local authorities known as LAHT5,[15] sought to impose the constraints of sustainable development as the basis for any decision on Heathrow. The LAHT5 went so far as to cite the 'precautionary principle' in order to counter the proposals for expansion (Vandermeer, 2001b: 342). Yet the inspector argued that the emergence of sustainable development and environmental concerns had done little to offset the overriding demand to meet economic need. He referred to discussions in 1995 in which the Major government had (re)asserted that

> there had been no change in the position taken by the Government in a statement issued in February 1995 to the effect that issues of global warming are of very limited relevance to decisions on the capacity of UK airports. (Vandermeer, 2001a: 21)

Interpreting the 1985 white paper, the inspector thus concluded that he was

> in no doubt that, at that time, the Government priority was meeting the need for airport capacity where and when it arose. While policy required that every effort should be made to minimise the environmental damage caused that was seen as a secondary stage. (Vandermeer 2001a: 23)

Nonetheless, as these exchanges demonstrate, new antagonisms were emerging in the domain of transport policy and aviation. What is more, the construction and sedimentation of the discourse of sustainable development, which became more prominent in the late 1980s, was to put into place the conditions for new equivalences to be drawn between protests against noise and local quality of life, on the one hand, and demands to challenge climate change, on the other.[16]

On taking office in May 1997, some six months before the organisers of the Kyoto conference aimed to forge international cooperation between nation-states in the fight against rising emissions of carbon dioxide and climate change, New Labour thus encountered relatively new demands for the regulation of aviation from environmental pressure groups, such as FoE, which highlighted the greenhouse effect of carbon dioxide and water vapour emissions from aviation, as well as the impacts of airports on local habitats, water quality and noise (FoE, 1997: 50–1). Equally, FoE researchers and campaigners were quick to draw equivalences between aviation expansion and the 'discredited' 'predict and provide' methodology of road transport planning.[17] At Manchester airport, the campaign against the second runway began to engender protean alliances between local residents and direct action environmentalists, who imported into the domain of airport protests the strategies and tactics of the anti-roads movement. Protesters at Manchester such as Daniel Hooper (aka Swampy) had been involved in the protests against the A31 road expansion in North Devon (Griggs and Howarth, 2002). Engaging in the campaign against airport expansion, these environmental activists began to challenge the ideological assumptions underpinning the politics of aviation expansion by highlighting the inconsistencies between plans to curb road expansion and continued support for aviation expansion.

Fledgling alliances like those assembled in Manchester began to take the first steps towards transforming the politics of the anti-airport expansion protest movement. They sought to reactivate the political exclusions and antagonisms associated with the social logics of 'predict and provide', which had in part constituted the post-war regime of aviation expansion. Their condemnations, and the chequered history of earlier protests and grievances against airport expansion, raise important questions about how and why the regime of aviation expansion had been installed and sedimented. In the light of these protests against expansion, how can we begin to critically explain this consistent vector of aviation expansion? Why and how did aviation achieve a privileged, not to say 'sacrosanct' position? It is to such questions that we now turn.

The ignoble origins of aviation

One way to answer these questions is to argue that once civil aviation had been established as a vital part of the UK's post-war manufacturing and transport strategy, and once it had been decided to concentrate civil airports in London and the south-east, then it became very difficult to dislodge these beliefs and assumptions. Much evidence points in this direction. For instance, governments and ministers, as well as their civil servants, believed that London should be a 'world transport centre', rivalling New York, Chicago and other European capitals. Central to this ambition was the associated belief that the UK could, and therefore should, retain its 'leading position on world air routes' (BAA, 1967: 11, 12). As an industrialised state that depended on overseas trade, officials and politicians argued that the UK required airports that could service trade and earn foreign currency. As early as 1952, the Secretary of State for Air in Churchill's government concluded in Cabinet that aviation was 'the all-important manufacturing industry' (cited in Engel, 2005: 2).[18] Later that year, in one of his first speeches to the House of Commons as Minister of Transport and Civil Aviation in July 1952, Alan Lennox-Boyd announced to his colleagues 'that we are on the verge of a great air age in which there can be no turning back'. He went on: 'I said that this is an air age, and there is no politics in that statement at all, and most certainly no party politics'. Making reference to 'the white cliffs of Dover' and their 'particular place in the sympathy and affections of our people', he predicted that 'the first sight of the greatest number of people who come to Britain will now be, and ever more so as the years go by, the sight of London Airport from the air'.[19] The 1953 white paper subsequently declared aviation to be a cornerstone of Britain's economic development, and it went on to draw comparisons between air transport and the role of shipping in the building of the British Empire (Ministry of Civil Aviation, 1953: 3).

In fact, as early as 1913, Winston Churchill had recognised the importance of the 'naval aeroplane service' to the UK and its empire, when he argued that 'the enduring safety of this country will not be maintained by force of arms unless over the whole sphere of aerial development', though as British Minister of War and Air he had initially been unsympathetic to helping the development of civil aviation companies. Having said this, the most positive appraisal of the UK government's air transport policy between the wars was that it did not actively prevent the growth of commercial aviation, which was developed by a number of small companies (Bagwell, 1988: 281). Although the UK was a pioneer in commercial aviation – the first commercial air service in the world was established in Britain on 10 August 1910, and there were sporadic efforts after the First World War to establish regular air services between London and Paris, and between other UK cities – its early commercial carrier, Imperial Airlines, quickly fell behind its continental rivals, especially with the development of Lufthansa in Germany and KLM in the Netherlands (Bagwell, 1988: 281; Brooks, 1961: 40–1).[20]

During the Second World War, however, as the UK rapidly expanded its manufacture of aircraft, constructed additional runways and quickly developed new aircraft technologies, the government came to the conclusion that the aviation industry was a decisive component of British manufacturing (Coopey and Lyth, 2009: 226–30).[21] Rapid military advances in aeroplane technology led to the growing realisation in government circles that civil aviation was to become a crucial industry in the post-war period, and a cross-party consensus emerged over the need for government support to expand aviation and its attendant transport infrastructure. Both parties of the wartime coalition thus agreed to appoint Lord Brabazon, a well known advocate of civil aviation, to chair an interdepartmental committee on the industry – the Ministerial Committee on Civil Air Transport – and to prepare plans for the future development of civil aviation in post-war Britain. The so-called Brabazon Plan, which was explicitly adopted in 1942, focused on the long-term development of technologically superior aircraft, which, through 'a vigorous and farsighted policy' of unprecedented business and government coordination, would lead to the production of superior aeroplanes in the 1950s. From lagging behind its competitors in the 1930s, the UK would now, Brabazon predicted, 'leap-frog' ahead of its rivals in international aviation by the late 1940s and 1950s, although there was more than a hint of hubris in the ambition (Hamilton-Paterson, 2010: 250).

Yet the consensus on civil aviation was constructed in the face of internal pressures and conflicts. On the one hand, there were struggles between different ministries and agencies about the appropriate balance between the war effort and commercial aviation. There were strong disagreements about separating civil aviation from the War Ministry, as well as the subsequent decision to create the Ministry of Civil Aviation. As the war entered its final phase, there were calls to transfer the Department of Civil Aviation at the Air Ministry to the Ministry of War Transport. On 14 June 1944 Lord Beaverbrook, the Lord Privy Seal, who had been Minister for Aircraft Production and Minister for Supply under Churchill, argued for an immediate transfer, as 'the existing machinery for development of Civil Aviation will not work'.[22] These calls reiterated arguments made by the Civil Aviation Planning Committee (which had been called the Brown Committee, before the Second World War).[23] But though these calls were actively resisted by the Secretary of State for Air, Sir Archibald Sinclair, who believed there were 'good military reasons' for delaying the decision until the end of hostilities with Japan, Churchill established a new Ministry of Civil Aviation later that year.[24] A few others in the Cabinet remained unconvinced about the prospects for commercial aviation. In their view, while 'British civil aviation should be developed to the utmost possible extent', it 'could not be expected that aviation would provide employment for more than a small fraction of the number of persons at present employed'; the 'probable small size of the Civil Aviation Industry' was used as a further argument in favour of keeping civil aviation within the Air Ministry even after the war.[25]

Internal struggles were also evident in the decisions about commercial airports, particularly the choice of Heathrow as the favoured location for the UK's main post-war international airport. The official narrative of the origins of Heathrow airport contends that it was initially built as an airfield for the Royal Air Force (RAF) in the Second World War and that at the end of the war it was developed into the main civil airport for London. In fact, there are at least two rival and equally ignoble accounts of the decision to locate the nation's principal international airport at Heathrow, which make extraordinary reading. The first account emerged in 1973, when Harold Balfour published his autobiography, *Wings Over Westminster*. Serving as the Parliamentary Under-Secretary of State in the Air Ministry between 1938 and 1944, he claimed to have misled a Cabinet committee over the procurement of land for post-war civil aviation by strongly arguing for the need to requisition land at Heathrow for a bomber airfield, even though there were other airfields in the Home Counties that could have been used. Balfour persuaded the Cabinet and the government to seize the land using emergency powers by invoking the Defence of the Realm Act of 1939, thus bypassing the normal peacetime procedures governing procurement. The decision permitted no right of appeal. BOAC was complicit in the ruse, yet still complained about the unsuitability of the proposed layout of runways for its civil aviation requirements. To maintain the deception, a runway was constructed that was inappropriate for civil purposes, which was subsequently abandoned.

The second account was presented by Douglas Jay in his auto-biography, *Change and Fortune* (1980). He writes that the Heathrow decision was made in 1943 at a meeting which 'lasted only 40 minutes'. As a civil servant in the Ministry of Supply, he claims he 'was asked to attend a meeting at the Air Ministry to decide on a site for a postwar civil airport, and protested at first that this was no business of mine at this stage of the war. But I was ordered to go, and about six of us assembled at assistant-secretary level' (Jay, 1980: 106). Forty minutes later, according to Jay, the fateful decision had been taken.

It is now accepted that each of these accounts distorts the true picture of events to different degrees. On the one hand, the official story conceals the way in which Heathrow was earmarked for civil aviation well before the end of the war. As Balfour records, the War Cabinet was misled into giving approval for its construction: Heathrow was destined to be a civil airport right from the start. At the same time, the development of the site for the RAF was merely a ruse to circumvent a public inquiry, while displacing criticisms that the war effort was being diverted to matters that could be tackled after the war. But though Balfour provides the most accurate account of events, recent research indicates that the possible location of a major international airport at Heathrow was discussed in late 1942 – it was proposed by S. A. Dismore, who had been assistant general manager of Imperial Airways before the war – and Air Ministry files show that the proposed airport was discussed in the early part of 1943 (Sherwood, 2009: 75). In fact, despite the various arguments about the urgent needs of the RAF, the latter never used the airport. These machinations and deceptions that characterised the ignoble origins of Heathrow airport were to haunt its subsequent development. The next sixty years were marked by a vicious cycle of expansion, agreements on the prohibition of further growth, and broken promises. This cycle was also to mark the development of the other major airports in London and the south-east, as well as some of the regional airports.

This 'improvisation' of a mass industry, as Correlli Barnett has put it, had many flaws and faced considerable difficulties in translating its wartime advances into commercial successes in the new global marketplace (Barnett, 1995). Yet its expansion still placed the UK at the forefront of commercial opportunity in the decisive post-war conjuncture. The destruction and weakening of its major European competitors led the UK government and manufacturers to harbour high hopes of competing with the US for the domination of global aviation. In fact, the key watchwords in this emergence of UK civil aviation were competition, conflict and deception, each of which was decisive in the development of this then new and highly promising technology. Competition, in terms of both the competitiveness of the UK aviation industry as well as the threat posed by rival countries and their aviation industries, was a critical driving force of UK aviation. As such, an important, if not decisive, factor in sustaining this emergent consensus on the future of civil aviation was the positing of an 'other' that threatened UK aviation and its future interests. Whereas the threats were once posed by competitors in Europe, it was now the power and might of the US that occupied the attention of politicians and producers alike. The Brabazon Plan was provoked by the desire to counter America's greater production capacity (Engel, 2005: 6; Engel, 2007, 33–9). Ministers in general were acutely aware of the dangers posed by the US. For example, in Cabinet discussions about the creation of a more autonomous ministry for civil aviation, those in favour argued that

> Unless substantial progress was made at once with the design and development of new types of civil transport aircraft, and with the negotiation of agreements with foreign countries, it would be impossible for this country to secure a fair share in the post-war development of civil aviation. This was all the more pressing given 'that the future of our aircraft manufacturing industry was largely dependent on the development of British civil aviation'.[26]

In the period leading up to the Chicago Convention in October 1944, explicit fears and anxieties about US domination were voiced. The newly appointed Minister of Civil Aviation, in his first memorandum on the 'organisation of civil aviation', stated that

> Civil aviation is first and foremost a Transport business. To make it efficient and compete against the United States we must have the best brains and experience in transport.... Everywhere else, in Europe, Asia and Africa, across the oceans, the competition will be against the highly efficient air services of the United States, and later of Dutch and other countries. This competition can only be met by equally good, or better, airlines.[27]

He also cautioned against internal disagreements about the relative merits of 'Socialism' and 'private enterprise' as the most efficient instrument of development. Instead, as he put it, 'our fight must be with foreign competitors and not amongst ourselves'.[28]

Stringent efforts were made to mobilise and organise the Empire against the US in the lead-up to the Chicago Convention towards the end of 1944. The Minister for Civil Aviation stressed the importance of consulting with Commonwealth delegates at Montreal before the Convention 'to secure close working arrangements between the various Commonwealth [air] services', and to oppose US plans for a period of unrestricted competition in aviation in the post-war period, during which 'the US would have a great advantage over all other countries'.[29] A clear strategy was outlined to counter US proposals:

> The line which the Minister proposed to take was to make a strong effort to secure the agreement of the United States to a Convention covering frequencies, quotas and rates on the lines set out in the White Paper (Cmd. 6581). If this failed, we should not attempt to establish a Convention excluding the United States but embracing the Dominions and such foreign countries as were willing to join it, since this would be regarded as a lining up of countries against the United States. Rather, we should try to secure a Convention with the United States on a narrower basis covering technical matters such as safety regulations and face the possibility of dealing with frequencies, quotas and rates by means of bilateral negotiations. In this event he would attach great importance to our acting in combination with the Dominions and not independently. We should also try in our bilateral negotiations to secure the adoption of standard clauses, so that in the course of time it might be possible to secure by a series of bilateral agreements very much the same results as would be achieved by a multilateral Convention.[30]

While British policy-makers accepted that they had to negotiate with their American counterparts, eventually signing up to the Chicago Convention, and then agreeing Bermuda 1 in 1946, they were extremely anxious about US intentions and policies, and sought various ways to escape the latter's growing power and hegemony (Dobson, 1991: 192–210). (These anxieties were evident, for example, in the development of the world's first jetliner – the Comet – and the tragic outcomes surrounding its untimely withdrawal from service – see Engel, 2005: 22–31; Engel, 2007).

The actual and perceived threats posed by US interests were to continue throughout the post-war period, as the British aviation industry was consistently impeded by American diplomacy and its security ideals. If anything, these anxieties intensified, as the UK sought to develop its aircraft technology in the face of US competition, while also seeking to support its nascent airline industry and maintain its 'national prestige' (Barnett, 1995: 228–46). In the face of financial constraints and US diplomatic pressures, coupled with the inherent organisational failings of post-war reconstruction, the circle proved difficult to square. For example, a major contradiction emerged between the development of an autochthonous aircraft industry, on the one hand, and the profitability and commercial viability of the nationalised airlines, on the other, with key ministries positioning themselves on different sides of the debate. The Ministry of Supply was determined to defend the development of an indigenous aircraft industry for commercial and strategic reasons, as well the mainten-ance of national prestige, especially in the eyes of the Commonwealth. As the Minister of Supply put the point in March 1947:

> If our public Corporations buy American one cannot expect the rest of the world to buy British. There is therefore a need for reaffirmation by the Cabinet of the general policy … that the Corporations would be required to use British types; if need be at the cost of increasing subsidies.[31]

The Ministry of Aviation for its part despaired about the poor quality of British planes, which jeopardised the commercial com-petitiveness of the recently nationalised airlines. In a joint statement by the Ministers of Supply and Civil Aviation on 19 April 1947, it was stated that

> the prestige of the British aircraft industry as a whole would be bound to suffer gravely from the decision to operate the main Empire routes with American aircraft (even if later to be powered with British engines); this would particularly tend to discredit the British interim types themselves, but the repercussions would be felt throughout the industry and earnings from exports … would be affected.[32]

Yet, at the same time, the joint statement acknowledged that

> there is a serious danger that the prestige and efficiency of our opera-tions will suffer gravely if they have for long to compete on the Empire routes with planes which are slower and less economic than the Constellations flown by our American, Dutch, French and Australian competitors.[33]

Eventually, the failings of British technological development and industrial reorganisation, coupled with the obstacles presented by US security ideals, proved too much for the fledging aviation industry, and the chance to compete globally was lost.

The overwhelming threat of US competition, as well as the constraints of US foreign policy, which had assumed a hegemonic position in the eyes of UK politicians and diplomats in the post-war period, was thus vital in causing and sustaining successive government investments in civil aviation. Yet the threats of the emergent superpower served only to enhance the desire to sustain UK aviation and the UK's leading position in global aviation. In short, the threat of foreign competition constituted something akin to a horrific fantasy for UK policy-makers and manufacturers, which if actualised carried the threat of destroying UK aviation and its drive to secure global markets in the post-war period. The political struggles and contentious decisions at the end of the Second World War put in place a powerful set of path dependencies for future developments.

But any regime must be installed and sedimented. It must not only become embedded in institutions and a regime of policy practices, but must gain some acceptance in the populace as a whole; it should, in short, grip politicians, officials and citizens. What is more, the reproduction of a regime is not automatic; it has, rather, to be managed and maintained through an array of strategies and tactics, which involve political practices and the operation of power. In the next section of this chapter, we first examine the grip of the fantasmatic narrative of aviation within government circles, before turning to analyse the multiple political logics through which the UK government endeavoured to manage the demands against airport expansion.

The grip of aviation

As our discussion of the politics of the ignoble origins of aviation intimates, the grip that aviation exerted on policy-makers and the public imagination owes much to the production and dissemination of what we have termed a fantasmatic narrative, which in our view has strongly marked the policy debates and political contests from the 1940s onwards. In this discourse, the (future) competitiveness of the aviation industry – and the growth of air travel itself – was portrayed as an essential ingredient in the economic modernisation and improved social well-being of the UK. In the rhetoric of successive white papers and government publications, aviation was consistently and regularly represented, not only as one of the few UK success stories, but also as a crucial component of the modern economy. Aviation thus held out the prospect of continued economic prosperity – the beatific dimension of the fantasy – while the failure to expand air transport evoked a horrific story of economic failure and national decline. Fantasmatic narratives of this kind persistently drew equivalences between the maintenance of London as a global financial centre and the growth of aviation, in which the latter would link the former to the rest of the world. These appeals and rhetorical constructions were reproduced across multiple arenas. In the early 1970s, for example, the Conservative Political Centre pointed to the dynamic role of airports in the growth of London and commerce, arguing that 'for both trade and tourism London will be the focus of [future] traffic and the airport the highway of commerce' (Conservative Political Centre, 1973: 5).

In the 1950s, 1960s and 1970s, this consensus about the centrality of civil aviation, as well as the need to expand airport infrastructure, grew stronger, even if there were some disagreements and minor hiccups about where and how this expansion was to be implemented. Not only did governments take rising passenger numbers as a given in their formulation of airport policy, but they also fêted the success of the UK aviation industry. In one notable celebration, the Wilson government in the late 1960s trumpeted the fact that 'few industries can match this record of sustained expansion' and it looked forward 'to continuing expansion at high rates for as far ahead as can be foreseen' (Cabinet Office, 1967: 2). Indeed, the expansion of air transport was frequently equated with social progress, for it promised to extend social opportunities to the mass of the population, when, until that point, air travel had been restricted to narrow sections of British society. Typically, for example, the 1967 white paper presented to Cabinet claimed that 'the ordinary citizen can now enjoy opportunities – the Mediterranean holiday, the visits to relatives in other continents – that were until recently the privilege of a minority' (Cabinet Office, 1967: 2). As Elliot Feldman concludes, basing his judgement on confidential interviews with civil servants in several agencies, by the late 1960s the 'development of civil aviation was an uncontested public good, in part because the British perceived themselves an island nation dependent on the highest technologies of transportation in order to guarantee trade and a favourable balance of payments' (Feldman, 1985: 58).

Statements and appeals of this sort were still evident in the rhetoric of the government inspectors who led various public inquiries at the end of the 1970s and in the early 1980s. For example, at the public inquiry into the construction of a fourth terminal at Heathrow in 1978, Inspector Sir Ian Glidewell approved the case for expansion using the rhetoric of 'national need' and he justified his decision to give the go-ahead to a fourth terminal in terms of its 'overriding national importance' (Glidewell, 1979: 97). He invoked once again the threats of external competition and the fear of capacity overload at the airport in his claim that 'the inevitable overloading of facilities', the 'diversion of some traffic to other airports on the continent' and the 'dissuasion of some potential passengers from traveling at all', particularly those visiting the UK, were all 'contrary to the national interest'. He also dwelled on the grave consequences of a failure to expand – the horrific dimension of fantasy – by declaring that 'the loss of traffic to foreign airports which have some spare capacity, and of foreign tourists who wish to come to this country, is clearly to be deplored' (Glidewell, 1979: 16).

Similarly, at the beginning of the 1980s, in his final report on the building of a second terminal and other works at Gatwick airport, Inspector John Newey lauded the economic benefits of aviation while raising the threat of international competition. The conclusion to his report made reference to the negative outcomes of 'overload conditions' at airports, which he related directly to national prestige. In his words, the

> acceptance of overload conditions in one or more British airports for a period of years would be most regrettable; it could create an unfavourable impression upon foreign businessmen and tourists and would also be unpleasant for British travellers and staff. (Newey, 1981: 28)

In fact, for the Conservative governments of the 1980s, aviation expansion gave greater credence to their belief in popular capitalism and individualised consumption, and it was intimately connected to the Thatcher government's support for finance capital and economic globalisation. Airlines and airports were depicted as an integral part of the growing service industry, which the government sought to protect from the threat of foreign competition. They were allocated a critical role in the continued prosperity of London and the financial dominance of the City. It was not surprising, therefore, that the Thatcher government extolled the competitive advantages of UK aviation over its rivals. In its 1985 white paper, for example, it praised the UK industry's 'leading place in international aviation' and delighted in the competitiveness of UK airports, 'particularly Heathrow as one of the most important air traffic centres in the world' (Department of Transport, 1985: 2). Repeating what we have termed the beatific narrative of aviation expansion, in which the growth of the industry went hand in glove with national and international economic success, the Department of Transport asserted that 'civil aviation is vital to our national prosperity. Aviation directly provides 85,000 jobs and contributes about £500 million a year to our balance of payments' (Department of Transport, 1985: 2). In the neoliberal ideology of Thatcherism, the growth of air travel and global tourism thus came to operate as a symbolic indicator of rising affluence and increased consumerism, and nowhere more so than at Heathrow airport – the 'jewel in the crown' – along with its privatised national flag carrier, BA.

Political arguments that promoted the strategic interests of the aviation industry were also employed at the long-running public inquiry into the construction of Terminal Five at Heathrow. The inspector, Roy Vandermeer, concluded in his report that the building of Terminal Five would meet the 'objective of fostering a strong and competitive British airline industry' set out in the 1985 white paper. In laying out the consequences of not building the new terminal, like previous inspectors before him, he raised the spectre of foreign competition, arguing that 'the real beneficiaries if Terminal 5 [is not built] will be the other major European airports, Charles de Gaulle, Schiphol and Frankfurt'. He also identified aviation and Heathrow as essential motors of the British economy, and the City of London, when he declared that 'unless [Heathrow] is able to maintain its competitive position there must be a substantial risk that London's success as a world city and financial centre would be threatened' (Vandermeer, 2001a: ii).

Important elements of this fantasmatic narrative continued to exercise their hold over departmental officials and senior politicians in the 1990s and into the new century. Reflecting in his diary on his experience as Aviation Minister within Blair's first New Labour government, for example, Chris Mullin notes that in May 2000, following a meeting to discuss the potential break-up of BAA

> the official in charge of aviation talked with, I thought, a little too much enthusiasm about the likely growth of passenger movements from 160 million a year at present to 400 million in 20 years time. At one point, he used the word 'inevitable'. (Mullin, 2010: 102)

In summary, therefore, a strong case can be made that, in important respects, the expansion of aviation in the post-war period was supported by a fantasmatic narrative, with its interconnected beatific and horrific dimensions. The growth of civil and military aircraft manufacturing, the development of more sophisticated and safer technologies, the very experience of flying and the promises it offered, as well as global trade and mass tourism, were intimately connected with a discourse of economic modernisation and social progress. Taken together they constituted an essential ingredient in sustaining the different regimes of accumulation that were installed in the post-war period, while countering threats of and warnings about the UK's inexorable economic decline. Aircraft manufacture, the building of modern airports and the growth of mass tourism appeared to embody Harold Wilson's invocation of the 'white heat of the technological revolution'.[34]

Resistance to airport expansion, by contrast, was more defensive. It was often associated with the protection and conservation of the countryside, the preservation of traditional communities, an opposition to economic growth and the stagnation of British society. Even some of the opposition to particular airport expansions did not necessarily challenge the fundamental logic of airport expansion. For example, in the campaign against the second runway at Manchester airport, local residents sought to make a case for the expansion of Liverpool airport rather than Manchester. Equally, in its opening statement to the public inquiry into Terminal Five at Heathrow, HACAN, the local resident organisation against expansion at the airport, made positive cases for other London and 'regional airports', such as Manchester. Moreover, with respect to the growth of Stansted, HACAN's opening statement drew attention to the way in which

> the centre of gravity of London is moving inexorably eastwards. Leading law firms move from the West End to the City. Leading banks are now moving from the City to Canary Wharf. *For these locations the airport of choice for international flights is in fact Stansted* – a short rail journey from Liverpool Street, conveniently situated within the Broadgate financial complex. (HACAN, 1995: 5; our emphasis)

It is thus not too far-fetched to claim that much of the local protest against airport expansion was still complicit with the fantasmatic narrative of aviation expansion. Accepting its contribution to economic growth and prosperity, and fearing overseas competition, campaigners were not so much opposed to the growth of aviation *per se*, but to particular manifestations of this growth, those which would adversely affect their communities.

But no matter how well this post-war regime of aviation expansion was underpinned and supported by a fantasmatic narrative, growth was still punctuated by the emergence of grievances and the construction of demands which did challenge certain practices or the policy regime itself. It is here in our approach that political logics come to the fore. If fantasy operates to prevent and displace the construction of antagonisms by concealing the contingency of decisions and events, as well as forms of domination, then an important component of political logics is to manage and control the effects of demands when they do occur. In others words, when dealing with the articulation of grievances and their possible translation into social demands, as well as the linking together of demands into alternative political projects, power-holders employ a diverse range of tactics, techniques and strategies. In the domain of aviation and airport politics, promises of limited impact, adequate compensation, environmental safeguards and curbs on future growth were often used to secure the consent of those affected by expansion.

It was relatively unusual, however, for these mechanisms and incentives fully to achieve their objectives, so that various techniques and tactics were used to short-circuit the translation of grievances into social demands. For example, at the end of the 1960s, faced with growing protests against the siting of the third London airport, the Wilson government attempted to depoliticise the issue by deferring the decision it had to make to the more technocratically orientated Roskill Commission. Named after the pre-eminent judge who chaired the investigation into the third London airport, the Commission drew extensively upon the 'scientific' decision-making tool of 'cost–benefit analysis' (Layard and Glaister, 1994). Similarly, the logic of 'predict and provide' installed a logic of difference – a veritable practice of 'divide and rule' – in the formulation and implementation of airport policy, so that decisions and policy debate focused upon particular sites for development, thus negating collective opposition to airport policy by not presenting national plans for development.

But the predominant means of attempting to deal with grievances against expansion in the domain of aviation policy were undoubtedly the logics of consultation and negotiation, which ranged from informal and formal local meetings to official hearings and fully fledged public inquiries. In 1948, the Ministry of Civil Aviation set up the London (Heathrow) Airport Consultative Committee (now known as the Heathrow Airport Consultative Committee) in order to promote dialogue and collaboration between the airport, users, local authorities and local residents and ministerial advisers.[35] It was followed in 1956 by the establishment of a consultative committee at Gatwick, although these bodies were formally constituted only by the 1982 Civil Aviation Act.[36] In 1987, guidance from the Department of Transport presented consultative committees as advisory and collaborative forums, which would meet at least three times a year.[37] That guidance suggested that consultation through the committees should be a 'positive and interactive process' and made reference to their roles in enabling 'the concerns of interested parties to be taken into account', as well as offering 'an opportunity to reconcile differences' and 'resolving difficulties through agreed voluntary action' (Department of Transport, 1987: para. 2). GATCOM, Gatwick's consultative committee, continues to recognise that 'its effectiveness depends entirely upon its powers of persuasion and on the goodwill of those involved'.[38] The work of the committees traditionally addressed a range of local concerns, from noise pollution and local quality of life to environmental impacts, as well as complaints about airport operations, particularly night flights.[39] In practice, however, noise pollution preoccupied much of the work of committees, which elicited fears that noise 'crowded out' other issues (Grimley, 2002: 3). Importantly, their capacity to generate local agreements was also called into question, with a survey of twenty consultative committees concluding that 'discussion of noise can be heated and differences do not seem to be reconciled', while airport representatives on committees were charged with 'taking defensive attitudes, possibly denial, obfuscation' (Grimley, 2002: 3).

In the post-war period, governments often reverted to the procedural mechanisms of public inquiries for justifying and managing the building of the large-scale infrastructure projects that are airports. Open to members of the public, the inquiries are chaired by government-appointed inspectors, who are charged to hear evidence from supporters and opponents of the development, and then submit a report of findings and recommendations to government. In theory, ministers have the option of accepting or rejecting the report; they can also modify its findings. In exchange for being heard and listened to, parties to the conflict are expected to abide by the rational decisions that are reached by the neutral and impartial inspectors (Appleyard, 1983: 112).

But public inquiries over airport expansion all too often became sites of political struggle and their decisions often provoked more hardened forms of protest and even resistance. In the 1970s, John Tyme, a famous anti-roads protester, sought to exploit the arena of public inquiries not only to raise awareness of opposition to road expansion but also to attack the independence of the inspectors, as well as the framing of the inquiries, which he felt were designed to exclude a consideration of broader questions pertaining to the national interest, so much so that 'participation was in any case irrelevant because the eventual outcome was a foregone conclusion' (Levin, 1979: 21). For critics, inquiries tended to come too late in the planning process; relied too heavily on legal discourses, which meant that opposition came to depend upon the hiring of experts and legal teams; and ultimately put the minister in the position of being both 'judge and jury' in the decision-making process (Appleyard, 1983: 113–14). Yet inspectors could, if they chose to, exercise discretion in the running of inquiries, which activists against road-building such as Tyme recognised when they sought to disrupt established practices and exploit inquiries as 'arenas without rules' (Dudley and Richardson, 2000: 121–4).

In the arena of aviation policy, the public inquiry into the expansion of Gatwick in the 1950s was condemned for its narrow framing of debates, which effectively constrained any questioning of the actual need for an alternative to Heathrow as a London airport, as well as the consideration of alternative ways of meeting that need (McKie, 1973: 45). Similarly, the 1965 Stansted public inquiry brought criticisms from local residents about the partiality and lack of preparation of government, as well as the alleged 'holes in the case', not least because of the vague calculations of the travel time from Stansted to London. Indeed, the management of the expansion of Stansted and the site for a third London airport was described by some critics as 'many years of partial and almost secret decision-making by Government' (Lichfield, 1971: 157). By the beginning of the 1970s, the practice of the public inquiry was thus under increasing pressure, with its capacity to deliver effective political settlement under question. As Sharman puts it,

> the British practice of seeking to expose and justify an airport proposal
> at a local public inquiry, though it has had good results in some cases,

has become increasingly inadequate to prevent a polarisation of forces for and against each proposal. (Sharman, 1975: 50)

Over time, defeats of local campaigners at public inquiries, preceded and followed by the increased polarisation of local communities, discredited the practices of the public inquiry as a means of scrutinising decision-making over airport developments. They also generated demands for open government and democratic decision-making. Residents around Manchester airport, for example, who invested heavily in the public inquiry over the second runway in the mid-1990s, dismissed its alleged neutrality, claiming that they had 'won' the rational argument but 'lost' the inquiry (Griggs *et al.*, 1998). Similarly, local residents within HACAN repeatedly experienced the personal dislocations of lost campaigns or of a 'pressure group not winning' (interview with local campaigner). HACAN fought and lost the public inquiry into a fourth terminal at Heathrow from May to December 1978. Partial concessions won at the inquiry were then overturned as the recommended ceilings on flight movements were disregarded and the Major government, despite recommendations against the construction of a fifth terminal, opened a public inquiry into such a development in May 1995.

The dilemma for local campaigners was also evident in HACAN's submission to the Terminal Five public inquiry. HACAN's chair, Dermot Cox, opened his organisation's submission with the statement that 'we have every confidence that the Inquiry will make a full and balanced assessment of the important issues before it' (HACAN, 1995: 1). At the end of the longest public inquiry in British history, and following the decision of New Labour to grant approval to the construction of Terminal Five, Cox was to resign from his position as chair (Griggs and Howarth, 2004). Commenting on the experience of local residents at the inquiry, John McDonnell, local MP for Hayes and Harlington in which Heathrow is located, reported that:

> For many of my constituents and others the ability of governments to ignore the planning process no matter how exhaustive the inquiry had been and how clear the planning inspector's recommendations had been, undermined their faith in both the planning process and in government policy making in this field. They felt that no matter how effectively they had presented their arguments at the inquiry and no matter what government they elected, their voice went unheard as ministers rode roughshod over the democratic process.[40]

In short, then, by the late 1990s, traditional strategies of fighting public inquiries, and indeed the practices and roles of those inquiries, found themselves increasingly discredited within the ranks of local protesters. Inquiries became associated with the rhetoric of 'broken promises' and the policy reversals of successive governments.

Conclusion

This chapter has delineated the contradictory regime of aviation expansion, which had its 'ignoble origins' in the political struggles of the aftermath of the Second World War, was sustained during the post-war consensus and then gathered momentum during the 1980s and 1990s, when the Thatcher government pursued an agenda of liberalisation, deregulation and privatisation. Despite the ups and downs, policy confusion and policy reversals, the exponential growth of air transport, airports and the consumption of air travel, aviation gelled with the all-important myths of post-war Britain. Aviation was an important symbol of Britain's victory in the Second World War – iconic images of Spitfires and Hurricanes taking on the might of the Luftwaffe – and the UK's apparent advantage in aircraft technology and design, alongside its extensive imperial and Commonwealth links, promised a bright future of global aviation domination. Yet this fantasy of global dominance was predicated on the fear of competition, especially US competition, which threatened the UK's hegemony in the field. Both elements – the beatific and the horrific – stimulated desires and investments in aviation.

Once inscribed into the key institutions of the British state, the major political parties and successive governments, as well as the social and cultural practices of its citizens, the pre-eminence of UK civil aviation and its expansion, as well as its concentration at Heathrow, Gatwick and other London airports, acquired a path dependence that proved difficult to dislodge. Moreover, although the means differed at different stages of its evolution – state-driven expansion as opposed to market-led expansion – the overall purpose and ends of aviation policy remained the same. Claims for the importance and benefits of civil aviation in all its facets were repeated by politicians, officials and business leaders. As the twentieth century wore on, aviation was bolstered less by the promise of technological and manufacturing ascendency, though this continued in the leading position of the UK's arms industry, and more by the promises that civil aviation was a critical component of the country's post-industrial path to economic prosperity. Here, the grip of aviation was sustained by exotic holidays and individualised consumption.

But the story of aviation expansion had its shadow, for there is another narrative that charts the emergence and articulation of demands about the character and future trajectory of aviation. Calls for more rational forms of planning in the field of aviation, in which expansion is taken as a given, coexist with darker demands, which have connected the aviation industry, and its insatiable need for airport expansion, to the problems of noise, air pollution, the social and natural environment and citizens' quality of life. What is more, the path dependence of the logic of aviation expansion was not in any way automatic. On the contrary, the sedimentation and maintenance of this regime involved the deployment of a battery of fantasmatic and political logics. Fantasmatic logics secured what we might term the ideological hegemony of aviation expansion as an indisputably positive goal for government and society alike. When working successfully, they served to naturalise the inexorable expansion of UK aviation, thus immunising the regime from potential dislocation and pressure. Aviation was also able to connect with other myths and goals of post-war Britain: the need for economic growth, the proper utilisation of new technologies, the acceleration of globalisation, the rise of mass consumerism, and so forth. Political logics, on the other hand, served to negate, co-opt, incorporate and manage challenges and threats to the regime of aviation expansion. They enabled politicians, officials, business leaders and experts to deflect and control pressures, thus ensuring the overall reproduction of UK aviation.

Notes

1 *New Labour, New Life for Britain*, 1997 Labour Party manifesto, www.labour-party.org.uk/manifestos/1997/1997-labour-manifesto.shtml (accessed 10 November 2011).

2 The Terminal Five Public Inquiry, which began on 16 May 1995, was destined to become the longest public inquiry in British history, ending on 17 March 1999.

3 HM Treasury, (undated) press release, 'Heathrow', 3–4, www.hm-treasury.gov.uk/d/foi_heathrow310306.pdf (accessed 12 January 2012).

4 See *Hansard*, House of Commons Debates, 17 December 1979, vol. 976, cols 35–8, http://hansard.millbanksystems.com/commons/1979/dec/17/airports-policy-1#column_37 (accessed 1 January 2013).

5 *Hansard*, House of Commons Debates, 5 June 1985, vol. 80, col. 309.

6 Based on CAA annual airport statistics, 1998 comparison with 1993, www.caa.co.uk/default.aspx?catid=80&pagetype=88&sglid=3&fld=1998Annual (accessed 2 January 2012).

7 Based on CAA annual airport statistics, 1998, www.caa.co.uk/default.aspx?catid=80&pagetype=88&sglid=3&fld=1998Annual (accessed 2 January 2012).

8 Based on CAA annual airport statistics, 1998, www.caa.co.uk/default.aspx?catid=80&pagetype=88&sglid=3&fld=1998Annual (accessed 2 January 2012).

9 Based on CAA airport statistics for 1990 and 2003, comparison with 1998, www.caa.co.uk/docs/80/airport_data/1990Annual/Table_01_Size_of_UK_Airports_1990.pdf and www.caa.co.uk/docs/80/airport_data/2003Annual/Table_01_Size_of_UK_Airports_2003_Comp_1998.pdf (accessed 2 January 2012).

10 A third national carrier, British South American Airways, was also created out of BOAC's routes, but it had merged with BOAC by 1949.

11 The alliance included the Airports' Policy Consortium, the Aviation Environment Federation, Friends of the Earth, the Council for the Protection of Rural England and Transport 2000. Its demand for noise controls came after a commitment by New Labour in its 1998 white paper, *A New Deal for Transport*, to enable airports to take measures against non-compliant airlines and to enable local authorities to enforce noise mitigation measures. Friends of the Earth press release, 'New Alliance to Fight Aircraft Noise', 14 December 1998, www.foe.co.uk/resource/press_releases/19981214150203.html (accessed 14 March 2008).

12 Here it is worth mentioning a number of landmarks: the publication in 1987 of *Our Common Future*, by the World Commission on Environment and Development chaired by Gro Harlem Brundtland, which articulated a discourse of sustainable development; the establishment in 1988 of the Intergovernmental Panel on Climate Change (IPCC); and the 1992 Rio United Nations Conference on the Environment and Development, the Earth Summit, which led, among other things, to the Agenda 21 programme on sustainable development.

13 RCEP press release, 26 October 2004, www.rcep.org.uk/news/94-4.htm (accessed 20 October 2008).

14 Cited in RCEP press release, 29 November 2002, http://web.archive.org/web/20030817105333/http://www.rcep.org.uk/news/02-05.html (accessed 2 January 2013).

15 For an overview of the membership of LAHT5 and other opponents to Terminal Five, see www.hacan.org.uk/news/press_releases.php?id=38 (accessed 1 January 2013).

16 For a first-hand account of the development of Gatwick and the shifting relationship of local villagers with the airport, see Sewill (2012).

17 Friends of the Earth press release, 'New Alliance to Fight Aircraft Noise', 14 December 1998, www.foe.co.uk/resource/press_releases/19981214150 203.html (accessed 14 March 2008).

18 Public Record Office, Cabinet Papers (hereafter PRO, CAB), 134/844, E.A. 52.69.

19 Debate on civil aviation reported in *Hansard*, House of Commons Debates, 16 July 1952, vol. 503, cols 2155–292, http://hansard.millbank systems.com/commons/1952/jul/16/civil-aviation#S5CV0503P0_19520716_ HOC_328 (accessed 25 July 2012).

20 The first airmail flight was between Blackpool and Southport, and was undertaken by G. Holt Thomas and C. Graham-White on 10 August 1910. The first regular daily air service within the UK was provided by Avro Civil Aviation between 24 May and 30 September 1919, and linked Manchester, Southport and Blackpool (see Stroud, 1962).

21 For good overviews and analysis of the British civil aviation industry and its links to government and public policy, see Devons (1958) and Hayward (1983, 1989).

22 PRO, CAB/66/51/22.

23 See *Flight Magazine*, 1 February 1940: 90.

24 PRO, CAB/66/51/36.

25 PRO, CAB/65/42/39.

26 PRO, CAB/65/42/39.

27 PRO, CAB/66/56/35.

28 PRO, CAB/66/56/35.

29 PRO, CAB/65/44/12.

30 PRO, CAB/65/44/12.

31 CAB 134/58, CAC(47)1, 6 March 1947, Purchase of Foreign Aircraft for the Government Corporations.·

32 CAB 134/58, CAC (47)9, Project X, 19 April 1947.

33 CAB 134/58, CAC (47)9, Project X, 19 April 1947.·

34 The iconic status of airports is captured, for example, in Gordon's (2008) study of the cultural history of airports.

35 The Committee currently has over forty members, including seventeen local authority representatives, an adviser from the Department for Transport and representatives from HACAN ClearSkies, Ealing Aircraft Noise Action Group, Local Authorities Airport Noise Council, British Air Transport Association, Association of British Travel Agents, Trades Union Congress, Consumers' Association and West London Business.

36 For further details on the organisation of Heathrow Airport Consultative Committee, see http://lhr-acc.org (accessed 23 July 2012). For the organis- ation of Gatwick Airport Consultative Committee, see www.gatcom. org.uk (accessed 21 July 2012). See also the Liaison Group of UK Airport Consultative Committees, www.ukaccs.info (accessed 21 July 2012).

37 For example, the consultative committee at Heathrow meets six times a year, while at Gatwick it meets four times.

38 See www.gatcom.org.uk (accessed 21 July 2012).

39 For a discussion of the development of airport consultative committees, see Barnes (1983) and Holdsworth (1980).

40 Statement by John McDonnell MP, 'Manchester Airport on Trial', www. manchesterairportontrial.org/wp-content/uploads/2011/02/McDonnell-witnessstatment.pdf (accessed 19 January 2012).

4

The new rhetoric of airport protest

The principal issue to address will be how to meet demand for aviation in the most sustainable manner. In our view, policies which limit consumer choice or seek to artificially constrain demand would lead to job losses, damage to the UK economy and undermine the freedom of consumers to travel at a reasonable cost to a broad range of destinations. Our own vision is of an aviation policy promoting a dynamic industry to support the British economy, provide consumer choice and deliver effective measures to protect the environment. (Ed Anderson; Airport Operators Association, 2002: 1)

The forecast increase in demand over the next 30 years is, at best, irrelevant to most business sectors as it largely consists of leisure travellers taking weekend breaks abroad. The fact that it is clearly relevant to the aviation industry – and some sectors of the travel industry – has clouded the Department's view. It fails to spell out that the demand is being artificially stimulated by the tax concessions the aviation industry enjoys. It fails to spell out that, if these tax concessions were removed, there would be no need for any increase in airport capacity. (HACAN ClearSkies, 2003a: 9)

In 1997, the accelerating regime of aviation expansion, which had gathered momentum from 1945 until the mid-1990s, left the newly elected Blair government facing a growing number of competing and intensely felt demands in the field of aviation policy, especially with respect to airport expansion. Those favouring more growth charged the government with 'dithering' and 'piecemeal development' and of failing to take the lead to provide adequate airport capacity (Caves and Gosling, 1997: 320). Airlines, airport operators, trade unions, air users, organised business and sections of the tourist industry thus called on the UK government to support an increase in airport capacity, especially at Heathrow. At the same time, local residents and environmentalists demanded more stringent regulation of air travel, especially of its negative environmental impacts, in particular in terms of noise and air pollution.

But despite the contradictory nature of the pressures on New Labour, they all coalesced around the single universal demand for a national aviation strategy, which most parties felt had been lacking since the saga of the third London airport in the 1960s and 1970s. In fact, there had been no white paper on aviation since 1985. This state of affairs had not been lost on the House of Commons Transport Select Committee, which in its May 1996 report on airport capacity added to demands for a national strategy in aviation (House of Commons Library, 2009). Typically, for example, with Labour now in office, having previously attacked the strategy of 'predict and provide' in aviation policy, the Aviation Environment Federation (AEF) and Friends of the Earth (FoE) jointly produced a pamphlet, *Plane Crazy*, which condemned the 'uncontrolled growth' in aviation, its ineffective regulation and the 'absence of a sustainable national airports policy' (AEF and FoE, 1999: 2–3). It also called for a national strategy in aviation. The environmental pressure groups argued that, in the 'absence of a national aviation policy', proposals for airport expansion were 'viewed in isolation, often without any consideration of other options, or whether demand could be met by using existing capacity at other airports' (AEF and FoE, 1999: 4). They suggested that government policy, which 'dates back to the mid 1980s ... scarcely considers the environmental or social impacts of air travel', and that without a national strategy 'the piecemeal expansion of airports throughout the United Kingdom continues' (AEF and FoE, 1999: 1).

In response to such demands, New Labour announced a review of policy in aviation in its August 1997 integrated transport consultation paper. Its initial scoping of this review revealed the competing pressures it faced, for the government invited responses on how the contribution of airports 'to regional and national competitiveness [could] be enhanced without detriment to environmental objectives' (DETR, 1997: para. 34). Advancing its environmental credentials, it drew attention to the global impact of aviation on climate change and sustainability, recognising that carbon emissions per passenger kilometre in aviation 'are higher than [in] most other ways of travelling' (para. 21). At Kyoto, in December 1997, it subsequently agreed to reduce UK greenhouse gas emissions to 12.5 per cent below 1990 levels by 2008–12, although international aviation was not included in the Kyoto protocols.[1] In the transport consultation paper, the New Labour government also drew attention to the problems of noise and air pollution around airports, while recognising that air transport had been growing dramatically and arguing, as had many previous governments, that better use might be made of regional airports (para. 19).

Yet, in more concrete policy terms, the New Labour government undertook measures to support regional airports when in June 1998 it announced the removal of public sector borrowing restrictions from those regional airports owned by local authorities that had 'sound finances', so as to enable them to take out commercial loans to fund capital investment (see House of Commons Library, 2011d: 5–6). (In April 1999, Manchester, Newcastle, Leeds/Bradford and Norwich airports took out such loans.) Equally, it oversaw the opening up of international access to regional airports, in exchange for British airlines being allowed to operate on the same routes (AEF and FoE, 1999: 3). Furthermore, the New Labour government's 'New Deal' integrated transport white paper, published in July 1998, named road transport, rather than aviation, as the 'fastest growing contributor to climate change' (DETR, 1998: 6).[2]

Against this policy background, the New Labour government opened consultation for its aviation white paper in December 2000. With much pomp and ceremony, it announced that it would develop a thirty-year plan for the long-term strategic development of air transport. Using the rhetoric of its 1998 integrated transport white paper, the government promised a 'fully integrated approach to air transport policy' (DETR, 2000a: 6). In the foreword to its consultation document, John Prescott, the then Deputy Prime Minister and Secretary of State for the Environment, Transport and the Regions, called for a 'long term framework that will maximise the beneficial aspects of aviation and minimise the negative effects', a framework which would 'ensure that, as a country, and as individual consumers, we are getting the most from our aviation services and that the future of the aviation industry is a sustainable one' (DETR, 2000a: 5). With its commitment to this framework, which it characterised as a policy of sustainable aviation, the New Labour government set itself the task of 'deliver[ing] economic, social and environmental goals while ensuring that the industry continues to operate efficiently and effectively' (DETR, 2000a: 7).

Unlike its predecessors, and in opposition to the piecemeal incrementalism of previous governments, including the market orientations of the Thatcher and Major administrations, New Labour claimed that it would address once and for all the challenge of increasing consumer demand for air travel, mounting capacity constraints at airports, and the growing contribution of aviation to climate change, as well as to local noise and air pollution. Ambitious policy objectives like these rested upon the brokering of a long-term settlement between competing and arguably incompatible demands for growth *and* the regulation of aviation's negative environmental impacts. Much thus came to depend upon the political management of the consultation process. But it was also dependent on being able to confer a hegemonic meaning to the signifier of 'sustainable aviation', which would then enable it to engineer an enduring policy settlement. If successful, these political and ideological manoeuvres would institutionalise equivalences between the competing demands that structured the field of aviation policy, while negating opposition to its plans for the strategic development of aviation.

This chapter analyses the politics of the consultation process leading to up to the publication of New Labour's white paper in 2003. We argue that the government's efforts to broker a long-term settlement between rival stakeholders backfired. Rather than resolving the heightened tensions and sharpening contradictions, the consultation process created the conditions for the development of two antagonistic discourse coalitions: the pro-expansionist Freedom to Fly and the pro-regulation AirportWatch. Political frontiers hardened as the consultation process unfolded, with rival hegemonic projects contesting the ideological battle over airport expansion, both within the space of the consultation process and beyond it. In this battle, as we suggest, the Freedom to Fly coalition was able to structure the terrain of public reasoning and debate in its own image, while negating or at least containing opposition to expansion. Its rhetorical redescription of the aviation industry, and its multiple stakeholders, as proponents of responsible growth and sustainable aviation, and not as threats to the environment, provided New Labour with the requisite ideological cover for supporting a policy of airport expansion, thus assuaging industry concerns that government might not endorse expansionist demands for fear of provoking a media backlash or the threat of intense political protest (Howarth and Griggs, 2006). By articulating a fantasmatic narrative in which the growth of aviation and environmental protection were both possible, the zero-sum game of airport expansion or environmental protection could potentially be reframed as a positive-sum game. If successful, this would constitute a heresthetic move that negated opposition to expansion by rendering environmental issues invisible, thus leaving oppositional groups unable to contest the terms of their own exclusion. We begin by characterising the limits of the consultation process which led up to the 2003 air transport white paper.

The consultation process

The political difficulties confronting the Blair government in engineering an acceptable policy of sustainable aviation were aptly demonstrated with the publication in 1999 of a report from Oxford Economic Forecasting (OEF) on the contribution of aviation to the UK economy. The report reproduced the sedimented narratives of air travel as a catalyst for economic growth by constructing aviation as an 'unusual industry' (OEF, 1999: 51), which, in contrast to other industries, 'boosts the rate of economic growth' and fulfils strategic needs for future growth sectors, which 'make relatively heavy use of aviation' (OEF, 1999: 6). Its 'banner headlines' thus portrayed aviation as an industry which contributed approximately £10.2 billion to Britain's gross domestic product (GDP), employed directly 180,000 people and supported the employment of three times as many through its supply chains (OEF, 1999: 5). Alongside such claims, OEF reiterated the horrific dimension of the fantasmatic narrative about UK aviation expansion by predicting that restrictions would threaten economic growth and international competitiveness. In the conclusions to its evaluation, the consultancy even sought to calculate the 'threat' of the failure to expand airports to the UK economy, positing that a '25 million a year reduction in the number of passengers, spread proportionately across all types of passengers would mean that GDP would be expected to be nearly £4 billion a year (in 1998 prices) lower by 2015'. The report thus positioned aviation as a central component of the UK's 'reputation as a good place for international business', evoking a 'spiral' of 'lost investment' should government fail to support aviation, with 'potentially damaging long-term effects on the competitiveness of the UK economy' (OEF, 1999: 51).

Importantly, the publication of the OEF report associated the Blair government, or rather the Department of the Environment,

Transport and the Regions (DETR), with the expansionist demands of the aviation industry. The report had been funded by the aviation industry, a fact that was openly recognised in its foreword, which was signed by Keith Jowett, the chief executive of the Airport Operators Association (AOA) and Dave Hopkins, the chair of the British Air Transport Association (BATA) (OEF, 1999: 1; Sewill, 2007: 1). But while it sought to convey the 'rigour' of the study, the foreword also celebrated the broad aviation consortium behind the study *and* its collaboration with government, declaring that 'for the first time, this report encompasses the entire aviation industry and has been produced with the co-operation and support of that industry, working with DETR' (OEF, 1999: 1). The DETR was alleged to have funded 10 per cent of the cost of the report (Sewill, 2007: 1). For local residents and environmentalists who were engaged in the consultation process, the DETR involvement in an industry-funded report, even before the start of the consultation, amplified doubts about the legitimacy of the Labour government acting as a 'broker' between competing demands in the field of airport expansion. Indeed, the Strategic Aviation Special Interest Group (SASIG) of the Local Government Association, which brings together some fifty local authorities, published its own rival report in December 2000, at the start of the consultation process. Labelling its own findings as 'independent research', the SASIG study explicitly refuted the OEF report by concluding that 'some restraint [on aviation] will be needed but that there will be little or no economic penalty to the UK' (SASIG, 2000: 2). In making such claims, it sought to deconstruct OEF's articulation of aviation as a 'special case', arguing that 'agriculture is more valuable than aviation' (SASIG, 2000: 9).

Between December 2000 and June 2003, the New Labour government undertook a wide range of consultative activities, including discussions with stakeholders, surveys and independent studies to contribute to its policy decisions. These were undertaken in the context of ministerial reorganisation, as the DETR, which was created in May 1997 and led by Deputy Prime Minister, John Prescott, was broken up in the aftermath of the 2001 general election. Transport was again separated from the environment portfolio, first through the creation of the Department for Transport, Local Government and the Regions (DTLR) in June 2001 (thus replacing the DETR), and subsequently in May 2002 through the creation of a separate Department for Transport (DfT), when the DTLR itself was disbanded (Smith, 2007:

586). For many in New Labour circles, this reorganisation was seen as the decline of the agenda of integrated transport planning and sustainability, as well as further evidence of ministerial conflicts between transport and the environment (Beecroft, 2002).

In the early stages of the consultation, between December 2000 and April 2001, the Labour government elicited approximately 550 responses about the main issues to be addressed in the forthcoming white paper and published its summary of these responses in November 2001 (DTLR, 2001). It then conducted an appraisal of the dynamics of regional air services (studies covering Scotland, Northern Ireland, Wales, the midlands, the north of England and the south-west were commissioned in parallel), with a second set of studies concentrating on the south-east (DETR, 2002b; DfT, 2002a, 2002b). These seven regional consultation documents were published from July to August 2002. In addition, the government commissioned the polling organisation NOP to publish seven questionnaires canvassing views covered in the consultation documents; over 66,000 completed returns were analysed and a series of consultation events and exhibitions were staged across the UK, at Manchester and Newcastle for example. The Treasury and DfT also published and put out for discussion a report, *Aviation and the Environment: Using Economic Interests*, in March 2003, which considered the most effective instruments for ensuring that the aviation industry factored in environmental costs to its fares and overall business costs, and reduced its contribution to global warming and noise pollution (HM Treasury and DfT, 2003). In February 2003, following a high court decision in November 2002, which effectively extended the consultation period, New Labour released revised versions of the south-east consultation documents to include options for runway development at Gatwick, and issued revised NOP questionnaires taking account of this development (DfT, 2003b). (Gatwick was previously excluded from the consultation process because local agreements limited its future expansion until 2019.) The whole consultation process finally closed at the end of June 2003.

By the end of the consultation period, more than 400,000 responses and representations to the exercise had been registered. These included intensive submissions by large stakeholders – such as British Airways (BA), the British Airports Authority (BAA) and the pro-expansion lobby Freedom to Fly – specific responses to questionnaires and many thousands of individual letters (DfT, 2003c: 6). Respondents were classified into five categories: 'wider stakeholder groups'

(which included both national and local environmental groups, consultative committees and airport development opposition groups),
'political stakeholders' (such as county, district and borough councils,
MPs, devolved administrations and regional assemblies), 'surface
transport organisations' (including bus, coach and rail operators),
'economic interests' (including regional development agencies, enterprise agencies, chambers of commerce and trade unions) and the
'aviation industry' (which included airlines, airports, aircraft manufacturers, aircraft maintenance providers and direct suppliers to the
aviation industry such as ground handling and aircraft catering) (DfT,
2003c: 7). Not surprisingly, in the regional capacity study of the
south-east of England, for instance, there was broad support for
additional capacity across all categories except 'wider stakeholders
groups'. More specifically, 'aviation industry' and 'economic interests'
offered 'virtually unanimous support' for expansion, while 'political
stakeholders' supported new capacity by a ratio of almost two to one
and over half of 'surface transport organisations' favoured growth.
In contrast, 'wider stakeholders groups' opposed new capacity
provision by a ratio of three to one, with forty-two environmental
groups 'broadly opposed to new capacity' and only three classified as
'broadly in favour' by the DfT (DfT, 2003c: 471).

On the surface, at least, the consultation exercise had the appearance of an inclusive democratic process: virtually all major
stakeholders and parties were invited to make representations and to
deliberate in a wide range of forums about the future expansion of
the aviation industry in the UK. Most groups and interested parties
accepted the opportunity to participate and to express their views in
the various spaces and through the sundry channels made available. In
the words of one aviation environmentalist, the consultation for the
white paper was initially 'second to none', with the DfT generating
at the opening of the consultation 'a sense of not having heard from
you [environmentalists] yet' (interview with environmental lobbyist).
Closer investigation, however, discloses a different interpretation of
the particular practices of consultation, the character of the actors
and subjects involved in the deliberation, the structural conditions
underlying the consultation process itself, and the broader set of
political practices surrounding the process. This alternative narrative
suggests that far from being a level playing field with access to all, and
far from being a process of democratic transformation in which actors
could converge on a rational consensus through deliberation and the

exchange of reasons, a more profound and classical political struggle between differently positioned actors with competing identities and interests took place.

First, as a highly complex industry and policy arena, which encompasses the planning of airports, as well as the environmental and economic impacts of the airline industry, the aviation policy sphere lends itself to a technocratic discourse. Many of the 'wider stakeholder groups', such as those involved in the local anti-expansion organisations HACAN ClearSkies and Stop Stansted Expansion (SSE), which were well versed in the industry and the planning and environmental issues, spoke nonetheless of being 'baffled by science' during the consultation process (interview with local campaigner). And while, in addition to written submissions and questionnaires, there were opportunities to discuss and debate the issues, it was suggested by some participants that these interactions tended to be elitist, managerialist and top-down. Participants spoke of 'being informed' about plans and developments, and their potential implications and effects – of what was being proposed and how it would happen – rather than being asked to contribute to particular solutions or to engage in the process of deliberation. One representative from the environmental pressure group Friends of the Earth (FoE) openly insisted after the close of the consultation that 'we were trying to get meetings with ministers, informally or formally, since the government brought out its consultation paper in December 2000. It just didn't happen' (*Guardian*, 6 December 2003). In FoE's response to the consultation, it did in fact argue that the consultation process had been managed such that it 'denied objectors to air travel and airport growth any real choice' (FoE, 2003: 1).

Secondly, personnel and symbolic linkages between the New Labour government and the civil service, on the one hand, and the aviation industry, on the other, reinforced the perception among opponents to expansion of a powerful set of structural and institutional connections between the state and big business. These perceptions were fuelled before the opening of consultation, as we suggest above, by DETR support for the OEF report on the contribution of aviation to the UK economy. They were reinforced by the decision in November 2001 to grant approval for the construction of Terminal Five at Heathrow, after the longest-running public inquiry in British history. Although Stephen Byers, the Secretary of State at the DTLR, had imposed limits on development at Heathrow (for example a new 480,000 annual ceiling on flights at Heathrow), the decision was interpreted as further evidence of the ongoing collusion between the government and the aviation industry, with the lobby for sustainable transport, Transport 2000 (T2000), construing the decision as 'another sign that the aviation industry is being allowed to grow out of control' (*Guardian*, 20 and 21 November 2001). Once again, local residents who invested their time and resources in the public inquiry process could only point to a Pyrrhic victory.

Many of the key players advocating growth on behalf of the airline and airport companies did have close relationships with New Labour. In July 2002, opposition groups questioned, for example, the role played by Joe Irvin, the director of the Freedom to Fly coalition, who was the former chief transport policy adviser to John Prescott, the Deputy Prime Minister and Secretary of State at the DETR. Irvin was to leave Freedom to Fly in 2003 to become director of policy at the Transport and General Workers' Union before taking up the position of director of public affairs at BAA in March 2006 and then rejoining government as part-time political secretary to Gordon Brown, the Labour Prime Minister. Environmental groups and campaigners, such as Jeff Gazzard from AirportWatch and Charles Secrett from FoE, publicly accused Irvin of using his access and influence to help secure from government a deal in favour of airport expansion, which Gazzard claimed the airline industry 'could have written themselves', and which Secrett described as a 'squalid political fix' (*Observer*, 28 July 2002). Indeed, New Labour's networks within the aviation industry included another former adviser to Prescott, Mike Craven, who ran a lobbying firm whose main client was BA, and Stephen Hardwick, corporate affairs director for BAA, who had also worked as a speech writer and adviser for Prescott (*Observer*, 28 July 2002). Brenda Dean, the chair of Freedom to Fly, was a Labour peer, and Dan Hodges, who was to replace Irvin as director of Freedom to Fly, had worked for his mother, former Transport Minister Glenda Jackson MP, the Road Haulage Association and the GMB trade union.

New Labour's links to the airline industry caused much suspicion among environmental and local resident groups. Throughout its campaign during the consultation process and beyond, the leadership of SSE, the local resident organisation formed in response to the consultation, made frequent use of the populist rhetoric of the 'underdog' fighting an unresponsive and corrupt London-based establishment (Griggs and Howarth, 2008). It repeatedly accused the DfT of 'over-indulg[ing] the aviation industry demands for growth' (SSE press release, 1 August 2003), of engaging in 'cosy' relationships (SSE press release, 2 March 2005) and 'stitch ups' with BAA (SSE press release, 27 May 2003) that 'disregarded heritage and environmental issues in favour of pursuing the aviation industry's agenda' (Brian Ross, SSE economics adviser, press release, 11 August 2003). It condemned the DfT for having 'clearly been overwhelmed by representations from BAA and the aviation industry and [having] completely ignored the voice of the people' (SSE press release, 25 February 2003). BAA itself was characterised as a privileged monopoly whose attempted bullying of local residents was symbolically rejected as 'Lord Haw Haw tactics', a reference which conjured up the national struggle against the Third Reich during the Second World War (Norman Mead, SSE deputy chair, press release, 23 December 2003).

Finally, the consultation process itself spawned the formation of two large rival hegemonic projects, thus intensifying rather than diminishing the struggle for ideological and political hegemony as the consultation exercise unfolded. Freedom to Fly (box 4.1) was launched on 14 January 2002 and drew together airport companies, airlines and trade unions, air users, organised business and sections of the tourist industry around a rhetoric of sustainable growth. It argued the case for the benefits of aviation expansion for a range of subjects (passengers, business, workers) while endeavouring to confer a particular meaning to the notion of sustainable growth, which was the object of ongoing ideological contestation. In contrast, AirportWatch (box 4.2), launched on 19 July 2002, brought together local airport protest groups and national environmental and conservation lobbies (such as the Council for the Protection of Rural England, FoE and T2000) in opposition to expansion. It argued for a policy of 'demand management' in aviation, insisting that further airport growth across the UK was unnecessary, while lobbying for the removal of the tax concessions enjoyed by airlines (Griggs and Howarth, 2004; Howarth and Griggs, 2006).

Over the course of the consultation, these rival projects sought to universalise their more narrow particular interests by articulating heterogeneous demands and identities in the aviation policy subsystem, and by reconciling or covering over the differences between the elements they aimed to combine. Hence the first task of those wishing either to oppose or to promote expansion was to forge a coalition of supporters who could speak with a united voice. But

---

Box 4.1 The backers of Freedom to Fly (January 2002 launch)

British Airports Authority (BAA); British Airways (BA); British Midland International (BMI); Virgin Atlantic; British Air Transport Association; Association of British Travel Agents; British Tourist Authority.; Confederation of British Industry; Trades Union Congress; Transport and General Workers' Union

---

Box 4.2 The backers of AirportWatch (July 2002 launch)

National organisations
Aviation Environment Federation (AEF); Friends of the Earth (FoE); Council for the Protection of Rural England (CPRE); National Society for Clean Air (NSCA); Transport 2000 (T2000).

Airport-based organisations
HACAN ClearSkies; Manchester Airport Environment Network (MAEN); Regional Airports Environment Forum; North West Essex and East Hertfordshire Preservation Society (NWEEHPA); Gatwick Area Conservation Campaign (GACC).

---

the political entrepreneurs who took up this challenge on both sides of the divide were confronted by the fact that they sought to represent a series of competing and potentially conflicting identities and interests. Across the pro-expansion network there were, for example, significant conflicts of interest between competing airlines, which did not necessarily agree on where the expansion should be, and between different airports and competing regional coalitions, as well as the difficulties of constructing a legitimate case for expansion in the eyes of the wider public. At the same time, for those seeking to build an anti-expansionist network, there were considerable tensions generated by proposals to expand airports at different sites, as well as conflicts between broader environmental campaigns and quality-of-life demands, and between local residents and direct action protesters. It is to the examination of how these rival projects sought to address these challenges that we now turn.

AirportWatch and the new politics of airport protest

As we argued in chapter 3, most previous campaigns against airport
expansion in the UK before the 1990s were mainly particularistic
protests that expressed conservationist and quality-of-life demands
against the building or expansion of specific airports in singular
places using traditional methods of campaigning. They had thus
focused primarily upon the impact of expansion on noise and air pollution, as well as the destruction of property and local congestion. But
stretching back at least to 1990, key opponents of airport expansion
at London's three major airports – Heathrow, Gatwick and Stansted –
had agreed to coordinate their actions and strategies. Employing the
language of international diplomacy and war, the different campaigns
had, in the words of Brendon Sewill, who was the chairman of
the Gatwick Area Conservation Campaign (GACC), 'got together
and agreed a "non-aggression pact"', which could form the basis
of a 'popular front' against unacceptable growth (Sewill, 2012: 54).
Reflecting on his involvement in the RUCATSE working group, which
was established in 1990, he notes how he and his fellow campaigners
had decided to 'fight our own corner but would not advocate putting
the runway in each other's patch, and would not criticise each other's
case' (Sewill, 2012: 55).

Elements of populist rhetoric and strategy became more pro-
nounced in the various local campaigns that were reactivated in the
space opened up by the 2000–03 consultation process. In the discourse
of the SSE campaign, for example, 'local communities' were depicted
as opposing 'irresistible' demands for a 'third Heathrow' in a battle
against 'covetous' airports (SSE, 2003a: 2–3); plans for expansion
at Stansted were described as a 'land grab'[3] and an 'act of environmental vandalism',[4] which would lead to the inexorable spread of the
'metropolis' intent on extending 'its urban tentacles in all directions
and without limit' (SSE, 2003a: 1). At the same time, populist appeals
urging the government to 'put people before planes'[5] were employed
to galvanise opposition to public authorities; in the language of the
SSE leadership, the government had effectively said: 'to hell with protecting the environment, our national heritage and local communities:
planes take priority'.[6] Such claims and demands also called into
question the openness of the consultation process which was presided
over by the DfT. Indeed, SSE leaders condemned this distrusted institution of the state for favouring BAA and the aviation industry,

while completely ignoring 'the voice of the people'.[7] The upshot of these machinations, it was asserted, would be a policy solution that sacrificed the environment and local communities, while furthering the interests of the aviation industry.

A key reason for using populist rhetoric of this sort was the desire to construct a political frontier between local communities living around Stansted and the interests of the aviation industry, which SSE leaders identified as BAA. BAA was named by the SSE campaign as a privileged monopoly that exploited its dominant position to bully local residents into submission. Its alleged campaign of 'intimidation and misinformation' was equated with an essentially undemocratic way of proceeding. At a well attended public meeting, for example, Norman Mead – the deputy chairman of SSE – alluded to BAA's 'dirty tricks' and excoriated its dubious methods:

> I won't be going into detail here because almost certainly we have within our midst at least one representative of BAA – who will report back to Terry Morgan [managing director of Stansted airport] in the morning. So if the person sitting next to you is wearing a grey suit, taking lots of notes and suddenly looking very embarrassed, you might just wish to whisper 'NO WAY BAA' into his ear![8]

So as to counter 'dirty tricks' of this sort, and as part of its overall media campaign, SSE activists, disguised as 'city gents', travelled to the City of London to 'brief institutional City investors and financiers on the dismal financial record of BAA's Stansted Airport'.[9] In addition, SSE campaigners exploited shareholder resolutions within BAA to end the practice of free car parking at airports for Members of Parliament, peers and Members of the European Parliament,[10] while endeavouring to force through a vote on the company's political donations, and to oblige the company's directors to obtain shareholder approval for major investments.[11]

As the campaign developed, the SSE leadership also began to link its particular demands with other demands voiced by contiguous protest groups opposed to expansion of airports outside the Stansted region. At its first meeting, the campaign group acknowledged the existence of AirportWatch – the national campaign to prevent airport expansion – and recognised the need to establish close links with protesters at Heathrow and Gatwick.[12] And during the period of consultation leading to the 2003 white paper, and beyond, SSE participated in a number of joint actions with other local campaigns (as discussed below). Significantly, it endorsed a more universal struggle against the construction of inland runways at any site in the south-east of England, advocating alongside AirportWatch and HACAN ClearSkies the policies of 'demand management', while condemning expansion through the policies of 'predict and provide'. In so doing, SSE sought to render equivalent a number of demands and grievances. These included calls for sustainable development, the demands for an end to the 'excessively favourable tax regime which aviation enjoys and its exemption, contrary to the "polluter pays principle"', as well as a challenge to government forecasts of the growth in air traffic and the alleged economic benefits of the aviation industry (SSE, 2003b:2). It thus appeared to reject a narrow localised campaign in favour of a populist politics that sought not to displace the development of runways onto other inland sites. In fact, its campaign was directed against inland runways *anywhere* in the south-east (SSE, 2003a: 7–8).

These linkages and connections were greatly enhanced and accelerated by the creation of AirportWatch during the consultation exercise for the 2003 white paper. Local protest groups began to extend their campaigns beyond the particular struggle of specific local campaigns into a universal struggle against *all* airport expansion across the UK, thereby attempting to forge chains of equivalence between local groups and, indeed, wider political struggles (Griggs and Howarth, 2004). Within this new politics of AirportWatch, local resident groups such as HACAN ClearSkies[13] endeavoured to inscribe its struggles against the expansion of Heathrow within more universal discourses and struggles against aviation growth. They attempted to go beyond tactical short-term, interest-based alliances that Sewill (Gatwick), Mead (Stansted), Evelyn Atlee (Heathrow) and Moira Logan (Airfields Environment Federation[14]) had agreed in the early 1990s when serving on the RUCATSE working group (Sewill 2012: 54–5).

Instead, they now sought to forge new collective identities, while engaging in a populist politics that linked together different demands and subject positions by constructing multiple antagonisms with the aviation industry and government. Alongside the old enemies of the BAA and the DETR were now added NIMBY groups that simply defended their own particular interests to the detriment of similar associations. Seen in this light, the birth of AirportWatch can be viewed as the product of a transformative strategy which built upon the protean alliances of local residents and direct action environmentalists (first witnessed in the campaign over the second runway at

Manchester), thus reproducing in the domain of anti-airport expansion many of the strategies and tactics employed by the anti-roads movement (Doherty, 1999; Griggs *et al.*, 1998).[15]

The knowledge and experience of these previous campaigns was brought into the arena of airport protest by political entrepreneurs such as John Stewart, who was a surface transport adviser with an established background in community action and anti-roads campaigning, having been chair of the anti-roads pressure groups Alarm London and Alarm UK. Stewart became involved in anti-airport expansion campaigns through his engagement with ClearSkies, which emerged in 1998 to tackle rising noise pollution from aircraft over Brixton and Lambeth in south London. ClearSkies merged with HACAN in 1999 and Stewart took over as chair of HACAN ClearSkies, the newly merged anti-Heathrow expansion resident group, in the aftermath of its defeat in the public inquiry into Terminal Five. He sought to reorientate HACAN ClearSkies away from the traditional politics of lobbying and formal representation towards the politics of community action. Thus, in the winter 2002 edition of *Take Off*, the organisation's newsletter, Stewart openly talked of the development of a 'parallel strategy' which aimed to bring together a wide-ranging coalition to act as a counterbalance to pressure for expansion from the aviation industry (*Take Off*, winter 2002: 5). Seeking to make sense of the perceived failure of HACAN's campaign at the Terminal Five inquiry, he believed that public inquiries should be viewed as 'part of a wider campaign' and that HACAN ClearSkies should take the campaign to government, 'campaigning on our territory, not theirs' (interview with local campaigner).

In November 2002, HACAN ClearSkies members duly undertook their first ever protest march through Whitehall (*Take Off*, winter 2002: 3). This followed high-profile demonstrations outside the annual general meeting of BAA in July 2002 and protests outside the meeting of Labour's National Executive Committee before the decision over Terminal Five, as well as support for the occupation of BAA's headquarters by Rising Tide, the direct action environmental protest network. Within HACAN ClearSkies itself, twelve new community groups were established to support community activism at the grassroots – another innovation ushered in by Stewart and his committee. Through local stunts and marches, these community groups aimed to create a 'more visible HACAN ClearSkies presence in their own areas' (*Take Off*, winter 2002: 3).

Similarly, SSE campaigners sought to mobilise community opposition to expansion, with its committee members speaking to around 2,000 people at eight public meetings in the six weeks following its launch at the beginning of August 2002. Over 250 of its supporters protested outside the DfT consultation exhibition at the Stansted Hilton at the end of August, while some 1,200 people pledged their support and signed up over the summer of 2002 to receive email updates from the local residents' anti-expansion group.[16] Campaigners at Stansted, who included the celebrity chef Jamie Oliver, as well as protesters against expansions at Cliffe, Luton and Rugby, also joined supporters of HACAN ClearSkies on a march through London in November 2002. The march ended with a rally at Trafalgar Square, after campaigners had delivered an open letter to Tony Blair condemning the government for 'failing in its duty' to 'strike the right balance' between aviation growth and environmental protection (Griggs and Howarth, 2008).[17]

In seeking to forge equivalences between local campaigns during the summer of 2002, AirportWatch staged meetings at all the major airports where expansion was being considered, culminating in a national conference on airport expansion attended by local and national protest groups and environmentalists at the end of September and a mass protest at Stansted Airport.[18] Its leadership appealed repeatedly to the collective nature of the struggle facing local anti-airport campaigners. At a meeting with SSE in October 2002, Jeff Gazzard from AirportWatch and John Stewart were thus anxious to quash rumours of splits in the emerging network of local campaigners. Responding promptly to claims that campaigners at Rugby airport had suggested expansion at Stansted, for example, they noted that 'emails have been flying to and fro and we are all good friends opposing the whole idea of the need for extra runways'.[19] Indeed, as we argue above, AirportWatch eschewed the rhetoric of NIMBYism, deeming any airport expansion in the UK to be 'unnecessary, unsustainable and irresponsible'.[20] When in June 2003, the Gatwick Area Conservation Campaign (GACC) was reported to have highlighted the benefits of expansion at Stansted airport, Gazzard quickly denounced such statements as 'churlish', declaring that 'Nimbyism has no place in this argument. Shifting things around is no good for anybody' (*Guardian*, 2 June 2003).[21] Similarly, Tim Johnson, director of the Aviation Environment Federation (AEF), was at pains to convey the united front of local resident groups against government and the aviation industry, declaring: 'what is interesting is that people are not saying "not in my back yard." They are challenging the Government to come up with a sensible and sustainable aviation policy, not one written by the aviation industry.'[22]

The discursive representation and sedimentation of this emerging transformative strategy pursued by AirportWatch rested upon three rhetorical devices: an attack on the crisis in, and unsustainability of, the 'predict and provide' paradigm; the discrediting of the government's impartiality and its broad failure to resist airport expansion; and an undermining of the supposed contribution of the aviation industry to the UK economy. In the pamphlet *Flying Into Trouble*, the failings of the 'predict and provide' paradigm were set against the benefits of measures designed to manage demand for air travel and promote integrated transport networks (AirportWatch, 2002a). The very internal logic of the dominant paradigm was targeted by AirportWatch supporters as failing to 'grasp basic economics', with claims that 'there will be a demand for anything if it is sold cheaply enough' (B. Sewill, GACC, cited in AirportWatch, 2002b: 3). Tax concessions and subsidies to the aviation industry were derided as fuelling demand and 'making forecasts come true by building the capacity needed to meet the forecasts' (P. De Zylva, FoE, cited in AirportWatch, 2002b: 3). AirportWatch activists thus sought to foreground the unsustainability of government and industry proposals. They generated counter-narratives in which fantasmatic visions of the looming threat of 'the equivalent of a new airport the current size of Stansted [being built] every year for the next 30 years' were juxtaposed with the industry's claims that economic decline and growing international competition would be jeopardised if expansion was not forthcoming (AirportWatch, 2002a: 1). We can conceptualise this rhetorical onslaught as an endeavour to *politicise* the 'predict and provide' paradigm by highlighting its ignoble origins, as well as the hidden background conditions that enabled it to become one of the dominant social logics of the regime of aviation expansion (a strategy that took on increasing salience following the anti-roads struggles of the 1990s).

AirportWatch thus blamed the UK government for the emergent crisis in the 'predict and provide' model in airport policy. The government was castigated for failing to regulate the aviation industry and for being incapable of engaging in rational decision-making. In the rhetoric of AirportWatch, the aviation industry was nothing less than an 'out of control' insider (AirportWatch, 2002a:3), with 'ministers listening only to the demands of the airlines and airport operators' (De Zylva, cited in AirportWatch, 2002b: 3). Government was repeatedly charged with 'irresponsibility', for failing to consider the interests of the majority, and for not learning from the past experiences of its own policies. Hence D.A. Franklin, a HACAN ClearSkies committee member, concluded that

> the Government should discard its obvious predilection for a policy of 'predict and provide' in aviation and implement instead a policy with a proper concern for people and their environment and their safety ... by legislating meaningful controls on flight numbers, flight paths, and noise and pollution levels. (Franklin, 2002: 8–9)

AirportWatch challenged the government to learn from road-building programmes, where the abandonment of 'predict and provide' policies had led some of its supporters to question publicly how the government could 'justify using the very same approach for aviation?' (Tim Williamson, National Society for Clean Air, cited in AirportWatch, 2002b: 4). It criticised the absence of policy coordination and the failure to consider alternative forms of transport on the part of the New Labour government, arguing that it should embrace demand management, an integrated transport policy and an end to the tax concessions offered to the aviation industry. Outlining an alternative policy agenda, AirportWatch advocated: an effective fiscal and charging regime to manage demand for air travel; high-speed rail links and videoconferencing; increased roles for local communities in the regulation of local airports; and the imposition of 'tough and legally-binding' targets for reductions in noise and pollution levels (AirportWatch, 2002a: 11). 'Demand management' was thus advocated as the opposite of the 'predict and provide' model which underpinned airport expansion. With its clear Keynesian overtones, the state was called upon to intervene actively in the regulation of 'big business' so that demand would be 'vigorously' managed and 'strongly constrained' in the wider public interest (SSE, 2003a: 6).

Significantly, rather than arguing for the consideration of environmental downsides to offset economic growth, in a well versed 'economy versus the environment debate', AirportWatch and its supporters challenged the basis of the economic arguments for airport expansion which, it argued, had been taken 'as read' in the past. In *The Hidden Cost of Flying*, Brendon Sewill, chair of GACC, exposed what he calculated to be the £9 billion tax subsidies enjoyed by the UK aviation industry, which were derived from the absence, for example, of value-added tax on fuel and air travel (Sewill, 2003: 18). He called instead for the introduction of a 'fair taxation' regime for the aviation industry. Challenging claims for airport expansion on the basis of the economic importance of aviation, he compared the aviation industry to the sewage industry, arguing that 'the sewage industry is important but that is not taken as self-evident proof that it must treble in size' (Sewill, 2003: 1). In fact, airports were variously charged with being 'cuckoos in the nest' (AirportWatch, 2002b: 2), having a 'privileged position to protect' (AirportWatch, 2002a: 7) and having a 'sole motive [of] profit without limit or constraint' (Franklin, 2002: 1).

In a four-page pamphlet compiled by John Stewart, *It's the Economy, Stupid*, a thinly veiled reference to 'third way' politics, HACAN ClearSkies (2003a) also questioned the perceived economic benefits of airport expansion. In a series of vignettes, it set out seven arguments to undermine the economic case for airport expansion, part of a strategic move to refute what Franklin had characterised in his pamphlet as 'unsubstantiated scare stories ... spread about the fearful consequences to the British economy if unlimited expansion to meet "demand" is not met' (Franklin, 2002: 1). Rather than an economic good, HACAN ClearSkies highlighted what 'air transport takes *out* from the economy', and was keen to point out equally how subsidies to the air transport industry allegedly equated to '2p on the standard rate of income tax' (Franklin, 2002: 4; HACAN ClearSkies, 2003a: 3). Indeed, in the pamphlet *Aviation Policy in the United Kingdom*, Franklin (2002: 1) further explained how 'the massive hidden subsidies' awarded to aviation hampered the operation of the market for aviation, enabling 'ridiculously low fares to be offered by many airlines – or recently, even free flights'.

In repeatedly enunciating doubts about the economic contribution of aviation during the consultation process, HACAN ClearSkies and AirportWatch sought to engineer possible splits in the pro-expansion coalition, while also constructing new 'friends' and broadening support for the regulation of the aviation industry. A crucial part of this quintessentially political operation was the attempt to widen the constituency affected by airport expansion. AirportWatch thus predicted that the

> impact [of expansion] will be huge – at every airport site in the country, and at some new ones, on the adjacent 'airport communities';

on towns near and far under the flight-path; and much further afield
as infrastructure and development impacts ripple outwards. (Airport-
Watch, 2002a: 2)

It posited that there would be no possibility for individuals to escape
the negative impacts of air transport expansion: 'the consequences of
meeting this growth will be felt everywhere: locally, around airport
site; nationally, as aviation competes unfairly against other forms of
transport and undermines the achievement of sustainable development; and globally, as aviation increasingly contributes to devastating
climate change' (AirportWatch, 2002a: 2). Notably, as we demonstrated above, in its report on the future expansion of airports, *Flying
Into Trouble*, AirportWatch constructed the category of 'airport
communities', thereby appealing to the common interests and identities that exist between those residents living near airports and under
their flight paths and those living at some distance from the airport
(AirportWatch 2002a: 9). Repeating these appeals, the Campaign to
Protect Rural England (CPRE), in its pamphlet *Flying to Distraction*,
set out the threat of noise pollution from new flight paths and aircraft
holding 'stacks' to the 'tranquillity of the countryside'. Additional
noise, it argued, would 'make hundreds of thousands of people's
lives a misery' and 'extend far beyond the environs of airports – it is a
problem that will affect the nation as a whole' (CPRE, 2003: 1, 4).

Most importantly, this aim of widening its constituency was
matched by the attempt to unify or join struggles, so that the campaign against airport expansion became equally the campaign of
others. In so doing, the leadership of AirportWatch introduced new
issue dimensions into the policy arena that they hoped would cut
across narrow environmental concerns or particular struggles at
specific airports, thus facilitating the identification of new enemies
and demands. In one such endeavour to connect with other struggles
to protect rural economies, fight poverty and support developing
countries, airport expansion was portrayed as an attack on the liveli-
hoods of UK farmers and tourist resorts:

> They will make it easier to jet in cheap food and to jet out
> holiday-makers on cheap flights. How does this help hard-pressed UK
> farmers or our traditional UK holiday destinations? (K. Thompson,
> Regional Airports Environment Forum, cited in AirportWatch, 2002b:3)

In addition, in an appeal to supporters of the countryside fearing
urban expansion, airports were articulated as a threat to rural

communities and 'our "green and pleasant land" [which] looks set to be ruined by runways and turned into sprawling suburban development zones' (P. Hamblin, CPRE, cited in AirportWatch, 2002b: 3). At the global level, the pollution caused by airlines was often construed as a threat to the commitments made by the UK government at Kyoto (Franklin, 2002: 6). In short, the rhetoric of AirportWatch and its supporters was employed to cultivate resonances and draw equivalences between the struggles of local residents against airports in the UK and putative 'friends' in other national and global protest movements, who were deemed to be fighting the same struggle.

An exemplary instance of this construction of 'friends' was evident in the way HACAN ClearSkies challenged the social justice of the Labour government's policy on airport expansion. In May 2003, it published a four-page pamphlet, *A Poor Deal*, another thinly veiled reference to 'third way' politics through its play on the New Labour government's 'New Deal' employment schemes (HACAN ClearSkies, 2003b). The pamphlet responded to a report from the government's Social Exclusion Unit (SEU) that highlighted the impact of poor transport on patterns of social exclusion. It condemned the injustice of tax concessions for airlines and high earners, when the poorest communities in society were said to suffer a 'double whammy' from air travel, by not having the money either to afford holidays or to move away from flight paths (HACAN ClearSkies, 2003b: 1). The aviation industry's tax concessions and cheap fares, it was argued, 'work against the interests of the poorest in society', with John Stewart, chair of HACAN ClearSkies, pointing out that only 11 per cent of people in social classes D and E flew in any one year (HACAN ClearSkies, 2003b: 2). Eliminating these tax concessions would, it was alleged, provide the funds to 'develop a decent transport system for socially excluded communities' (2003b: 1). In fact, *A Poor Deal* went on to argue that the SEU itself claimed that poor communities would benefit from surface transport initiatives, and it demonstrated how subsidies to the aviation industry – which were then calculated as approximately £7.5 billion – could be used to provide walking schemes, changes to road layouts in favour of all road users and more bus lanes (2003b: 4). By establishing an equivalence between the campaigns against airport expansion and the struggles against poverty and social exclusion, HACAN ClearSkies strived to redefine the problem of airport expansion as an issue of social justice. Indeed, in its own rhetoric such struggles extended beyond the UK to people in developing countries, where poor communities were 'the biggest losers' from aviation expansion (HACAN ClearSkies, 2003b: 1). These communities, HACAN ClearSkies argued, lacked any recourse to consultative forums, but experienced at first hand the negative environmental consequences of air travel.

As the rhetoric and arguments of the *Poor Deal* pamphlet illustrate, HACAN ClearSkies was seeking to forge chains of equivalences between its struggle against airport expansion and those discontented with 'big government'. Populist appeals were made to the common taxpayer, who it was alleged was opposed to those 'top 10% of income earners [who] benefit from most flights'. Equally, 'second-home owners' were articulated as privileged flyers who fuelled demand for cheap flights while benefiting from a subsidy from ordinary taxpayers to the tune of an additional £550 in income tax per year (for person on a wage of £25,000) (HACAN ClearSkies, 2003b: 1–2). Airport communities were equally portrayed as outsiders, 'the odds … stacked against them' (AirportWatch, 2002b: 9). In the pamphlet *Aviation Policy in the United Kingdom*, Franklin (2002: 1) painted a picture of ordinary people fighting government failure and its bias towards corporate capital, describing the expansion of Heathrow as a 'story of connivance, deceit and broken promises'. Echoing the sentiments of the SSE leadership, he threatened government that if it continued to expand airports 'the costs in civil strife within the British community from the unleashed anger of people driven beyond endurance by broken promises and their ignored distress will be immense' (Franklin, 2002: 9). Indeed, alluding to the 'winter of discontent' that brought down the Labour government at the end of the 1970s, AirportWatch campaigners threatened 'a summer, autumn, winter and spring of discontent and public backlash' (De Zylva, cited in AirportWatch, 2002a: 3).

But this populist strategy (Laclau, 2005), which sought to connect particular demands and struggles into a more universal project against airport expansion *per se*, while diversifying the strategies and tactics of local campaigns, was not without its difficulties. Traditional supporters of HACAN ClearSkies, and for that matter SSE, did not always readily embrace the new strategy and tactics of community activism (interview with local campaigner; interview with campaign director). The SSE leadership even warned against new forms of direct action protest, claiming that while 'some may wish to dig tunnels or chain themselves to trees … we must first use the democratic process and take it through to the end'.[23] In fact, as we have suggested, the leadership of AirportWatch had to go to great lengths to ward off actual and potential splits in the coalition, so that its more universal struggle against expansion did not give way to particularist demands against or for expansion at specific airports. For example, while arguing against the expansion of inland airport capacity, SSE also promoted the case for the development of an offshore airport as 'the least worst option' (Mead, SSE press release, 16 December 2002; SSE, 2003b: 3–4). Such an option was not included in the original consultation document and stood in opposition to the universal, environmental demands and strategies endorsed by AirportWatch and its supporters, who rejected increased airport capacity anywhere in the UK in favour of demand management.

Even more so, SSE's successful judicial bid to include for consideration the expansion of Gatwick airport in the consultation process betrayed the proclivities of a particularistic rather than a universal mode of struggle. In this instance, SSE campaigners successfully argued that the 1979 planning agreement between BAA and West Sussex County Council, which stated that there would be no further runways at Gatwick before 2019, should not prohibit the consideration of expansion at Gatwick. This was because the white paper was to plan airport expansion beyond 2019, and the government predicted a third runway would be required in the south-east in 2024. The bid and judgement delayed the consultation process. But it also called into question the engagement of SSE within the broader campaign of AirportWatch and it brought 'like-for-like' retaliation from the Gatwick campaign, which advocated expansion at Stansted (Griggs and Howarth, 2008).

Undoubtedly, of course, in the political battle to hold together a broadening constituency, AirportWatch and HACAN ClearSkies were aided by the government's decision to begin a national and regional consultation on the future development of air transport across the whole UK. This decision broke with the political logic of 'divide and rule', which had characterised previous attempts by government to manage the contradictory demands surrounding airport expansion. Put in a nutshell, then, its consideration of *all* airports in the UK facilitated the articulation of universal demands against expansion.

But the conditions for the emergence of this transformative strategy also rested in part on the dislocatory experiences of local residents at public inquiries into expansion, notably at Heathrow, where defeat at the Terminal Five inquiry undermined HACAN's commitment to traditional practices of political campaigning and led to the resignation of its chair, Dermot Cox (Cox, 2002). As one local campaigner put it, the 'eyes' of participants involved in that public inquiry were 'opened as to their [public inquiries'] real function'. Participants presented 'great arguments ... but lost' (interview with local campaigner). Such recognition of the dislocatory impact of failure at yet another inquiry echoed the testimonies of local residents at Manchester after their experience of the public inquiry into the second runway (interview with local campaigner; Griggs and Howarth, 2002). Indeed, Franklin, of HACAN ClearSkies, dismissed the neutrality of inquiries, arguing that

> civil servants who should have been impartial went out of their way to support BAA, BA and the industry in general while doing their utmost to rubbish the arguments of tens of thousands of objectors. (Franklin, 2002: 3)

These interpretations were fuelled by the overturning on appeal by the UK government of a 2001 European Court of Human Rights' judgement in favour of HACAN ClearSkies. The Court had concluded that the regulation of night flights at Heathrow unfairly infringed the local residents' rights in respect of their private and family lives. In early July 2003, however, the Court overturned its previous judgement, which the HACAN ClearSkies leadership interpreted as further evidence that 'the economic interests of the country are more important than the right of people living under the flight path to a decent night's sleep' (*HACAN ClearSkies News*, summer 2000, 4–5; *Financial Times*, 7 January 2002; *Guardian*, 9 July 2003).

Yet this new politics of airport protest cannot be divorced from the emergence of a new leadership in HACAN ClearSkies, which was spearheaded by its newly elected chair, John Stewart. Stewart brought new ideas and strategies, and he found support for his approach among the leadership of other anti-airport groups, notably Jeff Gazzard, who had orchestrated a broad media campaign and direct action against the second runway at Manchester, spanning the organisational boundaries between local residents and direct action environmentalists (Griggs and Howarth, 2004). Strategically placed political entrepreneurs were thus able to develop and symbolise rival strategies, in which the notion of demand management operated as an empty signifier that held together disparate demands and strategies, while also making possible the construction of antagonistic relations with new enemies.

Overall, therefore, the leadership of HACAN ClearSkies and AirportWatch worked assiduously throughout the consultation period leading up to the white paper to extend the boundaries of the constituency of those affected by airport expansion; to join up the struggle against expansion with wider social struggles; and to make populist appeals that would enable the forging of a wide social coalition against airport expansion. In harnessing the language of social justice in the name of a fairer and more egalitarian community, which could not be accomplished under a government beholden to large corporations and business interests, the campaign supplemented its usual NIMBY and environmental orientations by aligning itself with a series of broader political forces in the country, which called for the government and state to fulfil their properly impartial roles in a liberal democratic society. Its rhetorical and political strategies were pivotal in defining and isolating potential adversaries, while also binding together the emergent coalition. More than this, however, in the appeals to demand management, they also harboured a clear alternative to the trajectory of aviation expansion. Indeed, this signifier functioned as the glue that held this emerging coalition together and enabled anti-expansion campaigners to construct antagonistic relations with abstract targets such as the neoliberal economic policies of deregulation, as well as its main adversary, the Freedom to Fly coalition (see, for example, *Birmingham Post*, 15 January 2002). 'Demand management' was thus elaborated in opposition to the logic of 'predict and provide' and, in keeping with its clear Keynesian resonances, the state was called upon to intervene actively in the regulation of the aviation industry in the name of the wider public interest. For FoE, demand management was equated to sustainable aviation such that its response to the consultation began with the headline 'sustainable aviation = demand management' (FoE, 2003: 1). In the endeavour to cultivate resonances between diverse forces and to produce equivalential linkages among disparate demands by constructing novel lines of division among actors and groups, well placed actors such as Stewart and Gazzard played key strategic and tactical roles. They were thus able to constitute and maintain a powerful discourse coalition that engaged in a transformative campaign which brought into being a new politics of airport protest. Yet, as we have intimated, this is only half the story, because throughout the consultation process

AirportWatch was constantly engaged in a hegemonic battle with a rival political project – Freedom to Fly – that favoured expansion. Both coalitions sought to garner political and ideological support behind their respective demands, so it is to AirportWatch's 'other' that we now turn.

Providing ideological cover: the strategy of Freedom to Fly

While AirportWatch strived to bring together a broad coalition against expansion, there was a real fear among supporters of expansion that the Labour government, though intent on giving a strong ideological and policy lead on aviation expansion, would in the last instance prevaricate and defer any decisions to expand airport capacity. In this section, we examine how the supporters of expansion sought to strengthen their position and weaken opposition by deploying rhetorical strategies aimed at displacing and then restructuring the existing terrain of argumentation. This would enable them to display and advance their arguments in the best possible light. In launching Freedom to Fly, supporters of expansion sought, first, to construct a broad political coalition of all those forces in favour of increased airport capacity (see box 4.1) and, secondly, to articulate a viable public discourse that could hold the alliance together. In constructing this alliance, intellectuals and activists associated with the aviation industry sought to make equivalent a series of diverse particular demands by elaborating a common discourse that could provide a plausible and credible project for growth. More concretely, the purpose of such a discourse was to provide a defensible 'storyline' about the need for, and advantages of, aviation growth, which was built around the ideas of 'sustainable aviation' and 'freedom to fly', and to elaborate a persuasive set of counter-arguments designed to negate and disarticulate the political alliance opposed to growth.

In seeking to unify these different interests into a collective will, political entrepreneurs in the leadership of Freedom to Fly were able to locate a point of universality between the various demands and interests (voiced by competing airlines and airports, regional expansion coalitions, and producers and consumers of airline and airport services) to which all could agree to give their support. In other words, they managed to secure an agreement between interests that both supported growth and strongly opposed all those forces that were against expansion, in which the immediate and decisive support for aviation by the Labour government became the lowest common denominator or point of compromise between the different forces at play (interview with campaign director). Large corporations such as BAA, BA and Virgin Airlines, along with air users, business associations, trade unions and elements of the tourist industry, put aside their short-term interests – what Gramsci would have called their 'economic-corporate interests' (Gramsci, 1971: 160) – in maximising their individual preferences in order to construct a united front in favour of airport expansion *per se*.

To promote demands for growth, the leadership of Freedom to Fly sought to foreground the embedded constructions of air travel as an economic success story, not only in its own right, but also in its capacity to unlock new opportunities for both business and pleasure. In its pamphlet promoting airport expansion, *Flying Responsibly into the Future*, the coalition thus associated aviation with 'growth, prosperity and jobs', stressing equally its role as a catalyst for growth across all business sectors, although especially tourism: 'Aviation is vital for our country. It supports jobs, investment and tourism' (Freedom to Fly, 2002: 1). Or, as Brenda Dean, its chair, argued in a newspaper interview:

> Time is money. Modern businesses rely on fast, reliable transport both of people and high value, time sensitive goods. The UK's highest growth industries especially, such as pharmaceuticals, communication services, finance, insurance and consultancy, depend heavily on good international transport links. (*Observer*, 3 November 2002)

Claims of employment and business opportunities were presented in its promotional pamphlet as a series of uncontestable 'FACTs' (Freedom to Fly, 2002: 2–3; original emphasis):

> **FACT**: Aviation adds over £10 billion a year to the UK economy and generates half a million jobs.

> **FACT**: The Government estimates that throughout the UK some 260,000 extra jobs could be created through the proposals for expanding airport capacity by 2030.

In seeking to decontest and sediment its stylised empirical claims, Freedom to Fly invoked the OEF 1999 study on the positive contribution of aviation to the UK economy, and even the government's own consultation papers, which, it argued, 'are unequivocal that the UK's aviation industry is good for the economy and employment' (Freedom to Fly, 2002: 2). Reiterating General Motors' famous advertising slogan, the supporters of expansion asserted that 'what is good for aviation is good for the United Kingdom' (see Miliband, 1969: 69).

Alongside its rhetoric of aviation as an economic success story, Freedom to Fly also focused on the consequences of the failure to build new airport capacity, thus tapping into the horrific dimension of the fantasmatic narrative on UK aviation. Failure to expand was articulated as a threat to both the host of employment and investment opportunities unlocked by air travel and the global competitive position of the UK aviation industry. As Freedom to Fly was keen to point out, 'the cost to the economy of no growth could be in excess of £15 billion (net present value) and the economy would lose billions of pounds' (Freedom to Fly, 2002: 2). Without expansion, the pro-growth coalition threatened, the price of air travel would increase; up to 260,000 jobs would be put at risk; 73 million passenger movements in the UK would be prevented; and incoming tourism would be hit, threatening 4,700 jobs (Freedom to Fly, 2002: 12). And, as if to amplify the threat, the leadership continually noted with alarm that government indecision and the failure to build new capacity would also mean losing out to the UK's competitors in Europe. In the words of Brenda Dean:

> While we were labouring through the cumbersome inquiry about a Fifth Terminal for passengers at two-runway Heathrow airport, the French, Germans and Dutch were busy building the fourth or fifth runways at Paris Charles de Gaulle, Frankfurt and Schiphol. (*Observer*, 3 November 2002)

Notably, this inculcation of an external threat not only raised the prospect of economic decline, but it also invoked the priority of the collective good over the particular interests of individuals. Joe Irvin, for example, evoked the importance of aviation to economic well-being across the UK by declaring that 'If everyone says "not in my backyard", it'll be disastrous for consumers and the British economy' (cited in Clark, 2002). In other words, for the leadership of Freedom to Fly, 'community interests' were to be 'balanced with national priorities' (Freedom to Fly, 2002: 11). These appeals stood in marked contrast to those of AirportWatch.

Nevertheless, proponents of the expansion campaign were wary of presenting their case in terms of 'growth at any cost'. On the contrary, they were of the firm view that the environmental and social costs of expansion had to be carefully acknowledged and addressed. The leadership of Freedom to Fly was thus determined to elaborate a public discourse that would allay fears about the negative consequences of growth, and portray the aviation industry in the best light. Indeed, it was here that a first usage of what we have termed the technique of rhetorical redescription can be pinpointed, for those articulating the Freedom to Fly discourse sought to redescribe the aviation industry not as a threat to the environment, but as a proponent of sustainable aviation that could lead to sustainable growth. Drawing on radical environmental and development discourses – demands for sustainable development in the face of the limits to growth – 'organic intellectuals' (to use Gramsci's phrase) in the leadership of the pro-aviation network thus substituted a rival evaluative term based on the qualifier 'sustainable' to counter efforts by environmentalists and local protesters, who were intent on presenting the expansion of the aviation industry as 'unsustainable', 'unnecessary' and 'subsidised'. The upshot of this rhetorical redescription was that the demand for air travel had to be 'managed' and 'limited', though not in the draconian ways proposed by AirportWatch. In short, therefore, the metaphor of sustainable development, widely understood as 'development that meets the needs of the present without compromising the ability of future generations to meet their own needs' (World Commission on Environment and Development, 1987: 43; see also Weale, 1992: 135), was reiterated in the context of aviation to stave off potential criticism and adverse publicity. Using such rhetorical devices and mechanisms, the proponents of expansion sought to transform the zero-sum game of expansion or environmental protection into a positive-sum game where it was possible to achieve both growth and environmental protection.

The second director of Freedom to Fly, Dan Hodges, deployed appeals to environmental concerns to justify the rejection of proposals for the building of a new airport at Cliffe on the Thames estuary, claiming that 'Cliffe is simply unsustainable on environmental grounds'. He repositioned the aviation industry as defenders of the environment, declaring that 'the aviation industry has a long standing commitment to sustainable expansion'. Going further, he encouraged environmental groups to follow this example:

> All that is now required is a firm commitment from those environmental groups who went to court to oppose the exclusion of Gatwick that they will not repeat the exercise and unnecessarily maintain the

blight on local residents of North Kent. We are prepared to demonstrate our commitment to sensible aviation growth, and we call on
AirportWatch and Friends of the Earth to do the same.[24]

In a similar vein, Brenda Dean called upon the New Labour government to address the challenge of 'maximis[ing] the economic and
social benefits of air travel while mitigating harmful effects and environmental costs'. The then chair of Freedom to Fly was keen to
acknowledge that aviation growth

> must be responsible and sustainable. All human activity affects the
> environment. There is general agreement that aviation like all industries
> should meet the environmental costs it imposes, on a fair and equitable
> basis. (*Observer*, 3 November 2002)

But these claims sat alongside repeated attempts to cast doubt on
the extent of aviation's impact on the environment, as well as appeals
to future technological developments, mitigation and compensation, which would enable growth in air travel while minimising its
environmental costs. Appeals to technological fixes were reproduced
by Dean, who argued that the aviation industry should be encouraged to be 'greener by design' – a direct reference to the aviation
industry network Greener by Design, which was founded in 1999 and
sponsored primarily by the Royal Aeronautical Society (RAeS) and the
Department for Business, Innovation and Skills (BIS), with the aim
of delivering 'practical and environmentally and economically sustainable solutions to the challenge posed by aviation's impact on the
environment'.[25] As a portent of future debates, an emissions trading
scheme was acclaimed as an economic instrument that would enable
both continued expansion and environmental mitigation.

These rhetorical appeals were repeated by Mike Hodgkinson, chief
executive of BAA, in speeches at the Freedom to Fly conference in
July 2002 and to the RAeS in November 2002. In his response to the
environmentalist Jonathon Porritt at the July conference, Hodgkinson
reiterated the claims of the aviation industry to sustainable air transport, which he endorsed as one of the seven guiding principles of
Freedom to Fly, while arguing that 'I don't think the solution is to
stop growth'. Like Dean, he endorsed technological developments
within aviation, though he recognised that 'there is simply no credible
alternative aviation fuel to kerosene'. Hodgkinson also came out in
favour of emissions trading, for 'if aviation can't cut its own emissions
sufficiently, then it needs to pay other industries which can cut their

emissions more cost effectively'. But he typically negated opposition to the industry by insisting that aviation would continue in the future to represent a 'very small proportion' of global emissions and that 'those who express their concerns about the environmental impact of air travel have a responsibility to forge a new relationship with the industry, as partners not opponents'.[26]

As we suggest above, the desire to redescribe demands for more airport capacity in terms of a policy of sustainable aviation was driven by attempts to dispute the alleged environmental costs of air travel. Freedom to Fly (2002: 9–11) thus endeavoured to foreground the progress made by the aviation industry in combating noise pollution, lauding its commitment to meet new European Union standards for NO_2 and supporting emissions trading. Equally, it threw doubts on the significance of the contribution of air transport to existing global CO_2 emissions and to levels of air pollution surrounding local airports (attributed primarily in this instance to cars not necessarily travelling to airports). Any decision to impose further taxation on air travel to offset its environmental costs was challenged by the reasoning that 'If aviation covers its environmental costs (both by cutting pollution and paying for the remaining external costs) what justification is there for pricing people out of flying?' (Freedom to Fly, 2002: 9). Finally, it questioned the charges that demands for airport expansion were reducible to 'some simplistic form of "predict and provide" policy – an accusation previously levelled at roads policy' (Freedom to Fly, 2002: 7). Existing levels of demand, it was argued, already justified new infrastructure, and airport expansion, unlike roads, would incur no costs to taxpayers, who would have a marginal charge for using them because 'runways are built by airports who depend on customers paying to fly' (Freedom to Fly, 2002: 7).

Against this background, the collocation 'sustainable growth', which was made to serve as the universal demand of the coalition, was the product of a metaphorical redescription, which was then universalised by political entrepreneurs intent on developing what they thought was the most plausible and credible case for expansion. Similarly, the very name of the coalition – the catachretic moment *par excellence* – was an inspired creation that successfully tapped into a number of important beliefs, desires and discourses held by large swathes of the British populace. In this view, naming the coalition Freedom to Fly was a radical and inspired act that brought into being a new object – the coalition demanding sustainable growth – and provided the ideological means of representing a perceived threat or lack (being prevented from flying) that could be overcome by a particular policy (a pro-expansion strategy). The name, Freedom to Fly, framed the demand for sustainable aviation, and the discourse was structured around the fantasy that these two elements did not contradict or cancel each other out, but could be equally desired and achieved.

That Freedom to Fly was an inspired choice of name for the coalition, which also served to constitute the group and helped to frame its demands in ideological terms, is evident in the connotations and meanings of the signifiers it employed. On the one hand, the importance of the signifier 'freedom' in any political discourse is difficult to underplay. Historically, and in numerous contexts, freedom has connoted an exemption or release from bondage, liberation from sin, emancipation from slavery, breaking free from shackles, removal of obstacles or impediments to actions, and so forth. Just as it is difficult to be against measures that are protective of our natural environment, so it is politically difficult to be against freedom. The burden of proof seems inevitably stacked on the side of those who wish to interfere with our freedoms, or take away our liberties. In the discourse of political philosophy, and in the analysis of political ideologies, the basic concept of freedom is generally taken to mean an 'ability to choose without interference by others', and it has been commonplace, if somewhat misleading, to distinguish between at least two conceptions of freedom: a negative conception – 'freedom from' external constraint – and a positive conception – 'freedom to' (Berlin, 1969; but see MacCallum, 1967; Miller, 1991). The beauty of the name Freedom to Fly was that it seamlessly captured both dimensions: the 'freedom from' those who would prevent British people from flying by 'managing demand', for example, or by blocking the expansion of airports; and the 'freedom to' fly wherever they wished to at the lowest possible price and in the most convenient fashion.

On the other hand, 'to fly', as in 'flying in an aircraft' or 'flying to a destination', has also acquired powerful and positive connotations in the modern age. In the popular imagination, in novels, films, the world of advertising, the image of international airports, jet flight, pilots and stewardesses, as well as the exotic destinations which are put within easy reach, have become quintessential signifiers of the cosmopolitanism, excitement, speed and adventure of our increasingly 'small world'. As the story of Daedalus and his son Icarus attests, the exhilaration, thrill and danger of flight and flying –

connected strongly with ideas of escape and liberation – are deeply inscribed in ancient Greek mythology, and it continues to operate on contemporary popular consciousness as a sign of progress, freedom and pure possibility. As an appellation, Freedom to Fly resonated strongly with these fantasies and collective imaginaries that structure the mentalities of many subjects in the modern world, and it was used to try to displace the discourse of demand management, which the pro-expansion forces feared was beginning to take root as an alternative discourse on aviation.

Tapping into these fantasies and collective imaginaries, Freedom to Fly stressed the articulation between aviation and travel and holidays. In its pamphlet *Flying Responsibly into the Future* it claimed that aviation

> has opened up opportunities for ordinary people to fly for a holiday in the sun, visit friends and relatives or experience other cultures. Being able to fly away on holiday is a valued part of people's quality of life. (Freedom to Fly, 2002: 4)

Similar statements were publicly reiterated by Brenda Dean. She evoked romantic holidays in Venice and flights to visit grandchildren in Sydney, thus capturing the increasing popularisation of flying, which she declared was 'no longer the preserve of the wealthy' (*Observer*, 3 November 2002). Populist rhetoric of this sort persistently portrayed the aviation industry and flying as a force for social progress. Air travel was deemed, for example, to have 'broadened minds as well as mobility', with '15% of young people flying to the UK coming here to study' (Freedom to Fly, 2002: 5). Notably, in the rhetoric of Freedom to Fly, as a counter to AirportWatch's concerns with social justice, airport growth had enabled 'ordinary people to fly'. Additional environmental charges on aviation would, it suggested, threaten such progress, adding up 'to £340 for a family of four flying to holiday in Majorca. This would be unjustified, unfair and ineffective' (Freedom to Fly, 2002: 7). Through these populist appeals, airport expansion was rearticulated not as the agenda of profit-maximising companies, but as the necessary social response to rising consumer demand and social progress. Continued opportunities to experience such forms of enjoyment were, in the narrative of Freedom to Fly (2002: 7), said to be fragile; as it pointed out, for the predicted growth in demand to be realised, 'all that it would mean would be for each of us on average to take one summer holiday and one other return trip by plane each year (for example, a weekend break, a winter holiday, a study visit, a business trip or to stay with friends and relatives)'.

It is here that a second kind of rhetorical redescription can be discerned. Efforts were made not just to redescribe aviation as 'sustainable aviation', but to redefine the very terms of argumentation themselves. Richard Rorty, for instance, distinguishes between 'interesting philosophy' and philosophy that is simply concerned with examining 'the pros and cons of a thesis'. 'Implicitly or explicitly', the former approach amounts 'to a contest between an entrenched vocabulary which has become a nuisance and a half-formed new vocabulary which vaguely promises great things' (Rorty, 1989: 9). Furthermore, as he goes on to argue, the

> latter method of philosophy is the same as the method of utopian politics or revolutionary science (as opposed to parliamentary politics, or normal science). The method is to redescribe lots and lots of things in new ways, until you have created a pattern of linguistic behaviour which will tempt the rising generation to adopt it, thereby causing them to look for appropriate new forms of non-linguistic behaviour, for example, the adoption of new scientific equipment or new social institutions. (Rorty, 1989: 9)

Endeavouring to redescribe the predicament of the aviation industry in this way, those in the Freedom to Fly coalition attempted to shift the debate away from concerns about the environment, the control of demand and issues about equality and social justice, and more towards questions about our freedom to fly, and about the threat to jobs and economic competitiveness and our opportunities for pleasure, if expansion was blocked or threatened.

In this way, the discourse of Freedom to Fly provided an ideological framing device within which to locate the signifiers of 'sustainable aviation growth', 'sustainable aviation' and 'socially responsible development' more generally. The latter became floating signifiers which were the target of the two hegemonic projects, each intent on dominating the discursive field. Steering a *tertium quid* between leftist demands for state and governmental intervention to lower consumer demand, and demands from the right to leave the aviation industry in the hands of the market, Freedom to Fly sought to undercut both by articulating the notion of sustainability within the framework of a socially responsible corporate capitalism. Such a system would be sensitive to environmental and social concerns, on the one hand, and to the economic development of the UK as a whole, on the other. In short, by chance or design, the government was thus advantaged by the emergence of a powerful and effective organisation – Freedom to Fly – that was determined to provide it with the necessary ideological cover in the critical period surrounding the consultation process.

Conclusion

New Labour had hoped and expected to resolve the mounting crisis in UK aviation in its first two terms of office. Yet the consultation process it initiated in 2000 served mainly to provide the space for the emergence of two large discourse coalitions or hegemonic projects – AiportWatch and Freedom to Fly – pitted against one another. The formal constitution of these coalitions actually took place during the three years of the consultation period, and the struggle for ideological and political hegemony in this sector intensified as the consultation exercise unfolded. There was little or no transformation of the preferences of the major protagonists who were involved, so that rather than moves towards a rational consensus there was a hardening of political frontiers. Seen in this light, the politics of the consultation process backfired on New Labour, as it failed to provide the anticipated foundations for a new settlement in aviation policy. On the contrary, it produced two rival forces which struggled to impose their respective beliefs and values in the policy sub-system by hegemonising the various demands and grievances that were voiced.

In fact, while the government at the outset of consultation announced its desire to broker a new settlement in aviation, both discourse coalitions sought to drag the New Labour government into the fray by seeking its top-down endorsement of their particular sectional demands. AirportWatch, the anti-expansion coalition that called for a policy of demand management, ushered in a new politics of airport protest by forging novel linkages between rival groups and restructuring opposition to expansion by bringing new issue dimensions into the field of argumentation. Freedom to Fly, by contrast, strenuously made the case for more airport capacity by launching a coordinated media campaign and by mobilising its close links with the government. Both campaigns were able to generate considerable media attention and garner public support for their causes as they endeavoured to hook together various identities and constituencies. Yet by 2003, on the eve of the publication of the new white paper, neither force had landed a knock-out blow. Public opinion was divided and the lines of antagonism were as sharp as ever.

Importantly, however, what Freedom to Fly did manage to do was to provide the New Labour government with the requisite ideological cover for its expansion plans. It did so by successfully structuring the terrain of public reasoning and debate, and by temporarily negating or at least containing the emergent opposition to airport expansion. As we have shown, those propagating the Freedom to Fly discourse sought to redescribe the aviation industry not as a threat to the environment, but as a proponent of sustainable aviation and thus committed to sustainable growth. Indeed, while in its rhetoric Freedom to Fly constructed air travel as an economic success story, presenting the failure to expand airport capacity as a threat to employment and investment, as well as the enjoyment and mobility of the British people, it was the elaboration of a public discourse that redescribed the aviation industry as the proponent of sustainable aviation which was pivotal in its strategy to provide ideological cover for the New Labour government to expand the UK's airports.

Freedom to Fly and its allies were thus able to nullify some of the opposition to expansion by seeking to institute a positive-sum game in which growth in aviation and environmental protection were both achievable. Oppositional groups were left facing a tricky strategic dilemma: should they endorse the discourse of sustainable aviation, which would be in keeping with their avowed commitments to environmental protection but would appear to support their opponents' demands, or should they oppose it, and thus risk the opprobrium of the public by appearing to be concerned only with their narrow sectional interests? Would they be able to respond creatively to this novel challenge? We shall address this question when we explore the Labour government's attempts to implement the proposals set out in the 2003 air transport white paper. But first we shall turn to the form and content of the white paper itself.

Notes

1   The Intergovernmental Panel on Climate Change (1999) did draw attention to the potential impacts of air travel on climate change, particularly the uncertainty surrounding emissions at high altitudes.

2   For a review of New Labour's sustainable transport policy over its first ten years in office, see Docherty and Shaw (2008).

3 SSE press release, 22 March 2004, www.stopstanstedexpansion.com/press130.html (accessed 16 September 2009).
4 SSE press release, 12 May 2003, www.stopstanstedexpansion.com/press065.html (accessed 16 September 2009).
5 SSE press release, 25 February 2003, www.stopstanstedexpansion.com/press051.html (accessed 17 September 2009).
6 SSE press release, 16 December 2003, www.stopstanstedexpansion.com/press116.html (accessed 17 September 2009).
7 SSE press release, 25 February 2003, www.stopstanstedexpansion.com/press051.html (accessed 17 September 2009).
8 Norman Mead, notes of speech to public meeting, Stansted Mountfitchet School, 8 January 2004, p. 3 (emphasis in the original), www.stopstanstedexpansion.com/press118.html (accessed 15 October 2009).
9 SSE, press release, 18 November 2003, www.stopstanstedexpansion.com/press110.html (accessed 15 October 2009).
10 SSE press release, 14 September 2004, www.stopstanstedexpansion.com/press147.html (accessed 15 October 2009).
11 SSE press release, 18 January 2005, www.stopstanstedexpansion.com/press163.html (accessed 19 October 2009).
12 Roger Clark, notes of public meeting 'SERAS report on runway capacity in the south east', 1 August 2002, p. 1, www.broxted.org/pages/arpt/NWEEHPA20020801.doc (accessed 10 November 2009).
13 In July 2011, Fight the Flights, which opposed the expansion of London City airport, also merged with HACAN ClearSkies.
14 The Airfields Environment Federation was later to change its name to the Aviation Environment Federation (AEF). Moira Logan was assisted in her work on the RUCATSE working group by Tim Johnson, who was to become director of the AEF (Sewill, 2012: 54).
15 In pursuing what we have termed a transformative strategy, groups and social movements seek to respond to crises and dislocations by regenerating themselves. This involves the development of new tactics, practices and goals and the articulation of new discourses. In fact, in our view, all hegemonic projects have to reinvent themselves in the different contexts in which they operate, thus extending their demands in a metonymical fashion to contiguous domains of society in their efforts to articulate a wider set of political aims (Griggs and Howarth, 2004: 185).
16 SSE press release, 14 September 2002, www.stopstandstedexpansion/press010.html (accessed 15 January 2012).
17 See http://news.bbc.co.uk/1/hi/england/2505469.stm (accessed 5 January 2011); see also SSE press release, 23 November 2002 (accessed 5 January 2011).
18 FoE press release, 26 September 2002, www.foe.co.uk/resource/press_releases/0926airw.html (accessed 26 January 2012).

19 Jeff Gazzard, SSE press release, 30 October 2002, www.stopstansted expansion.com/news_archive01.html (accessed 27 January 2012).

20 The 'headline' of the AirportWatch homepage, www.airportwatch.org.uk (accessed 9 September 2003).

21 GACC was engaged in a relatively low-profile public campaign. It aimed to ward off expansion at Gatwick by convincing the aviation industry of the inefficiencies associated with any development at the airport and by holding government to the local planning agreement which prevented any expansion at Gatwick before 2019 (Sewill, 2012: 77–93).

22 FoE press release, 26 September 2002, www.foe.co.uk/resource/press_releases/0926airw.html (accessed 26 January 2012).

23 SSE press releases, 13 and 20 August 2002, www.stopstanstedexpansion.com (accessed 27 January 2012).

24 Freedom to Fly press release 19 May 2003; see also *Planning*, 30 May 2003, www.planningresource.co.uk/news/413341 (accessed 2 January 2013); BBC News, 19 January 2003, http://news.bbc.co.uk/1/hi/england/3039283.stm (accessed 2 January 2013).

25 The founding members of Greener by Design were the AOA, BATA, the RAeS and the Society of British Aerospace Companies (SBAC). See www.greenerbydesign.org.uk/about/index.php (accessed 15 January 2012).

26 Freedom to Fly conference speech, www.baa.com/assets/B2CPortal/Static%20Files/freedom_to_fly_conference.pdf; RAeS speech, www.baa.com/assets/B2CPortal/Static%20Files/royal_aeronautical_society.pdf (accessed 16 February 2012).

5

The Future of Air Transport: the 2003 white paper

[The 2003 air transport white paper] recognises the importance of air travel to our national and regional economic prosperity, and that not providing additional capacity where it is needed would significantly damage the economy and national prosperity. (DfT, 2003a: 9–10)

We have to recognise that simply building more and more capacity to meet potential demand would have major, and unacceptable, environmental impacts, and would not be a sustainable approach. (DfT, 2003a: 25)

In early 2003, the Blair government published its energy white paper (DTI, 2003), which committed the UK government to a 60 per cent reduction in carbon emissions by 2050. As far as aviation was concerned, the Labour government pledged to reduce emissions from aviation, to secure the long-term sustainable development of the sector and to ensure that the industry met its external costs (DTI, 2003: 72). Yet the government delayed setting out its strategy about how to deliver on these commitments, leaving this task until its forthcoming air transport white paper (ATWP), which appeared only at the end of 2003. It thus temporarily sidestepped the potential contradictions between its commitments both to lower emissions and to expand airport capacity (which at the time was widely expected to be the outcome of the consultations surrounding the ATWP). This strategy of deferment led to a public rebuke from the House of Commons Environmental Audit Committee (EAC). In its response to the energy white paper in July 2003, the Committee identified the future expansion of aviation as one of the major areas where the Labour government had failed to address the wider implications on government policy of the target of a 60 per cent reduction in carbon emissions (EAC, 2003: 8).

The ATWP, entitled *The Future of Air Transport*, was finally published amidst much fanfare in December 2003 (DfT, 2003a). As promised, it set out New Labour's strategic framework for the development of airport capacity for the next thirty years (DfT, 2003a: 17), with the DfT claiming to have finally put in place a 'policy framework against which the relevant public bodies, airport operators and airlines can plan ahead' (DfT, 2003a: 9). Strikingly, despite the emergence of competing discourse coalitions during the consultation process, coupled with the growing set of antagonisms in this policy sub-system and society at large, which we analysed in the last chapter, the new strategic plan for the future direction of air transportation in the UK strongly supported the case for expanding airport capacity to meet projected demand for air travel, with environmental concerns deferred to a relatively subsidiary role. Although plans were rejected for any new airports, extra runways were proposed for Stansted, Edinburgh and Birmingham, with another runway promised at either Heathrow or Gatwick. Expansion plans were also approved for runway extensions at a large number of regional airports as well as new terminals at Manchester, Glasgow and Cardiff (Dudley, 2004). The implications of these expansionist proposals, which we lay out in more detail at the end of the chapter, would dominate aviation policy for the rest of the decade and beyond.

In this chapter, we analyse the discourse and rhetoric of New Labour's proposals in the ATWP. Drawing in part on the tools of critical discourse analysis and rhetorical political analysis, which we articulate into our overall theoretical approach, we first explore the ATWP as a specific genre of political communication by investigating its logics of justification, instruction and consent. We then turn to an examination of the framing of the ATWP and its underlying prob- lematisation, before providing the concrete detail of the government's proposals for a viable policy of sustainable aviation. Here we concen- trate on the way in which the New Labour government envisaged the expansionist character of UK aviation as an 'inevitable' trajectory, though it also recognised the increasing environmental impacts of air travel. The problem of sustainable aviation was conceived to be one of achieving a balanced approach, and the ATWP outlined a series of strategies to realise this goal. We name and characterise these strategies as those of brokerage, deferred responsibility or individualisation, and incentivisation. In conclusion, we analyse how the rhetoric of sustainable aviation and its proposed resolution of competing demands enabled the government to come out in favour of the largest post-war programme of expansion of British airports.

The ATWP: genre and framing

White papers are an established and distinct genre of political communication in the British political system. Genres, in the words of Norman Fairclough, are the 'different more or less stabilised ways of acting and interacting in a semiotic aspect'. For example, editorials or stories in newspapers are a different genre from press releases, lectures or policy reports.[1] White papers are government documents that set out the direction of future policy across a sector. Often the forerunner of government legislation, they are not, however, specific consultative documents like green papers. But they do serve to trigger further responses from stakeholders before the formulation of a government bill.

In terms of its own particular format and structure, the ATWP consisted of a foreword signed by the Secretary of State for Transport, Alistair Darling, followed by an executive summary, twelve chapters and five annexes. The chapters themselves were subdivided into sections, which served to further circumscribe and guide the reader towards the key characteristics of the issues under discussion. After a first chapter on the purpose of the white paper, the second chapter addressed the strategic framework for aviation, while the third examined the environmental impacts of aviation and the fourth the air transport sector. Chapters 5–11 were devoted to the 'region-by-region case-by-case' conclusions drawn by government on the development of airport capacity across the UK. Here, England was divided into four regions (the north, the midlands, the south-west and the south-east) alongside Scotland, Wales and Northern Ireland. Chapter 12 concluded the white paper by setting out the 'next steps', while the five annexes presented UK air travel forecasts and the wider policy background to emissions trading, before setting out a glossary, a bibliography and an integrated policy appraisal.

While the first four chapters served to problematise and contextualise the policy challenges facing government, roughly the next two-thirds of the ATWP laid down the conclusions of the regional studies on the expansion of particular sites. These conclusions were foregrounded in the executive summary, which was just over six pages long. Over three pages were devoted to the case-by-case conclusions, which were presented in a series of bullet points, thus deploying a promotional genre associated with report writing to further frame action and interaction. With this foregrounding of the decisions about the capacity demands of individual airports, entwined as they were with questions of growth forecasting and maps of land to be safeguarded, the ATWP could not escape the 'predict and provide' ghost of previous white papers. This spectre repeatedly reduced airport policy to questions of capacity, demand and decisions over site locations. New Labour thus did not challenge the fundamental practices of what constituted a white paper in aviation. Importantly, its attention to particular sites for expansion arguably reverted to the 'divide and rule' logic of site location that would potentially create conflicts between particular local campaigns at different airports.

Of the regional studies in the full white paper, chapter 11, on the south-east, was by far the longest – approximately three times the length of other studies. Significantly, the south-east was the only region mentioned in the foreword by the Secretary of State. In that foreword, Darling acknowledged the environmental concerns of any expansion of London airports, but was at pains to recognise the 'importance of these [London] airports to the South East and to the UK's prosperity' (DfT, 2003a: 8). The status accorded to the south-east reflected the sedimented understandings of the spatial pressures on airport capacity in the UK: the issue of capacity was once again framed as a problem facing the south-east and particularly London and London Heathrow (see for example the ongoing debates over a third London airport from the 1960s onwards).

As a form of political action, the ATWP was characterised by a bureaucratic and programmatic rhetoric, which sought to justify (*probare*), instruct (*docere*) and persuade (*conciliare*) (Reisigl, 2008: 98). Yet in the repeated definition of the ATWP as a 'strategic framework' or 'policy framework', as opposed to a concrete set of policy proposals, the New Labour government underplayed the rhetoric of political instruction while resorting to appeals and statements that were designed to legitimise decisions and/or build support. In fact, the New Labour government made few directive commands or orders, except, significantly, in its conclusions for the south-east, where it supported the building of two new runways. Instead, the authors of the white paper stressed a number of times that the ATWP 'does not itself authorise or preclude any particular development but sets out a policy framework ... which will guide decisions on future planning applications' (DfT, 2003a: 9). The white paper thus accepted that 'policies may also need to evolve over time to reflect changing market conditions and expectations' (DfT, 2003a: 18). This positioning of the ATWP, which in many ways can be seen as typical of the multiple political aims of all white papers, and the reliance of government on airport owners to take forward developments, cannot, however, be divorced from the political strategies and tactics which strongly marked the ATWP.

Returning to the question of genre, the ATWP, like other white papers, is best conceptualised as a hybrid of multiple genres. On the one hand, it was itself composed of different genres, including the distinct genres of the promotional foreword and executive summary, as well as the promotional framing techniques of illustrative boxes and bullet points, coupled with the visual rhetoric of photographs of airplanes in flight and airport operations. On the other hand, the white paper was part of a chain of genres; its publication was punctuated by an interconnected series of national and regional consultation documents, public exhibitions, seminar briefing papers, press releases and parliamentary speeches. Many of these genres are explicitly reproduced in the ATWP, notably through short-hand references, which are interpolated in specific highlighted boxes. For example, the DfT deployed a promotion box to bring to the attention of the reader the studies, briefings, exhibitions, forums and workshops which were all part of the consultation process. In an attempt to provide political justification for its proposals, this specific box presented the conclusions of the ATWP as the outcome of the largest consultation exercise undertaken in aviation. Numerous appeals were made to the grounding of its analysis in an 'extensive consultation exercise', which 'closely informed our conclusions' (DfT, 2003a: 18–19). In his foreword, the Secretary of State thus sought to legitimise the conclusions of the ATWP by binding them to the 'half a million people [who] gave their views' (DfT, 2003a: 7). Significantly, there is no mention of any opposition to the proposals.

Problematising air transport

In his foreword, Darling declared that the challenge facing government was 'to deal with the pressures caused by the increasing need to travel whilst at the same time meeting our commitment to protect

the environment in which we live' (DfT, 2003a: 7). This problematisation of the policy challenges in the field of aviation replicated the
way in which the New Labour government had sought to frame the
consultation process. Here, we further analyse this particular problematisation, arguing that it rests on three fundamental 'facts', which
were constantly enunciated throughout the white paper. From a rhetorical point of view, it is worth noting that the logic of repetition plays
a significant role in the argumentative structure and performative force
of the ATWP. We first analyse this representation and employment of
'facts': that aviation is an economic success story; that demand for
air travel will continue to grow; and that there are increasing environmental costs associated with air travel. We then go on to explore how
these 'facts' constituted a particular set of policy problems for the
government.

1. Aviation is an economic success story

To begin with, the New Labour government constructed aviation in
the ATWP as one of the UK's economic success stories, which constituted an increasingly important driver of growth in a modern global
economy. The Secretary of State for Transport thus opened the white
paper with the statement that 'air travel is essential to the United
Kingdom's economy and to our continued prosperity' (DfT, 2003a: 7).
This opening assertion was reiterated seven lines into the foreword,
with a declamatory chain of economic 'facts', which stressed the
pivotal role of aviation in the modern British economy:

> Our economy depends on air travel. Many businesses, in both manu-
> facturing and service industries, rely on air travel; and it is particularly
> important for the fastest growing sectors of the economy. Visitors by
> air are crucial to UK tourism. Airfreight has doubled in the last 10
> years; one-third by value of all goods we export go by air. And 200,000
> people are employed in the aviation industry, with three times as many
> jobs supported by it indirectly. (DfT, 2003a: 7)

Aviation was thus directly and positively associated with a series
of modern growth industries. It was accepted by the ATWP that,
in a globalising world, effective air transport routes were 'vital' for
service industries (p. 9), the 'fastest growing sectors of the economy'
(p. 7), 'hi-tech knowledge-based sectors' (p. 9) and 'high-value com-
modities' (p. 52). In addition, UK airports and carriers were portrayed

as 'leaders in their field, whose success brings significant economic benefits to this country' (p. 22). They were frequently associated with a series of positive signifiers, including 'technological advances', 'cost efficiencies', 'strengthened competition', 'increasing affordability' and 'new destinations' (p. 21). Aviation itself was depicted as the 'aviation industry', a connotation which operated at times as a shorthand for the disparate range of stakeholders engaged in the delivery of air services, but which equally grounded air transport in the economic domain of production (p. 5). Claims like these were supported by a battery of statistics and 'independent' studies, which were all presented diagrammatically, and which all served to justify arguments about the positive economic significance of aviation. Such third-party endorsements did not just vindicate the direct economic benefits of aviation, but also its indirect benefits, as a trigger for inward investment and as an economic multiplier in the development of regional and national economies. Airports thus became in the white paper 'a magnet for other forms of development' (p. 22) or a 'focal point for "clusters" of business development' (p. 50). These assertions were not tested against comparative data on the impact of aviation in relation to other industries; aviation's impact remained in this sense decontextualised throughout the pages of the ATWP.

Chains of declamatory statements worked in this vein to establish 'our' wider dependence on aviation. This dependency was made visible by the mobilisation of key 'facts', which captured the importance of the economic contribution of aviation (especially, for example, in terms of jobs). It is noticeable that these 'facts' were often couched in emotional appeals, which were brought home to the reader by the use of signifiers such as 'depends', 'rely' and 'crucial' (and, indeed, 'vital'). Importantly, these economic benefits were regularly portrayed as under threat. UK airports and carriers were thus depicted as operating in 'a tough economic environment' (DfT, 2003a: 22), with the ATWP raising the spectre of the potential 'horrific' economic implications of failure to support the aviation industry. In fact, the failure to increase airport capacity, the DfT declared, would

> become a barrier to future economic growth and competitiveness. Airports would become more congested; air fares would rise as slots became increasingly sought-after; and much of the future growth in air travel – along with the associated economic growth – could in due course migrate elsewhere. In the case of international traffic, this would often mean to other European countries. (DfT, 2003a: 24–5)

Invoking such fears, the Secretary of State thus concluded his fore-word with an urgent appeal for action, declaring that 'it is essential we plan ahead now – our future prosperity depends on it' (DfT, 2003a: 8).

In short, then, the foregrounding of the economic 'success story' of aviation, as well as 'our' collective dependency upon it, brings out the horrific dimension of the fantasy structuring the perceptions of UK aviation by highlighting the threat posed to 'our' economic and social well-being if government failed to address the capacity con-straints facing UK airports. It thus displaced the problem of airport expansion from an issue facing local communities to one confronting the nation as a whole, thereby universalising the set of interests that would be negatively affected by the failure to expand. In typical fashion, Darling resorted more than once to this horrific dimension when pronouncing in the foreword that 'failure to provide some addi-tional capacity could have substantial repercussions in the country as a whole, as well as for us individually' (DfT, 2003a: 8).

In conjuring up threats of this kind, various allusions were made to the discounted future benefits of aviation, the acceptance of which rested itself upon the construction of a highly globalised, competitive and communication-based economy. Within this par-ticular logic of argumentation, the ease of international transport connections become a key driver of future economic success, with frequent assertions to the 'fact' that, 'in an increasingly competitive global marketplace, Britain's continuing success as a place in which to invest and do business depends crucially on the strength of our international transport links' (DfT, 2003a: 22). And, in this context, air transport was said to offer the necessary competitive advantages of 'rapid access', 'essential connections' and 'speed of delivery'. Such arguments typically surfaced in the ATWP's discussion of the future of air freight. Here, the government's support for the expansion of air freight was legitimised through its capacity to meet the demands of 'just-in-time practices' and 'world-wide rapid delivery and logistics requirements of modern businesses', which in the ATWP became 'an important factor in assuring the future competitiveness of both the UK and regional economies' (DfT, 2003a: 51–2).

2. Demand for air travel will continue to grow

A second tranche of facts, often embedded or backgrounded in the white paper, was used to affirm that demand for air travel would continue to grow (DfT, 2003a: 9). A constant refrain in the text was the idea that the demand for air travel would continue to rise; this was not questioned and remained unopposed throughout the ATWP. It was epitomised by the phrase 'all the evidence suggests' (p. 23). Growth was thus portrayed as one of the key constants of aviation policy, an assertion that was legitimised in part by multiple references to the five-fold increase in air travel since the 1970s (pp. 7, 9, 21). In fact, the DfT articulated three scenarios of projected growth – 'high', 'medium' and 'low' – all of which resulted in rising passenger numbers, with even 'low growth' scenarios predicting a doubling of passenger numbers, from approximately 200 million in 2000 to 400 million by 2030 (p. 23). Difficulties of long-term forecasting, the potential knock-on effects on air travel of rising oil prices, and the costs of addressing global climate change were each brought forward, but summarily dismissed, with the DfT asserting that its scenarios remained a 'reasonable indication of the likely scope of underlying future demand'. Indeed, it stressed to the reader that estimates of growth in earlier white papers had proved 'conservative' (p. 24).

In this way, the idea of rising demand formed part of the background of this policy text – it became part of the unsaid, against which other things could be said – as it was assumed to be an inevitable trend projected into the future, which we could not escape, nor should we want to, given its obvious association with economic prosperity and social progress (cf. Fairclough, 2003: 11, 17, 40; Foucault, 1972: 123–4, 135). Rapidly growing demand for air travel was thus understood to be outside the direct control of government, and divorced (at least for the most part) from the expansionary dynamics of previous government policies of liberalisation and privatisation. On the one hand, it made the provision of additional airport capacity itself a foregone conclusion. On the other hand, it constructed additional capacity at airports as a response to a policy problem – inevitable rising demand – rather than as a cause or driver of that very policy problem. Indeed, the DfT (2003a) set out a number of arguments explicitly designed to counter any alternative conclusion to airport expansion. These included 'the continued need to travel' (p. 7), the limited scope of rail as an alternative (p. 59) and the inexorable demand for air travel. In practice, this meant that 'the provision of some additional airport capacity will therefore be essential if we are to accommodate, even in part, the potential growth in demand' (p. 24). Put differently, the DfT accepted only one limit on the rise of passenger numbers, and that was limited airport capacity.

While the inevitability of rising demand in the arguments of the ATWP left government little choice but to mediate or balance rising demand against other policy drivers, the DfT, in an effort to distance its proposals from previous 'predict and provide' policies, brought into being the category of 'unconstrained demand'; in referring to this notion, the DfT implicitly valued its 'constrained' proposals as a form of demand management. What is more, the DfT repeatedly drew attention to the toughness or stringency of its proposed management of demand for air travel, playing out scenarios of 'what might happen' in the advent of unconstrained demand. Implicitly endorsing its claims to manage demand, it argued, for example, that by 2030 passenger numbers would, 'if sufficient capacity were provided … be between two and three times what it is today' (p. 19). Yet, at the same time, repeating arguments made Freedom to Fly, the DfT construed this expansion to be little more than 'an average of two return trips a year for each UK resident by 2030, compared to an average of just under one return trip each today' (p. 23). While it neatly sidestepped questions about the social inequalities which partly determine who is able to fly, this translation of rising demand into individual journeys reframed projected expansion by recalculating its impact on individuals, thus making increases appear less dramatic and raising the horrific threats to individual travel should airport expansion not continue.

This narrative of rising demand was further embedded by the DfT within a particular developmental logic of economic growth. Here, the argument employed by the DfT was that growing economic prosperity and wealth (rising in part due to the economic contribution of aviation) brings increased demand for travel, as 'wealthier' individuals 'can afford to travel further and more often' and 'afford to pay for goods and services from abroad' (p. 21). In the field of aviation, this developmental logic, the DfT suggested, had been 'amplified by technological advances, cost efficiencies and strengthened competition within the industry, which have brought air travel within the reach of many more people' (p. 21). Rising demand for air travel was thus transformed into an indicator of economic success, and a healthy industry. In this narrative, it was not a 'problem' to be solved, but a benefit that accompanies economic prosperity and social progress – a sign of the 'success' of British carriers and airports. In short, then, for the Secretary of State, working within the context of the economic and social pressures of globalisation, air travel became an unavoidable 'increasing need' (p. 7).

Statements and assertions like this were closely allied to the beatific dimension of the aviation fantasy, which associated air travel with holidays, foreign travel and an increasing opportunity for all. Airports and air travel were constructed as community 'goods', while the entry into the market of 'no frills' carriers was characterised as the popularisation and mass consumerisation of air travel, which was once within the economic capability only of the 'jet-set'. Thus, the ATWP often referred to the way in which air travel has come within 'the reach of many more people' (p. 54), to foreign travel being a 'common experience', to how 'increasing affordability has opened up the possibilities of foreign travel for many people' (p. 21), not to mention its use of categories like 'leisure flights', 'leisure travellers' (p. 112) and 'new destinations', which have 'expanded people's horizons, opportunities and expectations' (p. 21). In this way, the 'fact' of rising demand was progressively redefined not as an environmental challenge but as an important contribution to social progress. Aviation, and indeed its growth, thus came to represent in the ATWP a key tool for a Labour government aiming to reduce inequality and to increase opportunity for the many and not the few.

3. There are increasing environmental impacts from air travel

A third group of facts noted and acknowledged in the ATWP pertained to the negative environmental impacts of air travel on those communities living close to airports, as well as the contribution of air travel to global warming through its emissions of greenhouse gases. Local communities surrounding airports, the government accepted, have to 'live with the immediate effects of aircraft noise, air quality problems and increased congestion on local roads' (DfT, 2003a: 29). Again, in his foreword to the white paper, Darling was at pains to assert New Labour's 'commitment to protect the environment in which we live', thus legitimising demands for environmental regulation by accepting that 'environmental problems cause genuine concern for their impact on people near airports as well as for the global environment' (p. 7). Environmental impacts were classified as noise pollution, lower air quality and increased road traffic congestion for those living near airports, as well as the 'significant and growing' contribution of air travel to climate change (p. 29). Chapter 3 of the ATWP specifically discussed environmental impacts, while other sections of the document were peppered with references to sustainable approaches and the principles of sustainability, as well as repeated

---

Box 5.1 The air transport white paper and its appeals to
sustainability (DfT, 2003a: 10, 19)

'Airport growth needs to reflect the Government's wider objectives for sustainable communities.'

'... difficult decisions, but ones which should provide a sound
and sustainable basis on which to plan the future of aviation in
this country.'

---

commitments to sustainable development (p. 26; see box 5.1). But,
having established the economic and social benefits of aviation, the
white paper made no reference to the environmental costs of air
travel. Such costs were represented as 'environmental impacts' or
'environmental consequences' or 'environmental problems'. In the
whole of the white paper there was only *one* endeavour to quantify
the monetary costs of the environmental impacts of aviation, and
this was in the context of economic instruments, such as emissions
trading. Economic and social benefits were thus juxtaposed with
environmental impacts, rather than costs. As we demonstrate below,
this designation of 'impacts' rather than 'costs' cannot be dissociated
from the strategy of mitigation which New Labour put forward as its
policy response to noise and air quality controls at airports and the
contribution of aviation to climate change.

Against this background, the DfT clearly distinguished two
broad categories of environmental 'impacts', one which it associated
primarily with airports and the other with air travel. In the first
instance, the DfT delineated a broad category of localised environmental impacts, typically noise and air pollution, which hamper the
quality of life of communities leaving near airports. The DfT constructed such impacts as problems of collective action and fairness,
whereby 'the benefits [of aviation] are spread across society as a
whole, [but] many of the adverse impacts are distributed unevenly'
(p. 29). Those living near airports were thus constituted as 'injured
parties', for it was 'local communities' and not the general population
who 'had to live with the immediate effects' of airports (p. 29). Here,
the DfT recognised in part the demands of local residents for further
controls on the regulation of airport operations. Local concerns were

thus consistently reframed as environmental impacts, which could and should be addressed by national and local institutions, and the DfT pledged to support the elaboration of a series of principles, objectives and local controls designed to tackle negative environmental impacts (pp. 30–1).

In addition, turning its focus to air travel and, in particular, international aviation, the DfT identified as a distinct category of environmental 'impacts' the contribution of aviation to climate change and growing carbon emissions. It forecast that by 2030 carbon emissions from aviation 'could amount to about a quarter of the UK's total contribution to global warming' (p. 39). Two information boxes were used to summarise and explain aviation's impact on climate change (pp. 39–40). These boxes acknowledged that the release of CO_2 at high altitude amplifies the detrimental climate impacts of aviation, while recognising the absence in the short term of a viable alternative to kerosene as an aviation fuel (p. 40). At the same time, discussion of such challenges was framed within the wider commitments of the New Labour government to reduce carbon emissions by 60 per cent from current levels in 2050 and the policy framework put in place by the energy white paper in early 2003. Nonetheless, in contrast to the broad category of problems associated with airports, the DfT firmly situated any resolution of the impact of carbon emissions from air travel within the domain of international action, arguing that aviation's contribution to climate change could 'only be tackled effectively on an international basis' (p. 25). Climate change was thus backgrounded and rendered less visible, while airports – where aircraft take off and land – were sidelined in the policy debate surrounding climate change. Significantly, against the backdrop of the government's 2050 commitment to reduce carbon emissions, the DfT vividly presented in a coloured graph carbon emissions from aviation actually declining from the mid-2030s (although they remained at three times the level of the 1980s); no explanation for this decline was offered in the surrounding notes (p. 25).

The problem: 'a balanced strategy'
The collection of 'facts' informing New Labour's analysis of air transport constituted – and were in turn constituted by – a particular problematisation of aviation policy. Yet herein resides the nub of the conundrum confronting the New Labour government. Government was charged with the responsibility of 'balancing' the economic and

---

Box 5.2 The air transport white paper and the fantasy of
reconciling competing demands (DfT, 2003a: 9–10)

'Instead, a balanced approach is required which:

- recognises the importance of air travel to our national and regional economic prosperity, and that not providing additional capacity where it is needed would significantly damage the economy and national prosperity;
- reflects people's desire to travel further and more often by air, and to take advantage of the affordability of air travel and the opportunities this brings;
- seeks to reduce and minimise the impacts of airports on those who live nearby, and on the natural environment;
- ensures that, over time, aviation pays the external costs its activities impose on society at large – in other words, that the price of air travel reflects its environmental and social impacts;
- minimises the need for airport development in new locations by making best use of existing capacity where possible;
- respects the rights and interests of those affected by airport development;
- provides greater certainty for all concerned in the planning of future airport capacity, but at the same time is sufficiently flexible to recognise and adapt to the uncertainties inherent in long-term planning.'

---

social benefits of aviation, and the insatiable demand for flying, with its negative environmental impacts. Throughout the ATWP, the DfT thus constructed the role of government to be a mediator of competing demands (box 5.2) which should strive for a 'balanced' and 'measured' strategy (DfT, 2003a: 9–10). The ATWP, it argued, endorsed

> a strategic and sustainable approach to *balancing* the economic benefits of airport development, the social benefits of easier and more affordable air travel, and the environmental impacts that air travel generates. (DfT, 2003a: 17–18; our emphasis)

This 'balanced strategy' was depicted by the DfT as one which was to navigate between the unacceptable 'extremes [of] failing to provide additional capacity, or encouraging growth without regard for aviation's wider impacts' (p. 6). So the New Labour government claimed throughout the ATWP to address demands for a 'clear policy framework', thus responding to grievances about 'over-lengthy planning inquiries and unnecessary delay', as well as 'unnecessary blight, uncertainty and distress for many people' and the 'piecemeal and uncoordinated fashion' of past policy.

In its efforts to legitimise its claims, the DfT repeatedly sought to distance the white paper from the regime of 'predict and provide', not least through its unspoken contrast with its 'measured and balanced approach', as enunciated in the ATWP itself (p. 7). As we have demonstrated, the white paper constructed and employed the category of 'unconstrained demand', thus contrasting its 'balanced approach' with the unfettered expansionism associated with 'predict and provide'. The ATWP, though, made no direct reference to the 'predict and provide' policy frame, although it often attempted to register its opposition to such policies. For example, the Secretary of State for Transport reiterated how New Labour wanted to 'make best use of existing airport capacity'. He drew attention to the 'considered' proposals of the government, which rejected options for expansion, arguing that

> we have concluded against proposals to build new airports at a number of locations. In every case we considered the consequences would be severe and better options are available. (DfT, 2003a: 7)

The executive summary made claims that the white paper had proposed policies that would address an array of competing demands. It included measures that would

> support economic prosperity throughout the United Kingdom, will enable ordinary people to make flights at reasonable costs, and will manage and mitigate the environmental impacts of aviation, in particular noise, air quality and the contribution to climate change. (DfT, 2003a: 10)

Aspirations to 'balance' competing goals and beliefs rested on the credibility of the argument developed in the ATWP that competing demands in aviation were in some way commensurate. In other words, it was based on the view that it was possible to mediate or balance demands for growth against demands for environmental protection. This primary assumption provided one of the argumentative foundations of the discourse of sustainable aviation. In making such claims, the DfT sought to depoliticise demands in the field of aviation, thus transforming oppositional demands into managerialist challenges to be incorporated into the policy process through technocratic policy instruments, effective planning and the rationality of cost–benefit analysis. Bullish statements were made about the capacity of planning practices to resolve the political conflicts surrounding aviation. For example, Alistair Darling argued that

> we need to plan ahead so we can continue to benefit from the economic and social advantages of air travel, but also to deal with the impacts of increasing air transport for the environment. (DfT, 2003a: 7)

In short, then, the white paper constituted a 'strategic framework', which functioned via the construction of various fantasmatic appeals to the role of planning and strategy as a privileged site for the representation and mediation of demands, though it is worth noting that a key DfT strategy was to have already represented these demands as capable of mitigation. But in establishing this particular problematisation of the policy difficulties facing the New Labour government, the DfT again offered no alternative to the expansion of airport capacity. Noticeable by their absence are attempts to elaborate and consider potentially horrific narratives foretelling environmental degradation brought about by our increasing demand for air travel.

The political strategies of the air transport white paper

How did the New Labour government seek to navigate these complexities? What political and ideological strategies and tactics did it endeavour to articulate in order to deliver its 'balanced and measured approach'? Answers to these questions emerged in the ATWP, which adumbrated a complex of practices with which to resolve the problem. In this section, we name and delineate three potentially competing political strategies in the ATWP, which we name the strategies of brokerage, deferred responsibility or individualisation and incentivisation. We consider each in turn.

1. Strategies of brokerage
What we name the strategy of brokerage captures the way in which the Labour government sought to place itself above the conflict of interests within aviation, thus positioning itself as an 'honest broker', which could accommodate and balance the various interests and

demands in the field, so as to produce a partial and acceptable equilibrium. This strategy, which is well conceptualised as a particular logic of difference, claimed explicitly to reject the 'predict and provide' policy frame, which had previously grappled with the difficulties of forecasting and meeting increasing demand for air transport. Rather, in keeping with the primacy of airport expansion as a 'problem' of 'balance', the government came down in favour of a comprehensive strategy, in which it eschewed the course of 'simply building more and more capacity to meet demand [as it] is not a sustainable way forward' (DfT, 2003a: 9). Most importantly, this strategy of brokerage was predicated upon the fantasmatic appeal that competing demands are in some way reconcilable. In other words, it affirmed the possibility of reaching a policy consensus which would satisfactorily address the demands of rival stakeholders, who were in their own way striving to combat climate change, to protect local environments and to deliver further capacity for air travel.

The fantasmatic belief that government had the capacity to 'balance' competing demands was not founded on the elimination of the negative impacts of air transport, but on a process of mitigation, whereby, for example, in the domain of noise and air pollution, 'action can be taken to mitigate these adverse effects, but it is seldom possible to eliminate them altogether' (p. 29). In the ATWP, therefore, 'balance' increasingly stood in for 'mitigation', which in turn communicated the prospect of a positive and active role for government in addressing competing demands, while distancing Labour's new proposals from existing and somewhat discredited local mitigation schemes. At the same time, in making these appeals, the DfT drew upon a particular definition of sustainable development which privileged the compatibility of competing demands and offered, without apparent contradictions:

> social progress which recognises the needs of everyone; effective protection of the environment; prudent use of natural resources; maintenance of high and stable levels of economic growth and employment. (DfT, 2003a: 26)

Finally, in pursuing this strategy of brokerage, the ATWP presented government as a reflexive and unified actor, which was evident in its use of reflexive verbs, such as 'concluded' and 'considered'. It informed its decisions by a 'series of key principles' (p. 21), which were listed in bullet point form in chapter 2 of the text, in keeping with a promotional genre (p. 26). In the ATWP, government thus becomes the ultimate arbiter of the public interest and the defender of the common good. It was attributed the role of 'enabler and regulator' (p. 17) and thereby given responsibility for taking a 'strategic view' (p. 17). Typically, therefore, in its discussion of the proposals for runway expansion in the south-east of England, the DfT appealed to the reasoned and principled calculations underpinning its conclusions, arguing that 'taking all these factors into account, including the longer-term uncertainties, we propose to take a balanced and measured approach, based on the principles set out in Chapter 2 and Chapter 3' (p. 110). Yet it is important to stress that these strategies of brokerage operated in conjunction with the strategies of deferred responsibility or individualisation, to which we now turn.

2. Strategies of deferred responsibility or individualisation
The strategy of deferred responsibility or individualisation captures the way the New Labour government endeavoured to incorporate multiple stakeholders into the shared ownership or management of a desired policy outcome. In other words, New Labour privileged the mutual dependencies that hold government and stakeholders together, while at the same time shifting responsibility for outcomes away from the sole ownership of the Labour government and onto the aviation industry and citizens. For example, the DfT regularly claimed that it was not for government to take many of its proposals or policy instruments forward, making reference, for example, to having 'set stringent environmental conditions which developers will need to meet to take proposals forward' (p. 8). The setting of 'conditions' in this way enabled New Labour to appear authoritative in the domain of aviation, while keeping a regulatory distance from the political conflicts surrounding airport expansion by displacing responsibility onto the industry to deliver change and manage local policy development.

This strategy extended to the aviation industry, with the Labour government making claims to work with industry to encourage changing environmental practices. In the ATWP, it called for the better management of existing airport capacity through improvement and modernisation, new decision processes based on emissions cost assessments, investment in new technology to offset the noise and pollution of jet aircraft, and the funding of research into aviation and the environment (see, for example, the commitment of £5 million to the new knowledge transfer network called OMEGA, or Opportunities for Meeting the Environmental Challenge of Growth in Aviation). In proposing this strategy, New Labour invested in the promise of 'technological fixes' in aviation, in which it posited that future scientific and engineering advances would minimise the environmental impact of air travel and thereby enable further expansion and environmental protection. These plans were crucial to its particular development of the policies and practices of sustainable aviation. For example, the DfT claimed in the ATWP that fuel reduction technology would result in 50 per cent reductions in CO_2 emissions from planes by 2050, and it cited 'research targets' endorsed by the Advisory Council for Aeronautical Research in Europe to legitimise its claims (p. 40). Such beliefs about the capacity of the industry to offer policy-makers a suitable 'technological fix' to cope with rising emissions go hand in hand with the strategy of displacing or deferring responsibility onto other actors.

The ATWP also invited thirty airports (where major development was planned or the airport was expected to deal with 20,000 flights or more by 2030) to prepare or revise master plans to inform the planning process and blight schemes and to provide a mechanism for local community engagement. Master plans, which called upon airport operators to set out proposals to mitigate noise and local air pollution, constitute further evidence of the strategy of deferred responsibility (pp. 7, 35). Government was thereby distanced from the process of airport development, with the DfT declaring that it was 'for airport owners and operators to bring forward such proposals' (p. 17). This was because the government was 'not the primary provider of civil airport capacity' and because airports were operated by private sector companies and local authorities (p. 17). Master plans, however, were to be taken into account by regional spatial strategies and local development, a move which offered a further means for government to locate expansion plans within local and regional planning strategies (Mander and Randles, 2009: 278; FoE, 2004).

In a similar vein, the white paper shifted responsibility for addressing climate change onto the aviation industry, calling for voluntary action by the industry to meet its external costs. The DfT asserted that 'we expect' the industry and international bodies 'to address the "polluter pays" problem seriously' (DfT, 2003a: 31). The ATWP also declared that 'the aviation sector needs to take its share of responsibility for tackling this problem [that is, its contribution to global warming]' (p. 39). The use of signifiers such as 'expect' and 'needs' demonstrated the symbolic commitment of the government to environmental protection, while shifting responsibility onto airlines and airport operators to deliver such policy outcomes. They also offered a veiled threat to potentially recalcitrant stakeholders.

Importantly, the Labour government extended the chain of responsibility up to various actors in the international arena, as it blamed international regulators of aviation and other nation states for many of the difficulties it faced in tackling climate change (in keeping with its categorisation of environmental problems). To highlight the difficulties of addressing carbon emissions at the national or local level, promotional boxes were deployed in the white paper to 'educate' the uninitiated in the complexity of regulations produced by the International Civil Aviation Organisation (ICAO) and European Union (EU). The UK government positioned itself as one responsible actor among many, constrained in its capacity to undertake unilateral action. So that while it committed itself to undertake 'a major role in seeking to develop new solutions and stronger actions by the appropriate international bodies' (p. 29), the international regulation of aviation was put forward as a constraint on any unilateral actions that might hamper the competitiveness of the UK aviation industry. The ATWP thus summarily dismissed any unilateral imposition of fuel tax on aviation to manage demand, given the limits on government action posed by 'international legal constraints' (p. 40). In contrast, it affirmed the commitment of New Labour to strategies of incentivisation, which constitutes the third element of its solution to the problem.

3. Strategies of incentivisation

What we term 'strategies of incentivisation' in the ATWP indicate the way in which the government promoted a hands-off approach to the environmental regulation of the air transport industry, notably through its support for the development of an emissions trading scheme. Fearful not to jeopardise the economic competitiveness of the UK aviation industry, the 2003 white paper claimed that

> as a matter of principle, any additional action to tackle the environmental impacts of aviation will take full account of the effects on the competitiveness of UK aviation and the impact on consumers. (DfT, 2003a: 41)

With this principle in place, air passenger duty was, much like fuel tax, quickly dismissed, in this case as 'too blunt an instrument'

(p. 41). The government sought to take its 'distance' from the market in aviation, choosing instead to work through steering mechanisms, which favour or incentivise particular policy outcomes, and that thus operate as 'carrots', rather than the top-down 'sticks', which were alleged to constrain the effective working of market mechanisms.

Assertions like these brought to the fore emissions trading as the principal instrument through which New Labour envisaged tackling the contribution of air transport to climate change. The white paper extolled emissions trading as an 'economic instrument', which 'use[s] price signals to drive improvements', and it devoted yet another educational and promotional box to 'developing economic instruments', as well as an appendix to emissions trading. In fact, within the 2003 white paper, emissions trading operated as a justificatory argument, in which aviation expansion could continue unabated without compromising demands for sustainability and climate change. Underpinning these claims was the acceptance that aviation could expand and trade emissions with other industrial sectors, where 'reductions … can be produced more cheaply' (p. 40). Arguments of this type embedded the principle of air travel as a 'special case', whose rising emissions *should* be countered by reductions in other industries. For example, the ATWP declared that government must 'ensure that growing industries [such as aviation] are catered for within a reducing total' (p. 40). In this way, emissions trading effectively relieved the aviation industry of any control over or responsibility for its own emissions, thus offering the conditions for aviation expansion *and* sustainable growth. Indeed, it is in its role as a key policy instrument in the ATWP, marrying economic competitiveness, the regulation of demand and environmental protection, that emissions trading became pivotal to the maintenance of the fantasmatic discourse of sustainable aviation.

The fantasy of sustainable aviation

Taken together, the political strategies and tactics sketched out in the ATWP reproduced and fleshed out the dominant fantasmatic discourse on aviation in the post-war period, in which competing demands for growth and environmental protection were in some way reconcilable. By articulating and propagating a discourse of sustainable aviation it would be possible to reach a policy solution which simultaneously and satisfactorily addressed the demands of those stakeholders who sought to combat climate change and protect local environments, on the one hand, while delivering further capacity for air travel, on the other. Strategies of incentivisation thus operated in tandem with those of displacing responsibility onto other national and international actors.

New Labour was thus keen to establish the limits of any unilateral action. As the ATWP put it, the policy instrument of emissions trading was not within the 'gift' of any national government. It rested upon an international response, leaving the white paper to commit government to lobby for the inclusion of aviation in the EU emissions trading scheme from 2008, which was described as a priority for the UK's 2005 presidency of the EU (p. 146). Again, New Labour sought to demonstrate its commitment to addressing such impacts by asserting its determination to act and by concocting a sense of urgency, stating that 'we reserve the right to act alone or bilaterally with like-minded partners if progress towards agreements at an international level proves too slow' (p. 41).

But its political strategies and rhetorical manoeuvres were not without contradiction, and they were exposed by Labour's appeals to the strategy of brokerage. As against the strategies of deferred responsibility or individualisation and incentivisation, which distanced the government from the delivery of outcomes, the logic of brokerage presented government as the ultimate arbiter of the public interest and the defender of the common good. In addition, the privileging of brokerage as a means of finding a 'balance' between competing demands framed the work of government in terms of mitigation – not elimination – of the negative impacts of air transport, thus raising particular challenges about how government would effectively address the demands of the antagonistic coalitions inhabiting the consultation process.

The proposals within the white paper

Each of the individual studies of airport capacity in the white paper offered the reader summaries of key issues, conclusions on future capacity, as well as land safeguarding maps, forecasts of demand growth and discussions of existing and future noise contours and local air quality issues. As we have argued, much of the policy legitimacy of the ATWP rested on the legitimacy of New Labour's claims to offer the oft-repeated 'balanced and measured' strategy. But closer examination of the proposals contained within the ATWP shows that the government came down firmly on the side of expansion,

Box 5.3 The air transport white paper and its support for expansion (DfT, 2003a: 13–15)

- New runway at Stansted for 2011–12
- New runway and additional terminal capacity at Heathrow for 2015–20
- Safeguarding of land for a new runway at Gatwick after 2019 (in the event that environmental conditions at Heathrow are not met)
- New runway at Birmingham
- Additional terminal capacity at Manchester
- Land safeguarded for terminal development and an additional runway at Edinburgh
- Increased terminal capacity and potential runway extension at Liverpool John Lennon airport
- Substantial terminal development at Glasgow
- Safeguarding of option to provide an additional runway at Glasgow until 2030
- Development of terminal and other facilities at Prestwick, Aberdeen and Dundee
- Recognition of potential need for runway extensions at Aberdeen and Inverness, as well as improvements at smaller airports in the Highlands and Islands
- Terminal development at Cardiff
- Support for increased capacity at Belfast International
- Consideration of proposals for the development of City of Derry airport
- Support for expansion of terminal facilities and runway extension at Newcastle
- Scope to expand terminal facilities and runway at Teesside
- Additional terminal capacity and extended runway at Leeds Bradford
- Expansion of passenger and freight operations at East Midlands
- Runway extension and new terminal at Bristol
- Additional terminal capacity at Bournemouth
- Support in principle for development of existing south-east airports, including London City, Norwich and Southampton

thus relegating environmental principles and concerns to a secondary position (see box 5.3).

In the traditionally privileged space of the south-east, the DfT (2003a: 13) declared that 'there is an urgent need for additional runway capacity'. It supported the construction of two new runways by 2030, concluding that there should be a new runway at Stansted by 2011 or 2012, as well a further runway and additional terminal capacity at Heathrow between 2015 and 2020, after the completion of the new runway at Stansted. In the event of Heathrow expansion not going ahead, land was also to be safeguarded for the possibility of an additional runway at Gatwick after 2019. The latter was a possibility because expansion at Heathrow was contingent upon the meeting of environmental conditions relating to air and noise quality.

However, New Labour sought persistently to counterbalance the expansionary logic of the white paper. On the one hand, repeated commitments were made to use existing airport capacity in a better and more efficient way, notably at Luton and Stansted. Better use of existing capacity was also preferred over expansion, where the latter was narrowly defined in terms of the construction of new infrastructure rather than increases to capacity. On the other hand, it sought persistently to foreground the demands for development that it had considered but ultimately rejected in its decision-making. This foregrounding of rejected proposals bolstered arguments that the white paper was a 'balanced approach' to airport expansion. Indeed, the public airing of the expansionary demands that it might have endorsed served to reposition government once again as the guardian of the public interest, which had implicitly warded off demands from the industry to expand. The DfT was thus keen to point out that a whole series of options were considered and then rejected, including new airports in central Scotland, south-east Wales, in the midlands between Coventry and Rugby, to the north of Bristol, not to mention the construction of a new runway at East Midlands airport. In the case of the south-east, the DfT also emphasised its rejection of a new airport at Cliffe and the development of Alconbury for passenger or freight services, as well as its refusal of two or three additional runways at Stansted, two new runways at Gatwick, a second runway at Luton and 'other proposals put forward during the consultation for new airports at alternative locations' (DfT, 2003a: 14). Noticeably, these rejections were strategically inserted within the summary conclusions of the ATWP, alongside the decisions of the government to expand capacity at particular airports. Thus, in the list of summary conclusions for the south-east, composed of fifteen bullet points, eight decisions against expansion were made visible, including the decision not to overturn the 1979 local planning agreement, which prevented the construction of a second runway at Gatwick before 2019 (DfT, 2003a: 13–14). Many of these rejected options, however, had in fact never been considered as viable alternatives on the policy agenda of the DfT. Nonetheless, their inclusion served to generate scenarios of 'what might have happened' under governments which did not endorse New Labour's 'balanced' approach to airport expansion.

Finally, in its particular forms of argumentation, the ATWP emphasised the environmental conditions attached to many of these developments, which were deployed to bear witness once again to the legitimate balance of its decisions. Environmental conditions were attached to a number of proposals for airport expansion, more specifically on noise levels at Leeds, Bradford, Bournemouth, Birmingham and Manchester (as well as air quality standards, notably NO_2 in the last case). Further, the runway extension at Liverpool John Lennon airport was approved on condition that it did not encroach on environmentally sensitive areas surrounding the airport. Most importantly, for the legitimacy of the white paper, 'stringent environmental limits' were attached to the third runway at Heathrow, notably on noise levels (no net increase in the total area of the 57 dBA noise contour compared with summer 2002) and air quality (compliance with the EU mandatory air quality limit values for NO_2 to apply from 2010). In his foreword to the white paper, Alistair Darling attempted to soften the decision to support the construction of a third runway at Heathrow by emphasising the stringent environmental controls on its development. Despite past public inquiries and rulings against further runways by inspectors at the international hub, expansion at Heathrow was thus made possible by attaching conditions to mitigate its environmental impacts.

Conclusion

The ATWP came down firmly in favour of expanding capacity at British airports, while making claims to have delivered a 'balanced approach' that took into account the demands for environmental protection and demand management within aviation. It rearticulated many of the rhetorical appeals and tropes used by the Freedom to Fly coalition, thus exploiting the ideological cover provided by the latter. This cover comprised frequent references to the economic contribution of aviation, the inevitability of rising demand for air travel and the popularity and positive social impact of air travel. Environmental demands were accommodated as part of a 'balance' between growth and sustainability in a strategy of mitigation. This was made possible by the fact that the authors of the white paper borrowed from the discourses of 'ecological modernisation' and 'high modernism' (Scott, 1998: 4; World Commission on Environment and Development, 1987). In these discourses, promises of green technology, market innovation and science could ensure a positive-sum game in which growth and environmental protection were both possible.[2] The DfT thus sought to reframe the impact of aviation on the environment, so that it could be seen as a manageable set of risks. Given the right economic incentives, these risks could be mitigated through technical innovation and human ingenuity. Here, the government's commitment to emissions trading schemes, as well as technological developments or technical 'fixes' within the aviation industry, took on a particular strategic importance for New Labour's discourse of sustainable aviation.

But, following the publication of the ATWP in December 2003, it remained to be seen whether the government's articulation of a discourse of sustainable aviation, as well as its proposed resolution of the competing demands for expansion and demand management, would garner sufficient support from the competing coalitions that had emerged during the consultation process. Senior New Labour politicians believed that they had responded to demands from both coalitions, claiming, for example, that they had resisted expansionist proposals from trade union leaders who were intent on maximising economic growth.[3] Yet, there were still doubts about how far the strategies of brokerage, deferred responsibility or individualisation and incentivisation would go in effectively negating or placating the opposition to expansion. In fact, these strategies exposed contradictions in New Labour's rhetoric on aviation, as well as its governance of this growing dilemma. These contradictions were epitomised by its commitment to the logic of brokerage, as against those of deferred responsibility and incentivisation, which positioned the government as the ultimate arbiter of the public interest. It is to such questions and contradictions that we turn in the next chapter.

Notes

1 R. Rogers (2004) 'Interview with Norman Fairclough', on the companion website to R. Rogers (ed.) *An Introduction to Critical Discourse Analysis in Education* (New York: Routledge, 2nd edn), p. 10, http://cw.routledge. com/textbooks/9780415874298/data/Fairclough_Interview.pdf (accessed 20 April 2012); see also Fairclough and Fairclough (2012: 82).

2 See Hajer (1995), Hulme (2009), Mol (2000, 2001), Mol and Sonnenfeld (2000), Mol *et al.* (2009), Weale (1992).

3 Personal communication with senior New Labour politician.

6
Resignifying airports and aviation

Earlier this year the government published an Energy White Paper setting out its strategy for tackling global climate change, and set challenging but necessary targets for greenhouse gas emissions. Today's Aviation White Paper undermines those targets and continues to favour commerce over vital carbon dioxide reduction measures. (Sir Thomas Blundell, chair of Royal Commission on Environment and Pollution, press release, 16 December 2003)

Alistair Darling's decision to massively expand aviation will not only be felt by people living near airports, it will affect people worldwide and impact heavily on generations yet to come. Today's announcement is yet another missed opportunity to put the air industry on a sustainable course. (Tony Juniper, director of Friends of the Earth, press release, 16 December 2003)

This was the Government's big opportunity to dampen down demand for aviation and bring its environmental and social problems under control but it hasn't taken it. By opting for significant growth, the Government has issued a passport to much greater carbon emissions, pollution and noise nuisance in the future. (Stephen Joseph, director of Transport 2000, press release, 16 December 2003)

The publication of the air transport white paper (ATWP) in December 2003 was greeted with an expected flurry of press releases and public debate, as the competing discourse coalitions stepped up to condemn or praise the Labour government and in particular Alistair Darling, the Secretary of State for Transport. Rod Eddington, chief executive of British Airways (BA), applauded the government's support for the third runway at Heathrow, while claiming that 'for the first time we have an effective forward-looking aviation policy'. He was joined by Richard Branson, owner of Virgin Atlantic, who praised Darling for having 'shown real courage'. Nonetheless, there were isolated pockets of criticism across the industry about the government's promotion of Stansted expansion over that of Heathrow, notably from Sir Michael Bishop, chair of the low-cost carrier British Midland International (BMI). Yet measured criticism like this was in marked contrast to the attacks on the ATWP from environmental campaigners and anti-airport expansion groups. The Campaign to Protect Rural England (CPRE) bemoaned the government's failure to 'grasp the nettle of environmental sustainability for air transport', while the National Trust condemned the ATWP as an 'inadequate, short-sighted and unsustainable policy response to the rising demand for air travel'.[1] Warning of future protests against expansion, John Stewart, chair of HACAN ClearSkies, announced that campaigners at Heathrow would 'continue to stand shoulder to shoulder, with our fellow campaigners at the other airports', claiming that although the ATWP had 'left Heathrow up in the air', local residents had 'won' the first stage of their battle against the third runway.[2]

Far from resolving the grievances facing the Department for Transport (DfT) and the Blair government, the publication of the ATWP thus engendered new political conditions and contingencies that were to lead to a reshaping of the post-consultation policy space. These challenges were intimately related to the constitutive function of the ATWP in naming 'aviation policy' (Laclau, 2005: 100). Put differently, the new aviation white paper crystallised New Labour's policy of sustainable aviation, marking the end of the Blair government's strategy of deferment, in which it repeatedly argued that the ATWP would resolve any potential policy contradictions, though ignoring calls to clarify how it would do so. However, with the publication of the ATWP, the government's ability to meet both its expansionary and its environmental objectives was increasingly open to challenge from other actors and forces, which articulated opposed discourses. Thus, while the ATWP made provision for a 'measured and balanced approach', the ideological and political commitments of New Labour were now made more visible and thus more contestable.

Importantly, for our analysis, the plans for airport expansion and commitments to sustainable aviation within the ATWP were soon confronted by a series of methodological, epistemological and substantive challenges, which sought to elaborate alternative understandings of sustainability in the field of aviation policy. This chapter investigates the argumentative strategies and rhetorical mechanisms employed by various expert actors in their efforts to rearticulate the meaning of the signifier 'sustainable aviation' in the wake of the publication of the ATWP. What emerges, we suggest, was a weakening of the fantasmatic narrative of sustainable aviation, as opponents to expansion successfully exposed the tensions and ambiguities in the ATWP, especially when set alongside other government policies and commitments. This process had begun in anticipation of the publication of the ATWP and was evident, for example, in the intervention of the House of Commons Environmental Audit Committee (EAC), when it drew attention in July 2003 to the failure of the 2003 energy white paper to take into account the impact of aviation emissions (EAC, 2003). Opponents of airport expansion thus made sustained efforts to discredit the empirical evidence and scientific analyses of the ATWP, which they portrayed as a further example of 'predict and provide', while connecting aviation to the problem of global warming. In such representations, the growth of aviation and flying was directly related to the problem of climate change and thus rendered complicit with the horrific dimension of the dominant fantasmatic narrative.

Having described and analysed these rhetorical strategies, we then examine how New Labour reacted to such challenges by endeavouring to recycle the tropes, political strategies and tactics embedded within the ATWP. But, we argue, these responses failed to counter the increasingly fragile narrative of sustainable aviation, which began to lose its fantasmatic grip in a changing political context, marked by heightened public concern about climate change and the collapse of the New Labour project. In short, following the publication of the ATWP, we show how aviation began to function as a nodal point that condensed disparate grievances and demands, some distant from aviation policy, and how they were increasingly directed at New Labour's plans for airport expansion (Laclau, 2005: 97).

The evolving context of 'sustainable aviation'

In the consultations and debates leading up to the 2003 white paper, the government and supporters of aviation expansion, notably Freedom to Fly, engaged in practices of rhetorical redescription. Acknowledging the growing importance of environmental concerns in the field of air transport, these actors augmented their previous arguments by using signifiers like 'sustainable' and 'responsible' in order to justify their positions and persuade their critics. The notion of sustainable aviation functioned as a new metaphor which redefined both terms of the expression: aviation expansion must be sustainable and properly regulated, while the values and principles of sustainable development could be made compatible with the overall logic of aviation expansion (Howarth and Griggs, 2006).

The New Labour government would have liked to fix and naturalise the meaning of aviation policy around this signifier, for it would be seen to have responded positively to the various dimensions of the environmental challenge. Ideally, from the government's perspective, 'sustainable aviation' would have started to function as an empty signifier or a generative metaphor which fixed and naturalised the meaning of its policies, while accommodating the contradictory sets of demands that had been knitted together in the conjuncture surrounding the publication of the ATWP. Ecological protesters and local residents would thus have accepted the government's efforts to create a more sustainable environment, while those calling for expansion would acknowledge its efforts to take the lead and promote the UK aviation industry.

But though the creation and acceptance of an empty signifier such as 'sustainable aviation', which was underpinned by a beatific fantasy in which aviation expansion and environmental sustainability could be linked in a harmonious and mutually reinforcing fashion, would have proved an astute strategic manoeuvre to displace environmental concerns and stabilise the meaning of aviation policy, this proved difficult to achieve. In practice, it rendered the government vulnerable to further critique and challenge, especially from those who questioned the scientific evidence and empirical basis upon which New Labour's public policy was meant to have been grounded. In order to account for the growing authority and power of this critique, we need to explore the evolving context of the UK's aviation policy. This changing context marked the emergence of a new terrain of argumentation, which disclosed untenable contradictions in the government's policy discourse.

It is somewhat ironic that at just about the same time as the Secretary of State for Transport, Alistair Darling, sought to justify the decision to give the go-ahead for the expansion of the UK's airport infrastructure by using the rhetoric of sustainable aviation, the issue of climate change began to dominate the political agenda in the UK and many advanced industrial states. Of course, the environment (especially in the field of transport policy) had been an important political issue for some time. However, a peculiar set of events and intellectual interventions in the period following the publication of the ATWP in December 2003 heightened the problem for the government and the public alike. First, there was a publicised set of natural phenomena and events – dramatic temperature rises, extreme events like melting glaciers, droughts and flooding, all of which were symbolised by the highly publicised Hurricane Katrina and the destruction of New Orleans in August 2005 – that began to be taken as evidence of rapid climate change. The understanding that these natural phenomena were closely linked to climate change was bolstered by a growing scientific consensus that the events and phenomena associated with climate change were a human creation. In early January 2004, Sir David King, the UK government's chief scientific adviser, declared that climate change was a far greater threat than international terrorism; in fact, it was declared to be 'the most severe problem we are facing today'.[3]

The sum total of these changes was also reflected in an important shift in public opinion and in the environmental movement. In November 2005, an IPSOS-MORI poll found that 91 per cent of the British public believed that the world's climate was changing (IPSOS-MORI, 2006). Similarly, a Pew Global Attitudes Survey, undertaken between March and May 2006, showed that over 90 per cent of British people considered that climate change was a 'serious problem'. To cap it all, a poll-of-polls study, tracking IPSOS-MORI surveys from May 2005 to May 2007, revealed increasing public recognition of the 'environment/pollution' as a 'main issue facing Britain' (for poll data, see Gill and Humphreys, 2007). At the same time, the issue of climate change was rising up the agenda of national environmental campaign groups, having been initially defined as an international issue. Rising Tide was formed in November 2000 to organise protests at The Hague sixth sessions of the United Nations Framework Convention on Climate Change (UNFCCC), which ultimately broke down because of US demands over carbon sinks and the promotion of nuclear energy (Carpenter, 2001). The Campaign Against Climate Change came into being in 2001, following the US rejection under George Bush of the Kyoto agreement on cutting emissions.[4] Friends of the Earth (FoE) and other environmental groups were also to enter the fray of climate change to lobby against growing support for nuclear power, which was suddenly being touted as the carbon-friendly 'solution' to climate change. In May 2005, FoE launched its 'Big Ask' campaign, which demanded a new climate change law that would commit the government to reducing carbon emissions by 3 per cent year on year,[5] while the Stop Climate Chaos coalition, which brought together Greenpeace, the Royal Society for the Protection of Birds, Oxfam, the World Wide Fund for Nature and FoE organised the Stop Climate Injustice rally at Trafalgar Square in November 2006 (Rootes, 2012).

Concerns about climate change were strengthened in the wider popular imagination by a series of political and cultural interventions. In 2006, the former US Vice-President Al Gore presented the documentary film *An Inconvenient Truth*, which detailed the threat of climate change, and became the fourth-highest-grossing documentary film to date. Closer to home, in September 2004, Tony Blair gave a highly publicised speech on climate change, in which he argued that 'the emission of greenhouse gases, associated with industrialisation and strong economic growth from a world population that has increased sixfold in 200 years' and was 'causing global warming at a rate that began as significant, has become alarming and is simply unsustainable in the long-term' (Blair, 2004). Blair's speech made it clear that the scientific and anecdotal evidence of global warming and climate change was indisputable. He extolled the virtues of the UK's excellence in science, especially in the environmental field, where 'the world-renowned Hadley and Tyndall Centres for climate change research' were singled out for praise. Such claims were soon reiterated in the Stern review, published in October 2006. (As we shall see, it was more than a little perverse that these very scientists and research centres were soon to question important aspects of the Blair government's aviation policy.) But this brings us to the way in which the discourse and policy of sustainable aviation were confronted by a new threat: the concerted critique of those whom the government regarded as scientific experts on climate change.

The rhetoric of scientific expertise: challenging the logic of sustainable aviation

The concerted critique of the ATWP, which began in earnest after its publication in late 2003, was part of a complex political battle in which rival forces sought to define and fix the meaning of sustainability in the aviation field. In this section, we argue that persistent challenges to the ATWP by parliamentary committees, public agencies, academic institutions and think-tanks ultimately rendered the idea of sustainable aviation a floating signifier, thus making possible its hegemonisation and resignification by other forces and coalitions. In advancing this claim, we focus on the rhetoric of the EAC in its reports from 2004 onwards, as well as those of the Sustainable Development Commission (2004), the Tyndall Centre (2005) and the Stern review (2006). Such reports formed part of a much wider corpus of documents and publications which were launched between 2004 and 2006. They reflect, however, a concourse of critical expertise on sustainable aviation, which was generated in the wake of the publication of the ATWP, while offering different genres or chains of genres of political communication.[6] Collectively, they reveal how the construction of a new knowledge base came into being, as successor reports began to reproduce and cite arguments articulated within earlier reports to legitimise their positions.

The Environmental Audit Committee (EAC)

The EAC was established as a Select Committee of the House of Commons in November 1997.[7] Its creation followed New Labour's manifesto commitment to establish a single parliamentary committee that would scrutinise the contribution of all government departments, non-departmental public bodies and broad policy programmes, regarding environmental protection and sustainable development. The Committee has a cross-party membership of MPs, and at the time of the publication of the reports under discussion here, it was chaired by a Conservative politician. From July 2003, the chair was Peter Ainsworth MP, who was previously a shadow Secretary of State for the Environment, Food and Rural Affairs, and from December 2005 it was Tim Yeo MP, who was previously the Minister of State for the Countryside and the Environment in the Major government.

After the publication of the ATWP in 2003, the Committee was quick to condemn New Labour's strategic plan for UK airports as a 'lost opportunity', berating the multiple 'failures' of the New Labour government to

> begin the arduous task of changing hearts and minds ... to utilise available policy instruments to promote sustainable – rather than unsustainable – growth; and ... to learn from our experience in other related areas such as road transport. (EAC, 2004b: 12)

It dismissed the 2003 proposals as little more than another round of 'predict and provide' policy-making in aviation (EAC, 2004a: 7).

Moreover, proposals to expand airport capacity invalidated the legitimacy of any claims of the Labour government to have put in place a policy framework for sustainable aviation. Putting it bluntly, the Committee concluded that 'such a conviction in favour of growth belies claims of a balanced approach' (EAC, 2004a: 14).

In developing this challenge, members of the Committee persistently countered attempts by the New Labour government to equate the expansionist plans of the ATWP with the discourse of sustainability. The ATWP, the EAC argued, lacked an adequate understanding of sustainable aviation, because it was marked by an economic interpretation of sustainability, which 'places insufficient weight on the environmental dimension of sustainable development' (EAC, 2004d: 17). The EAC thus called for a 'formal statement' from the DfT, clarifying how it understood 'sustainable consumption' in air travel (EAC, 2004a: 16). In the words of the Committee:

> Our fundamental concern with the aviation White Paper is that it uses the language of sustainability without demonstrating a deeper understanding of what is really involved. The DfT claims it is not actively supporting growth. We therefore consider that there is an urgent need to promote a wider public debate before specific expansion plans are brought forward; and that it would be appropriate for the DfT to subject its plans for airport expansion to a Strategic Environmental Assessment. (EAC, 2004c: 4)

Importantly, the EAC criticised the break-up in June 2001 of the Department of the Environment, Transport and the Regions (DETR), arguing that its demise and the separation of Transport from the Environment had 'had a negative impact'. This was evident, for example, 'by the failure to incorporate a deeper understanding of sustainable development within the Aviation White Paper' (EAC, 2004d: 34–5).

Against this background, the Committee challenged the DfT's analysis of the evidence informing the ATWP and stressed the inadequacy of some of its judgements and evaluations. For example, members of the EAC declared themselves to be 'astonished' at the lack of research by the DfT into the incorporation of aviation into the European Union emissions trading scheme (EU ETS) (EAC, 2004b: 21). They also criticised the 'particularly weak' integrated policy appraisal undertaken by the DfT (EAC, 2004b: 3), notably the validity of assuming stable oil prices in the future (EAC, 2004b: 8). Equally, the Committee accused the DfT of deliberately attempting 'to massage the aviation percentages downwards by including non-CO_2

greenhouse gas emissions at a fixed level until 2050' (EAC, 2004b: 11). Such allegations carried with them concerns over the limited democratic accountability of the DfT and its capture by aviation interests, which hampered open and informed decision-making. Members of the Committee thus drew attention to the DfT's delayed publication of supporting studies that informed the consultation process, which appeared two months after the ATWP, and they suggested that this delay 'raise[d] questions about the extent to which such analyses were fully available during the autumn at the time when the key decisions contained in the White Paper were being made' (EAC, 2004a: 9, 13).

Yet the primary charges launched at New Labour by the EAC lay in the failure of the ATWP to recognise the overriding and universal imperative of the fight against climate change. Climate change, the EAC argued, necessitated that plans for all airport expansion should be subservient to the wider commitment to a 60 per cent reduction in carbon dioxide emissions by 2050, as set out in the 2003 energy white paper.[8] Its rhetoric delineated explicit connections between climate change and aviation, in which aviation was constructed as a major contributor to climate change. Attributing increasing and human-induced climate change to aviation began to shift the dominant terrain of argumentation surrounding aviation away from questions of capacity and towards its carbon emissions, thereby putting in place the conditions for a new narrative of aviation, in which it was transformed into a growing environmental 'problem' framed by the demands of climate change. The Committee thus confronted New Labour with the rhetoric of aviation as the undeniable and greatest threat to climate change:

> the underlying truth is not in dispute: that the global warming impacts from aviation are forecast to increase *massively* just as we are striving to make huge cuts in emissions from all other sectors of the UK economy. (EAC, 2004b: 11; our emphasis)

The Committee accused the DfT of having 'failed to recognise ... or to accept the disparity between its policy on aviation and the major commitments the Government has given to reduce carbon emissions and develop a sustainable consumption strategy' (EAC, 2004a: 7). Furthermore, it derided the effectiveness of emissions trading as a policy instrument; questioned the capacity of the government to bring about the inclusion of aviation in the EU ETS; and highlighted the government's ultimate reliance on limited technological fixes within aviation to address rising emissions (EAC, 2004b: 20–2). In so doing, the EAC doubted the environmental leadership of government and its understanding of the potential impacts of emissions trading on the price of carbon, claiming that 'we are disappointed at the failure of Government to show leadership in this area' (EAC, 2004a: 10). Increases in aviation emissions would, for the EAC, make the government's own target of 60 per cent reductions in carbon emissions by 2050 'meaningless and unachievable'; the 'most we could hope to attain would be about 35 per cent' (EAC, 2004a: 8).

In its contestation of the ATWP, the Committee thus generated 'horrific' narratives in which aviation expansion threatened any attempt to address climate change, while the government and the DfT were named as the 'bad guys', who had failed in their responsibilities to address climate change by regulating the demand for aviation. Its members positioned themselves in opposition to the New Labour government, openly stating that 'there remain fundamental and apparently irreconcilable differences between the DfT and ourselves' (EAC, 2004c: 4). In its rival narratives, climate change was projected as the universal challenge facing government, and to which all policies, particularly aviation, had to defer. The plans for expansion expounded in the ATWP were thereby summarily dismissed as contradicting the urgent battle against climate change, while any claims by New Labour to have delivered sustainable aviation and controls on aviation emissions were delegitimised through the constitution of alternative discourses of sustainability. In making these rhetorical appeals, the EAC revealed the 'have your cake and eat it' appeal of sustainable aviation, in which aviation growth and environmental protection were presented as compatible objectives. In contrast, the EAC raised the necessity of government taking the lead and determining the necessary trade-offs between different policy objectives (EAC, 2004d: 18). It urged government to act, placing responsibility for future action firmly within the domain of the state. Its 2006 report on carbon emissions from transport thus lamented the 'slow progress' in the introduction of financial measures to reduce emissions from aviation, characterising the government and the aviation industry as 'intransigent', while calling upon the DfT to 'implement demand management measures straightaway' (EAC, 2006: 59, 60). These demands were to resonate with other expert challenges to the ATWP, notably those of the Sustainable Development Commission, to which we now turn.

The Sustainable Development Commission (SDC)

The Sustainable Development Commission (SDC) was established in October 2000 as an independent advisory body to government. It operated as a non-departmental public body, which worked at arm's length to the then Department of the Environment, Transport and the Regions (DETR). Emerging from the discussions surrounding the UK Round Table on Sustainable Development, as well as the British Government Panel on Sustainable Development, its role was to advise ministers across government, mainly by generating 'evidence-based reports' on controversial environmental, social and economic questions.[9] Its first chair, appointed by Tony Blair, was the prominent environmentalist Jonathon Porritt, who had been the co-chair of the Green Party in the early 1980s and director of FoE from 1984 to 1990. In the wider public domain, he was well known as a personal adviser to Prince Charles.

In the consultation running up to the publication of the ATWP, the SDC had defined rates of growth in aviation as 'unsustainable' and had demanded that government implement policies 'to manage growth rates towards more sustainable levels' (SDC, 2002: 3). Like the EAC, it was quick to condemn the ATWP. Reiterating the arguments made by the EAC, it castigated the 2003 white paper as a 'missed opportunity' (SDC, 2004: 1). It also denounced the absence of effective leadership by the New Labour government in addressing the environmental impact of aviation. The SDC named the rapid growth in aviation as 'one of the most severe threats to the global environment today', which, it argued, 'governments have failed completely to confront'. Given this, the Labour government should move 'towards restraining rather than encouraging growth in air traffic' (SDC, 2004: 2). Reproducing the arguments of the EAC, the Commission thus condemned the New Labour government for lacking 'urgent conviction' in its attempts to incorporate aviation into the EU ETS and for failing to address the 'fundamental contradictions' of its aviation policy, which belied the government's claims to 'joined-up thinking'.

Significantly, given its standing as an 'arm's length' public agency, the SDC even went so far as to reiterate the claims of institutional bias, which had figured strongly in the campaign rhetoric of Airport-Watch, accusing the DfT of being 'too closely respondent to the industry it is supposed to regulate, and resistant to outside influences and wider policy considerations' (SDC, 2004: 3). It reprimanded the DfT for not having responded to either of its earlier reports or its 'offers … to help', which was interpreted by the SDC as further evidence 'of a departmental culture that is in danger of becoming semi-detached from the sustainable development imperative, which the Government has wanted to put at its heart' (SDC, 2004: 3). The SDC thereby disputed the government's capacity in the arena of climate change policy 'to carry conviction through leading by example' (SDC, 2004: 3) and it attributed blame to New Labour, using very similar rhetorical figures to those mobilised by the EAC.

Alongside these explicit critiques of partial and ineffectual government, the policy rhetoric of the Commission, again like that of the EAC, distanced the ATWP from any understanding of a 'balanced and measured' approach to aviation. First, despite the assurances of the New Labour government, it repositioned the ATWP as a direct continuation of previous policies, which, the SDC argued, had left aviation 'outside' measures to constrain CO_2 and greenhouse gas emissions (SDC, 2004: 2–3). The SDC did not directly name the white paper as an example of 'predict and provide' policies. Nonetheless, it clearly set out how the logic of 'predict and provide' – its underlying set of rules, assumptions and practices – were reproduced within the pages of the ATWP. It thus claimed that the white paper

> reads as though the increasing demand for air traffic is an ineluctable fact, and one that is automatically linked with increased growth and prosperity for the country. It assumes that the primary responsibility of government must simply be to ensure that this demand is catered for as smoothly and efficiently as possible. It urges acceleration in the process of designating and constructing new airports and facilities, whose effect will be to sustain and encourage further growth of traffic many decades into the future. (SDC, 2004: 3)

Secondly, the SDC frequently dismissed the ATWP for failing to conform to the principles of sustainable development and the wider strategic commitments of the Labour government. It concluded that the white paper 'violates no fewer than five out of the six Principles of the Sustainable Development Commission' (SDC, 2004: 5) (see box 6.1). Like the EAC, it depicted the ATWP as advancing a commitment to sustainability within a framework dominated by an economic model of cost–benefit analysis. The proposals thus legitimised decision-making in terms of 'crude trade-offs' between economic and environmental benefits, while ultimately justifying decisions solely on economic grounds. These 'trade-offs' were

---

Box 6.1 The principles of sustainable development – excerpts from the SDC's appraisal of the air transport white paper (SDC, 2004: 4)

'Putting Sustainable Development at the Centre: ... This Principle rejects "crude trade-offs", in favour of "the pursuit of mutually reinforcing benefits". The ATWP makes absolutely no attempt at such a pursuit. It clearly violates this Principle.'

'Valuing Nature: the ATWP values nature, in the sense of giving it monetary value, in order to justify the trade-off it is proposing. This is not what is meant by this Principle.'

'Fair Shares: expansion of aviation is not about meeting people's basic needs – but its contribution to climate change will make it more difficult for some of the world's poorest people to meet their basic needs in future.... The ATWP clearly fails to be consistent with this Principle.'

'Polluter Pays: the ATWP ... recommends no firm measures to ensure that this will be achieved ... the ATWP as it stands is therefore inconsistent with this SD Principle.'

'Adopting a Precautionary Approach: ... expansion of aviation as envisaged in the ATWP threatens to render meaningless the Government's targets on greenhouse gas emissions ... the ATWP therefore clearly violates this Principle.'

---

designated by the SDC as running counter to the principle of sustainable development (SDC, 2004: 3). By mobilising similar arguments to those put forward by the EAC, especially the latter's questioning of the evidence and the 'facts' informing the analysis of the ATWP, the Commission cast doubt on the calculations of the costs and benefits of airport expansion, thus juxtaposing questionable benefits in output, investment and employment with definite increases in carbon emissions (SDC, 2004: 3–4).

Thirdly, the SDC placed demands for airport expansion under the overriding and universal challenge of climate change and (like the

EAC) it emphasised the failure of the ATWP to take into account the carbon reductions set out in the 2003 energy white paper. This, as the SDC put it, was its primary 'bone of contention' with the proposals. Again, in the rhetoric of the SDC, airport expansion became the primary 'threat' to the UK's laudable carbon reduction strategy, with the Commission reiterating scientific estimates by the EAC and the Royal Commission on Environmental Pollution (RCEP), which predicted that aviation by 2050 would account alone for 66 per cent of the total of the UK's contribution to 'radiative forcing' (SDC, 2004: 5).[10] In addition, the SDC insisted that the aviation industry faced its own 'special challenges' if it was to address its environmental impacts, thus inverting the 'special case' status attributed to the aviation industry by government and Oxford Economic Forecasting (OEF). It thus claimed that aviation's reliance on fossil fuels would not be offset by technological advances, as indicated by government. It also argued that aviation's contribution to radiative forcing at high altitudes acted as a multiplier of its carbon emissions – the extent of which was not fully understood by scientists (SDC, 2004: 5).

Finally, the SDC challenged the government's commitment to emissions trading, which it identified as the 'only policy measure' in the ATWP, while simultaneously deriding the commitment of the Labour government as little more than 'an expressed intention' to include aviation in the EU ETS from 2008 (SDC, 2004: 5). The Commission again sided with the EAC criticisms of the limits of emissions trading. But it challenged the unexpected consequences of the logic of emissions trading by setting out a future policy narrative which claimed that if airport expansion went ahead, the price of carbon permits for aviation would 'go through the roof', thereby increasing the price of flying for customers and leading ultimately to falling demand for air travel. Falling demand thus produced the central contradiction of the ATWP's endorsement of emissions trading, which was that the planned expansion of airports facilities would not actually be required if New Labour succeeded in including aviation within the EU ETS (SDC, 2004: 6).

In summary, in the immediate aftermath of the publication of the 2003 white paper, the SDC (like the EAC) began to contest the government's airport's policy, as well as the fantasmatic discourse of sustainable aviation within which it was embedded, by directly challenging the validity of proposals that aimed both to increase airport capacity and to bring about falling emissions, a policy which, in the rhetoric of the Commission, 'defies objective credibility' (SDC, 2004: 6). It rebuffed the efforts made in the ATWP to recontextualise airports policy within the framework of sustainable aviation by calling into question the measures proposed by government to combat the contribution of aviation to climate change while foregrounding the internal ambiguities within government policy, which planned both to expand aviation and to reduce emissions to 60 per cent of current levels by 2050. In its attacks on the institutional bias of the DfT, it also reproduced the demands made by AirportWatch for open government. These interventions resulted in the rearticulation of aviation as an industry confronting 'special challenges', while air travel was redefined not as an economic multiplier but as a threat to climate change. At the same time, the aviation industry was seen to benefit from the embedded institutional support of the establishment. By reproducing and validating the estimates of the EAC and the RCEP in its own 2004 report, the SDC (and similarly colleagues in other scientific and environmental bodies) thus legitimised its own work and that of others, and worked to bring about a scientific and expert consensus in the realm of aviation. It is to the world of science and academia that we now turn.

The Tyndall Centre for Climate Change Research
Named after John Tyndall, the nineteenth-century physicist who pioneered investigations into the earth's natural greenhouse effect, the Tyndall Centre pursues trans-disciplinary research into sustainable responses to climate change, engaging with the broad research community, business, policy-makers and the media. More specifically, it brings together physical scientists, engineers and social scientists in a consortium drawn from across six British universities and is funded by three UK research councils.[11] 'Decarbonising the UK' was one of the four themes which guided the work of the Centre in the early 2000s. For our purposes, we examine the rhetoric of its working paper *Decarbonising the UK: Energy for a Climate Conscious Future*, which was published in 2005, and which was coordinated by the Universities of Manchester and East Anglia, with additional financial support from the DTI, the SDC and private industry, including BP, EON and Alstom.

In *Decarbonising the UK*, the Tyndall Centre made use of its carefully established academic credentials and scientific objectivity to substantiate its empirical claims and prescriptions. To put it in rhetorical terms, the Centre's report emphasised the role of *logos*, rather than *ethos* or *pathos*. It thus framed its working paper as the work of seventy researchers across seventeen academic institutions (Tyndall Centre, 2005a: 10). The report itself is punctuated by graphs, pie charts and tables, as well as discussions of methodology, which are typical of this genre of scientific report. In the words of its foreword, which was penned by Colin Challen, who was then chair of the All-Party Parliamentary Group on Climate Change and a member of the EAC, the report is presented as a moment of science speaking truth to government. The Tyndall Centre is also firmly located in the world of academia, whose members are characterised by Challen as '"cool heads"', who '(unlike the occasional politician!) seek to demonstrate their hypothesis before rushing to judgment' (p. 3). Importantly, Challen's endorsement of the report served to reinforce the growing scientific and expert consensus which was coming together to demand a reduction of emissions in aviation.

In its report, the Tyndall Centre outlined a number of climate change scenarios in order to give a 'whole systems' understanding of how the UK could meet its 2050 target of a 60 per cent reduction in carbon emissions. These scenarios were given what were termed 'neutral descriptors' (p. 6), based on different colours (red, blue, turquoise, purple, pink and orange). Across each of these future scenarios, aviation growth was constructed as the primary problem or challenge facing government if it was to reduce carbon emissions and meet its 2050 targets. Air travel was thus depicted as a kind of fantasmatic obstacle, one which threatens economic and social well-being. At various points in the text, air travel is described as one of the 'main culprits' (p. 7) responsible for climate change, aviation is viewed as a 'high-stakes issue' (p. 49) and, significantly, air travel is described as a 'looming problem in the sky' (p. 47). In fact, airport expansion was charged with imposing an inappropriate and unfair charge on other sectors of the economy and their attempts to lower carbon emissions. In all but one of its scenarios,[12] the Centre thus argued that with 'carbon emissions from aviation *dwarfing* those from all other sectors' (p. 7; our emphasis), all other sectors would have to reduce their own emissions by more than 60 per cent if the UK was to meet its 2050 commitments (p. 5).

Replicating arguments made by the SDC, the Centre confronted the aviation industry with its own particular challenges over and above those facing other sectors if it was to address its growing emissions (box 6.2). These challenges have emerged, the Centre

Box 6.2 The rhetoric of the Tyndall Centre (2005a: 47)

'Unless the UK Government acts to significantly reduce aviation growth, the industry's emissions will outstrip the carbon reductions envisaged for all other sectors of the economy. Moreover, the Government's own 60% carbon reduction target will be impossible to achieve if aviation growth exceeds just two-thirds of its current rate – even allowing for year-on-year efficiency improvements and assuming all other sectors completely decarbonise.'

suggested, from aviation's 'continued reliance on kerosene and its high growth rate' (p. 49), as well as the multiplier effect of its emissions at high altitude through contrails and cirrus clouds (p. 50). Uncertainties were also raised about the capacity of the aviation industry to deliver technological fixes or alternatives to kerosene (p. 50). Indeed, the Tyndall Centre left the reader with no room for doubt over the requirement for demand management in aviation, reporting as 'fact' that

> an unequivocal and dominating conclusion in relation to carbon emissions is that growth in aviation must be dramatically curtailed from both its current level and historical trend. (Tyndall Centre, 2005a: 7)

Informed by this conclusion, the Tyndall Centre called upon the New Labour government to act to ensure the management of the growing demand for air travel (echoing again the demands of the EAC and the SDC). Blame was directed squarely at government departments for 'their singular inability to seriously recognise and adequately respond to the rapidly escalating emissions from aviation' (p. 50). It regretted government's 'serious underestimation' (p. 4) of the actions required to meet its 2050 targets and its failure to take account of emissions from aviation in its formulation of the ATWP. It repeatedly pointed out the policy contradictions both between government departments and between the ATWP's plans for growth and the energy white paper's plans to reduce carbon emissions (pp. 4, 50). All in all, it demanded that the Blair government address the 'urgent need for coherent climate policy across key departments, including DEFRA, DfT, DTI, HM Treasury and ODPM' (p. 4). Interestingly, the aviation industry itself was constructed as a 'victim' of such government inaction, caught as it was

> in the unenviable position of seeing the demand for its services grow at unprecedented rates, whilst at the same time being unable to achieve substantial levels of decarbonisation in the short to medium-term. (Tyndall Centre, 2005a: 50)

The Centre's deconstruction of the government's proposals added further weight to attempts to reconstitute the policy frame within which airport expansion was to be considered and decided. Aviation was no longer viewed as a 'special case' that deserved government sponsorship. Rather, it was named as a 'special challenge' facing government, which, more than other industry, posed a serious threat to any realistic attempt to address climate change. This particular representation of aviation, as with the rhetorical strategies of the EAC and the SDC, relied upon the successful reframing of the terrain of argumentation, which would make the universal criteria for the assessment of any policy rest on its contribution to rising emissions and climate change. Within these rhetorical framings, the ATWP and the aviation industry came to occupy the position of a fantasmatic obstacle or threat to the beatific visions of sustainable growth in the combat of climate change. Thus, in the rhetoric of the Tyndall Centre, sustainable growth was 'within our grasp' (p. 4), but government had to decide whether to

> permit high levels of aviation growth whilst continuing with their climate change rhetoric or to convert the rhetoric into reality and substantially curtail aviation growth. (Tyndall Centre, 2005a: 50)

The economics of climate change: the Stern review

The Stern review was announced by Gordon Brown, then Chancellor of the Exchequer, in July 2005. The review led by Sir Nicholas Stern, the head of the Government Economic Service and former World Bank chief economist, was given the task of investigating the economics of moving to a low-carbon global economy, evaluating potential approaches to adapting to changes in the climate, and identifying specific lessons for the UK. Stern reported to Brown and Prime Minister Tony Blair at the end of October 2006.

The 700-page review conformed to the genre of an independent official publication, replete with the language of expertise, science and claims of impartiality. More specifically, like the Tyndall Centre report, it was imbued with the rhetoric of economics and science, which had the effect of depoliticising the arguments and policy positions expressed within its pages. Its opening statements set out to establish the objective status of its findings, thus informing the reader that 'we start with the science' (Stern, 2006a: iv). Recourse to the authority of science was also used to convey the relevance and indisputable nature of the review's findings and policy recommendations. Appeals to the evidence and authority of scientific discourse were thus deployed to support demands for coordinated action by governments across the world. For example, it was frequently claimed that the scientific evidence 'warrants strong action' (Stern, 2006a: iv) or that 'the scientific evidence is now overwhelming' (Stern, 2006b: 1).

While depicting climate change as a 'threat' which was 'immediate', Stern also validated the effectiveness of the measures the review proposed to address the problem. The executive summary claimed, for example, that 'there is still time to avoid the worst impacts of climate change, if we take strong action now' (Stern, 2006b: 27). The designation of climate change as a tractable problem added to the weight and urgency of the review's proposals for government action against aviation expansion. With respect to this issue, the review presented air transport as a growing and future threat to climate change, projecting the tripling of its contribution to CO_2 emissions by 2050. Echoing the interventions of the Tyndall Centre, the SDC and the EAC, aviation was singled out as a particular challenge to efforts to address climate change, and it was identified in the review as being among 'the fastest growing sectors' (Stern, 2006a: 172) or the 'second fastest' growing sector (p. 176), while facing 'difficult challenges' (p. 341), namely that it was 'unlikely to see technological breakthroughs' (pp. 207, 337, 356–7) and that it was difficult 'to envisage cost-effective approaches' in aviation (p. 247).

The portrayal of aviation as a 'threat' to measures to tackle climate change was amplified in the review by references to the growth potential of the demand for aviation, not least as 'people with lower incomes in developed countries, are now able to travel globally due to low-cost flights' (p. 485). Here, the oft-repeated appeals to the alleged social benefits brought about by the popularisation of air travel were redesignated by the Stern review as a threat to climate change. Similarly, it increased existing assessments of the impact of aviation on global warming, as did the EAC, the SDC and the Tyndall Centre, by adding in estimates of the impact of its emissions at high altitude, which was predicted to increase aviation's contribution to total warming effects to 5 per cent in 2050 (p. 172). These 'impacts over and beyond the CO_2 effects', which included condensation trails and the uncertainty over the effect of cirrus clouds created by aircraft (p. 342), were deemed by Stern to make aviation 'particularly problematic' (p. 181).

Like the emerging challenges to the sedimented narratives of air travel developed by the EAC, the SDC and the Tyndall Centre, the Stern review helped to turn aviation into an intractable problem, which required concerted action by national governments. It focused on the way in which congestion and capacity limits at airports operated in practice as an 'inefficient way of regulating demand', drawing attention to the low levels of aviation taxation in comparison with road transport fuel taxes (p. 341). The review thus invited governments to intervene in the field of aviation by creating new regulatory forms for air transport and its carbon emissions. It endorsed the principle of 'polluter pays', in that the 'level of the carbon price faced by aviation should reflect the full contribution of emissions from aviation to climate change', and advocated carbon pricing and carbon trading schemes (p. 341), as well as suggesting new policy instruments such as auctioning allowances to raise revenue (p. 485) and imposing adaptation levies on air tickets (p. 558). Notably, it threw doubt on the capacity of governments and politics to address aviation emissions, suggesting somewhat negatively that, in the field of aviation, the selection of policy instruments would have more to do with political viability than economic effectiveness (p. 341).

However, and significantly for the Blair government, Stern's policy recommendations also partly reproduced elements of the political strategies put forward by the DfT in the pages of its 2003 ATWP. Thus the review acknowledged the challenges and constraints of international regulation and bilateral agreements on the capacity of national governments to introduce carbon pricing, as well as the difficulties posed by the international coordination of taxes. Here, it privileged the leading role of the International Civil Aviation Organisation over national governments in determining the bulk of air transport policy (p. 341). Hence it replicated the arguments developed by the DfT in the ATWP against the current regime in air transport.

For example, it problematised the lack of incentives to reduce inter-national aviation emissions, 'blunt national policy instruments, the existence of large aviation markets outside Kyoto and the fact that only domestic flights [are] allocated to national emission inventor-ies' (p. 485). Indeed, the ATWP had dismissed any increase in air passenger duty on British flights as one such 'blunt instrument'.

In short, the Stern review, not least through its repetition of sci-entific and expert arguments already voiced in other forums and to different audiences, supplemented ongoing political challenges to the expansion of air travel. In contrast to the work of the EAC, the SDC and the Tyndall Centre, it highlighted the constraints facing government in tackling the growing emissions from aviation, thus reproducing many of the political strategies adumbrated in the ATWP. Nonetheless, it still positioned aviation as a threat to climate change strategies, while further reframing the policy problem of aviation within the dominant terrain of argumentation, which was climate change and carbon emissions.

Resonance, repetition and the reframing of aviation

When considered cumulatively, and over time, the repetition of these scientific and expert interventions began to forge a clear connection between air travel and climate change. In the process, they consist-ently linked aviation policy to the universal challenge of climate change, naming aviation as a 'culprit' that threatened 'our' capacity to address the wider and crucial challenge to humanity of climate change, and which thus required government intervention and demand management to curb its accelerating emissions. Implicated in the shifting public discourse about climate change, as well as the heightened public awareness of its effects, air travel was thus transformed from its privileged position within a beatific narrative of economic modernisation and mobility, to that of a threatening obstacle in a horrific narrative, which could block the action that was required to ward off the totalising threat of global warning and thus realise the eventual promise of a genuinely sustainable future. In this crucial reframing, the ATWP, which had been characterised as 'a missed opportunity', was regularly condemned: for departing from the principles of sustainable development and privileging an economic approach to sustainability; for lacking an analytical grounding in relevant evidence; and for contradicting wider government policy commitments to reduce carbon emissions by 2050. Such rhetorical moves undermined New Labour's promises to deliver a policy of sustainable aviation by presenting the latter's discourse as little more than a fantasmatic narrative, whose false prospectus claimed to offer a balanced approach that could reconcile demands for airport expansion and environmental sustainability.

Consciously or unconsciously reproducing AirportWatch's demands for open government, these expert discourses blamed the New Labour government for its lack of effective leadership and for its practices of partial and 'closed' policy-making in the field of aviation. Underpinning these demands for government to take the lead was a sustained attack on emissions trading, which was singled out as *the* policy response to aviation emissions. It is noteworthy that even the Stern review recognised the political difficulties of moving towards demand management in air travel. On the one hand, the inclusion of aviation in the EU ETS attracted the attention of commentators, simply because it was one of the few concrete policy initiatives in the ATWP that addressed rising aviation emissions. On the other hand, its emergence as one of the primary nodal points that structured the terrain of argumentation in aviation policy can be explained by its key function within the fantasmatic narrative of sustainable aviation: carbon trading was the mechanism which, in theory, through the buying and selling of carbon rights, enabled both the expansion of aviation and environmental protection.

Finally, the repetition of the arguments and findings of this body of work in different arenas and through multiple genres brought new knowledge claims into the field of aviation policy. At least for the media, they helped to manufacture a scientific consensus on the contribution of aviation to climate change and raised the significance of air travel on the policy agenda of national environmental groups. In the wake of the 2003 ATWP, the reports formed part of a corpus of work on aviation that resonated across the media and wider networks of stakeholders engaged in aviation policy. Notably, in September 2006, FoE published its critique of aviation expansion, *Pie in the Sky*, and the Environmental Change Institute at Oxford University released its final report into aviation and climate change policy in the UK, *Predict and Decide*, an earlier version of which had been submitted to the Stern review in 2005 (Environmental Change Institute, 2006). The Oxford University report made reference to the work of the Tyndall Centre and the reports of the EAC. Of course, the publication of each report triggered further features in media news coverage. The travel section of one national newspaper even felt obliged among its articles on holiday destinations to ask the question: 'Is it ok to fly?' (*Guardian*, 20 May 2006).

Yet the institutional bias of the DfT and the status of the ATWP also came under pressure from developments within other ministries. In 2005, the Department for Environment, Food and Rural Affairs (DEFRA) published its revised sustainable development strategy, which was followed by the release of the UK Climate Change Programme in 2006. Its sustainable development strategy, *Securing Our Future*, recognised the policy priority of raising the problem of aviation emissions for the UK presidency of the EU (DEFRA, 2005: 76). DEFRA's summary of the 'Taking It On' consultation processes, which accompanied the development of its 2005 strategy, also recognised that aviation was 'singled' out in the consultation as 'needing better regulation' (DEFRA, 2005: 73). How did the DfT and New Labour respond to these policy expectations of different stakeholders and the argumentative challenges to the 2003 white paper? And how did the Labour government seek to address or counter such opposition? It is to these questions that we now turn.

The rhetoric and political strategies of New Labour

In the 2003 ATWP, the DfT committed itself to publishing a progress report on the implementation of its proposals within three years. Its publication in December 2006 (DfT, 2006a) was one of a battery of interventions in the public domain through which the Labour government, now faced with growing contestation, sought to manage politically the sustained attacks on its ATWP. The DfT, the Secretary of State for Transport and indeed Gordon Brown at the Treasury reiterated the economic contribution of aviation and defended the ATWP as a policy of sustainable aviation across an array of publications. These included the DfT's responses to the EAC, the Treasury's pre-budget reports and the Eddington report on the contribution of transport to economic well-being. Most importantly, the DfT sought to recontextualise the white paper by reinscribing its proposals into a new discourse, which now emphasised the role of the environment and sustainable development. The aim was to recharacterise the ATWP as a response to the universal challenge of climate change.

The ATWP progress report thus foregrounded a number of appeals to the environmental policy commitments of the wider government, asserting that climate change is 'the biggest single issue we face', while underlining the commitment in the ATWP that aviation should meet its 'external costs' under the 'polluter pays' principle (DfT, 2006a: 7). It also drew equivalences between the approach of the 2003 white paper and the government's broader response to tackling climate change, thus seeking to counter arguments that the ATWP contradicted the commitments of the 2003 energy white paper. In so doing, the progress report explicitly referred to the climate change commitments of the Labour government, which were expressed in the 2006 Climate Change Programme, the Energy Review and the 2006 Queen's Speech. It is noteworthy that the DfT positioned the ATWP as a precursor to the Stern review into the economics of climate change, where the latter had endorsed carbon trading and offsetting, by arguing that the approach of the white paper was to ensure that aviation

> reflects the full costs of its climate change emissions, which will influence the amount of traffic growth that will occur ... [this] is the same approach Sir Nicholas Stern recommended right across our economy. (DfT, 2006a: 3)

Associated with these rhetorical moves to defuse opposition, the DfT rearticulated the very demands and policy problematisations expressed by opponents of the ATWP. For example, the progress report incorporated demands for aviation to be included in the government's climate change strategy to reduce emissions by 60 per cent by 2050 (DfT, 2006a: 3). It also recognised the problem of rising emissions from aviation and the contradictions of expanding air travel for climate change policy, estimating that even if the UK reduced its carbon emissions by 60 per cent in 2050

> within that total, domestic aviation emissions rise from 0.8 to 1.6 million [tonnes]. This means that in 2050 domestic aviation would represent 2.4 per cent of UK carbon emissions. (DfT, 2006a: 12)

In part, the rhetoric of the progress report thus began to accept the metaphor of air travel as a 'culprit'. However, these arguments were still accompanied by concerted attempts within the DfT to reconstitute the strategic commitments of the white paper as instances of sustainable aviation. In the foreword to the progress report, the then Secretary of State for Transport, Douglas Alexander, restated the problematisation of the 2003 white paper as being that of 'sustainable

economic growth requir[ing] recognition of our environmental responsibilities' (DfT, 2006a: 2), thereby re-establishing the ambition of
the ATWP to balance 'the growing aspirations we have to travel and
the needs of our economy with the need to protect our environment'
(DfT, 2006a: 3). In its second written response to the first report of the
EAC, the DfT (as reported by the EAC) redefined the white paper as
'reflect[ing] the economic, social and environmental pillars of sustainable development and [being] consistent with the environmental goals
of the Energy White Paper' (EAC, 2004c: 7).

In fact, the Labour government retreated back to its tried-and-
tested narratives about the economic importance of aviation,
repeatedly focusing on the 'horrific' threats of non-expansion to
economic well-being, while conjuring up affective appeals about the
joy of flying. In his 2005 pre-budget report, the Chancellor of the
Exchequer, Gordon Brown, thus reiterated the 'unique role' of Heathrow in the economic productivity and competitiveness of the UK
economy (HM Treasury, 2005: 73). Twelve months later, in his 2006
pre-budget report, he drew upon the Eddington transport study, which
was commissioned by the Treasury and the DfT, and undertaken
by Sir Rod Eddington, the former chief executive of BA, to make
the case for the 'important role of international gateways such as
airports in contributing to the productivity and competitiveness of
the UK economy, and the costs imposed by congestion in and around
airports' (HM Treasury, 2006: 175). Brown even went so far as to
invoke the 'natural growth' of aviation, thus reiterating the established
rhetoric about the 'net benefits' of expansion and the 'economic
consequences of constraining aviation growth', while also raising the
threats of congestion, the risk of growing demand outstripping supply
and 'reduced choice and higher prices for passengers', if expansion
was not to take place (HM Treasury, 2006: 175).

Such tropes recurred in the ATWP progress report (box 6.3), which
was published just a few days after Brown's 2006 pre-budget report.
Like Brown's pre-budget statement, the progress report reproduced
the claims of the 2006 Eddington study, which stressed the contribution of aviation, and transport more generally, to economic
development, trade and service industries, claiming that 'from the
invention of the wheel onwards, transport has been fundamental to
economic progress and has led to huge improvements in our quality
of life' (HM Treasury and DfT, 2006: 9). The progress report even
noted Eddington's estimates that 'an additional two runways in the

---

Box 6.3 The economic success story of air transport – the *Future of Air Transport Progress Report* (DfT, 2006a)

'a substantial employer, providing around 200,000 jobs directly and many more indirectly. The industry also contributes around £11 billion directly to the economy (approximately 1 per cent of UK economic activity).' (p. 24)

'On average airports have increased the number of overseas routes they offer by 44 per cent between 2003 and 2005, with new routes and markets being opened up with countries such as India, China, Russia, Brazil and Australia, stimulating further business and travel opportunities. In turn, the UK's inbound tourism industry is now the fifth largest in the world. Around 30 million overseas visitors came to Britain in 2005, over two-thirds of them arriving by air and spending some £14 billion here.' (p. 24)

'About a quarter of UK visible trade by value goes by air.' (p. 24)

'In the south-east of England, for example, 90 per cent of companies surveyed by the OEF regard Heathrow as either vital or very important to their organisations.' (p. 24)

'The aviation industry also invests in the skills and training of its workforce. Since 2003, new Centres of Excellence for aircraft maintenance have opened in Prestwick, South Wales and Newcastle, providing training and employment for a new generation of skilled aircraft engineers and technicians.' (p. 25)

South East would deliver net economic benefits of £17 billion' (DfT, 2006a: 24). Throughout the report, the DfT thereby advanced the case of expansion by drawing upon updated economic assessments from OEF, which had reworked its 1999 and 2003 consultancy reports into the impact of aviation on the economy (Sewill, 2007). In short, the progress report rehearsed the chain of positive social and economic opportunities that constructed aviation expansion as a necessary response to the demands of globalisation, the driver of rising disposable incomes, the provider of increasing opportunity for greater numbers of people travelling into and out of the UK, as well as foregrounding the economic successes of UK airports as international hubs (DfT, 2006a: 5). Once again, however, these economic benefits were portrayed as under threat if the government stalled in its plans for expansion. It thus echoed the ATWP's appeals to the 'horrific' fantasy of declining UK competitiveness and increasing threats from EU competitors, as well as the looming spectre of China, which, the progress report claimed, 'plans to invest $17.5 billion on launching 71 airport expansion projects, relocating 11 airports and building 49 new airports' (DfT, 2006a: 5).

Alongside the recourse to these horrific narratives, the progress report reactivated affective appeals about the mass popularity of air transport and the enjoyment that flying brings to greater and greater numbers of the population, thus emphasising the role of airport expansion as a means of enhancing social equality. In making these arguments, the DfT again portrayed the rising demand for air travel as an inevitable consequence of factors outside the control of government. The latter included the increasing number of journeys by 'leisure travellers', which it related to the positive outcomes of rising incomes, lower fares, greater choice and economic progress (p. 25). It drew upon an October 2006 Attitudes to Air Travel survey to demonstrate rising patterns of, and aspirations for, air travel, identifying the increasing proportion of journeys undertaken by leisure travellers as evidence of its claims to the popularisation of air travel (p. 25). Echoing the fantasmatic logics embedded in the discourse of Freedom to Fly, the DfT thus constructed the growing opposition to aviation expansion as an attack on the normal lifestyles and preferences of the wider population.

Such rhetorical devices show that, when faced with contestation, the New Labour government continued to follow the political strategies devised in the ATWP: those of brokerage, deferred responsibility or individualisation, and incentivisation. The DfT again described the ATWP as the embodiment of 'honest' brokerage. In its view, the white paper 'rejected a predict and provide approach' and provided 'a comprehensive strategy', which had 'rejected proposals for new capacity at several airports and at new greenfield locations, and instead promoted making much better use of existing airport capacity' (DfT, 2006a: 3). It reproduced the fantasmatic narrative that competitive demands for growth and environmental protection were in some way reconcilable, and that by appealing to the 'sustainable development of aviation capacity' (DfT, 2006a: 13) it was possible to reach a policy solution which satisfactorily addressed the demands of stakeholders to combat climate change and protect local environments, while delivering growth and further capacity for air travel. Yet New Labour could not escape the fundamental contradiction that the privileging of broker-age, which involved finding a 'balance' between competing demands (box 6.4), framed the work of government not as an elimination of the negative costs of air transport but merely a mitigation of its negative environmental impact on climate change.

In its second written response to the EAC, the DfT continued to displace responsibility for managing emissions onto international regulators, thus making favourable comparisons of its own plans for expansion with those of foreign competitors. Alluding to the competition from Amsterdam, the US and China, it drew attention to the 'major expansion of airport infrastructure ... underway, for example in the United States and China, that dwarfs the balanced and measured proposals in our White Paper' (EAC, 2004c: 7). Inter-national developments, in the arguments of the DfT, thus undermined

---

Box 6.4 The continued appeal to 'balance': the *Future of Air Transport Progress Report* (DfT, 2006a)

'it [the ATWP] strikes the right balance between economic, social and environmental goals.' (p. 3)

'Our objective is to strike a fair balance between the local and national benefits that can be gained from airport expansion, and the local costs that might be imposed.' (p. 15)

'We consider that for each airport the outcome represents an ap-propriate balance between the need to protect local communities from excessive noise and the economic benefits that night-time air services can bring.' (p. 16)

'There is a strong demand for air travel, but this must be de-livered in a way that balances the need to manage aviation's environmental obligations.' (p. 6)

the effectiveness of self-imposed demand management. This was because:

> arbitrarily constrain[ing] the UK air transport industry could poten-
> tially cause lasting harm to the UK economy and the interests of
> the travelling public without delivering the worldwide environmental
> benefits which both the [Environmental Audit] Committee and the
> Government wish to see. (EAC, 2004c: 7)

Shifting the blame for limited progress in reducing aviation emissions away from the UK government and onto international actors and other nation-states, the Labour government again questioned the commitment of international actors to agree economic instruments to address climate change. It also disparaged the non-inclusion of international aviation emissions in its Kyoto targets, the 'out of date' Chicago Convention on international air routes and the limited progress within the International Civil Aviation Organisation on aviation emissions since 1998 (thereby reproducing many of the arguments of the Stern review, which itself reiterated claims in the ATWP) (DfT, 2006a: 7).

Similarly, the Labour government continued to incorporate individual citizens and the aviation industry in the shared management of aviation emissions, particularly in its claims to be working with industry to encourage changing environmental practices (DfT, 2006a: 9, 11). On the one hand, the progress report thus set out how government would simplify the processes for individual passengers to offset their carbon emissions to 'help people to take responsibility for tackling their contribution to climate change' (DfT, 2006a: 4). It did not fail to point out in the process that officials and ministers offset their own carbon emissions from their air travel (p. 4). On the other hand, the DfT welcomed a number of 'best practice' policies across airports (pp. 16–20), devoting an annexe to airport master plans that informed planning processes, blight-mitigation schemes and community engagement (p. 18). It also designated as an example of 'best practice' the participation of the British Airports Authority (BAA) in the EU ETS and its commitment to reduce absolute carbon emissions from fixed sources by 15 per cent by 2010 compared with 1990 (p. 11).

Most importantly, the progress report gave a special endorsement to the industry-led 2005 Sustainable Aviation initiative 'as a mark of greater commitment to address aviation's environmental impacts ... lodg[ing] sustainability firmly at the forefront of the sector's strategic planning' (p. 10). The Sustainable Aviation network brought together 'key players' (Sustainable Aviation, 2005: 8) in commercial aviation, including British Airways, Virgin Atlantic, National Air Traffic Services, Airbus UK, BAE Systems and Rolls-Royce (Sustainable Aviation, 2005: 8). In a foreword to its launch strategy document, Tony Blair offered his support to the industry-led network, declaring:

> I am delighted that such a wide range of organisations have worked together on Sustainable Aviation. By working with government and society to tackle the environmental issues associated with aviation, the industry can demonstrate that economic success, social progress and respect for the environment can go hand in hand. (Sustainable Aviation, 2005: 3)

Equally, the Aviation Minister, Karen Buck, proclaimed in a DfT press release that 'we look to the industry to take their strategy forward energetically so that aviation contributes to a sustainable society'.[13]

Against this background, the progress report also referred to technological improvements or 'fixes' in aviation. In a section entitled 'How Industry Is Delivering', it supported the aviation industry's setting of fuel efficiency targets (50 per cent improvements per seat kilometre in new aircraft in 2020 compared with 2000) (p. 10). It repeated demands for improved management of existing airport capacity, emissions cost assessments and investment in new technology. (Here, once again, it mentioned the £5 million commitment to the new knowledge transfer network, OMEGA, or Opportunities for Meeting the Environmental Challenge of Growth in Aviation.) This shift of responsibility to external stakeholders was equally discernible in the 2006 Civil Aviation Act, which granted powers: to airports to tackle aircraft noise; to put into place 'economic measures' that encouraged aircraft to stay on noise-minimisation routes; and to set charges that reflected levels of local aircraft emissions (DfT, 2006b).

In conjunction with these proposed strategies and tactics, the Labour government increasingly relied upon its logics of incentivisation and its 'hand offs' environmental regulation of aviation through emissions trading. It did make one symbolic concession, responding to growing demands for increased taxation on air travel. The 2006 pre-budget report thus announced the doubling of air passenger duty from the beginning of February 2007. This can be seen as a political concession to the growing calls for demand management, for it was derided in the 2003 white paper as a 'blunt' instrument, which was 'not the ideal measure for tackling the environmental impacts of aviation' (DfT, 2003a: 41). Nonetheless, emissions trading schemes formed a key nodal point in organising the government's response to aviation's impact on climate change. References to emissions trading were peppered throughout the government's policies on the environment, notably in the 2005 sustainable development strategy (DEFRA, 2005: 86) and its 2006 UK climate change programme (DEFRA, 2006: 71–2). Equally, the progress report legitimised emissions trading as a policy measure, which worked in tandem with the Stern report on the economics of climate change, with its 'strong belief that market mechanisms are the most effective way of reducing carbon emissions' (DfT, 2006a: 8). As we suggest above, it was in its particular construction as a policy instrument that married economic competitiveness, demand regulation and environmental protection that emissions trading became pivotal in the maintenance of fantasmatic narratives of sustainable aviation. Indeed, it was argued in the progress report that the inclusion of aviation in the EU ETS was

> the most efficient and cost-effective way to ensure that the sector plays its part in tackling climate change [as] it avoids artificial targets for each sector which would distort economic decision-making. (DfT, 2006a: 4)

In making such claims, the emissions trading scheme was contrasted positively with 'industry-specific carbon targets', which, the DfT feared, 'can constrain growth and be arbitrary and inflexible' (p. 9). The scheme was extolled as one of the most 'cost-effective ways of reducing carbon emissions while responding to the strong demand for air travel' (p. 9). This strategy of incentivisation enabled government to take a certain distance from the market for aviation *and* establish steering mechanisms that favoured particular policy outcomes. In other words, it offered government the possibility of squaring the circle of sustainable aviation. However, in the conclusion to this chapter, we analyse the limits of such political strategies and show how, by the summer of 2007, rather than planning for major expansion, the aviation industry was in fact experiencing a 'summer of discontent'.

Conclusion

In the three years following the publication of the ATWP, the political credibility of New Labour's attempts to frame a policy of sustainable aviation collapsed, as expert and scientific interventions successfully highlighted the contradictions of the ATWP, especially when they were viewed alongside other government policies and commitments to reduce carbon emissions. As we suggest, the constitutive function of the ATWP in setting out a comprehensive aviation policy made the ideological and political commitments of New Labour more visible and thus able to be confronted. After its publication in December 2003, there were sustained efforts to discredit its conclusions, which were pictured as little more than a repetition of the discredited 'predict and provide' model, and to connect aviation to the problem of climate change. In part, this attack on New Labour's policy of 'sustainable aviation' was led by scientists and expert scrutiny bodies, whose challenges to the ATWP, especially its lack of consideration of aviation's contribution to rising carbon emissions, resonated with the changing public mood, which was now exhibiting a growing concern about the dangers of climate change. A corpus of expert reports, which emanated from the EAC, the SDC, the Tyndall Centre and Stern, drew a robust connection between growing aviation emissions and climate change, so that to be against climate change was also to be against aviation expansion. At the same time, they gave the campaigns against airport expansion greater legitimacy while bringing into the public domain new knowledge claims about aviation's wider environmental impacts, which stretched beyond local communities, thus extending the constituencies affected by air travel. In other words, aviation and flying were now made synonymous with climate change, and both were associated with a catastrophic future that required immediate and concerted action in the present.

The Labour government responded to these challenges by restating its belief that a 'balance' could be achieved in aviation without adversely affecting economic growth and expansion. It thus continued to seek to adopt the overarching role of an honest broker, and effectively abdicated its directing function, by employing the logics of steering and incentivisation. It thus endeavoured to displace or decentre responsibility by offloading decisions to other groups, individuals and constituencies. Within this panoply of political strategies, emissions trading became the primary policy instrument to achieve the goal of sustainable aviation. But the obvious difficulty with this logic of difference was that it exposed the government's weak position in taking decisive action to shape the policy agenda in a definitive way, that is, in determining the appropriate balance between national and local interests, as well as the trade-offs between economic and environmental benefits. These difficulties were exacerbated when the policy of emissions trading also came under severe criticism, as scientific and environmental bodies attacked its effectiveness in reducing aviation emissions. The government thus found itself facing a twin effectiveness and legitimation crisis. Yet its main response to these crises and deficiencies was once again to retreat back to the construction of fantasmatic narratives – 'having your cake and eat it' forms of justification and representation – such as 'sustainable aviation', even though these ideological representations ultimately betrayed its inability to shape the policy agenda and exude a credible leadership function.

In fact, with the failure of the government's strategies to manage the growing contestation of its ATWP, aviation came to function as a nodal point for a range of disparate grievances and demands, as the scientific and policy scrutiny of the white paper foregrounded a new dimension in national policy debates, effectively restructuring the terrain of argumentation around aviation's contribution to climate change. Local residents, anti-aviation lobbies, environmental groups and the media all quickly seized upon New Labour's contradictory pledges both to expand air travel and to reduce carbon emissions by reiterating, in different genres and political arenas, the headline summaries of scientific reports and discourse, which represented aviation as a growing contributor to climate change. For example, opponents of expansion skilfully deployed the arguments of the Tyndall Centre and the EAC, thus seeking to integrate aviation policy within the more universal policy demands of climate change and the commitments to lower carbon emissions (for example in the formulation of the 2008 Climate Change Act). Typically, in an Aviation Environment Federation (AEF) booklet, *Fly Now, Grieve Later: How to Reduce the Impact of Air Travel on Climate Change*, which was published in June 2005, and was penned by Brendon Sewill, a former Treasury economist and chair of the Gatwick Area Conservation Campaign, who also wrote the *The Hidden Cost of Flying* in 2003, it was claimed that 'there is unanimous agreement among scientists that the world is heating up at a dangerous rate, and that air travel adds to the damage' (Sewill, 2005: 4). In defence of this claim and through the booklet, Sewill cited recent reports by the Environmental Audit Committee, the Sustainable Development Commission and the Tyndall Centre. Similarly, Tony Bosworth, an aviation campaigner working at FoE, characterised aviation as 'the fastest-growing source of carbon dioxide emissions' and claimed that 'if the government is serious about tackling climate change it must abandon its airport expansion plans' (*Guardian*, 14 November 2006). Following the publication of the ATWP progress report, FoE subsequently repeated these charges, accusing the New Labour government of 'greenwash' (*Guardian*, 15 December 2006). However, this restructuring of aviation politics was best brought to the fore at the opening of the public inquiry into expansion plans for the existing runway at Stansted at the end of May 2007. In its opening statement, the Stop Stansted Expansion (SSE) campaign characterised the ATWP as reading as if

> from another age – *before* the Government's Chief Scientist, Sir David King, advised the threat from climate change to be 'far more serious than that of terrorism'; and *before* the Prime Minister, Tony Blair, asserted climate challenge is 'the world's greatest environmental challenge'.[14]

By the summer of 2007, the UK aviation industry was experiencing something of a summer of discontent. In August 2007, the Camp for Climate Action targeted Heathrow airport, despite the intensive attempts by BAA to gain legal injunctions against its organisers and supporters (*Guardian*, 27 July, 2 August 2007). The protest action was conceived as a means of drawing public attention to 'the world's busiest airport', which was 'a bigger source of CO_2 emissions than most countries'.[15] Camp organisers also called upon the public to 'remember [that] we cannot stop climate change without stopping airport expansion',[16] and they insisted that the campaign against the aviation industry would be 'one of the most important environmental battles in Western Europe'.[17] They accused BAA of being 'climate criminals' and labelled the decision to expand the airport as 'sheer lunacy in this time of ecological crisis'.[18] Accusations were also often phrased in terms of populist critiques of 'irresponsible corporations', which 'threaten the safety and future of all humankind'; government failure; and the predominance of economic growth over all other considerations.[19] Indeed, camp activists called upon 'so-called ordinary people' to campaign and protest, so as 'to solve the world's problems, largely in spite of the actions of governments and corporations'.[20] Importantly, camp activists attacked industry claims that demands to regulate aviation were an attack on the pleasures and lifestyle choices of UK citizens by situating their perceived fear-mongering within the context of climate change and the dangers it poses to the world's population. They thus endeavoured to generate alternate affective appeals, which juxtaposed the benefits of holidays abroad with the threat of climate change:

Air passengers are not our enemy. But [nor] are the 160,000 people already dying every year as a direct result of climate change. It is not our intention to ruin holidays, only to stop the planet going to ruin.[21]

At the same time, Heathrow airport came under further attack from ministers for its congestion and for the excessive delays experienced by travellers,[22] while BAA's control of the major London airports was called into question by airlines and the Competition Commission. The Commission was considering the potential break-up of BAA, which controlled the major airports in London and Scotland, in a shake-up of the regulatory regime, which had been established in the shift to liberalisation and privatisation during the 1980s (*Financial Times*, 4 and 9 August 2007). On 30 July 2007, the newly appointed City Minister, Kitty Ussher, publicly criticised what she termed the 'Heathrow hassle', voicing her concerns that queues at passport control, the effect of security measures and the very layout of the airport would undermine the attractiveness of London as a financial and commercial centre. The government, she announced, was committed to maintaining the competitiveness of London, declaring that 'I don't want their New York or Dubai executives saying, "Oh God, I don't want to go through Heathrow".' The minister was joined by a chorus of support, including: Tony Douglas, Heathrow's former chief executive; Giovanni Bisignani, the director general of the International Air Transport Association (IATA); Colin Stanbridge, chief executive of the London Chamber of Commerce; Ken Livingstone, mayor of London; and, for good measure, the chief executive of Ryanair, Michael O'Leary.[23]

While talk about the 'Heathrow hassle' might have appeared to enhance demands for expansion at the international hub, it also fuelled demands for the more effective regulation of UK airports, thus adding support to the inquiry opened by the Competition Commission. In October 2007, for example, the House of Commons Transport Select Committee announced its own inquiry into the future of BAA (House of Commons Transport Select Committee, 2008: 3). In equal fashion, these discourses cast doubt on the dominant pro-aviation narrative, which presented aviation and airports as an economic 'booster'. By 24 August 2007, BA's chief executive, Willie Walsh, was for the first time openly calling for the break-up of BAA's London airport monopoly, arguing in particular that it should not own both Heathrow and Stansted, where the former operation was cross-subsidising the latter (*Financial Times*, 24 August 2007).

There were increasing tensions between BAA and carriers, with public concerns surfacing over whether Ferrovial, the new Spanish owner of BAA, might abandon the expansion of Heathrow because of financial difficulties (*Guardian*, 21 and 26 June 2007). At the beginning of October 2007, the Competition Commission condemned passenger delays at BAA airports as 'unacceptable.' The Commission sided with the Civil Aviation Authority's proposal to reduce the return on capital at Heathrow between 2008 and 2013, a key factor in BAA's financial well-being, because the latter accrued much of its profit from its terminals and operations (*Guardian*, 3 October 2007). And, for equal measure, carriers again condemned the 'mismanagement' of London airports in their written evidence to the Transport Select Committee, which American Airlines alleged had cost it 'millions in higher landing fees, reduced operational performance and lost revenue as passengers chose to connect through other European hubs (House of Commons Transport Select Committee, 2008: 104). In his oral evidence to the Committee, Toby Nicol, the communications director of easyJet, alluded to BAA profit margins 'which would make Tutankhamen blush'. He accused BAA of irresponsible spending while 'we [carriers] are the ones who have to pick up the bill'.[24] In short, as one national transport correspondent put it, 'since the terror scare [in] August [2006] brought Heathrow to a near standstill, unrelenting criticism of BAA's perceived incompetence has appeared in print, on the airwaves and in everyday conversation' (*Guardian*, 21 June 2007).

Overall, therefore, following the expert scrutiny of the white paper and the growing contestation of the management of UK airports, the conditions for the reactivation and resurgence of anti-expansion coalitions were rapidly put in place. New narratives and appeals were made possible, and new demands were voiced. Government ministers publicly condemned the 'Heathrow hassle' which was experienced by many travellers using the London airport; the Competition Commission intimated that the break-up of BAA was one possible outcome of its inquiry into the regulation and ownership of UK airports; airlines complained about the poor services and the high fees charged at Heathrow; environmental protesters set up the Camp for Climate Action near Heathrow airport; and local residents at Stansted vigorously opposed any capacity increases to the existing runway. This growing contestation symbolised the negative experience of air travel, and it thereby challenged the once sedimented narratives of aviation's economic success and international competitiveness, by pinpointing the existence of privileged monopolies as well as partial insider government.

But, more importantly, for our analysis, these various practices helped to create equivalences between demands in the aviation field and demands in climate change politics, so that air travel and airports were increasingly resignified as 'culprits' or 'horrific' threats, thus undermining beliefs about their 'special status' as a key motor of social mobility and economic growth. Indeed, in an IPSOS-MORI poll for the Commission for Integrated Transport in February 2007, 34 per cent of respondents, when asked, unprompted, to identify causes of climate change, singled out emissions from planes, while 79 per cent of the public could recall having had information about aviation and climate change (IPSOS-MORI, 2007: 33–6). Half the public were 'very or fairly concerned' about the effects of air travel on climate change, with 39 per cent of those who were at least fairly concerned basing that on the belief that 'air travel is a growing contributor to climate change' (IPSOS-MORI, 2007: 37).

In the next chapter, bearing in mind this changing political context, we examine how an emerging climate change coalition against air travel was assembled and mobilised. We then explore how campaigners against expansion defeated plans to construct the third runway at Heathrow, thus delivering (for some) the biggest transport policy reversal since roads policy in the 1990s.

Notes

1 These and the further responses to the 2003 air transport white paper, issued as press releases on 16 December 2003, are available at www.stop stanstedexpansion.com/white_paper_responses.html#BA (accessed 19 August 2011).

2 HACAN ClearSkies, press release, 16 December 2003, www.hacan.org.uk/news/press_releases.php?id=54 (accessed 19 August 2011).

3 See http://news.bbc.co.uk/1/hi/sci/tech/3381425.stm (accessed 19 August 2011).

4 See http://risingtide.org.uk/about/political and www.campaigncc.org (accessed 9 February 2012).

5 See www.foe.co.uk/news/big_ask.html (accessed 9 February 2012).

6 We borrow the term 'concourse' from Q-method approaches, where it is used to describe the range of different discourses around particular issues.

7 The origins of the EAC lay in the 1994 Labour Party policy review, *In*

Trust for Tomorrow, and the 1990 FoE submission to the House of Commons Procedure Committee. For a discussion of its role and its history see www.parliament.uk/eacom (accessed 24 February 2013).

8 The 2003 energy white paper accepted the recommendation of the Royal Commission on Environmental Pollution (RCEP) of carbon-reduction strategies by government, stating in its introduction that 'climate change is real' (DTI, 2003: 6).

9 The institutional status of the SDC changed in 2006 when it became a non-departmental executive public body and took on the role of government watchdog.

10 In general terms, climate scientists define radiative forcing as the difference between radiant energy received by the earth and energy re-radiated to space. See Carbon Offset Research and Education programme, introduction to radiative forcing, at http://www.co2offsetresearch.org/aviation/RF.html (accessed 3 January 2013).

11 The universities in the consortium were East Anglia, Manchester, Southampton, Oxford, Newcastle and Sussex. The three research councils were the Natural Environment Research Council, the Economic and Social Research Council and the Engineering and Physical Sciences Research Council. For further details, see www.tyndall.ac.uk (accessed 24 February 2013).

12 However, this stand-alone scenario projected aviation growth at lower levels than those experienced at the time of writing in 2004 and 2005.

13 DfT press release 2005/0067, 20 June 2005, www.dft.gov.uk (accessed 28 June 2005).

14 SSE, opening statement to the public inquiry into expansion plans at Stansted airport, 30 May 2007, p. 10, www.stopstanstedexpansion.com/press277.html (accessed 19 August 2011).

15 Camp for Climate Action, www.climatecamp.org.uk (accessed 28 August 2007).

16 Response to injunction, www.climatecamp.org.uk/injunction.php (accessed 28 August 2007).

17 See www.climatecamp.org.uk (accessed 28 August 2007).

18 Camp for Climate Action press release, 6 August 2007, www.climatecamp.org.uk/pr6-8.php (accessed 28 August 2007); see also *Guardian*, 2 August 2007.

19 Response to injunction, www.climatecamp.org.uk/injunction.php; www.climatecamp.org.uk/views (accessed 28 August 2007).

20 See www.climatecamp.org.uk/views.php (accessed 28 August 2007).

21 Response to injunction, www.climatecamp.org.uk/injunction.php (accessed 28 August 2007).

22 The House of Commons Transport Select Committee (2007) published its own critical conclusions on the declining quality of passenger experience at UK airports.

23 *Financial Times*, 30 July 2007; *Telegraph*, 31 July 2007; *Guardian*, 31 July 2007; www.bbc.co.uk/news (accessed 1 August 2007).
24 House of Commons Transport Select Committee, *The Future of BAA*, 28 November 2007, Evidence Heard in Public Questions 146-342, uncorrected transcript, http://www.publications.parliament.uk/pa/cm200708/cmselect/cmtran/uc119-ii/uc11902.htm (accessed 5 January 2013).

7

The third runway at Heathrow

185 million people to die in Africa this century alone because of climate change and people are still hopping over to Barcelona for the weekend and saying 'Sorry, it's part of our way of life'. (Joss Garman, Plane Stupid, on *Newsnight*, BBC television, 17 October 2006)

First, some of the large proportion of aviation growth represented by short-haul fights can feasibly be transferred to rail. Second, unconstrained growth in short-haul aviation is creating air-dependent lifestyles and increasing the UK's tourism deficit. Third, limiting aviation growth is unlikely to price poorer people off planes. Finally, short-haul dominated demand growth can be constrained without damaging the business and long-haul leisure markets of most benefit to the economy. (Conservative Party's *Blueprint for a Green Economy* – Quality of Life Policy Group, 2007: 357)

Britain's economy was built on shipping, which carried manufactured goods to every corner of the globe and brought raw materials from all over the world to be processed in the UK. Today, Britain exports services and high-value manufactured goods to pay for the import of essential raw materials and goods that other countries can produce at lower cost. Britain will have to continue to do this in an increasingly competitive and globalised market to sustain GDP growth. Without GDP growth Britain would face lower earnings, a higher risk of unemployment, and less funding for public services. (BAA, 2008: 11)

Despite the growing furore about its 2003 air transport white paper (ATWP) and the shifting terrains of argumentation that framed the aviation debate, the Labour government remained publicly wedded to its plans for airport expansion. And while plans to expand Stansted airport continued unabated, the construction of a sixth terminal and a third runway at Heathrow remained the preferred option for much of the industry and for the Labour government. Towards the end of 2006, the ATWP progress report claimed that investing in Heathrow would offer 'a higher economic value than at any other UK airport', with a third runway 'worth £5 billion' (DfT, 2006a: 45–6). Indeed, support for a third runway at Heathrow arguably increased in the Cabinet with Tony Blair's resignation in June 2007, following a negotiated transfer of power to Gordon Brown, who was a persistent supporter of expansion at the international hub airport. The long-serving Labour Chancellor had supported further expansion of Heathrow in his 2005 and 2006 pre-budget reports. He had lobbied forcefully against Blair during the formulation of the 2003 ATWP for expansion at Heathrow rather than Stansted (*East Anglian Daily Times*, 25 October 2003). Importantly, Brown's unqualified public support for expansion was to continue, even as the New Labour political project began to collapse in the polls and as short-term capacity constraints on UK airports eased in the aftermath of the 2008 banking crisis and the subsequent global economic downturn. With falling economic growth, and rising oil prices and costs for carriers, passenger numbers through UK airports actually declined by almost 2 per cent in 2008 compared with 2007. This was the first fall in passenger numbers since 1991. It was followed in 2009 by a fall of over 7 per cent, the largest fall for some sixty-five years and the first ever consecutive fall in passenger numbers across two years.[1]

In this chapter we explore the struggles over the proposals to build a sixth terminal and a third runway at Heathrow airport. The Labour government finally approved expansion at Heathrow in January 2009. But this decision provoked widespread condemnation, exposed splits in the Cabinet and triggered another high-profile protest campaign against expansion by local residents, environmental and conservation lobbies, direct action environmentalists, as well as celebrities and even members of the government's own parliamentary majority. In fact, within days of Labour being ousted from office in the May 2010 general election, the incoming Conservative–Liberal Democrat coalition government placed a moratorium on new runways in the south-east, thus reversing the decision to expand both Heathrow and Stansted and effectively consigning to history the strategic plan for the future of UK aviation that was the 2003 ATWP (although New Labour had promised in its manifesto not to give the go-ahead for a new runway at Stansted during the next Parliament). The foundations for this policy reversal, we argue, had been laid much earlier with the formation of a climate change discourse coalition against aviation expansion; the tactical diversification of anti-airport protests; the provision by HACAN ClearSkies and AirportWatch of the 'ideological cover' for the Conservatives and Liberal Democrats to oppose expansion; and the failure of the Labour government and the leaders of the pro-aviation expansion discourse coalition to respond to the shifting context of aviation policy and the cultural resignification of air travel.

In analysing this complex set of events, we focus in particular upon the campaign of local residents and environmentalists against expansion, critically accounting for how, in the domain of aviation policy, the perpetual 'losers' became 'winners'. We first examine the coming together of a broad climate change coalition against expansion at Heathrow airport, exploring how AirportWatch and HACAN ClearSkies engineered a transformative campaign which equated anti-airport struggles to opposition to air travel *and* to climate change. Equally, we analyse how the campaign against airport expansion diversified its strategies and tactics, and linked together local resident campaigns, communities and direct action protests, in particular activists in Plane Stupid, who exploited new high-profile media-friendly campaigning tactics. We then investigate the work of HACAN ClearSkies and others to influence the changing politics of the Conservative Party, which was to reject expansion at Heathrow (and Stansted) in 2008, while endorsing the policy alternative to short-haul flights of high-speed rail. Here we argue that AirportWatch and HACAN ClearSkies provided ideological cover for the Conservatives and Liberal Democrats, negating economic arguments in favour of aviation expansion and making visible new dimensions of conflict.

Against this background, we examine in greater detail the dynamics of the consultation and decision-making processes surrounding the third runway and sixth terminal at Heathrow. We explore the political and ideological practices through which the Brown government endeavoured to displace contestation to expansion, as well as underlining the vain attempts of the expansionist lobby to continue to provide ideological cover for government. In so doing, we demonstrate how the changing strategies of the anti-expansion movement provoked the collapse of political support for air travel in sections of the Labour Party and parts of the core executive. In conclusion, we suggest that the resignification of air travel as a 'problem' of climate change cut across traditional alliances. In our terms, it was a heresthetic moment *par excellence,* in which campaigners provoked new cleavages and fractures in the pro-expansion discourse coalition and structured the decision over the third runway at Heathrow in a way that compelled previous supporters of expansion to oppose it (Riker, 1996: 9).

Building the climate change coalition and the politics of Plane Stupid

Public declarations of support for expansion at Heathrow by the Labour government through 2005 and 2006 triggered intermittent skirmishes between supporters and opponents of the third runway. John Stewart, chair of HACAN ClearSkies, thus met the publication of the ATWP progress report with the threat of a major political showdown should government give the go-ahead for expansion (*Guardian*, 15 December 2006). During this 'phoney war' before the opening of consultation on the third runway and sixth terminal, campaigners brought together a loose coalition against expansion, including local residents and local authorities, MPs, environmental and conservation lobbies, direct action environmental groups, anti-capitalist activists, global justice movements and high-profile celebrities (see box 7.1). Indeed, as it progressed, the campaign gave birth to loose umbrella groups, such as Stop Heathrow Expansion, which was created in October 2007, as well as to new direct action groups, such as the women's groups WeCan and the Climate Suffragettes (Stewart, 2010).

Yet in contrast to the 2003 consultation process, in which HACAN ClearSkies and AirportWatch linked individual airport struggles together in a broad anti-airport struggle, the more universal demand

---

Box 7.1 Organisations and people supporting the campaign against the third runway at Heathrow (Stewart, 2010: 19)

HACAN ClearSkies; NoTRAG; 2M; Greenpeace; World Wide Fund for Nature; National Trust; Campaign Against Climate Change; Plane Stupid; Royal Society for the Protection of Birds; Campaign to Protect Rural England; AirportWatch; Campaign for Better Transport; Aviation Environment Federation; West London Friends of the Earth; Enough's Enough; Society for the Protection of Ancient Buildings; Rising Tide; Alistair McGowan; Emma Thompson.

voiced by this anti-Heathrow coalition was for action against growing carbon emissions from aviation and their impact on climate change. The repeated claims by scientists and policy experts about aviation's peculiarly destructive and growing impact in terms of climate change had restructured the policy discourse in aviation. At the same time, as they had started to do in 2003, protesters also constructed equivalences between opposition to aviation and opposition to climate change, thus extending the chain of demands beyond noise and air pollution to claims and grievances about the consequences of air travel's impact on the planet's climate. Put differently, the leadership of the anti-expansion campaigns established a series of resonances and connections between the struggle against Heathrow expansion and the struggle against climate change. These overdetermined demands also exposed new fault lines in the pro-expansion coalition, with the universal demand to address climate change dividing elements of the business community and also amplifying potential lines of antagonism between trade unions representing the rail and aviation industries.

Attempts to cement this emerging coalition gathered momentum as the campaign against Heathrow expansion increasingly became the *cause célèbre* for the environmental movement, local MPs and even 'Tory Swampys' (*Observer*, 1 January 2006). Its strategies and tactics began to surface at the Stansted public inquiry in July 2007, when, for example, Aqqaluk Lynge, an Inuit leader from Greenland, spoke as a witness for Stop Stansted Expansion on the impact of climate change on traditional ways of living. He concluded his statement by calling for an end to airport expansion in the UK and elsewhere (Stop Stansted Expansion press release, 21 July 2007). Similarly, as discussed in the previous chapter, the Camp for Climate Action took place at Heathrow in August 2007, when aviation was explicitly connected to the problem of climate change. The growing linkages between climate change and aviation also brought Greenpeace and Friends of the Earth (FoE) into the battle to stop expansion. FoE was perceived to have lessened its involvement in aviation campaigning after the 1997 protests against the second runway at Manchester airport. As with Greenpeace, however, the campaign against expansion at Heathrow brought FoE back into the fray to invest resources into what became a symbolic battle against productivism and climate change (interview with environmental campaigner).

Typical of this new climate change discourse coalition was the launch of Plane Stupid, which was a non-violent and non-hierarchical direct action grassroots network of activists against aviation expansion. Its launch established a new front in the fight against aviation expansion and climate change, and the network hit the headlines in 2006 after a number of high-profile media actions. These stunts included: a memorial for the victims of climate change on a runway at East Midlands airport; occupying easyJet's offices in protest at short-haul flights; and activists chaining themselves to the doors of the offices of the British Airports Authority (BAA).[2] In its demands for an end to short-haul flights, it derided what it coined the pathology of 'binge flying' (*Guardian*, 25 May 2007), as well as aviation's impact on the environment and social justice. Aviation was declared to be 'mostly unnecessary', while 'diverting money away from public services' and offering 'cheap' flights was denounced as a 'perk for the rich'.[3] Its public discourse often employed populist rhetoric which condemned Labour as a failing and biased government, while invoking war-like metaphors to describe future protests:

> The lines are drawn. The government is showing a blatant disregard over the dangers of climate change by flying in the face of the scientists' warnings, and pushing ahead with plans for airport expansion. Aviation is the fastest growing cause of climate change and they won't succeed without a fight. Let the battle commence.[4]

When Plane Stupid activists chained themselves to the doors of BAA's offices, one of their spokespersons derided tax concessions of £9 billion to aviation, questioned the need for those 45 per cent of flights in Europe that were less than 500 km and dismissed emissions trading schemes, unless they were tied to a kerosene tax and VAT on aviation transactions. The threat of the third runway to the village of Sipson outside Heathrow was described as representing 'one of the biggest forced dispersals of people in the UK since the Highland Clearances', while it was claimed that the plans for expansion would 'also lead to the destruction of communities throughout Africa, Asia and even Europe, as the world begins to feel the full consequences of climate change'.[5]

Plane Stupid's discourse chimed with much of the rhetoric of the Camp for Climate Action, as its activists distanced themselves from traditional forms of lobbying, and even raised question marks about the conventional forms of campaigning pursued by AirportWatch, which comprised mostly petitions or legal challenges.[6] Instead, its supporters engaged in high-profile actions that could capture the attention of the mainstream media. It thus strengthened the media strategy of the coalition, which was also reinforced by national environmental lobbies like Greenpeace, with its professional media expertise and broader experience of radical campaigning (Stewart, 2010: 19). HACAN ClearSkies, for its part, went as far as to employ professional lobbyists and to publish advertisements in the national press, which were funded by Enough's Enough, the environmental network.

In the media, Plane Stupid quickly became associated with a group of young university graduate environmentalists, who included not only its founders, Joss Garman, Richard George and Graham Thompson, but also Leo Murray, Tamsin Omond and Olivia Chessell.[7] The public face of the network sparked further media interest in its actions, with one commentator arguing that the fact 'that they are young, attractive and, in some cases, Oxbridge-educated … may stimulate media curiosity' (*Guardian*, 1 March 2007). At the very least, the particular identities and backgrounds of these activists facilitated the forging of alliances with local residents (interview with local campaigner). John Stewart, chair of HACAN ClearSkies, endeavoured to bring together local residents with wider environmental lobbies and a new generation of direct action environmental activists, who were generally under thirty years old and for whom 'climate change was the big concern' (Stewart, 2010: 9). It was Stewart who invited Plane Stupid activists to share platforms at meetings organised by HACAN ClearSkies (interview with local campaigner) and who organised direct action training sessions, which served in part to radicalise the tactics and strategies of local residents at Heathrow (*Guardian*, 8 March 2007; McFlynn and Gordon-Farleigh, 2011). In February 2007, Dr John Hunt, a Hounslow resident, unfurled a 'No Third Runway' banner on the stage during a speech by Transport Secretary Douglas Alexander to the aviation industry. Hunt was reported as saying that

> we're glad to be joined by our eco-warrior friends from Plane Stupid…. They've done this kind of thing before and have been helpful with their direct action training over recent weeks. I think it's safe to say there's more of this to come.[8]

Thus, the fight against global warming served primarily to weave together particularistic demands against the third runway at Heathrow with more universal demands against national airport expansion and air travel, as well as for concerted action by government against climate change. Stewart aptly expressed this emerging concatenation of demands against expansion when he argued that the challenge against the third runway would

> come not just from residents, but from the broadest and biggest coali-
> tion ever assembled against airport expansion in this country: all the
> local councils, virtually every MP in the area, the mayor of London, the
> London assembly, leading environmental organisations such as Green-
> peace and the National Trust, as well as the direct action movement.
> (*Guardian*, 26 November 2007)

The presence of Plane Stupid and Greenpeace in the campaign sharpened the media focus of the protest, while forging networks with a new generation of climate change activists. Moreover, it is worth noting that, in many respects, this nascent discourse coalition copied the politics of the anti-roads movement, a movement in which Stewart was intimately involved during the 1980s and 1990s. It was not coincidental that Plane Stupid itself was established in November 2005 by Garman, George and Thompson following informal meetings with Stewart, who, with Garman, held a Plane Stupid workshop at the 2006 Climate Camp at the Drax power station (Stewart, 2010: 26).

Of course, this alliance was not without its tensions, for its leaders, not least Stewart, had to balance the demands of local residents in HACAN ClearSkies (who were mainly concerned about protection against local noise impacts) with those of local authority supporters such as 2M, who announced themselves 'not against Heathrow' (i.e. they positioned themselves against a third runway, but not the airport itself) and the supporters of Plane Stupid, who called for an end to all short-haul flights. To manage potential tensions, the emerging coalition was kept 'loose' and not convened as a new organisation; it was held together by its members supporting a set of general principles against airport expansion. There was no single spokes-person for the campaign and regular meetings were ensured through the use of email and internet (including Facebook) (interview with prominent campaigner). In fact, because the broad membership of HACAN ClearSkies was reluctant to engage in direct action tactics and protests, there was an emergent division of labour within the campaign, whereby another residents' organisation – NoTRAG (No Third Runway Action Group) – embraced a more public role than HACAN ClearSkies.

NoTRAG was created in 2002 as a local resident group working in defence of the communities threatened by expansion at Heathrow:

the towns and villages of Sipson, Harmondsworth, Harlington and West Drayton. Following the publication of BAA's interim plan for Heathrow in June 2005 (BAA, 2005), and the election as chair of Geraldine Nicholson, NoTRAG 'really sprang to life' (Stewart, 2010: 20). Its largely female leadership and activists became, for John Stewart, the public face of much of the protest campaign: telling 'stories of real people' affected by the planned expansion; addressing party conferences and appearing on television; and protesting alongside direct action campaigners. In contrast, the membership of HACAN ClearSkies appeared to take a more backseat role, broadly playing the role of the organisational 'hub' and coordinator of the coalition, while providing core networking functions as one of only two organisations involved in the campaign with a specific focus on Heathrow (the other being NoTRAG) (Stewart, 2010: 20–5). HACAN ClearSkies continued therefore to build political support against expansion within cross-party networks, which mobilised those MPs whose constituencies were affected by Heathrow expansion (Stewart, 2010: 33; interview with environmental campaigner). In short, for this anti-expansion climate change discourse coalition, the guiding principle was, according to one prominent campaigner in interview, 'unity of purpose, diversity of tactics' (see also Stewart, 2010: 27).

Building cross-party networks: shifting thinking within the Conservative Party

In its role as an organisational hub, HACAN ClearSkies acted as the secretariat for a cross-party parliamentary group against Heathrow expansion, which was chaired by the Labour MP for Hayes and Harlington, John McDonnell.[9] Local MPs, such as McDonnell, as well as Justine Greening, Conservative MP for Putney, and Susan Kramer, Liberal Democrat MP for Richmond Park, were to play very public roles in the 'no' campaign. HACAN ClearSkies and its campaigners looked to exploit political networks, lobbying local elected representatives, including the mayor of London and the London Assembly. As it turned out, the main candidates for the London mayoral election all came out against expansion in January 2008. In a rare show of unity, they all featured in an advertisement against the third runway, published in the *London Evening Standard*, *Guardian*, *Independent* and *Times*, and funded by Greenpeace, AirportWatch and Enough's Enough.[10] NoTRAG's chair, Geraldine Nicholson, also networked with local authorities, as did supportive local councillors such as Ruth Cadbury, deputy leader of the Labour group in Hounslow Council. As the campaign developed, over twenty-six local authorities were ultimately to join the campaign (Stewart, 2010: 18).

In seeking to provide ideological cover for politicians and parties opposed to the runway, HACAN ClearSkies took upon itself the task of promoting high-speed rail as an alternative to short-haul flights. For example, in June 2007, HACAN ClearSkies and NoTRAG staged a race between Eurostar and plane from London to Paris to demonstrate how trains could effectively substitute for short-haul flights on many European routes.[11] In November 2006, HACAN ClearSkies had published a pamphlet on the benefits of rail over aviation. Entitled *Short-Haul Flights: Clogging Up Heathrow's Runways*, the HACAN ClearSkies study claimed that over 100,000 short-haul flights could potentially be cut at Heathrow by switching from air to rail, thereby lowering the number of flights at the airport to 'below the levels they were 10 years ago' (HACAN ClearSkies, 2006: 1). The authors of the pamphlet also took the opportunity to point out that Heathrow's top destination was Paris, followed by Amsterdam and Dublin, and that apart from New York all the popular destinations at Heathrow were European. Thus the switch to rail, it was argued, made plans for the third runway and the ending of runway alternation 'increasingly irrelevant' (HACAN ClearSkies, 2006: 1). By calling for rail instead of air travel, HACAN ClearSkies offered opponents to expansion a requisite 'solution' to airport capacity limitations, but it also made visible new potential conflicts within the trade union movement, not least between the rail unions and other manufacturing unions. Significantly, the RMT, the rail workers' trade union, was subsequently to commission from John Stewart a report into the capacity of high-speed rail as a substitute for short-haul flights (RMT, 2008).

In lobbying political parties, the campaign leadership focused on the Conservative Party, which, under the leadership of David Cameron, had begun to review its environmental policy commitments (Bale, 2010; Connelly, 2009; King, 2011). In a high-profile media stunt, Cameron was photographed in 2006 on a sledge in the Arctic, putting environmental action at the core of the rebranding of the Conservative Party as 'modern' and 'compasssionate'.[12] Earlier, in December 2005, as part of this policy review, the Conservative leader had established the Quality of Life Policy Group, which was chaired by John Gummer, the former Conservative Environment Minister. It was given the task of setting out policy proposals to address the implications of climate change and social unease across a range of sectors, including transport (Quality of Life Policy Group, 2007: 3). HACAN ClearSkies and the ranks of AirportWatch had established networks with individuals on this Conservative internal policy review committee. Its vice-chair was Zac Goldsmith, editor of the *Ecologist* magazine, who, as well as being close to Cameron, had organised a charity cricket match in support of HACAN ClearSkies (Stewart, 2010: 25). Equally, the transport committee of the Policy Group was chaired by Stephen Norris, the former Conservative Transport Minister, who opposed a third runway at Heathrow, and whom Stewart 'had known in the 1990s and liked'. As it turned out, the transport committee within the Quality of Life Policy Group was to consult members of Airport-Watch as part of its aviation subgroup, including Brendon Sewill (GACC), Tim Johnson (AEF) and John Stewart (HACAN ClearSkies) (Stewart, 2010: 29; Sewill, 2012: 98).

By the summer of 2007, leaks to the media indicated that the Quality of Life Policy Group would ultimately recommend the rejection of new runways at Heathrow and Stansted in favour of high-speed rail routes (*Observer*, 1 July 2007). Its final report, *Blueprint for a Green Economy*, subsequently endorsed much of the platform of AirportWatch, coming out in support of demand management over technological fixes in aviation (Quality of Life Policy Group, 2007: 351).[13] It thus proposed 'a hold on all plans for further airport expansion in the UK' (p. 356). Characterising aviation as a 'uniquely greenhouse-gas-intensive mode of transport' (p. 350), it made frequent mention of the threat posed by the creation of 'air-dependent lifestyles that are highly carbon intensive' (pp. 308, 351, 357), while deriding the environmental consequences of Labour's 'predict and provide' aviation policies (pp. 13, 355, 423). The Conservative Party report also reiterated attacks on the contradictions of the 2003 white paper, arguing that it 'has often seemed that Britain has had two governments – one committed to preventing climate change, and one committed to causing it' (p. 13), while recycling claims that 'the Government's policy of actively encouraging aviation growth [was] at odds with the UK's commitment to tackle climate change' (p. 351). Explicitly alluding to the demands and arguments of the Sustainable Development Commission, the House of Commons Environmental Audit Committee (EAC) and AirportWatch, the Policy Group called for government to take the lead in addressing rising carbon emissions from aviation. Going further, its authors ultimately called upon a future Conservative government to manage proactively competing demands for air transport and moves towards sustainability (pp. 14, 352, 430). Finally, it recognised the limits of the market, which, it deemed, 'must be our servant and not our master' (p. 58).

Importantly, the Policy Group challenged the twin pillars of the post-war hegemonic policy of aviation expansion, with its sedimented narratives about the economic and social benefits of aviation. First, along with AirportWatch and others, it contested the economic benefits of aviation growth by claiming that rising demand was fuelled by growth in short-haul leisure flights by UK passengers, with 'much slower' growth in business and long-haul flights. It suggested that this rising demand was 'the wrong sort of growth' for the UK economy, as short-haul flights 'exacerbate the country's tourism deficit ... which already stands at around £15 billion' (p. 355). Challenging the 'special status' of aviation, the Policy Group reiterated claims that aviation was 'lightly taxed compared to other industries and private modes of transport' (p. 351), drawing attention to tax exemptions on aircraft fuel (fuel duty) and air tickets (VAT), which, it argued, 'reduc[ed] Treasury revenues by around £9 billion a year'. Indeed, the Policy Group dismissed these tax exemptions as

> indirect subsidies [which] flatter the economic case for airport expansion and stoke demand growth.... Such preferential treatment is not warranted in a mature sector. (Quality of Life Policy Group, 2007: 351)

Secondly, the Policy Group challenged those populist appeals that constructed air travel as a social benefit or contributor to social progress. Notably, it disputed industry claims that a policy of demand management, which would be achieved through increased taxation, should be dismissed as socially regressive, thus reproducing arguments made by AirportWatch that any additional airport capacity would be accessed by 'wealthier frequent flyers' on short-haul leisure flights, while 'half of the population do not fly in any one year' (Quality of Life Policy Group, 2007: 356). The Group equally foregrounded the lack of social equity in offsetting rising emissions in aviation against disproportionate compensatory cuts in other industries (as did the Tyndall Centre) (p. 351). It drew attention to the potential social injustice associated with compensatory cuts and questioned the fairness of cuts in other industries if and when, for example, 'aviation emissions were to drive up the prices of heating millions of homes' (p. 353).

In contesting these twin pillars of aviation expansion, and in support of demand management measures in aviation, the Policy Group produced a panoply of policy proposals, including: the imposition of rigorous caps on aviation within the European Union emissions trading scheme (EU ETS); acknowledgement of aviation's non-CO_2 impacts on global warming; the incorporation of international aviation emissions into national emissions inventories; accredited offset schemes and the replacement of air passenger duty by a per-flight duty for both passenger and freight aircraft. The Policy Group also called for strategies at airports to minimise aircraft ground movements and to promote low-carbon technologies, while also considering the introduction of fuel duty and taxes on domestic flights (through levying VAT on tickets for domestic air flights) (pp. 351–7). Significantly, it restated its call for a moratorium on airport expansion as a market response to 'capacity overload', as it would lead to slot reallocation at airports away from short-haul to long-haul flights – those 'part[s] of the markets that value them most' – and would thereby negate the 'need to expand airports in the way the Government proposes' (p. 355). Underpinning such arguments was the broader commitment to replace short-haul flights with high-speed rail, both for its environmental benefits and for its easing of capacity constraints at Heathrow. Reasserting the claims of HACAN ClearSkies in its 2006 study into rail substitution, the Policy Group argued that flights to Paris, Manchester and Brussels could be substituted by high-speed rail and it suggested that '100 000 flights from Heathrow could be cut and replaced by rail to 10 destinations' (p. 430).

In its framing of aviation policy, the Policy Group thus reiterated the fundamental demands, environmental rhetoric and argumentative logics of the climate change coalition. In so doing, it drew directly upon the reports by HACAN ClearSkies, the Tyndall Centre, the Aviation Environment Federation, the EAC, the Environmental Change Institute, the Sustainable Development Commission and the Institute for Public Policy Research (see box 7.2). For example, as we demonstrate above, the Policy Group took up the arguments put forward by HACAN ClearSkies in 2006 about the possibility of rail replacing short-haul flights. It rearticulated the EAC's concerns on the processes by which air transport would be incorporated into the EU ETS (pp. 352–3). And it even cited the work of Brendon Sewill, who was the chair of the anti-airport expansion Gatwick Area Conservation Campaign (GACC), and whose 2003 report, *The Hidden Cost of*

Box 7.2 Anti-airport expansion reports cited by the Conservative Quality of Life Policy Group (2007)

- Tyndall Centre for Climate Change Research (2005b), *Growth Scenarios for EU and UK Aviation: Contradictions with Climate Policy*, report for Friends of the Earth
- Sewill (2003), *The Hidden Cost of Flying* (Aviation Environment Federation)
- Sewill (2005), *Fly Now, Grieve Later: How to Reduce the Impact of Air Travel on Climate Change* (Aviation Environment Federation)
- RCEP (Royal Commission on Environmental Pollution) (2002), *The Environmental Effects of Civil Aircraft in Flight*
- Institute for Public Policy Research (2003), *The Sky's the Limit: Policies for Sustainable Aviation*
- HACAN ClearSkies (2006), *Short-Haul Flights: Clogging Up Heathrow's Runways*
- Environmental Change Institute (2006), *Predict and Decide: Aviation, Climate Change and UK Policy* (University of Oxford)
- IPSOS-MORI (2006), *Climate Change and Taxing Air Travel* (poll for the Airfields Environment Trust)

Flying, had informed the position of local residents and protesters against expansion in the 2003 ATWP consultation. Sewill's intervention, skilfully set alongside reports from the AEF, the EAC, the Tyndall Centre and others, was used by the Conservative Party in its consultation document *Greener Skies*, which it published in March 2007. The report set out the party's emerging principles on the reform of aviation taxation (Conservative Party, 2007a; see also Sewill, 2012: 98).

In short, therefore, the resignification of aviation as a threat to the environment through climate change, itself a product of the coordinated attacks on the ATWP by scientific bodies and scrutiny commissions, made possible the conditions for the broadening of the campaign against airport expansion. Leading political entrepreneurs such as John Stewart drew equivalences between the fight against expansion at Heathrow and the fight against global warming, thus inserting air travel and the aviation industry into a horrific narrative in which climate change was portrayed as a growing emissions problem and obstacle to action. This widening of the coalition against airport expansion brought about the emergence of new actors, such as Plane Stupid, while pulling groups like Greenpeace and FoE firmly back into the aviation fray. The entry of these new groups and actors reinforced the armoury of AirportWatch and HACAN ClearSkies, especially their capacity to embrace new media strategies and to generate high-profile direct action media events. At the same time, HACAN ClearSkies and AirportWatch activists, who adroitly exploited the shifts in the Conservative Party following the election of David Cameron as its leader, started to provide ideological cover for the Conservatives to oppose airport expansion. Their reports and statements, as well those of reputable scientific and scrutiny bodies, furnished the opposition to New Labour's proposals with knowledge and rhetorical arguments to negate the case for aviation expansion. The electoral appeal of an anti-expansion stance in key marginal seats in and across west London strengthened the emergent opposition to the third runway within the ranks of the Conservative Party leadership.[14] How, then, did the Labour government and the aviation industry seek to manage these challenges and potential contradictions? We shall now explore this question by examining the politics of the consultation over the third runway at Heathrow.

Preparing for take-off

It will be recalled that the ATWP had deferred the construction of a third runway at the London international hub until 2015–20. The project was to go ahead only after the expansion of Stansted, and after investigations by the Department for Transport (DfT), in conjunction with BAA and other relevant stakeholders, into how expansion could meet a series of environmental conditions, notably EU air quality limits on NO_2 levels in the atmosphere, noise pollution controls and improved public transport provision to the airport. These investigations duly opened in early 2004, when the DfT established the Project for the Sustainable Development of Heathrow (PSDH), which consisted of a set of working groups designed to evaluate the projected environmental impact of a third runway at the airport. The working groups for the PSDH brought together BAA, National Air Traffic Services (NATS), the Civil Aviation Authority (CAA), DfT Rail, the Highways Agency and external scientific experts. The Aviation Environmental Division of the DfT was given the role of coordinating three technical panels of air-quality experts and academics, which were lauded by the DfT for their 'balanced membership' and methods of 'independent peer review', as well as the involvement of 'representatives from recognised best practice working groups' (DfT, 2007a: 2–3). But it is striking that this initiative did not include representatives from local communities or environmental lobbies. On the contrary, the PSDH was an initial attempt to anchor the decision over Heathrow within the technical and scientific realms, rather than the political domain, thus legitimising the processes of decision-making through the mobilisation of, and appeal to, scientific discourse.

Formal public consultation on the expansion of Heathrow opened on 22 November 2007, only to close on 27 February 2008. The consultation proposed a new runway at 2,200 m operational length, a sixth passenger terminal, which would require additional land, and the loss of approximately 700 properties, including the village of Sipson. The building of the runway, it was estimated, would increase the capacity of the airport to around 605,000 air traffic movements a year from 2020 onwards, and 702,000 or around 122 million passengers a year in 2030. The consultation also brought forward plans in the short term for mixed-mode operations on existing runways (to cease once the third runway was built), changes to easterly departures off the northern runway and the westerly preference for operations at the airport, as well as the ending of runway alternation at night and early morning (DfT, 2007b). The proposal of a longer than previously planned runway was justified by the DfT on the grounds that it would enable mixed-mode operations of short- and long-haul flights by carriers' strategic alliances (DfT, 2007b: 44). Indeed, the shifting market strategies of carriers were more than once put forward as a rationale for expansion at Heathrow. In March 2007, some seven months before the opening of consultation, the signing of the first stage of the 'open skies' agreement between the EU and the US, which permitted all EU carriers to operate routes to the US, had reportedly raised fears within the DfT of carriers switching their capacity from internal UK routes to higher-revenue US routes, thus impacting negatively upon regional economies. For example, one government official was reported as arguing:

> You will begin to see a pattern of carriers squeezing out regional links from Heathrow. The transport white paper flagged the economic benefits of a third runway at Heathrow and the open skies deal underlines

the importance of increasing the capacity there, particularly if we are going to keep links between London and the regions. (*Observer*, 25 March 2007)

The run-up to the opening of the consultation was marked by a heightening of public demonstrations and direct action protests. In early November 2007, anti-runway groups released a film of local Heathrow residents and green campaigners setting out their opposition to the expansion of Heathrow – the film was screened during a month-long tour, accompanied by 'voices blaring out through loudspeakers' (*Guardian*, 8 November 2007). John McDonnell MP, whose Hayes and Harlington constituency included the airport, condemned the plans as an 'absolute betrayal', arguing that the commitment to expansion relegated the 'green' claims made by Prime Minister Gordon Brown to 'spin'. FoE echoed such concerns that Heathrow expansion would threaten commitments to reduce carbon emissions, and Theresa Villiers, the Conservative shadow Transport Secretary, said: 'in a week when Gordon Brown tried to shore up his green credentials by talking about 80% cuts in emissions, [the Secretary of State for Transport] has got some very tough questions to answer about Heathrow expansion' (*Guardian*, 22 November 2007).

As with the 2003 consultation process, however, pro-aviation lobbies once again began to position themselves to place demands on government to maintain its commitment to expansion. The construction of a third runway at Heathrow generated, as to be expected, support from major carriers (British Airways and Virgin Atlantic), airport operators, pro-business lobbies such as the Confederation of British Industry (CBI) and London First (which, in its own words, is an organisation that 'supports London's global competitiveness'), tourist operators, hoteliers, aircraft manufacturers, trade unions and even Kenyan organic farmers (if not Inuit leaders) (see box 7.3).

Future Heathrow, an industry-based expansionist lobby, of which BAA was a founding member, was formed in early 2005, just before the launch of BAA's interim plan for Heathrow. Its logo encapsulated its mission of 'supporting sustainable growth' and it characterised its role as one of voicing the 'wider public support', which 'is often overlooked because of the highly vocal minority which opposes the airport' (Future Heathrow, 2008: 9). Typically, its campaign director, Clive Soley, a Labour peer and former MP for Acton and Shepherd's Bush, strenuously called on government to approve expansion and to act on its 2003 commitments. He declared that 'doing nothing is

Box 7.3 The collective membership of Future Heathrow and Flying Matters[a]

ABTA (the Association of British Travel Agents, now the Travel Association); African Organic Farming Foundation; Airbus; Airport Operators Association (AOA); Air Transport Action Group; Air Transport Users Council; Amicus section of the UNITE trade union; Association of Corporate Travel Executives; Baltic Air Charter Association; Board of Airline Representatives in the UK; Blue Skies Holdings; Boeing; British Airline Pilots Association; British Airports Authority (BAA); British Air Transport Association (BATA); British Airways (BA); British Business and General Aviation Association; British International Freight Organisation; British Midland International (BMI); Confederation of British Industry (CBI); DHL; easyJet; Emirates; Farmers Own; Federation of Tour Operators; Flybe; Fresh Produce Consortium; GMB trade union; Guild of Travel Management Companies; Kenya Organic Agriculture Network; International Air Transport Association (IATA); London Chamber of Commerce and Industry; London First; London Heathrow Airline Operators Committee; Macquarie; Manchester Airport Group; Monarch Airlines; National Air Traffic Services; Prospect; QinetiQ; Rolls-Royce; Scottish Passenger Agents' Association; Society of British Aerospace Companies (SBAC); T&G Workers section of UNITE trade union; Thames Valley Economic Partnership; Thomas Cook; Tourism Alliance; Trades Union Congress (TUC); Transport and General Workers' Union (TGWU); TUI travel and tourism company; Virgin Atlantic Airways; West London Business; XL Airways.

[a] This listing includes membership of Flying Matters in July 2008 and that of Future Heathrow at its launch on 23 May 2005.

emphatically not an option. Heathrow can either grow or London and the UK will be worse off' (Future Heathrow, 2008: 9–10). He had earlier suggested that 'no one will thank us for ducking difficult decisions now if we store up greater problems for the future'.[15] In a press release that focused on the employment concerns of the trade union Amicus over the future of Heathrow, Soley amplified the threats of economic competition to Heathrow's international position, which fitted the dominant fantasmatic narrative on UK aviation, when he likened the potential collapse of the airport in the absence of expansion to the collapse of the London docklands and that of manufacturing industry across the UK (Future Heathrow press release, 28 November 2005). This analogy was regurgitated in other arenas, notably by Willie Walsh, chief executive of British Airways (BA), in his 2006 speech to the Royal Aeronautical Society (*London Evening Standard*, 13 November 2006).

The launch of Future Heathrow was followed in June 2007 by the formation of Flying Matters, a broad pro-aviation coalition which positioned itself as a successor to Freedom to Fly. Flying Matters was chaired by Brian Wilson, the former Labour Minister for Trade and Energy, after its first chair, Sir Digby Jones, the former head of the CBI, resigned shortly after its launch, to join the Labour government. In the wake of the ATWP, the decision had been taken to curtail Freedom to Fly's strategic and media operations, though this move was not universally supported by all its members. In the words of one leading aviation representative: 'me, I didn't want it stopped … big mistake' (interview with aviation representative). In fact, for some time after the closing down of Freedom to Fly, proponents of expansion ceded vital rhetorical and discursive ground to the emerging climate change coalition. With the formation of their new organisation they did eventually acknowledge that winning the battle over the ATWP did not mean they had won the war over the future of UK aviation. But Flying Matters was not to have the same impact on policy discourse of Freedom to Fly, down even to the comparative political resonance of its naming.

In contrast to the consultative practices of the ATWP, the Brown government endeavoured to impose clear boundaries on the process of consultation over Heathrow: what we characterise as the logic of managed consultation. New Labour's earlier attempts to engage in what we have termed a process of 'therapeutic consultation', in which it sought to create the apparent conditions for a consensual dialogue, had backfired amidst the formation of competing coalitions and the construction of multiple social antagonisms. In the Heathrow consultation exercise, the DfT held only eleven public exhibitions in the communities surrounding the airport, and there were none in the communities whose homes were directly threatened by expansion, allegedly due to the absence of 'suitable venues' (*Guardian,*

22 November 2007). The consultation ran for little more than three months, including the Christmas period. The London mayoral office condemned the 'partial' and biased' nature of the consultation, because of the lack of involvement of the Greater London Assembly in discussions with the PSDH, the limited distribution by the DfT of nothing more than a summary consultation leaflet, and the absence of any strategic environmental assessment to inform the consultation (Mayor of London, 2008: iv, 6, 28). In fact, the practice of managed consultation continued attempts from the ATWP onwards, including the PSDH, to anchor decision-making in the realm of technical and scientific discourses and practices, rather than the political sphere. In its 2007 consultation document, the DfT thus elevated the scientific evidence about whether or not the new infrastructure would meet the environmental conditions previously laid down in the white paper as the sole criterion for judging the expansion proposal (DfT, 2007b: 3, 114–18). The consultation did not formally offer the opportunity to question the case for a third runway, which for the DfT had already been decided in the 2003 ATWP. In addition, any environmental impacts were categorised as 'local', thus restricting contestation to debates about the appropriate levels of air quality and noise at Heathrow. Such limitations prevented protesters from formally taking into account broader environmental questions about carbon emissions and global warming (DfT, 2007b: 18).

Equally, the DfT reiterated claims that technological advances in aviation offered a means of balancing expansion and sustainability, which is a characteristic trope of the discourse of ecological modernisation. Even with a third runway, technological fixes, it was argued, would deliver reductions in emissions from commercial aviation and even result in a diminishing of certain emissions in the Heathrow area (DfT, 2007b: 60–1). These reductions, the DfT claimed, would emanate from improvements to road vehicle emissions and 'trends in cleaner aircraft engines', as well as future 'moves towards a higher proportion of twin-engined, as opposed to four-engined aircraft, with lower emissions' (pp. 59, 67, 115). It came as no surprise that the Labour government resorted to the availability of technological fixes to strengthen its case for approving the third runway, without 'the need for radical mitigation measures' (pp. 36, 60–1).

It is striking that this technical narrative was developed in conjunction with promises to alleviate the extent of the environmental impact of expansion. For example, the DfT argued that predictions of local air quality were 'much more positive than at the time of the White Paper', as new modelling techniques were able to 'represent future emissions much more accurately than at the time of the white paper, reducing a significant element of over-prediction in that work' (pp. 59–60). In these terms, the government argued that the proposed third runway 'could be delivered consistent with the environmental conditions, without the need for radical mitigation measures', albeit with some restrictions on capacity in the years following 2020 (p. 36). Even mixed-mode operations and the increased length of the proposed runway, which would increase the capacity of Heathrow by an additional 6 million passengers a year, would not, according to the DfT, 'imply more carbon emissions', as it would not impact upon the forecast mix of short-haul and long-haul traffic across the airport. Indeed, in a report on improving passenger experiences, the DFT claimed that capacity constraints at the airport led to the stacking of planes over London, releasing some 50,000 additional tonnes of carbon dioxide into the atmosphere (DfT, 2007c: 25).[16] Such claims and guarantees enabled expansion to be constructed once again as a positive-sum game: it was possible with little or no increase in emissions.

HACAN ClearSkies condemned the very terms of the consultation, arguing that the third runway would be almost impossible to block, given the focus on proving or disproving the environmental evidence of the impact of a third runway on air quality and noise pollution. John Stewart, its chair, argued that

> if Ruth Kelly [the Secretary of State for Transport] wanted to ruin the opposition, this is a good way to do it. If we had to spend millions of pounds on research, we could not spend any money on campaigning. (*Guardian*, 22 November 2007)

These views were shared by a *Guardian* newspaper editorial, which suggested that the process was 'not a consultation, nor even an attempt at conversion', but 'a lecture'. This editorial prompted a response from the Secretary of State for Transport, in which she defended the 'consultation' as an integral 'part of a transparent public process. This is not a "closed debate", this is democracy' (*Guardian*, 23 and 26 November 2007).

Yet when local campaigners quickly picked up on the technical findings of the DfT's own report from November 2007, *Attitudes to Noise from Aviation Sources in England* (*ANASE*), such expertise was summarily dismissed. HACAN ClearSkies argued that the report proved that people complain of aircraft noise at lower thresholds than had been previously believed by government (levels of 50 rather than 57 decibels) (DfT, 2007d). Local campaigners were quick to suggest that this finding scuppered the government's promise that expansion at Heathrow would not increase the numbers of people affected by noise pollution (based on 2002 estimates). On the contrary, campaigners argued that 'about 10 times as many people – over 2 million – are affected by a 50 decibel cut-off point than the Government's favoured 57 decibels'.[17] The government responded by questioning the credibility of its own report. Although it praised the work of the 'independent consultants' who undertook the study on its behalf, it also cited peer reviewers who denounced the evidence of the *ANASE* study as 'unclear, partial or subject to different inter-pretations' (DfT, 2007b: 47). At the same time, it should be noted, the DfT proffered the fantasy of 'neutral scientific evidence', though in rejecting the *ANASE* report it also disclosed the latter's limits, thus making visible the political dimension involved in the naming of certain discourses as 'evidence'.

In fact, campaigners did not overinvest their resources in the official consultation exercise, having learnt the lessons of the anti-roads movements and earlier campaigns against airport expansion. Rather, they created alternative spaces, which were beyond the formal con-sultation exercise, where they promoted their campaign messages, thereby exploiting the tactics of media-friendly direct action. In the words of John Stewart, the DfT

> showed no interest in speaking with us. That suited us fine. After all, what was there to say: they wanted a third runway, a sixth terminal and an end to runway alternation. We wanted none of those things. End of conversation. (Stewart, 2010: 28)

Instead of consultation and deliberation, the politics of protest sometimes required a different maxim: 'if you are faced with power, only power can challenge power' (interview with campaigner). On 28 November 2007, one week after the opening of the consultation, protesters disrupted a hearing of the House of Commons Trans-port Select Committee, just as Sir Nigel Rudd, chair of BAA, began to give his evidence (*Independent*, 29 November 2007; *Telegraph*, 29 November 2009). This was the first of a series of high-profile media-focused actions during the consultation. On the final day of the formal consultation, and two days after Greenpeace activists climbed onto the tail fin of a British Airways Airbus at Heathrow, Plane Stupid activists unfurled two banners on the roof of the Houses of Parliament, one saying 'No Third Runway' and the other declaring Parliament to be 'BAA HQ' (*Guardian*, 27 February 2008; *Sunday Times*, 2 March 2008). On the eve of the closure of the consultation, campaigners duly organised a rally of anti-expansion supporters at Central Hall in Westminster, which attracted over 2,500 protesters. Those gathered were addressed by both Nick Clegg, the leader of the Liberal Democrats, and Peter Ainsworth, Conservative shadow Secretary of State for the Environment (*London Evening Standard*, 26 February 2008; Stewart, 2010: 35).

As in the 2003 ATWP consultation exercise, allegations of collusion between New Labour, the DfT, BAA and BA figured prominently in the campaign against expansion (as clearly articulated in the 'BAA HQ' banner). Publishing departmental minutes gained through the Freedom of Information Act, Justine Greening, the Tory MP for Putney, and a leading parliamentarian in the 'no' campaign, publicly condemned BAA's provision of noise and air pollution data to the DfT. She declared:

> to have somebody who is benefiting from any decision to expand Heathrow providing and modelling data to prove it's OK raises questions about the credibility of the information that the public will be asked to respond to. (*Observer*, 18 November 2007)

Further allegations circulated throughout the consultation process and beyond, with the *Sunday Times* publishing, for example, its own dossier on BAA collusion in the generation of data for the PSDH. The dossier revealed internal memos from the Environment Agency that were critical of the 'robustness' of the scientific data, and even cited one official involved in 'Project Heathrow' as claiming that the evidence represented 'a classic case of reverse engineering. They knew exactly what results they wanted and fixed the inputs to get there. It's appalling' (*Sunday Times*, 9 March 2008). With ongoing allegations in the media, Greening called in March 2008 for the parliamentary ombudsman to investigate the 'sham Heathrow consultation'.[18]

Repeated accusations about the capture of the DfT by the aviation industry resurrected allegations made during the ATWP consultation process, when campaigners targeted the connections between Labour and Stephen Hardwick at BAA, the former adviser to John Prescott, as well as Brenda Dean, chair of Freedom to Fly and a Labour peer, and Dan Hodges and Joe Irvin. For example, Irvin, an ex-director of Freedom to Fly, had subsequently become an adviser to Gordon Brown, while Michelle Di Leo, the director of Flying Matters, was the partner of Dan Hodges, who had also been the ex-director of Freedom to Fly. Among others, Tom Kelly, an ex-spokesperson for Tony Blair, had been appointed as BAA group director of corporate and public affairs in late 2007, while Julia Simpson, an ex-adviser to Blair, had become head of BA's corporate communications in 2007 (*Sunday Times*, 16 March 2008; *Observer*, 18 January 2009). At the same time, Digby Jones, the first chair of Flying Matters, had joined the Labour government in June 2007, while his replacement at Flying Matters was Brian Wilson, a former Labour Minister for Trade and Energy. The campaign director of Future Heathrow, Clive Soley, was, as we note above, a former Labour MP and subsequently a Labour peer. At the same time, Greenpeace, FoE and BAA were all invited to give oral evidence to the Public Administration Select Committee (PASC) inquiry about the practices of lobbying and their democratic implications across Whitehall (PASC, 2009).

Importantly, as in 2003, in its continued efforts to provide ideological ammunition for the Conservative Party, HACAN ClearSkies and AirportWatch attacked the economic case for expansion at Heathrow. To coincide with the opening of the consultation, HACAN ClearSkies (2007a) published its pamphlet *Aviation and the Economy*, in which it challenged once again the basis of both the 1999 and the 2006 studies by Oxford Economic Forecasting (OEF) on the economic benefits of airport expansion. In a second pamphlet, it systematically challenged the economic claims of Future Heathrow by negating the latter's attempts to draw analogies between Heathrow and the London docklands. It did so by sketching out an alternative narrative, which tied the failure of the London docklands to 'outdated work practices' and containerisation, while suggesting that 'serious economists just don't accept that argument [that Heathrow will go the way of London docklands]' (HACAN ClearSkies, 2007b: 3).

Attacks on the economics of Heathrow expansion were accompanied by appeals to business, as opposition campaigners sought to divide support for expansion within the business community. Echoing the notion of 'Heathrow hassle', its rhetoric acknowledged that the airport was a 'mess', 'clogged up' and not 'serving the needs of business' (HACAN ClearSkies, 2007b: 3). In its place, HACAN ClearSkies envisaged a rose-tinted image of Heathrow 'where business travellers feel valued' and congestion was abolished. It recommended a series of policy measures designed to improve the experience of travellers, including reducing the number of slots available to short-haul flights and setting higher taxes on interchange passengers. Appealing to the broad constituency of the Conservative opposition, HACAN ClearSkies declared that any higher aviation taxes had to be offset by reductions in other business taxes, while advocating that once government had put the right framework in place, it should 'let the market decide!' Reiterating the rhetorical appeals of the Conservative Party leadership, it thus concluded that 'the evidence suggests that a bigger Heathrow is not necessarily best for the economy' (HACAN ClearSkies, 2007b: 4). In short, by repeating the case for rail and shedding doubt on the economic case for expansion, HACAN ClearSkies sought to offer ideological cover for the Conservatives in the party's growing opposition to the third runway.

The provision of ideological cover was also evident in February 2008, shortly after the close of the consultation process, when HACAN ClearSkies, in association with NoTRAG, launched its commissioned report on the economics of Heathrow expansion. The report by CE Delft, an independent environmental research and consultancy organisation, questioned the overestimations of suppressed business demand at Heathrow, which were put forward by the OEF 2006 report, and queried the failure to consider the costs of aviation subsidies and tax breaks for government (CE Delft, 2008). Its launch, which took place in the City, was hosted by Stephen Norris, who was an ex-Transport Minister and member of the Conservative Quality of Life Policy Group (*Financial Times*, 15 February 2008). Significantly, the second section of this independent report concluded that interventionist options are 'less desirable than the introduction of market mechanisms' (CE Delft, 2008: 51). HACAN ClearSkies was thus prepared to acknowledge that these sorts of mechanisms were part of a policy solution, if they were incorporated into its proposals for demand management. Attacks on the economic case for expansion were also circulated in *Flaws Galore* – a report from the Aviation Economics Group for AirportWatch – which set out over twenty flaws in the DfT's economic case for expansion at Heathrow. These included the flawed assumptions that: there would be a fall in the price of oil; increases in tax on aviation were unlikely; a third runway would generate net tourist spending; capacity constraints would lead to fewer routes; and major European airports were expanding at the expense of Heathrow (Aviation Economics Group, 2008: 2–7).

New Labour strategies and tactics and the failure of ideological cover for expansion

The disputes about the practices and process of the public consultation, as well as the role of government, revealed the limits of New Labour's efforts to create a legitimate terrain of argumentation, which could frame certain demands as acceptable and tractable while excluding and concealing others. Government ministers and officials repeatedly stressed the economic importance of Heathrow and its role in generating jobs and maintaining the economic competitiveness of the UK. For example, a few days after the launch of the consultation, in a speech to the CBI, Gordon Brown returned to well rehearsed claims that aviation was a crucial motor of economic growth. He argued that his government had

> to respond to a clear business imperative and increase capacity at our airports.... Our prosperity depends on it: Britain as a world financial centre must be readily accessible from around the world.[19]

These oft-repeated assertions and aspirations were important ingredients of a continuing narrative that plotted various threats to economic well-being, as well as affective appeals to the joys and freedoms associated with flying. It was stated once again that economic benefits would be threatened if the government stalled its plans for expansion. The threat of international competition, which not only challenged Heathrow's market position but threatened to absorb any fall in capacity and thus negate any reductions in carbon emissions at the London airport, was repeatedly invoked to undermine any attempts to constrain expansion at Heathrow. In a speech to London business leaders, just the day before the launch of the consultation process, Ruth Kelly declared that

> if Heathrow is allowed to become uncompetive, the flights and routes it operates will simply move elsewhere. All it will do is shift capacity over the Channel. It will make us feel pure, but with no benefit to the rest of the planet. (*Guardian*, 22 November 2007)

Worries were also expressed by the aviation industry, when Steve Ridgway, head of Virgin Atlantic, stated at the London Stock Exchange that 'capping Heathrow isn't green. It just shifts business to our competitors'.[20]

More importantly, the Brown government continued in its efforts to resignify the proposed expansion at Heathrow as one element of a sustainable aviation policy programme. This was part of an ongoing rhetorical practice of redescribing airport expansions as consistent with a form of sustainable and responsible aviation. Expansion at Heathrow was represented as a type of demand management, so that, in the words of the DfT, the third runway 'would only be satisfying around 70 per cent of the unconstrained demand forecast for 2030' (DfT, 2007b: 44). In fact, over the consultation period, Brown and his colleagues regularly sought to recontextualise expansion at Heathrow by presenting it as a 'green' option. Such redescriptions relied in part upon successfully highlighting the threat of international competition, which would immediately absorb falls in capacity. But they also depended upon the argument that the construction of Heathrow would lower emissions through easing congestion and the stacking of planes over London (see DfT, 2007c). When questioned by a national newspaper at the height of the consultation process, Brown thus declared that

> the use of energy in aircraft is partly the means by which aircraft come in to land, the amount of holding that they have to do in the air, and the transition that airlines have to make through national traffic control systems ... so it's not simply a decision about the number of passengers, it's also a decision about the ways that we actually operate our airlines. (*Observer*, 6 January 2008)

Increasingly, in order to justify its decisions and policies, the Brown government came to rely upon variations of what we have termed the fantasmatic logic of sustainable aviation, in which aviation expansion and environmental protection were presented as compatible objectives. During the consultation over the third runway, the DfT released its strategy paper *Towards a Sustainable Transport System*, in which it described economic growth and carbon reduction as 'both essential and mutually consistent' objectives. It thus dismissed the 'stark choice between being "rich and dirty" or "poor and green"' as a 'false dichotomy' (DfT, 2007e: 7–8). Like Ruth Kelly's use of the signifier 'pure' to deride radical environmental claims, this DfT strategy paper also contrasted the 'irresponsible moralists' or 'doom mongers' of the environmental movement with the 'realists' within the Labour government. 'Cake and eat it' storylines like these were designed to mask over the contradictions of New Labour's expansionist policy, though they cannot be divorced from the highly contested claims about the supposed benefits of future technological changes, including the spread of twin-engined aircraft, which provided the conditions for expansion 'without the need for radical mitigation measures' (DfT, 2007b: 60–1).

Of course, what we have termed the logics of reframing and fantasy coexisted with – and indeed relied upon – a wider set of political strategies through which the Brown government pursued its goals of deferred responsibility or individualisation, incentivisation and brokerage. Not unlike the rhetorical underpinning of the ATWP progress report, in which the Eddington report provided 'evidence' of the positive contribution of transport to economic growth, the Stern review was again mobilised to provide the market tools to make transport more sustainable, namely emissions trading, price incentives and carbon offsetting. The recourse to emissions trading remained the nodal point around which the government's response to aviation's impact on climate change was articulated, thus enabling it to maintain its 'distance' from the market for aviation, while establishing steering mechanisms that would allegedly favour particular policy outcomes.

Such rhetorical manoeuvres and political strategies were also evident in the broad expansionist coalition, which was fronted in 2007 by Flying Matters and Future Heathrow. BAA situated its project for expansion within a narrative that stressed the economic and social benefits which were likely to accrue from Heathrow expansion: its economic significance in a global competitive economy; its high level of transfer passengers; and the extensive network of routes to growing markets in India and China (BAA, 2008: 10–15). Future Heathrow praised the contribution that the international hub made to London as a business centre, to tourism and to local employment, as well as its social benefits for people visiting friends or relatives and for keeping 'talent' in the UK (Future Heathrow, 2008). The pro-expansion lobby also replicated the arguments of the Brown government by similarly citing the Eddington report, which claimed that the third runway would generate a '£7 billion additional GDP a year' (Future Heathrow, 2008: 6; BAA, 2008: 12). In its submission to the consultation, BAA did not fail to point out the key social benefits of air travel, be it the 'ability of the 184,000 Americans who live and work in the UK to go home for Thanksgiving' or the opportunity to visit relatives for '11 of the 15 largest immigrant groups in the UK [who] come from countries that are predominantly served by Heathrow' (BAA, 2008: 15).

Demands for expansion were often couched in terms of the hegemonic narrative of UK aviation, in which the failure to expand would spell a horrific world of lost opportunities and decline, whereas increased capacity at Heathrow was synonymous with economic growth, well-being and a beatific future. Pro-expansion groups stressed the threats to Heathrow because of 'shrinking route network[s]' and rival European airports, the prospect of lost jobs for the UK, lower earnings, less funding for public services and the relocation of businesses outside the UK (Future Heathrow, 2008: 6–7; BAA, 2008: 11–12). To counter grievances about falling levels of service at Heathrow, capacity constraints were blamed for the declining consumer experience and choice at the airport. The third runway was presented as the only possible answer to the 'Heathrow hassle', thus diverting attention away from managerial or regulatory solutions to congestion and the poor passenger experience, while combating appeals to a 'better not bigger Heathrow' (BAA, 2008: 6).

Also exhibiting the fantasmatic logic that we discerned in the Brown government's discourse, demands for expansion were articulated within a discourse of responsible growth. BAA thus entitled its contribution to the consultation exercise *Making the Case for Responsible Growth* (BAA, 2008). Endorsing the Stern review, the principle of 'polluter pays' and emissions trading (p. 25), while re-articulating the DfT's rejection of the choice between 'rich and dirty or poor and clean' policies (p. 21), BAA asserted that 'the aviation industry can continue to grow and help achieve the UK's emissions targets' (p. 24). Central to these fantasmatic constructions was the acceptance of emissions trading, although support for the EU ETS was set alongside demands for a 'global system', or, in the words of Michelle Di Leo of Flying Matters, 'full international agreement', which implicitly raised concerns about the potential cost advantage to non-EU carriers (Flying Matters press release, 27 October 2007).

Yet BAA continued to rely upon contested definitions of sustainability, which defined the concept in terms of the protection of the economic and social benefits of infrastructure and environmental mitigation (BAA, 2008: 21). At the same time, it challenged well grounded scientific predictions about aviation's impact on climate change, describing aviation as a 'small contributor' to carbon emissions, whose contribution would increase over time only if it was assumed that the 'rest of the economy reduces emissions by 60%' (BAA, 2008: 24). Similarly, Future Heathrow compared the additional three million tonnes of carbon dioxide per year from aircraft using the third runway to 'about 0.6% of the UK's current annual carbon dioxide emissions and less CO_2 per year than China will produce in the next five hours' (Future Heathrow, 2008: 9). In raising the spectre of China's aviation expansion, which had been noted by the DfT in the 2006 ATWP progress report, Future Heathrow sought to displace responsibility for tackling carbon emissions to the international arena, claiming that this manoeuvre ought not to be viewed as 'an excuse for inaction', but one that 'highlights the need for solutions to global warming that spur international action' (Future Heathrow, 2008: 9). In fact, Future Heathrow, like BAA, sought to displace responsibility for carbon emissions from airports and on to carriers, arguing that 'if airlines want to fly more then they will have to pay for other industries to reduce their emissions' (Future Heathrow, 2008: 8; see also BAA, 2008: 25). Subsequently, at the end of November 2008, in a further attempt to ward off criticisms about the unsustainability of the third runway, BAA did publicly agree to the establishment of a government-appointed assessor to regulate its environmental performance (*London Evening Standard*, 27 November 2008).

But the pro-expansion coalition also sought to hold Labour to its 2003 commitments to airport expansion by reinstating the legitimacy of the ATWP (Future Heathrow, 2008: 1). For example, in its formal response to the consultation, BAA lauded the white paper as having 'delivered clarity and certainty where none previously existed' (BAA, 2008: 30). It also attributed to the ATWP 'an unequivocal status as a definitive, up-to-date statement of national policy' (p. 29). Like the Labour government, it attempted to delimit the boundaries of the consultation process to environmental feasibility, rather than support a consideration of the desirability of a third runway, which, it claimed, had 'been settled by the previous policy statement' (p. 29). Nonetheless, supporters of expansion made demands on the Labour government to take the lead, with BAA urging government to 'maintain … its strong support for the ATWP' (p. 31), while venting its frustrations at the delays in the development of Terminal Five and the proposed second runway at Stansted (pp. 29–30). In addition, Future Heathrow 'urged' government to confirm its existing policy that a third runway should be provided at Heathrow as soon as possible because it has been demonstrated that this can be delivered within the strict environmental limits set out in the 2003 Air Transport White Paper. (Future Heathrow, 2008: 1)

Indeed, BAA even threatened to withdraw its plans to construct the third runway if the government was not adequately clear in its commitments, warning that

airport operators need greater certainty if they are to invest money, time and resources in the assembly of planning applications for projects of national significance. (BAA, 2008: 30, 31)

Throughout this consultation process, the rhetoric and arguments of the New Labour government, as well as those of the pro-expansion coalition, harked back to earlier strategies and tactics designed to reframe the zero-sum game of airport expansion *or* environmental protection as a positive-sum game, where both growth in aviation *and* environmental protection were deemed achievable. Hence Labour's primary response to the growing political contestation surrounding the construction of the third runway at Heathrow was to rearticulate its discourse of sustainable aviation, which contained various intertwined fantasmatic narratives. Yet, as with the 2003 ATWP, the reliance on ideological representations betrayed its inability to shape the policy agenda and exude a leadership function. More importantly, its dependence on fantasmatic logics and tropes to mitigate opposition to expansion at Heathrow meant that Labour was hampered by the changing political and policy context, which scuppered the credibility and resonance of its rhetoric of sustainable aviation.

On the one hand, the Brown government suffered from the absence of effective 'intellectual and moral leadership' (to use Gramsci's expression) for its expansion plans. Unlike six years earlier, when the Freedom to Fly coalition successfully provided ideological cover for the Labour government during the formulation of the 2003 white paper, Flying Matters was unable to perform the same role for the Brown administration. On the other hand, and partly explaining the failure of the pro-aviation lobby to offer Labour the necessary symbolic and ideational resources to argue convincingly for expansion, the changing political salience of climate change politics produced a new terrain of argumentation. This new terrain, which had in part been put in place by the oppositional forces, disclosed untenable contradictions in the government's policy discourse and the political strategies which it had formulated from the ATWP onwards. Rather than concealing contradictory imperatives, it rendered the government more vulnerable to challenge and critique. As we will now show, this became more evident in the run-up to the decision to approve the third runway and sixth terminal in January 2009.

The run-up to the decision

After the closure of the consultation, there followed almost a year in which the government repeatedly delayed the public announcement of its decision over the third runway. (The DfT blamed the delay, in part, on the requirement to evaluate the more than 70,000 responses to the consultation.) But a wider set of uncertainties surrounded the future of Heathrow. After its takeover by the Spanish transport group Ferrovial, BAA was persistently dogged by board-room shuffles and growing publicity over its financial troubles, not to mention the fiasco of the opening of Terminal Five at Heathrow in March 2008.[21] In early 2008, Stephen Nelson stepped down as chief executive of BAA, to be replaced by Colin Matthews, a former BA executive (*Telegraph*, 27 February 2008; *Guardian*, 22 April 2008). The group's financial difficulties were reportedly eased at the beginning of June 2008, when Ferrovial gained the backing of nine banks for its refinancing programme (*Independent*, 3 June 2008).

At the end of August 2008, however, the Competition Commission (CC) called for BAA to sell off three of its seven airports, including two of its three airports in London – Heathrow, Gatwick or Stansted – as well as either Glasgow or Edinburgh.[22] Its provisional report criticised the regulatory regime in civil aviation, but also challenged BAA's dominant ownership of UK airports, especially in London, which, the CC claimed, limited competition, delayed infrastructure investment and contributed to a 'lack of responsiveness to the interests of airlines and passengers that we would not expect to see in a business competing in a well-functioning market' (CC, 2008: 9). The intervention of the CC fuelled those grievances and demands which were symbolised by the signifier 'Heathrow hassle', which had been coined in the pages of the *Financial Times* in the middle of 2007, further delegitimising BAA's claim to being an economic success story. Instead, it was progressively redescribed as a privileged monopoly that needed dismantling. Indeed, while recognising the lack of capacity in the south-east, the CC concluded that 'common ownership of BAA's airports can no longer be considered an engine of capacity development. Rather, it has become a brake on it' (CC, 2008: 287). The public criticism from the CC triggered further attacks on BAA, with Heathrow designated a 'national disgrace', which had 'skewed … business away from flying towards high-profit shopping' (*Independent*, 21 August 2008: 34). In fact, in September 2008 BAA put Gatwick airport up for sale, which was widely interpreted as an attempt to pre-empt further rulings from the CC (*Guardian*, 18 September 2008).[23]

Amidst this uncertainty, opposition to the third runway did not relent as environmental experts continued to offer support to the 'no' camp. The EU warned that the third runway would breach European air pollution limits, and it was soon to be joined by the Environment Agency (led by the former Labour minister Chris Smith), the Sustainable Development Commission and Sir David King, who was the former government climate change adviser. They all came out publicly against the third runway.[24] At the beginning of October 2008, the *Financial Times* carried reports that the third runway would not meet noise or air pollution controls (3 October 2008). At the same time, protesters drew upon the UK banking crisis and economic recession to undermine calls for expansion, as airlines, hit by the economic slowdown, had begun to cut flights (*London Evening Standard*, 3 November 2008). Notably, on 21 July 2008, *Panorama*, the prime-time BBC current affairs programme, aired allegations of collusion between BAA and the DfT. In the programme, entitled 'Friends in High Places', viewers were shown a mock-up of an airplane interior in which the front rows of seats were entirely occupied by Labour dignitaries working for the aviation industry. During the programme, the *Panorama* team also cast doubt on the technological advances claimed by the industry, dismissing evidence for the introduction of long-haul twin-engined aircraft, which formed a key 'technological fix' in BAA's and the Labour government's case for the third runway meeting the environmental conditions imposed by the ATWP.

The opposition Conservative Party also declared itself against expansion at Heathrow, and it pushed instead for a 'better not bigger Heathrow', as David Cameron put it, which tapped into growing criticisms of the regulation of British airports and business demands to address the 'Heathrow hassle' (*Times*, 17 June 2008; *London Evening Standard*, 16 June 2008). Echoing the demands of campaign groups, the Conservative leadership also called for government to abandon the second runway at Stansted, while promoting high-speed

rail links as a credible alternative to airport expansion.[25] Opposition
parties thus came to operate as the 'voice' for environmental and
local residents' demands. The Liberal Democrats had long opposed
the third runway, with their transport spokesperson typically dismissing the 2006 ATWP progress report on the grounds that it 'would be
absolute folly to make any plans to expand airports in the south east
of England'.[26] For his part, in the autumn of 2008, Boris Johnson, the
Conservative mayor of London, upped his concerns over expansion
at Heathrow by calling for a new airport in the London estuary and
donating some £15,000 to the campaign against the runway (*Daily
Mirror*, 22 September 2008; *Guardian*, 12 and 17 November 2008).

Significantly, the rhetoric of a 'better not bigger' Heathrow made
visible new lines of division within the expansionist camp, where frontiers were drawn between those who privileged improved regulation
and service improvement and those who favoured greater expansion.
For example, in early May 2008, Bob Ayling, a former chief executive
of BA, feared that expansion at the international hub would be a
'costly mistake' (*Sunday Times*, 4 May 2008). Indeed, at the end
of June 2008, London First, the pro-business lobby and stalwart of
Heathrow expansion, went so far as to suggest that BAA should
axe 5,000 flights at Heathrow as a means of addressing capacity
constraints (*Guardian*, 25 June 2008). In a study entitled *Imagine a
World Class Heathrow*, which was published in June 2008, London
First criticised the price-cap regulation of Heathrow, because it meant
that the low price of servicing passengers encouraged the airport to
increase its passenger throughput in order to raise revenues (London
First, 2008). While Heathrow was a 'handicap' to London's competitiveness, it argued, the negative impact resulted not just from capacity
constraints, but also from price and lack of competition.

The 'no' campaign, for its part, looked to exacerbate these points
of discord within the expansionist coalition. In June 2008, HACAN
ClearSkies published a further pamphlet, *Turning Heathrow into
London's Premium Airport*, which foregrounded Cameron's message
that the 'aim should be to make Heathrow the best airport in the
world, not the biggest' (HACAN ClearSkies, 2008: 4). HACAN
ClearSkies also continued to mobilise support for high-speed rail,
thus fostering cleavages within the trade union movement. It concentrated its efforts on systematically negating the economic grounds
for expansion, thus offering ideological and rhetorical support for
the opposition parties and giving them greater room for political

and strategic manoeuvre. On 14 October 2008, six trade unions – the public service trade union UNISON, transport workers' unions TSSA, ASLEF and RMT, the civil servants' union PCS, and the communications workers' trade union CONNECT – came out against the third runway in a one-page advertisement in *The Times*.

The Labour government found itself increasingly isolated in its support for the third runway. Tony Blair stepped down as Prime Minister in June 2007, as part of a negotiated transfer of power to his Chancellor, Gordon Brown, with whom he had modernised the Labour Party. By the autumn of 2008, however, Brown's premiership was under growing attack as his electoral popularity waned, and as he faced allegations of a sexist-macho leadership style, as well as persistent rumours about challenges to his leadership. Amidst one of the many leadership crises he faced, at the end of September 2008, Ruth Kelly, the Secretary of State for Transport, resigned (*Telegraph*, 24 September 2008). The decision over the third runway was then further postponed, when Geoff Hoon, Whip and Parliamentary Secretary to the Treasury, replaced Kelly as Secretary of State for Transport.

What is more, by late October and early November 2008, reports were circulating of intensifying Cabinet and backbench opposition to the expansion of Heathrow, which was deemed to threaten the green credentials of the Labour Party, especially its capacity to deliver planned reductions in carbon emissions, as well as its capacity to win marginal seats in the south-east.[27] In the Cabinet, opposition to expansion was led initially by Hilary Benn at the Department for the Environment, Food and Rural Affairs (DEFRA) and Ed Miliband at Energy and Climate Change, as well as Harriet Harman, the Leader of the House, and David Miliband, the Foreign Secretary; they were later joined by John Denham, Secretary of State for Innovation, Universities and Skills.[28] Brown was reported to have met with Labour MPs at the end of October to assuage their concerns, but he encountered demands to delay any decision on the runway until after the general election. Outside the Cabinet, forty-one Labour MPs, sufficient to overturn the government majority, gave their support to an early-day parliamentary motion calling for a rethink on the third runway (*Guardian*, 3 and 6 November 2008; *Financial Times*, 6 November 2008). Significantly, the motion, which was tabled by the Labour backbencher John Grogan, declared that 'the consultation paper Adding Capacity at Heathrow Airport was deeply flawed, as it paid insufficient regard to the costs of air and noise pollution in the surrounding areas and the commitment to curb carbon dioxide emissions to tackle climate change'.[29]

The gathering momentum against expansion at Heathrow was not without its rebuttals, as the pro-expansion coalition strived to re-articulate the hegemonic discourses and rhetoric which had governed airports policy since 1945. Appeals to the national interest, promises of improved economic performance and threats of international competition were repeated by the industry and its supporters. In early October 2008, for example, Willie Walsh, the chief executive of BA, condemned Conservative aviation policy. He argued that 'the Conservatives apparently want to undermine the UK's efforts to succeed in a global economy – and condemn Heathrow to permanent status as the most delay-prone airport in Europe' (*Guardian*, 2 October 2008; *Telegraph*, 1 October 2008). Ian Godden, the chief executive of the Society of British Aerospace Companies, accused Cameron of privileging the interests of Tory MPs in marginal seats over the national interest (*Independent*, 21 October 2008). Pro-expansionists also seized upon the advice of the International Business Advisory Council for the newly elected mayor of London, Boris Johnson, when they implored him to rethink his position on the third runway (*London Evening Standard*, 6 October 2008). Even Geoff Hoon, the new Secretary of State for Transport, waded in, declaring that the demand of the Business Advisory Council 'just goes to demonstrate the lack of leadership shown by both Boris and David Cameron on this issue'.[30]

Typically, in a briefing letter to MPs published on 10 November 2008, Flying Matters affirmed the economic case for expansion, while setting out arguments for the aviation industry's commitments to sustainability. Its chair, Brian Wilson, extolled the virtues of an international hub airport in a globalised economy, which was essential for 'UK plc', while he conjured up the threat of international competition. He warned MPs that 'a lack of sufficient air transport capacity will encourage investment to be made in other places in Europe at a big cost to UK plc'. Dispelling concerns about the impact of aviation on climate change, Flying Matters reaffirmed the industry-wide commitment to 'tough targets to reduce and mitigate its emissions', thus reasserting its fantasmatic narrative of sustainable aviation. In this picture, aviation was depicted as 'a small but growing contributor to climate change', and it was affirmed that 'economic sustainability and environmental sustainability must go hand in hand'. The pro-expansion lobby thus directed MPs to read the briefing papers of the Society of British Aerospace Companies and the Sustainable Aviation initiative, which recognised the role of technological improvements and alternative fuels in reducing emissions. It also came out in support of aviation's inclusion in the EU ETS, which, it suggested, meant that the third runway would not increase carbon emissions, as, in practice, 'any growth in aviation emissions above those in 2004 would have to be found by reductions elsewhere and paid for by aviation'. Given these mitigating measures, Flying Matters called upon MPs to take the lead 'to ensure businesses and individuals can move forward with certainty', and thus benefit from 'a once in a generation opportunity to ensure that the UK has the infrastructure it requires – air, rail and road – to play its full part in a global low carbon economy'. The discourse of Flying Matters even took account of the financial crisis by pointing out to MPs: that the third runway would not require any public expenditure; that economic crises are 'cyclical'; that the 'test' is to 'plan now for the economic upturn to ensure that we can take full advantage of it rather than be sidelined in global trading'; and that failure to do so, using the rhetoric of Kelly, would produce 'no environmental gain, only economic pain' (Flying Matters press release, 10 November 2008).

At the beginning of December 2008, Hoon announced the suspension of any decision on expansion at Heathrow until January 2009 (Ames, 2008; *Financial Times*, 5 December 2008). After entering the DfT, Hoon had overturned the decision by the local authority to block an increase in flight capacity at Stansted, allowing a 10 per cent increase at the airport. The Brown government continued to try to confine debate about Heathrow expansion within the parameters of the environmental conditions set out by government, in which it assumed that the need for a third runway had already been accepted in the 2003 white paper (see Hoon's interventions in the early November debate in the House of Commons).[31] But in December 2008 the Committee on Climate Change (CCC) added further uncertainty to the runway controversy by publishing its report on emissions reductions, *Building a Low-Carbon Economy* (CCC, 2008). The Committee, an independent body created by the Labour government under the Climate Change Act to offer advice to government and to monitor progress regarding emissions targets, had a statutory obligation to report annually to Parliament. Its 2008 report came out in favour of constraining demand in aviation, as it estimated that, by 2050, aviation's emissions would account for 'a very significant proportion' of

UK emissions. The Committee also warned about the potential limits of technological improvements and new fuel sources in the sector, concluding that international aviation should be included in the UK's 80 per cent emissions reduction target for 2050, which had been upped from 60 per cent in 2008 (CCC, 2008: 318, 464). Its intervention, coupled with further delay, brought a flurry of activity from lobbyists, as opposition groups sought to frame the delay as a first step towards a policy reversal by the Labour government on Heathrow. On 8 December 2008, for example, Plane Stupid activists occupied Stansted airport, shutting it down for several hours (*Guardian*, 9 and 13 December 2008).

Opposition within the Cabinet and the ranks of the Labour Party continued in what was increasingly portrayed in the media as a battle between Ed Miliband and Peter Mandelson, the Business Secretary (*London Evening Standard*, 15 December 2008). But these protagonists were joined by Hilary Benn, who also intervened in the developing public debate, when he declared in an interview with the *Sunday Times* (14 December 2008) that the UK was not able to breach EU air pollution limits – the key issue at stake in the government decision over Heathrow. It was later reported that Benn and Miliband had discussed ways of limiting the environmental impact of the third runway with Simon Retallack, who had developed 'green aviation' proposals in a policy pamphlet by the Institute for Public Policy Research (*Guardian*, 16 January 2009). Equally, backbench MPs prepared for a cross-party revolt, when in mid-December Martin Salter, vice-chair of the Labour Party with responsibility for its environment portfolio, tabled a motion for a vote in the Commons on the third runway.[32] Nonetheless, just before Christmas, Brown, in his monthly press conference, gave further support for large infrastructure projects as a means of ensuring the UK would benefit the most from economic recovery. This was widely translated as support for Heathrow expansion, not least because it reproduced the arguments articulated by Flying Matters in its November 2008 briefing letter to MPs. The year thus closed with Mandelson, now apparently close to Brown, coming under intense pressure from Labour MPs to put electoral politics and the party before business (*Guardian*, 29 December 2008).

The New Year was marked by an intervention from the Transport Minister, Lord Adonis, who publicly endorsed a £4.5 billion international rail exchange for Heathrow airport, although he was keen to distance his support for this scheme from the impending decision on a third runway (*Financial Times*, 4 January 2009). Putting further pressure on backbench Labour MPs, Greenpeace published an ICM survey of voting intentions in Labour-held constituencies under or near the Heathrow flight path, which warned that 23 per cent of voters would be less likely to vote Labour if the runway was given the go-ahead, suggesting that Labour would lose four seats across London (*Guardian*, 12 January 2009).[33] On 12 January, Nick Raynsford, a former Labour government minister, announced the formation of a cross-party group in support of a London estuary airport, a development that had received support from London mayor Boris Johnson (*Guardian*, 12 January 2009). Brown again met with Labour MPs, and the press carried reports that Labour whips were ringing around to ensure support for the expansion of Heathrow. To make matters worse for Brown, Cameron proposed to use one of the opposition days in the Commons to debate the third runway, amidst rumours that the government was on the verge of announcing its support for the third runway and sixth terminal (*Guardian*, 14 January 2009).

On 15 January 2009, Hoon did indeed finally announce to the Commons the government's approval of the third runway and sixth terminal at Heathrow, although the go-ahead for mixed-mode operations on existing runways was refused. While making the expected appeals to the economic significance of the approval for the third runway as part of a policy of 'sustainable economic growth', Hoon set out a whole range of environmental conditions on the operation of the third runway. These included: granting the CAA a statutory environmental duty as well as compliance measures on noise and giving similar compliance measures to the Environment Agency on air pollution; a limit on the use of the runway to 125,000 air traffic movements a year (having consulted on 220,000); the principle of 'green slot' allocation on the runway to encourage low-noise and low-emission aircraft; support for ultra-low-emission road vehicles to offset increased emissions at Heathrow; requests for the Committee on Climate Change (CCC) to investigate ways forward for global climate change 'deals' on aviation; and new targets for aviation emissions in 2050 to be below 2005 levels. There were also assurances that future capacity increases at Heathrow could be approved only after a review by the CCC in 2020, which would investigate whether plans were on track to achieve the 2050 emissions target. Indeed, Hoon closed his parliamentary statement with the claim that, 'taken together, that gives us the toughest climate change regime for aviation of any country in the world, which gives Ministers the confidence that we will achieve our 80 per cent emissions reduction target'.[34]

Lobbying by Benn and Ed Miliband had forced concessions from the Transport Secretary. In his allegedly 'bruising encounters with Hoon', Miliband had delivered what was termed a 'half runway', as any additional capacity was open only to what were deemed to be 'green slots' and mixed-mode operations were abandoned (*Guardian*, 16 January 2009). Martin Salter, the Labour Party's vice-chair for the environment, was reported as saying that:

> there aren't enough jumbo jets to drag me into the lobby to vote for the third runway. But you can't doubt that it is radically different from that of 11 November, when he [Hoon] spent time arguing the case of mixed mode and he spoke for 45 minutes before he mentioned climate change. (*Guardian*, 16 January 2009)

However, on the announcement of the decision, John McDonnell, local MP and opponent of expansion, stood up and grabbed the mace, the symbol of the office of the Speaker, in a very public and widely reported gesture of opposition. He was asked to leave the House and later received a five-day suspension from the Commons (*Telegraph*, 15 January 2009).

There was no formal vote on the decision but the opposition did, as proposed, devote one of its parliamentary opposition days at the end of January to expansion at Heathrow, although the vote at the end of the debate would have no direct consequence for government policy. The day before that vote, Andy Slaughter, one of the leaders of the Labour backbench opposition to Heathrow expansion, resigned from his junior government post as parliamentary private secretary to Lord Malloch-Brown at the Foreign and Commonwealth Office in order to vote with Conservative and Liberal Democrats against the third runway (*Guardian*, 28 January 2009; *Telegraph*, 28 January 2009). Ultimately, twenty-eight Labour MPs voted with the opposition – the biggest Labour rebellion on an opposition day debate since New Labour came to power in 1997 – but the government successfully defended its majority in the Commons (*Guardian*, 29 January 2009). The concessions announced by the government, pressure from party whips and the Conservatives' inability to rule out indefinitely future expansion in the south-east had helped ensure the government's majority (*Daily Mail*, 29 January 2009). Yet the Labour government remained isolated in its support for the third runway and, with a general election looming in just over a year, campaigners moved to hold the Conservative Party to its public commitments to reverse expansion (interview with environmental campaigner).

Holding the Tories to the commitment against expansion

In the aftermath of its decision to approve the expansion of Heathrow, New Labour engaged in a media offensive, with Geoff Hoon seeking to legitimise government policy (which included a public spat with the actor Emma Thompson over the flying habits of those celebrities opposing expansion) (*Daily Mail*, 17 January 2009; *Guardian*, 17 January 2009). At the same time, BAA published a full-page advertisement in national newspapers in which it stated that it recognised that 'the consequences of the decision will be difficult for some' but pointed out that 'growth has not been agreed at any cost' (*Guardian*, 19 January 2009). However, Conservative and Liberal Democrat opposition to the runway, and the falling electoral prospects of the Labour Party, meant that the leadership of the climate change coalition met the decision with a certain indifference. Anti-aviation activists like John Stewart began to scent an important change in the politics of aviation policy. As he put it,

> a strange thing happened … we began to realise that Geoff Hoon's decision was pretty irrelevant.… It had become plain that the Conservatives were serious about their plans to scrap a third runway. (Stewart, 2010: 43)

Stewart's assessment was corroborated when Boris Johnson, the Conservative mayor of London, announced just a few days after the formal go-ahead for the third runway that it would 'never happen', as Labour would lose the forthcoming general election (*Guardian*, 22 January 2009).

Against this background, the strategy of protesters shifted even more firmly towards holding the Conservative Party to its commitments to stop any further expansion at Heathrow and Stansted. This relied in part on maintaining the public profile of the campaign, while continuing to support the alternative of high-speed rail and to challenge the economic case for expansion; there were also plans to undertake measures to delay the construction of the runway in the unlikely event that Labour won the forthcoming election (Stewart, 2010). For example, activists bought one acre of land designated for development, with the aim of selling small parts of it to as many individuals as possible in order to force the government to engage in up to 4,000 drawn-out compulsory purchase orders (*Daily Mail*, 13 January 2009). Notably, the Conservative leader, David Cameron, and Nick Clegg, the Liberal Democrat leader, sponsored a tree on the site, as did the actor Alison Steadman and the Poet Laureate Carol-Ann Duffy.[35] Plane Stupid protesters also continued to take part in high-profile media events, such as throwing green custard over Peter Mandelson (*Telegraph*, 6 March 2009). In addition, Greenpeace circulated further claims of collusion between BAA and the DfT (*Guardian*, 27 March 2009 and 7 April 2009). Finally, campaign organisations (including Greenpeace, the World Wide Fund for Nature, the Royal Society for the Protection of Birds and the Campaign to Protect Rural England) and seven local authorities, which were backed by Boris Johnson, launched a legal challenge against the third runway on the grounds that the decision breached noise and air pollution targets. It was also claimed that the new infrastructure project would hamper efforts to reduce emissions and that the plans were different from those upon which communities were consulted.[36]

In spring 2009, this strategy of holding the Conservatives to its pre-election commitments was given further impetus, as reports emerged that BAA would not be able to submit its planning application for the third runway before the next general election, which was due at the latest by May 2010 (*Guardian*, 27 March 2009). The CAA also published data suggesting the capacity constraints on UK airports were lessening, because passenger numbers following the economic slump of 2008 had fallen for the first time since 1991 (CAA press release, 16 March 2009). Cracks began to appear in the business support for expansion. In May 2009, for example, Russell Chambers of Credit Suisse and Justin King of Sainsbury's launched a business network opposed to the third runway at Heathrow (*Sunday Times*, 3 May 2009). In the same month, Nicholas Stern also came out against the third runway (*AirportWatch Bulletin* no. 27, May 2009, p. 5), as did Greenpeace protesters the following month at the Glastonbury festival, when they formed a human 'NO' in a field (*Observer*, 28 June 2009; *Daily Mail*, 1 July 2009). Shortly afterwards, the Liberal Democrats added to the undermining of the case for expansion by arguing that any economic benefits of expansion would be wiped out by the additional costs of emissions trading (*Guardian*, 17 September 2009). Its report correlated with the findings of the New Economics

Foundation (NEF), which had in January 2009 accused the government of 'fantasy economics' and predicted that economic benefits from expansion would not meet the cost of emissions from expansion of between £8 billion and £20 billion over seventy years (*Guardian*, 16 January 2009). The NEF report, entitled *Grounded*, which was published April 2010, reassessed the impact of the third runway at Heathrow and concluded that its construction 'would destroy rather than create value, demolishing any case for Heathrow expansion' (NEF, 2010: 3).

In contrast, supporters of expansion sought desperately to supply the Labour government with the intellectual arguments and political justifications to implement its proposals. One strategy was to undermine the economic case for high-speed rail. First, the British Chambers of Commerce (BCC) published a report into the positive economic impact of hub expansion in July 2009. The report was written by Paul Buchanan of the transport consultancy Colin Buchanan and Partners Ltd, whose founder, Professor Colin Buchanan, had been a member of the Roskill Commission that had looked at the possible location of a third London airport. The report was funded by members of Future Heathrow. It deliberately ignored the environmental impact of expansion and endeavoured to reorientate ongoing debates back onto the economics of the case. Revisiting the once dominant economic narratives about aviation's contribution to the economy, the report made reference to the 'substantial economic gains to UK plc' from hub airport expansion, in which it estimated gains of £8.8–12.8 billion in direct productivity and £20 billion in wider economic benefits (in present value). Equally, Heathrow expansion was endorsed as the better infrastructure investment for the UK, with the report arguing that the third runway would generate more than could be expected from high-speed rail projects, with expansion at the hub airport having the additional advantage of shifting costs for expansion onto the private sector (BCC, 2009: 7). In fact, the report claimed that high-speed rail would not sufficiently reduce capacity constraints at Heathrow, which was itself 'uniquely able to deliver the economic benefits', with each year of delay costing the UK economy 'an estimated £900 million–£1.1billion' (p. 8).

Secondly, in December 2009, the House of Commons Transport Select Committee endeavoured to recontextualise – and thus resignify – the decision about the third runway in terms of economic arguments. The Committee came out in favour of the third runway, while endorsing the 2003 ATWP as a 'sound basis for aviation policy' (although it did argue that the case for expansion at Stansted had yet to be made) (House of Commons Transport Select Committee, 2009: 8). More importantly, it sought to mobilise 'economic factors' as 'the key justification for difficult decisions' in airport expansion, 'when it is necessary to weigh the economic benefits against the environmental and social costs' (p. 25). The report included a detailed annex on the economic contribution of aviation, which recognised the need to reduce carbon emissions from aviation. But the Committee still endorsed the political strategies of deferred responsibility and incentivisation, concluding, like the Labour government, that meeting the challenge of rising emissions required global solutions and measures that had to take account of the economic value of the aviation industry. In short, in attempting to counter the construction of aviation as a 'culprit' and an obstacle to meeting the challenge of climate change, the Committee pleaded that the industry 'should not be demonised or assigned symbolic value beyond its true impacts' (p. 19).

These competing political projects clashed head on, however, in December 2009, when a battle broke out in the media about how to interpret the long-awaited report on aviation by the CCC (2009a). The Committee had been invited to advise government on options for meeting the 2050 target of keeping aviation emissions at 2005 levels, which was announced as part of the package of measures mitigating the increased emissions from the construction of the third runway at Heathrow. Taking into account projected fuel efficiencies, biofuels and air management efficiencies, the CCC concluded that a 60 per cent growth in passenger demand for aviation was 'compatible' with reducing carbon emissions from aviation by 2050 to the levels of 2005 (CCC, 2009b: 10). Importantly, its 60 per cent projected increase in demand was clearly presented as a demand management scenario, for without strategies of carbon pricing or constraints on expansion it was predicted that demand could rise by up to 200 per cent. Indeed, with carbon pricing and the 'capacity constraints' of the 2003 ATWP, the CCC still predicted that passenger growth would rise by 115 per cent by 2050. Yet, in its accompanying press release, it was at pains to emphasise its juxtaposing of predicted and 'permissible' passenger expansion with its claims that such demand could not 'exceed' a 60 per cent increase (CCC, 2009c). In meeting such targets, it supported the 'useful contribution' of high-speed rail as a substitute for domestic and short-haul flights, as well as fuel efficiencies and the potential of videoconferencing; although the Committee cast doubt on the future role of biofuels, it came out in favour of EU and global emission caps and trading, and pointed to the requirement to include in future targets the non-CO_2 impacts of aviation on global warming (CCC, 2009b).

The release of the CCC report sparked a media battle as various forces struggled to 'make sense' of its ambiguities and nuances. AirportWatch argued that Labour's aviation policy was effectively 'murdered' by the Committee on Climate Change, especially in light of its judgement that the predicted doubling of passenger numbers was not compatible with wider commitments to keep CO_2 emissions from commercial aviation in 2050 no higher than they were in 2005.[37] Yet the suggestion that the 60 per cent growth in aviation was possible while still meeting government targets was met positively by supporters of expansion. Jill Brady, chair of Sustainable Aviation, welcomed the report, arguing that 'limiting emissions is the answer rather than limiting people's ability to travel'.[38] Lord Adonis, Transport Secretary, interpreted the report as confirmation that the third runway could go ahead as planned (*London Evening Standard*, 9 December 2009). London First suggested that the report might indeed trigger a rethink by the Conservative opposition (*Observer*, 13 December 2009).

But these debates did little to derail the opposition to Heathrow expansion or to reframe the terrain of argumentation within which aviation policy was constituted. At the end of March 2010, campaigners won a high-court ruling that the government had not sufficiently addressed the issue of climate change in its deliberations over the construction of the third runway. Although this judgement did not reverse the decision to expand Heathrow, the judge did call upon government officials to reconsider the decision in light of the Climate Change Act, thus requiring the DfT to offer a new national policy statement that took into account the climate change priorities of the government.[39] Yet, in truth, much of the steam had already gone out of the campaign, especially as the general election loomed. With Labour and Gordon Brown running behind in the polls, both the Conservatives and the Liberal Democrats entered the election with manifesto commitments against expansion at Heathrow and Stansted. In the words of John Stewart (2010: 43), the 'media' had 'largely lost interest in the third runway. It was no longer a story. They, like most people, believed it just wouldn't happen.' In fact, the media and most people were soon proved right. A few days after taking office in the first coalition since the Second World War, the Conservative–Liberal Democrat government abandoned the construction of new runways at Heathrow and Stansted.[40] BAA then followed suit, announcing that it, too, had abandoned its projects for the development of Heathrow and Stansted (*Guardian*, 25 May 2010). Amidst the excitement about the UK's first coalition government in sixty years, it was difficult not to believe that local campaigners and environmentalists had pulled off the biggest victory in transport policy since the roads movement of the 1980s and early 1990s.

Conclusion

In the campaign against Heathrow, the perpetual losers of airport protest campaigns – local residents and environmental campaigners who had battled against the fourth terminal, the fifth terminal, changes to night flights and so on – had eventually become winners. On the surface, this was because of the formation of the new Conservative–Liberal Democrat coalition, which promised to be 'the greenest government ever', and the changes to the Conservative Party brought about by its new leader, David Cameron. But their victory owed much more to the cultural resignification of aviation and the symbolic reframing of airports policy during the first decade of the new century. Airports and aviation had been successfully represented by a complex assemblage of groups and movements as a threat to the global climate and an important obstacle in the path of the UK government's commitments to reduce carbon emissions. Campaigners had painstakingly established equivalences between struggles to stop airport expansion, the growth of the aviation industry and the battle against climate change. Expressed in rhetorical terms, airports, air travel and the emissions generated by aviation had been transformed into a synecdoche of climate change: they were the part that signified the whole problem. In an important respect, the exposure of 'sustainable aviation' *as* a fantasmatic narrative, that is, as a narrative which endeavoured to conceal the ambiguities and contradictions of Labour's pro-expansion policies, was a crucial condition for the construction of new alliances and the rearticulation of established positions against airport expansion.

Importantly, the scientific and expert critiques of the ATWP had rendered the government's plan unsustainable. But for anti-expansion forces at Heathrow (and elsewhere), they also made possible a powerful heresthetic move, in which campaigners were able to make visible the wider environmental threat of aviation expansion, thus resignifying aviation as an issue of climate change, while nullifying the pro-expansion arguments about the economic contribution of airports and aviation to the UK economy. The leadership of HACAN ClearSkies and AirportWatch had creatively linked together a number of demands into new chains of equivalence, which tied increasing carbon emissions from air travel to demands against congestion and for the improved regulation of UK airports. Equally, they highlighted the problem of congestion and the 'Heathrow hassle', thus calling into question the sedimented narrative of aviation as a veritable economic 'success'. Finally, the demand for better regulation opened up new policy alternatives to runway expansion, which resonated with the challenges posed by opponents to aviation and provoked splits among the traditional supporters of expansion.

Strategically placed individuals like John Stewart drove the anti-expansion campaign. Stewart was able to forge links with Plane Stupid and thus made strategic use of spaces outside the formal consultation process to lobby government, while drawing equivalences between competing demands so as to hold together a broad climate change coalition. In this instance, Plane Stupid and the stunts of its members, which were picked up by the media, offered much to the campaign, bringing in new forms of direct action and raising the profile of the protest, as did the winning over of well known personalities and celebrities. Networking with the Conservative opposition and holding it to its policy commitments, as well as coordinating opposition from local MPs, were also key ingredients in the success of the campaign. In fact, attempts to negate the economic case surrounding aviation and to provide alternatives to aviation expansion offered ideological cover for the Conservative opposition to come out against the third runway at Heathrow and the second runway at Stansted. Campaigners against expansion thus offered up media images of significant opposition to the runway, provided the alternative of high-speed rail and derided the economic case for expansion. They were also able to rearticulate the narrative of 'Heathrow hassle', the reports of the Competition Commission and the fiasco of the Terminal Five opening, not as issues of capacity, but as issues of limited competition, inadequate regulation and poor performance. These interventions split the expansionist camp by putting pressure on the support of London First and business, by engendering tensions between carriers and airport owners, and dividing the trade union movement.

Yet the 'no' campaign was aided and abetted in its victory by the failings of both the Labour government and the pro-expansion lobbies. Faced with mounting opposition, the Labour government retreated back to its discredited arguments in favour of a policy of sustainable aviation, thus reproducing political strategies that had failed to break up opposition, and had failed to convince the wider public, since the publication of the 2003 white paper. What is more, these moves occurred within a changing political context, where aviation had been discursively resignified as a major cause of climate change. In other words, Labour had failed in its efforts to rhetorically redescribe its expansion plans as a policy of sustainable aviation, which would be underpinned by a beatific fantasy in which aviation expansion and environmental sustainability could be linked in a harmonious and mutually reinforcing fashion, and it was unable to turn this signifier into an empty signifier that could fix the meaning of airports and air travel, and hold together a wider and hegemonic pro-expansion coalition.

In this task, at least during the Heathrow consultation, Flying Matters and Future Heathrow were unable to offer the Brown government the ideological cover that Freedom to Fly had offered the Blair government in the consultation over the ATWP. In fact, the aviation industry lobby was caught napping, partly because it had disbanded Freedom to Fly under the mistaken belief that it had won the case for expansion in 2003. Its arguments in favour of responsible growth were persistently discredited and failed to resonate within a changing political context in which aviation was signified as a threat to the environment and a major contributor of carbon emissions. Even ministerial appeals to solve the 'Heathrow hassle' misfired, because they were tied to criticisms of the monopoly of BAA and 'poor' regulation, rather than fears over capacity constraints at the international hub. Finally, despite internal splits within his own party, Gordon Brown had overinvested in the expansion of Heathrow. Along with other critics and media commentators, one can only wonder why Labour held on to its discredited plans for so long. Answers can be found in the hegemony of the productivist and growth orientations in the Labour Party, as well as Brown's position within his own party and his particular style of leadership. But Labour's close relationships with key sections of the aviation industry were also a significant factor. Unfortunately for Brown, his public support for expansion at Heathrow was caught up in the collapse of the Labour project in the opinion polls, as well as growing public concerns over his government and his leadership of it. Indeed, it is difficult to deny that the Labour government, while recognising the challenge of reducing carbon emissions from commercial aviation, failed decisively in its efforts to constitute a legitimate policy consensus around a discourse of sustainable aviation. In our concluding chapter, we delve deeper into this failure, while seeking to critically explain the important policy change it helped to make possible.

Notes

1 Civil Aviation Authority press releases, 16 March 2009, www.caa. co.uk/application.aspx?catid=14&pagetype=65&appid=7&mode= detail&nid=1726, and 15 March 2010, www.caa.co.uk/application. aspx?catid=14&pagetype=65&appid=7&mode=detail&nid=1846 (accessed 22 December 2012).

2 *Sun*, 3 April 2006; *Sunday Times*, 8 October 2006; *Guardian*, 12 April 2006; *Guardian*, 1 March 2008.

3 See www.planestupid.com (accessed 28 October 2009).

4 Plane Stupid press release, 2 January 2006, www.planestupid.com/ content/battle-lines-drawn%3A-green-activists-plan-halt-airport-expansion-2nd-january-2006 (accessed 22 December 2012).

5 Plane Stupid blog, 11 April 2006, www.planestupid.com/blog?page=97 (accessed 23 December 2012); see also *Guardian*, 12 April 2006.

6 See www.planestupid.com/home (accessed 30 October 2009).

7 *London Evening Standard*, 27 February 2008; *Guardian*, 31 May 2008; *Daily Mail*, 10 June 2009.

8 Plane Stupid, newsletter no. 7, www.planestupid.com/newsletter7 (accessed 30 October 2009).

9 Other members included Labour MPs and Lords such as Alan Keen, Ann Keen, Joan Ruddock (Climate Change Minister) and Lord Faulkner; Conservatives such as Adam Afyrie, John Randall, Nick Hurd; and Liberal Democrats such as Susan Kramer, Vincent Cable and Tom Brake (Stewart, 2010: 16–17).

10 See the Greenpeace website, www.greenpeace.org.uk/blog/climate/london-mayoral-candidates-unite-against-heathrow-expansion (accessed 5 January 2013).

11 See www.hacan.org.uk/news/press_releases.php?id=184 (accessed 10 February 2012).

12 BBC News, 20 April 2006, news.bbc.co.uk/1/hi/uk_politics/4925444.stm (accessed 10 February 2012).

13 The September 2007 policy report also recommended *inter alia* taxes on fuel-inefficient cars; a power station waste heat levy; curbs on

energy-wasting household goods; feed-in tariffs for small-scale low-carbon technologies; restrictions on energy-wasting stand-by lights; and a cap on energy use by domestic appliances (Connelly, 2009: 143). Indeed, policy papers like *Power to the People: The Decentralised Energy Revolution* and *The Low Carbon Economy: Security, Stability and Green Growth*, which were published in December 2007 and January 2009 respectively, added to this new environmental focus of the Conservatives (Conservative Party, 2007b, 2009).

14 In his assessment of the Conservative and Liberal Democrat coalition government and its environmental policy, James Connelly (2011: 125) raises the question of how far the commitment to oppose further runways in the south-east was more a question of 'symbol than substance'.

15 Future Heathrow, launch press release, 23 May 2005; see also BBC News, 14 December 2006, news.bbc.co.uk/1/hi/england/london/6178867.stm (accessed 20 November 2007).

16 The DfT report on passengers' experiences at UK airports negatively compared delays at Heathrow with the performance of its European counterparts. Significantly, it noted that Paris and Frankfurt, which outperformed Heathrow on delays to either arrival and/or departure rates, had more runways than the London airport (DfT, 2007c: 26).

17 HACAN ClearSkies press release, 6 November 2007, www.hacan.org.uk/news/press_releases.php (accessed 20 November 2007).

18 Justine Greening press release, 10 March 2008, www.justinegreening.co.uk/outside-parliament/view_detail.php?id=446238df65b2dfa6da9295e44e1f3dc8 (accessed 9 February 2011).

19 See www.cbi.org.uk/ndbs/press.nsf (accessed 20 April 2010).

20 See www.flightglobal.com/news/articles/industry-backs-third-heathrow-runway-as-consultation-opens-219826 (accessed 5 January 2013).

21 *The Times*, 'BAA Takeover by Ferrovial as Bad as Rover Deal', 23 April 2008; http://news.bbc.co.uk/1/hi/uk/7314816.stm (accessed 2 April 2009).

22 See CC (2008: 287–98) and the CC press release of 20 August 2008, www.competition-commission.org.uk/assets/competitioncommission/docs/pdf/non-inquiry/press_rel/2008/aug/pdf/24-08 (assessed 22 December 2012); see also *Independent*, 21 August 2008; *Guardian*, 18 and 21 August 2008.

23 Gatwick was sold to Global Infrastructure Partners in October 2009. Stansted was sold to Manchester Airports Group in January 2013.

24 *Guardian*, 18 August 2008; *Sunday Times*, 23 November 2008; *Independent*, 21 May 2008; *Independent*, 21 December 2008; *Observer*, 21 December 2008.

25 *Guardian*, 30 June, 29 September and 13 October 2008; Stop Stansted Expansion press release, 1 October 2008, www.stopstanstedexpansion.com/press338.html (accessed 22 December 2012).

26 BBC News, 14 December 2006, news.bbc.co.uk/1/hi/uk_politics/6177543.stm (accessed 23 September 2011).

27 *New Statesman*, 29 October 2008; *Times*, 2 November 2008; *Financial Times*, 10 November 2008.

28 *London Evening Standard*, 29 October 2008; *Telegraph*, 14 December 2008; *Guardian*, 21 December 2008.

29 Early day motion 2344, session 2007-08, tabled 27 October 2008, www.parliament.uk/edm/2007-08/2344 (accessed 22 December 2012).

30 See the Labour Party website, www.labour.org.uk/tories_letting_down_business_on_heathrow_-_hoon,2008-10-06 (accessed 16 August 2011).

31 *Hansard*, House of Common Debates, 11 November 2008, vol. 482, cols 641–3, www.publications.parliament.uk/pa/cm200708/cmhansrd/cm081111/debtext/81111-0005.htm (accessed 23 December 2012).

32 Early day motion 339, session 2008–09, tabled 17 December 2008, www.parliament.uk/edm/2008-09/339 (accessed 21 December 2012). See also news.bbc.co.uk/1/hi/uk_politics/7788763.stm (accessed 21 December 2012).

33 For the full details of the 'west London third runway' poll for Greenpeace, see www.icmresearch.com/pdfs/2008_dec_greenpeace_heathrow_poll.pdf (accessed 10 January 2012).

34 See www.publications.parliament.uk/pa/cm200809/cmhansrd/cm090115/debtext/90115-0005.htm (accessed 19 August 2011).

35 See www.hacan.org.uk/news/latest.php, 3 December 2009 (accessed 14 September 2011).

36 AirportWatch press release, 7 April 2009, airportwatch.org.uk/news/detail.php?art_id=3051 (accessed 19 September 2011).

37 AirportWatch press release, 8 December 2009, airportwatch.org.uk/news/detail.php?art_id=352 (accessed 9 May 2010).

38 Sustainable Aviation press release, 8 December 2009, www.bata.uk.com/Web/Documents/media/Pressreleases/SA%20CCC%20Media%20Release%2081209.pdf (accessed 19 September 2011).

39 BBC News, 26 March 2010, news.bbc.co.uk/1/hi/england/london/8588220.stm (accessed 10 April 2010); *Guardian*, 27 March 2010.

40 BBC News, 13 May 2010, www.bbc.co.uk/news/10112386 (accessed 17 May 2010).

Conclusion

> UK air travel has increased five-fold over the last 30 years. Half the population now flies at least once a year. And freight traffic at UK airports has doubled since 1990. Britain's economy increasingly depends on air travel, for exports, tourism and inward investment. The aviation industry directly supports around 200,000 jobs and indirectly up to three times that. Airports are important to the economies of the English regions and of Scotland, Wales and Northern Ireland. Aviation links remote communities and helps people stay in touch with friends and family around the world. It brings businesses together and has given many affordable access to foreign travel. All the evidence suggests that air travel will continue growing over the next 30 years. *But if we want to continue enjoying its benefits, we have to increase capacity.* (DfT, 2003d: 2; our emphasis)

> There is an urgent need for a genuinely sustainable framework to guide the aviation industry in planning its investment and technological development in the short, medium and long term. The previous government's 2003 White Paper, *The Future of Air Transport*, is *fundamentally out of date*, because it fails to give sufficient weight to the challenge of climate change. In maintaining its support for new runways – in particular at Heathrow – in the face of the local environmental impacts and mounting evidence of aviation's growing contribution towards climate change, the previous government got the balance wrong. It failed to adapt its policies to the fact that climate change has become one of the gravest threats we face. (DfT, 2011b: 4; our emphasis)

Global aviation is increasingly pictured as both a promise and a threat in the modern age. For many, powered air travel is a symbol of progress, growth and modernity, an integral and exhilarating part of the accelerating logic of late capitalist societies. It is widely considered to be a driver of economic development and connectivity in an increasingly mobile world, which plays a vital role in bringing together families, friends, businesses and workers, while transporting commuters, tourists, holidaymakers, spectators and pilgrims to far-flung places of the globe. Yet the massive expansion of global aviation, with its insatiable demand for more airport capacity and its growing contribution to carbon emissions, makes it a critical societal problem. Alongside traditional concerns about noise and air pollution and the disruption of local communities, airport politics has been connected to the problems of climate change, peak oil and social inequalities.

Our book has explored various aspects of this paradox in the UK context, especially the intensifying contradiction between aviation as a progressive force for growth, modernisation and mobility, and aviation as a cause of disruption, political unrest, policy vacillation and environmental degradation. Focusing on attempts by the New Labour government to engineer an acceptable policy of sustainable aviation, we have examined the way in which the problem of airport capacity in the UK, and especially in the south-east of England, has been transformed into a wicked policy issue that defies a rational and equitable policy solution. In explaining this transformation, we have stressed the way in which aviation and airports were discursively resignified in the first decade or so of the new century. Where for most of the twentieth century they were viewed as unquestioned forces for good, at the start of the twenty-first they were increasingly conceived as destructive and negative components of the modern transportation system. In developing our explanation, we have also emphasised the challenges posed to government by the power of scientific discourse and expert knowledge, which was produced and disseminated by bodies like the Environmental Audit Committee, the Sustainable Development Commission and the Tyndall Centre for Climate Change Research, and how the campaign against the third runway at Heathrow turned local residents and environmental campaigners, the perpetual 'losers' of aviation expansion, into apparent 'winners'.

In tarrying with these evolving problems and policy shifts, our study has furnished a thick descriptive analysis of the protest campaigns and policy-making practices that have marked British aviation since the murky origins of Heathrow airport during the Second World War. Grounded in documentary analysis, policy texts, media representations, and interviews with key actors, the study has delineated and explained the rival rhetorical and discursive strategies articulated by the coalitions seeking to shape public policy. Throughout the book we have used our distinctive poststructuralist approach to policy analysis, which we elaborate in the first chapter, to construct and analyse five key problematisations, which are enumerated below. More specifically, building on a range of critical and interpretivist traditions of research, we showed how our concepts of hegemony, rhetoric, heresthetics and fantasy offer novel twists in explaining policy change and stabilisation. We also demonstrated how these notions can be set to work in concrete policy research by outlining Glynos and Howarth's logics of critical explanation, and by conceptualising our objects of research and empirical data in terms of text and discourse.

In this concluding chapter, we shall draw together the various threads of our argument by returning to the key problematisations that orient our study, before integrating our main findings and explanations. We shall also make explicit the critical dimension of our analysis, before assessing the challenges facing environmentalists and government in the face of concerted pressures from the aviation industry to expand. We thus provide an evaluation of the emergent discourses on aviation, with a view to sketching out future directions for airports policy in the UK. In the policy stalemate brought about by the Conservative–Liberal Democrat coalition government, and faced with the exhaustion of Labour's ideological appeals to garner support for what we have termed a fantasmatic discourse of sustainable aviation, we conclude that government has to take the lead in aviation policy, constructing and defending a clear line which embraces the logic of sufficiency (Princen 2003, 2005), while offering a credible balance between economic growth and environmental protection.

Problematisations and solutions

In chapter 2 of the book, which draws upon Michel Foucault's concept of problematisation, which we have connected to policy problems, we presented the five main problematisations we discerned and explored in our study. These are: (1) the institution and installation of the regime of aviation expansion during the Second World War; (2) the struggle over the expansion or regulation of aviation at the start of the twenty-first century; (3) the subsequent reframing of aviation, not least as a threat to carbon emission targets; (4) the governmental and industry response to the resignification of aviation; and (5) the ensuing policy stalemate. Below, we address the first four problematisations, after which we present a more extended discussion of our fifth problematisation, which enables us to return to some of the fundamental questions we address in our research.

1. *The regime of aviation expansion*

Our first problematisation concerned the debates about the location, character and extent of the major commercial airport infrastructure in post-war Britain. In chapter 3 we elaborated a genealogical narrative of post-war British aviation by delineating the social, political and fantasmatic logics that worked together to institute and prolong the contradictory regime of aviation expansion. Our analysis demonstrated the ignoble origins of UK airports policy by focusing on the contingent choice of Heathrow as the major airport, and then the development of Gatwick and Stansted. Importantly, we argued that successive governments bought into, and helped to perpetuate, what we have termed a fantasmatic narrative on aviation. This narrative foregrounded both the beatific benefits of aviation expansion for the British economy, and the horrific threats of overcapacity at British airports and of competition from the United States in the aftermath of the Second World War. Once etched into the key departments and discourses of the British state, as well as the wider social and cultural habitus, the logic of aviation expansion acquired a path dependence, which proved difficult to change.

Chapter 3 also delved into the debates about the logic and character of aviation expansion during this period. Of particular interest in this regard was the Thatcher government's decisions to deregulate, liberalise and privatise key components of the UK aviation industry during the 1980s, so that aviation and airports became integral elements in the shift from a Fordist to a predominantly post-Fordist regime of capital accumulation. In the process, aviation, airports and their associated practices became less connected to the state and its imperatives, and more involved with the market, tourism and private consumption.

Finally, we dwell upon the campaigns of local residents opposed to the state-led and market-driven logics of airport expansion in the post-war period. We argue that these political struggles, along with the ideological and policy disputes about the preferred mode of aviation expansion in the 1970s and 1980s, show the contingency of the regime of aviation that was installed in the middle of the twentieth century, as well as the options and paths that were closed off in the process. Nonetheless, we conclude that the regime of aviation expansion resonated with the crucial myths and fantasies of post-war Britain. Indeed, as we suggest above, with the ostensible success of the Thatcher governments' policies of privatisation and liberalisation in aviation in the 1980s and early 1990s, air transport was once again strategically placed at the centre of Britain's economic prospects.

2. Expansion or regulation?

Our second problematisation arises from the resultant expansion of aviation in the last third of the twentieth century and the growing demands for greater airport capacity. Here the problem was represented to be the unresolved and contested role of government and the state in either planning for airport expansion, or endeavouring to manage demand in a more constraining fashion. We showed how the dislocations that were generated by the contradictory regime of aviation expansion led to the production of new grievances and demands, notably in the struggles about the location of London's third airport, the ongoing expansion of Heathrow and the proposed building of a second runway at Manchester airport in the 1990s. More particularly, we demonstrated how the latter struggle, and the growing awareness of the impact of aviation emissions on the environment, brought into being new political alliances and strategies, as direct action protesters joined forces with local residents and established environmental pressure groups like FoE and Greenpeace. Temporary equivalential linkages were constructed between different demands by naming and opposing Manchester airport's expansionist plans and its supporters as a common enemy, a strategy later redeployed in the struggle against expansion at Heathrow and other airports.

Entering office in May 1997, the New Labour government sought to resolve the mounting problems about airport capacity, by convening a national consultation exercise on aviation, which ran from 2000 to 2003, followed by the announcement of firm proposals. Yet the government's logic of therapeutic consultation and its efforts to broker a long-term settlement between rival stakeholders misfired, so that rather than resolving the heightened tensions and sharpening contradictions, the consultation process served mainly to create the conditions for the construction of two opposed discourse coalitions – the pro-expansionist Freedom to Fly and the pro-regulation AirportWatch – that each sought to impose its own solution on government. Our analysis of the emergence and formation of these coalitions in chapter 4, as well as their rhetoric, strategies and political impact on the UK aviation industry, highlighted the fact that Airport-Watch was able to construct equivalences between the demands voiced in particular airport campaigns into a more universal challenge that was directed against the threat of airport expansion across the whole country. But, importantly, we also concluded that Freedom to Fly's rhetorical redescription of the aviation industry as a proponent of responsible growth and sustainable aviation provided New Labour with the requisite ideological cover and intellectual justification for supporting a policy of airport expansion.

New Labour's policy proposals were set out in its 2003 air transport white paper, and in chapter 5 we developed an in-depth textual analysis of its form and content, supplementing our poststructuralist approach with tools drawn from critical discourse analysis and rhetorical political analysis. Conceptualising the 2003 ATWP as a specific genre of political communication, we examined its framing and underlying problematisation of aviation policy. We demonstrated that New Labour envisaged aviation expansion as an 'inevitable' trajectory, though it also recognised the increasing environmental impacts and adverse social consequences of air travel. The problem of sustainable aviation was thus conceived to be one of achieving a balanced strategy, and the ATWP outlined a series of strategies to realise this goal. Based on our analysis of the white paper and the surrounding policy documents, we named and characterised these strategies as those of brokerage, deferred responsibility or individualisation, and incentivisation. Chapter 5 thus concluded that the rhetoric of sustainable aviation and its proposed resolution of competing demands enabled New Labour in 2003 to come out in favour of the largest postwar expansion of British airports.

3. The resignification of UK aviation
Our third problematisation explored the subsequent resignification of aviation, not least as a threat to carbon emission targets and the world's climate, which occurred in the aftermath of the 2003 white paper. Chapter 6 described the discursive practices and processes that enabled the reframing of aviation in the first decade of the new century. By systematically analysing a broad corpus of expert texts and scientific reports, we demonstrated the strong correlations between the scientific statements enunciated in the reports and

findings of the Environmental Audit Committee, the Sustainable Development Commission, the Tyndall Centre, and the Stern review, and we showed how the repeated public interventions of scientists and experts in aviation policy paved the way for the collapse of the fantasmatic narrative of sustainable aviation, which was put together during the consultation process. In particular, we provided copious empirical evidence of the way in which opponents to expansion discredited New Labour's 2003 air transport white paper (ATWP), and sought to draw equivalences between demands to regulate aviation expansion and demands to tackle climate change, such that aviation and flying became synonymous with climate change. The upshot of these discursive practices was a growing resignification of aviation, so that rather than being understood as an unquestioned good, it became widely acknowledged as a horrific 'threat' or 'culprit' responsible for climate change and environmental destruction. Finally, we suggested that this resignification of aviation, following the expert scrutiny of the white paper, put in place the conditions for the resurgence of anti-expansion coalitions, making new narratives and appeals possible and articulating novel sets of demands.

4. Counter-strategies

Our penultimate problematisation of the problem of aviation concerned the governmental and industry's response to the cultural resignification of aviation. Our problematisation focused on the ways in which the government and industry sought to negate the growing challenge to the logic of aviation expansion, while seeking to develop the means to address the policy problems that emerged. How could those who favoured expansion counter the growing pressures to change the overall direction of aviation policy? What strategies and tactics were elaborated and followed in an effort to offset the growing political and ideological challenges?

In addressing these questions, we concentrated our analysis on the rhetorical devices, ideological practices and governmental rationalities through which the Labour government sought to deal with the problems brought about by the reframing of aviation. Our analysis highlighted the logic of difference at work in this regard, as the government pursued specific strategies and tactics that were designed to negate opposition and then make possible the implementation of its plans. Attempts were made to break up the chains of equivalence that connected aviation to the destruction of the countryside, the disruption of local communities, environmental degradation, social inequality, and climate change, thus making possible the implementation of its expansion proposals. Included in the latter were its own endeavours at ideological reframing; appeals to 'technological fixes' and rival scientific expertise; the deployment of the 'horrific' threats of European, US and increasingly Chinese expansion; the discursive positioning of government as an honest broker; the logic of deferred responsibility in which, for example, New Labour laid blame for lack of regulation on its international partners; the shift from what we have termed a 'therapeutic' to a more 'managed' mode of consultation; and the diverse tactics and practices associated 'the conduct of carbon conduct' (Paterson and Stripple, 2010). We drew particular attention to New Labour's advocacy of emissions trading, which acted over time as a nodal point for its policy of sustainable aviation, mainly because it offered the promise of simultaneously maintaining competitiveness, managing demand and protecting the environment.

But we also exposed the contradictions and ideological ambiguities in the various rationalities that were employed by the Labour government in dealing with what had evolved into a wicked policy problem. We show, for example, that in its commitment to a logic of brokerage the government presented itself as the arbiter of the public interest and defender of the common good. Yet this commitment was compromised by the fact that it had also devised the strategies of deferred responsibility and incentivisation, which tended to bracket out the role of government in delivering substantial outcomes. We also showed that Labour's attempts to recycle the rhetoric, political strategies and tactics embedded within its white paper failed to counter the collapse of its fantasmatic narrative of sustainable aviation, which began to lose its grip in a changing political context, marked by heightened public concern about climate change and the collapse of the New Labour project. Nonetheless, despite these limitations, in January 2009 the Brown government went ahead with proposals to build a third runway at Heathrow, which brings us neatly to our fifth and final problematisation. But, because this problematisation returns us to the dominant concern of the book, it requires a little more elaboration.

Losers and winners, equivalences and differences

Just a few days after assuming power in May 2010, the Conservative–Liberal Democrat coalition government announced that there would be no new runways at Heathrow, Gatwick and Stansted airports. The coalition proposed instead a more efficient use of existing resources – a 'better not bigger' Heathrow – as well as plans for high-speed rail as an alternative to expansion. These commitments stemmed from the Conservative and Liberal Democrat election manifesto pledges, which ruled out airport expansions in the south-east of England. The Liberal Democrats promised to 'cancel plans for a third runway at Heathrow and other airport expansion in the South East', while aiming 'to fully meet European air quality targets by 2012' (Liberal Democrats, 2010: 42). The Conservatives also came out in favour of the 'reform [of] Air Passenger Duty to encourage a switch to fuller and cleaner planes' (Conservative Party, 2010: 23). Its 2010 election manifesto acknowledged that 'because travel abroad is so important for our economy and for family holidays, we need to improve our airports and reduce the environmental impact of flying'; but it maintained that the party's goal was 'to make Heathrow airport better, not bigger' (Conservative Party, 2010: 23). In fact, speaking on the BBC's Daily Politics Election Debates, the Tory MP Greg Clark went so far as to declare that 'we've got no plans to build any more runways in the South East', though this statement and others were subsequently amended.[1]

Of course, this moratorium on new runways did not usher in a definitive settlement of the problems afflicting the field of aviation policy and practice. On the contrary, as we intimated in chapter 7, a range of powerful interests and forces remained persuaded of the need to expand UK aviation in the face of growing international competition, and these voices continued to express deeply held beliefs about the role of aviation as a driver of economic growth and jobs.[2] Yet, despite its precarious and uncertain status, it is clear that a significant political and cultural shift had taken place in the politics of airport expansion and aviation policy. As we have documented in the book, all previous UK governments and administrations since the Second World War had assumed that the expansion of the aviation industry and its attendant infrastructural needs was an inevitable and necessary boon to the UK economy and society. In the view of Chris Mullin, for instance, Minister for Aviation in the Blair government from July 1999 to February 2001, the demands of the aviation industry have been 'insatiable' and 'successive governments have usually given way to them'. Writing in the *London Evening Standard* on 14 January 2003, he noted that 'although nowadays the industry pays lip service to the notion of sustainability, its demands are essentially unchanged. It wants more of everything – airports, runways, terminals.' Yet the Conservatives and Liberal Democrats had still made their opposition to a third runway at Heathrow and further expansions at Gatwick and Stansted an emblematic issue in the lead-up to the 2010 election. From their converging perspectives, economic growth did not automatically trump the environment, while quality-of-life issues were not subsumed by powerful economic logics and interests. How, then, are we to provide a critical explanation of this important shift? What are the conditions that account for this policy reversal? And how and why were perpetual losers able to become winners?

At first glance, the change of government in May 2010 was the decisive factor in ending the previous administration's plans to expand Heathrow and other airports in the south-east of England. In its joint programme, the coalition immediately advanced its environmental credentials, promising that

> this coalition has the potential for era-changing, convention-challenging, radical reform [as] we both want to build a new economy from the rubble of the old. We will support sustainable growth and enterprise, balanced across all regions and all industries, and promote the green industries that are essential for our future … with radical plans to reform our broken banking system and new incentives for green growth. (HM Government, 2010: 7)

It is clear that the formation of the coalition government in May 2010, with its aspiration to become 'the greenest government ever', was an important condition in accounting for the shift, though this in turn presupposes the transformation of the Conservative Party under David Cameron, and his efforts to detoxify and rebrand the Tories following his election as leader in 2005. But, as we argued in chapter 7, both of these facts have to be seen in relation to the practices of key anti-airport expansion social movements and pressure groups, which were able to highlight the perils of aviation and its connection to climate change, while providing ideological cover for the Conservative and Liberal Democratic parties on the issue of airport expansions in the south-east of England. At the same time, we also stressed the importance of scientific experts and knowledge in exposing the fantasmatic narrative of sustainable aviation, as well as the changing institutional and structural conditions of the UK following the global financial crisis.

There is no doubt that one important reason why the anti-expansion campaigns were able to influence sections of the major political parties, while getting their messages heard in the mass media, was that their demands resonated with the problem of climate change, as it became increasingly prominent during the first decade of the new century. The focus on resonances among dispersed events and forces in various contexts provides a useful way of examining the way in which heterogeneous elements can coalesce into broader projects or assemblages. This notion informs Maarten Hajer's account of ecological modernisation discourses in the Netherlands and the UK, as well as William Connolly's exploration of the intertwining of evangelical Christianity, neoliberalism and neoconservatism in the US during the last ten or fifteen years (Hajer, 1995; Connolly, 2008).[3]

Yet it is not in our view sufficient to explain these forms. To begin with, resonance requires the repetition of key arguments and ideas in various contexts by different forces and agencies. We have already noted in our analysis of the construction of broader anti-airport coalitions since the mid-1990s that different organisations repeated the same rhetorical themes and messages with respect to the connection between growing aviation emissions and climate change. Along with the reverberations of various forces and demands, as well as the repetition of selected rhetorical statements and ideas, we also need to bring out the strategic dimension in the making and breaking of political coalitions. It is here that the logics of equivalence and difference, as well as the role of heresthetic, assume their importance. As we have suggested, the leaderships of AirportWatch and HACAN ClearSkies were aided by the Labour government's decision to open a national consultation, which broke with the political logic of 'divide and rule' and facilitated the articulation of universal demands against expansion. But resonances have to be noticed and constructed by the interventions of key actors and agents; they are never simply given. More precisely, in our view, the various grievances and demands have to be linked together into a common project, and this common project is often unified by reference to a common enemy or opponent.

With respect to the creation of linkages between different demands, we have shown in this book how the anti-expansion activists successfully displaced their demands to stop the expansion of Heathrow, Gatwick and Stansted to other social relations (such as the economy and concerns about social justice), while simultaneously representing their grievances and claims in terms of concerns about aviation and climate change. The traditional concerns with property expropriation, noise and air pollution – the particularistic roots of much (if not all) local campaigning – were thus supplemented and overdetermined by the more general and universal issues thrown up by the aviation industry and climate change: 'airport expansion' came to signify the 'aviation industry', and the 'aviation industry' came to signify the problem of 'climate change'. The meanings of both elements were thus fused together in the successful transformation of the campaigns.

But this transformative political campaign was possible, in part, only because of the way in which local residents at public inquiries into expansion (notably at Heathrow) were dislocated by their experiences of the process and by the eventual outcomes, and because of the campaigning of strategically placed political entrepreneurs, such as John Stewart and Jeff Gazzard, who developed novel strategies and tactics. It was also made possible by the availability of demand management, which operated as an empty signifier that enabled the construction of equivalences between competing demands, as well as the construction of antagonistic relations between differently positioned agents.

Put more fully, especially in the period following the publication of the 2003 ATWP, those groups and associations that were opposed to airport expansions in the south-east of England articulated demands that resonated with similar demands that were being voiced about the problem of climate change. These resonances and affinities were repeated by various actors and organisations in multiple spaces and arenas. Yet, as we have argued, the connections between the emergent carbon coalition and the anti-airport expansion campaigns were not given, but had to be socially as well as politically constructed. Equivalences between airports, property expropriations, noise and air pollution, aviation and climate change were established by key individuals and activists connected to the various campaigns against particular expansions.

However, the construction of a discourse coalition by creating equivalences between disparate elements is not sufficient to capture the dynamics of protest and the policy shifts we have been charting, for these projects invariably interact with rival forces, which are also striving to impose their own interests and values. It is here that the intersecting logics of equivalence and difference have to be stressed, as projects seek simultaneously to interrupt each other's aspirations through practices of disarticulating the demands and identities that are connected in an opposed assemblage, and then rearticulating these demands in their own project. This is also the point at which various heresthetical operations come into play, for, as we have suggested, the art of political manipulation involves the way in which certain issues or dimensions or politics are rendered visible or invisible, and then acted upon.

We have noted, for example, how in our case the aviation industry, with its hunger for more airports and other transport infrastructure, was presented by its advocates as an essential component of economic growth, jobs and prosperity. On the other hand, however, a key part of the anti-expansion campaigns was to negate the claims made by the pro-aviation camp about the benefits of aviation to the UK economy. In other words, those opposed to the proposals of the 2003 white paper were not only successful in highlighting the connections between airports, the aviation industry and climate change, but they also raised significant doubts about the overall benefits of the aviation industry to the UK economy and society. They commissioned reports to investigate the economic contribution of aviation and they used the conclusions to nullify the pro-expansion arguments. For example, in 2005 Friends of the Earth commissioned a report from the Dutch environmental consultancy CE. The conclusions of the report, entitled *The Contribution of Aviation to the Economy: Assessment of Arguments Put Forward* (CE, 2005), were used to nullify the pro-expansion arguments, particularly those articulated in the pro-expansion reports of Oxford Economic Forecasting. Similar practices were repeated by other anti-expansion groups as part of an onslaught of reports tackling the economics of aviation. Notably, the anti-expansion lobby returned to CE some three years later to commission another report into the economics of aviation expansion, this time to break up the economic arguments in favour of the third runway and sixth terminal at Heathrow (CE Delft, 2008).

In short, opponents of airport expansion either sought to make the economic case for expansion invisible, or sought to challenge the alleged benefits of expansion in the name of alternative forms of economic growth, which did not rely so heavily upon the aviation industry (interview with local campaigner). In conjunction with such rhetorical moves, the anti-expansion coalition made visible the contribution of aviation to carbon emissions and climate change, thus introducing and simultaneously redefining the environmental dimension in an effort to divide the pro-aviation forces and to win over supporters not directly affected by particular expansions at specific airports. New discursive articulations were thus deployed to disrupt the pro-aviation project.

In chapter 7, we charted the effects of the new environmental issue in splitting the pro-aviation coalition and uniting different elements in a novel political project. Part of this logic of disarticulation and rearticulation occurred at the interface between local groups and the major political parties. Resonance, repetition, equivalence and heresthetic were thus essential in binding together the anti-expansion demands and in catapulting their campaign into the forefront of political debate.

The resignification of aviation and environment by opponents of airport expansion also resulted in the production of a wicked policy problem. Whereas previous struggles around particular airports tended to focus on the location of new airports or the expansion of existing infrastructure, the new emphasis on climate change and the global impacts of carbon emissions caused by airlines transformed a difficult though tractable issue into a seemingly irresolvable one. But again, the emergence of airport expansion as a wicked problem was not given or automatic. In important respects, it was partly constituted as an intractable policy controversy by the political actions and practices of its opponents.

Our analysis of this process drew attention to the hegemonic practices that informed the decisions and actions of groups and movements opposed to airport expansion, while using our distinctive category of hegemony to assess the effects of their campaigns. In fact, apparently victorious campaigns, like all successful hegemonic practices, are fragile and precarious constructions, particularly at heightened moments of success, when followers may often perceive the initial goals of the movement as having been achieved (Chong, 1991). Having blocked the construction of a new runway and terminal at Heathrow, as well as runways at Gatwick and Stansted, the leadership of HACAN ClearSkies and AirportWatch thus now faced new and ongoing challenges, which we discuss below.

Nonetheless, the resignifying operations and political practices of campaigners brought the policy of aviation and airport expansion to at least a temporary standstill. But this judgement has to be refined in the light of our more complex concept of hegemony, which includes the policy, institutional and cultural dimensions. Restricting our focus to the policy domain, it could be concluded that, following the victory of the coalition in May 2010, the losers of 2003 became the winners in the battle over the future of air transport in the UK. Their actions have resulted in the production of a wicked policy issue, which may in turn lay the basis for a policy fiasco (Bovens and 't Hart, 1998).

Yet this policy victory has also to be tempered by a consideration of the other dimensions of hegemony that we have explicated in our theoretical chapter and genealogical narrative of airport expansion in the UK. A successful policy reversal in this field does require institutional changes and reorganisations, especially (in this case) in the DfT. A fully fledged sea-change in government attitudes and policy towards aviation, something approximating the change in roads policy in the UK during the 1990s, not to mention the changes in economic policy that occurred in the 1970s and 1980s – the movement from Keynesianism to neoliberalism – would require changes of belief among key civil servants, as well as the reorganisation of the department itself. For well over fifty years the DfT (or its functional equivalent) has been at the forefront of supporting and promoting the UK's aviation sector. This imperative is written into its institutional materiality so to speak, and its desire to realise this goal may prove (and has proved) difficult (if not impossible) to dislodge (interview with local campaigner; see Roffey, 2013; Vidal, 2009). For example, as we pointed out in our characterisation of the post-war regime of aviation expansion in chapter 3, officials had already decided in their minds in 1953 that Stansted airport was their preferred choice for London's third airport. After much debate and contestation over the best part of three decades this ambition was eventually realised in 1991, when Stansted did emerge as London's *de facto* third airport. Perhaps a similar logic pertains to the ongoing debates about the third runway and sixth terminal at Heathrow, and the more general need for airport expansion in the south-east of England, especially in the light of the continued and intensifying pressures for expansion from those within the aviation industry? Bringing in the role of the state and its institutional configuration thus problematises the simple assertion that policy hegemony has been achieved by the anti-expansion forces.

What, then, about the societal or cultural aspect of hegemonic struggle, which points to the deepest and most extensive dimension of the concept? On the surface, here the picture seems to support the anti-expansion campaigns, as the wider public appears to accept the connection between the expansion of the industry and its impact on climate change. What is more, local campaigns, which are traditionally associated with the narrow self-interest of middle-class groups, are now integral to a more universal and moral set of concerns. Yet there are important queries about the solidity of citizen opposition to airports and aviation. Citizens may reject aviation expansion and binge-flying when asked, but their actions continually contra-dict the beliefs they espouse. As we noted in our problematisation of aviation in chapter 2, large numbers of citizens in the UK and across the world continue to travel by airline for their leisure and business, despite rising costs, growing delays and their supposed ideo-logical commitments. In some quarters of the population, concern for climate change, and recognition of aviation as a contributor to global warming, has arguably been falling in recent years (Office for National Statistics, 2011: 6, 9). The creation of a post-expansion consensus in the field of aviation is thus fragile and precarious. In short, unless a hegemonic consensus at all three levels of society – policy, institu-tional and cultural – has been attained, coupled with the elaboration of feasible and desirable alternatives to air travel, then sustainable aviation in the UK (and elsewhere) remains a distant dream. These reflections bring us to considerations about the future of the aviation and airports in the UK context.

Critique

Our genealogical narrative of airport politics and policy in the UK during the last sixty or so years was designed to explain the current policy impasse, as well as the dynamics of coalition-building and cam-paigning that brought it about. But what are the ethical and normative implications of our account? Where is the *critical* dimension of our critical explanation? It is here that our logics of critical explanation come fully into view, for they allow us to detect moments of radical contingency, in which other ways of thinking and acting are possible, and they enable us to explore the various modes through which policies and practices come to cover over the radical contingency of things and processes (which prompted the emergence and formation of policies and practices in the first place). As Foucault made explicit in his later writings, exhibiting the *contingency* of a practice, identity or regime provides a vital inroad into its critique and evaluation. His genealogical studies were thus carried out in part to 'separate out, from the *contingency* that has made us what we are, the possibility of no longer being, doing, or thinking what we are, do, or think' (Foucault, 1984b: 46).

At the outset, our use of social logics has enabled us to characterise the post-war regime of aviation expansion in the UK. Based on policy instruments like 'predict and provide' and governmental techniques like cost–benefit analysis, though constrained by various forms of public consultation, the logic of airport expansion appeared in the eyes of the great majority to be natural and inevitable. But it is important to stress that this regime of practices and policies represented only one way of organising social relations and that it was always vulnerable to challenge and contestation. In part, this is because it was the product of bitter power struggles and political decisions, in which various forces competed to impose their visions of airports and aviation. As we have argued, before the novel challenges to the expansion of Manchester airport in the mid-1990s, then the formation of the antagonistic discourse coalitions in the run-up to the 2003 white paper, and finally the broad coalitions that opposed expansions at Heathrow and Stansted following the pro-expansion policy of the New Labour government, the regime of aviation was an obvious and taken-for-granted fact. (Indeed, some parts of the anti-expansion campaign focused their energies on disputes about the precise location of airport expansion, rather than the desirability of aviation expansion *per se*.) Yet these struggles exposed the fact that the logic of expansion was not natural or inevitable; there were alternative policies and practices that had to be considered by governments, the aviation industry, affected communities and citizens in general. The moratorium on airport expansion in the south-east by the coalition government reinforces the contingent nature of airport and aviation policy in the UK. Of course, as we have suggested, this commitment is itself contingent; it is by no means certain that it will remain unchallenged and may even be reversed.

Our analysis of the construction of the rival coalitions struggling to shape aviation policy enables us to show other possibilities of social organisation at each key conjuncture, when the 'ignoble origins' of a practice or regime are reactivated and challenged, and when new decisions are taken and instituted (Nietzsche, 1994). This complex operation of political logics – the intersecting logics of equivalence and difference – reveals the contingency of things, as well as the structural undecidability of seemingly natural rules and practices. Political logics thus indicate those points of conflict or antagonism when policies, practices and regimes can be formed and transformed in different ways.

Exposing the contingency of practices and regimes by discerning the political origin of social logics is important in developing our critical explanation. But we also need to explore the ideological justification and grip of those practices, policies and regimes which seek to conceal the contingency of decisions and social relations. Our recourse to the idea of ideological cover represents one of the ways in which we have explored this dimension of our problem. We have used the concept to characterise both the pro-expansion and the anti-expansion campaigns, though our analysis discloses important differences in the ideological discourses that have been articulated.

First, we need to say a word about the idea itself. The provision of ideological cover does not mean that groups like Freedom to Fly or AirportWatch articulated a form of distorted consciousness, which functioned as a series of false representations about an essentially true state of affairs. It is not an epistemological category. But nor is it a purely descriptive one that simply captures the beliefs and argumentative structures of groups seeking to advance their cause. Instead, the notion draws attention to the way in which (individual and collective) agents operating at a distance from the government and the state are able to construct and mobilise narratives that can advance their interests, as well as those of the elected government and the state, in ways that the latter are not able to. Ideological cover thus provides a government with a greater degree of freedom and more space for political manoeuvre in pursing policies that may attract intense criticism from affected interests, as well as adverse popular opinion.[4]

In providing ideological cover for the pro-expansion lobby, a group like Freedom to Fly (and later Flying Matters) elaborated a discourse of sustainable aviation, which emphasised the need for responsible and sustainable growth. But as its name suggests, Freedom to Fly was also able to make more strident expansionist arguments in terms that overtly stressed values like personal freedom and individual mobility, while emphasising demands for greater economic growth and aviation expansion, which would not have been fully consistent with New Labour ideology. Crucially, moreover, its distance from New Labour gave it licence to criticise and debunk anti-expansion claims. These negative tactics did not preclude personal attacks on key supporters of the anti-expansion campaign. For example, at the height of the public debate about the future of air transport in June 2003, Dan Hodges, the director of Freedom to Fly, said: 'We think it is hypocritical that Terry Waite and Jamie Oliver should be campaigning against expansion when they fly so extensively themselves' (*Cambridge News*, 21 June 2003). Similar allegations were made about other activists and prominent supporters of the anti-expansion groups. Freedom to Fly also placed advertisements in a series of local newspapers (such as the *East*

Anglian Daily Times) under the headline: 'They fly. Why shouldn't you?' These interventions drew attention to the fact that celebrities and campaigners against expansion were regular airline passengers.[5] The important point about these tactics is that they operated below the official public discourse of the New Labour government and the UK state. The latter would have been publicly embarrassed to be persistently associated with the making of these kinds of accusations and yet they directly benefited from their construction and dissemination.

The New Labour government, for its part, relied exclusively on the discourse of sustainable aviation to justify and garner support for its policy of airport expansion. The notion of sustainability was often used by New Labour politicians like John Prescott to describe various activities and policies; aviation was quickly subsumed under this rhetorical manoeuvre. But the metaphor of sustainable aviation, which, as we have argued, was put forward as a putative empty signifier that could bind together disparate and contradictory economic, environmental and cultural demands, failed to grip subjects and thus square the circle of balancing aviation expansion and environmental protection. Instead, as we made clear in chapter 6, this discourse was widely criticised by scientists, anti-expansion groups and media commentators, because it was based on a fantasmatic narrative that was perceived not to conceal the contingencies and ambiguities of aviation expansion. For government to support a policy of aviation expansion and to be seriously concerned with climate change was viewed by many as a desire to have their cake and eat it.

In our terms, then, 'sustainable aviation' failed to function as an empty signifier, because it could not mask the differences between contradictory impulses and because it was unable to cover over the lack of rational agreement to which it aspired. Instead, it functioned as a floating signifier – an object of hegemonic contestation – as various forces sought to fix its meaning. Indeed, the very notion of sustainable aviation left the government exposed to criticism and vilification, as the anti-expansion coalition successfully pointed to the *unsustainable* character of its proposed policies. This meant that the discourse of sustainable aviation, with its pro-growth policies, carried a further risk: a severe undermining of trust in government on this issue. The experience of the consultation process, which we analysed in chapter 4, followed by the attempt to dress up a policy output of airport expansion in terms of sustainable aviation, was taken by opponents of expansion as an insult and an affront. It stimulated more intense and direct forms of campaigning, which ran the risk of further eroding trust in democratic government.

In short, the myth of sustainable aviation put forward by the pro-expansion forces was perceived to be little more than a fantasmatic narrative, which covered over the contingency of the post-war regime of aviation expansion, thus naturalising its domination over airport policy. This made it difficult, if not impossible, to transform the myth of sustainable aviation into a stable social imaginary, which could organise the thinking and practices about airports and aviation in the UK. Any future proposals for the growth of airports and aviation would now have to be presented to the public as a straight trade-off between, on the one hand, economic growth, jobs and international competitiveness and, on the other hand, the protection of the environment and local communities.

What, then, of the anti-expansion forces? We have noted how these groups and networks articulated the myth of demand management as one possible response to the crises and dislocations spawned by the growth of aviation and airport expansion. The idea of demand management required government and state intervention to curb what anti-expansion groups claimed was excessive passenger demand for aviation. As their campaign progressed, 'excessive' airport expansion mutated into an 'unsustainable' demand for growth, where the concept of unsustainable was extended to include not only local communities but all those affected by carbon emissions and climate change. In much the same way as Freedom to Fly afforded protection to the Labour government in 2003, proponents of demand management offered ideological cover for the Conservative and Liberal Democrats to impose a moratorium on airport expansion in the south-east.

A compelling case can be made that the discourse of demand management, which has, over time, come to include an explicit concern with the impact of aviation on carbon emissions, is more in line with the dominant strands of scientific thinking about climate change (IPCC, 2007; but see also Hulme, 2009: 106–7). The discourse also displays a greater attentiveness to the radical contingency of objects and processes, which resonates with our particular conception of ethics. It will be recalled that, in our approach, the ethical dimension of social relations captures the way in which subjects relate to the contingency and fragility of things (Glynos and Howarth, 2007: 197–9; Howarth, 2008, 2010). Do their practices and actions conceal contingency and thus naturalise domination, or do they acknowledge it, and thus seek to cultivate more appropriate responses to it? Whereas pro-expansion forces either deny contingency in the name of a fantasmatic narrative of sustainable aviation, or cover over the fragility of things by invoking a technological fix or by investing in various forms of emissions trading, the calls for demand management are more sensitive to the dangers of airport expansion and its effects on communities and the environment. We return to these points when we consider the normative content of current discourses on sustainable aviation.

Before we do so, it is important to note that 'demand management' also functions as an empty signifier that holds together a range of forces, all of which are at the very least opposed to unsustainable airport expansion in the south-east of England (and possibly the UK). But there are also difficulties and tensions with this discursive strategy. For one thing, any broad alliance of forces is composed of different and often contradictory elements that emphasise various strategies and employ different modes of argumentation. Typically, these elements are precariously linked together. Demand management is no exception to this rule. It brings together those who espouse more moderate demands about the curtailment of airport expansion with those who want radical changes to the UK transport system, including those who wish to transform a wide range of social relations and practices which they associate with destructive forms of capitalism. It also incorporates those with a narrow interest to stop a particular expansion in a specific location with those who want to address the problem at the national, regional or even global level. What is more, the anti-expansion coalition gathers together arguments and appeals that can be positioned on a continuum bordered by the rational and affective dimensions. For example, some are concerned with the technical and scientific aspects of airport expansion, whereas others focus on emotional appeals to local communities, traditional ways of life, or the impact of aviation on climate change and its damaging effects on animal habitats and eco-systems. The question of economic growth also divides the anti-expansion forces, with some favouring alternative forms of green growth, which do not entail airport expansion, and others favouring the curtailment of growth altogether. Finally, it embraces those who found themselves ministers within the coalition government, those who occupy respectable positions in established social movement organisations and those who remain committed to continuing the campaign from locations beyond the state, still willing to use radical strategies and tactics, including direct action.

The anti-expansion coalition, therefore, has to balance conflicting demands, interests, identities and modes of campaigning. Even maintaining a minimal opposition to further airport expansion in the south-east of England involves a careful practice of mediating between those forces that wish to displace the problem of expansion from their particular location to another and that those that are attracted to the building of a completely new airport (for example on the Thames estuary), so long as it will not affect any local communities. Campaigners also have to balance demands between those who are anti-aviation and those who are just against the expansion of airports in particular places. Narrow calls for demand management and the restriction of airport growth in particular places are often more focused and rational, but they are opposed by more emotional demands about jobs, economic growth and international competition. The broader appeals of climate change have more emotional resonance for larger swathes of the population, but they can weaken the intensity of bread-and-butter appeals to property expropriation, noise and air pollution – the quality-of-life issues that are the mainstays of most local campaigns (Feldman and Milch, 1982).

Campaigners may also be tempted to overplay the impact of aviation on climate change, or stress too strongly the catastrophic consequences of climate change. This may in turn lead to accusations that anti-expansion groups are peddling a fantasy of horrific climate change, which may produce public resignation and helplessness. Indeed, these difficulties facing the anti-expansion groups cannot be divorced from the challenge of developing new strategies, practices and goals, which may enable them to transform themselves in a context in which they appear to have become the dominant players. There is a strong argument to suggest that this challenge requires a further round of transformative political campaigning, so that they can generate alternative visions that go beyond a simple opposition to expansion and towards more desirable and feasible alternatives to mass air travel (Griggs and Howarth, 2004). These and other considerations bring us, finally, to the content of the discourses under consideration, which in our terms concerns the normative dimension of our study.

Moving forward: normative evaluation

It is clear that our focus on radical contingency is connected to the practice of critique, as this focus can disclose points of political contestation and moments of possible reversal. Our critique is also connected to our analysis of the provision of ideological cover by pro- and anti-expansion forces, as well as the pinpointing of fantasmatic narratives, which conceal contingency and perpetuate certain regimes and practices. Yet we most certainly concur with the view of critical theorists like William Connolly, who urge poststructuralists to go beyond the strategy of simply inverting existing hierarchies and binary oppositions in order to project more 'positive ontopolitical presumptions' (Connolly, 1995, 2008). Negative critique goes hand in hand with normative evaluation. But how is this possible, and under what conditions?

Here, it is important to distinguish between ethics and our grounds for normative evaluation. Ethics, in our perspective, involves an acknowledgement of the radical contingency of social existence – the 'lack' inherent in any identity or order of being – and a particular way of responding to 'its' demands: an *ethos* that faces up to the fact that each of us is necessarily marked by our identifications with an object that fills the lack, and which defines *who* we are and *what* we stand for. By contrast, questions of normativity are directed at the concrete relations of domination in which subjects are positioned. Normative questions thus require the analyst to characterise those relations that are perceived to be oppressive or unfair in the name of alternative values or principles (Howarth, 2008, 2010).

Two elements come into play here. First, there are the values that are brought to any interpretation by the theorist (in our case, for example, the values associated with a project of radical democracy that is attentive to environmental challenges) as well as the accompanying tasks of continually clarifying, justifying and modifying them. Secondly, there is the task of pinpointing and remaining attentive to those new values and identities encountered in the practices interpreted: what might be deemed the 'counter-logics' of social domination and oppression. These counter-logics, which may amount to little more than 'marginal practices' that are not subsumed by relations of domination, must themselves be evaluated in terms of their own internal standards and in terms of our contestable values and ideals. Yet they may, in turn, lead us to revise the normative grounds of our judgements and justifications (Glynos and Howarth, 2007).

How, then, does this relate to the case of UK airports? What should be done about airport expansion in the UK and the growth of the aviation industry more generally? Are there any policy prescriptions and strategic implications that emerge from our story? These are complex and controversial questions that require much reflection and deliberation. In practice, any policy of sustainable aviation is likely to be a somewhat 'messy' or 'clumsy' affair, as it brings together a package of policy instruments that are designed to address the multiple problematisations and contingent outcomes of interventions in the field of airport expansion (Griggs and Howarth, 2012). Indeed, the political and scientific uncertainty currently structuring airport politics may well lend itself to such 'messiness', which allegedly avoids the exclusion of one or more of the different 'problem solution' dynamics that inform aviation policy and practice (Verweij et al., 2006: 16–19).

'Clumsy' solutions tend to prosper where decision-making processes generate uncertainty rather than certainty. But they can also create an open culture throughout the formulation and implementation of policy so as to capture learning and forge consensus (Priemus, 2010). Megaprojects such as new airports, rail routes and road networks are inherently risky affairs, which engage multiple actors with conflicting interests and which frequently rely on poorly informed cost–benefit analyses. They are often undertaken with a limited consideration of alternatives and inadequate problem analysis, as particular project concepts are 'locked in' or 'captured' early on by producer interests (Flyvbjerg, 2009; Priemus, 2008: 108–10). Decisional optimism and the strategic misrepresentation of information thus combine in megaprojects to produce a formula of underestimated costs and overestimated benefits (Flyvbjerg, 2005: 15; Flyvbjerg et al., 2009). Creating an open culture, that gives sufficient weight to problem analysis, that considers alternatives and that facilitates stakeholders by challenging the very assumptions underpinning project approval throughout the decision-making cycle, may well support the construction of 'clumsy' solutions that forge consensus (Priemus, 2010).

The practices of decision-making informing the 2003 ATWP and the approval for the third runway at Heathrow failed to engineer such conditions. Despite extensive consultation, the limits of what we have termed Labour's 'therapeutic consultation' left local residents and environmentalists excluded from the deliberative exercise. Political debate was polarised between competing coalitions. What is more, as Flyvbjerg et al. (2003: 5) suggest, this polarisation was exacerbated by the clash of competing 'truths' and rival constructions of social reality. Efforts to communicate 'authoritative claims' (Hajer, 2009) via the white paper were further blighted by an unconvincing identification of the public interest, especially with respect to issues of environmental sustainability, as well as its commitment to the discourse of sustainable aviation. Like previous governments, which had sought to act as both the 'promoter' of the aviation industry and the 'guardian' of the public interest, New Labour found itself on the horns of a dilemma (Flyvbjerg *et al.*, 2003: 138).

Difficulties like these serve to shed further light on the intrinsic political and ideological dimensions of megaprojects and the limitations of information and consultation strategies in forging a consensus or workable compromise. In our case, calculations about the costs and benefits of airport expansion were structured by the dominant fantasmatic narratives on UK aviation, which outlined the opportunities and looming disasters that would befall government and local communities should approval for new runways or terminals be given or refused. Equally, as we have shown in our empirical analyses, such appeals were often part and parcel of attempts by rival coalitions to provide ideological cover for government or opposition parties. Managerial or technocratic strategies were repeatedly embroiled in antagonistic rivalries and societal divisions. As David Apter and Nagayo Sawa reveal in their poignant analysis of the protests and mass mobilizations against Narita airport in Japan during the 1960s and 1970s, bargaining and reconciliation processes can be severely circumscribed 'once deeply felt principles have been invoked' (Apter and Sawa, 1984: 225–6). This observation was borne out in our investigation of the UK case. What is more, as our analysis of the campaign against the third runway at Heathrow demonstrates, principled oppositions in the field of airport politics are often brought into consultations as the legacy of earlier failed campaigns and engagement in decision-making processes.

In his analysis of the persistent conflicts over climate change, Mike Hulme (2009: 339) ultimately casts doubt on the effectiveness of 'clumsy' solutions to tackle the unexpected and contradictory outcomes that typify efforts to address wicked issues. He argues that disagreements in this domain are rooted not merely in contested understandings of scientific knowledge, but also in competing webs of ethical and ideological beliefs, attitudes to risk and technology, as well as rival interpretations of the past and visions of the future (Hulme, 2009: xxvi). These competing perspectives are sustained by opposed climate change 'myths', that is, 'powerful shared narratives which bind together otherwise quite different perspectives and people' (Hulme, 2009: 341). He contrasts, for example, myths 'presaging apocalypse', in which climate change poses radical threatening changes to our planet, with those 'constructing Babel', in which scientific and techno-logical innovations and human ingenuity enable humanity to master any challenges posed by global warming (Hulme, 2009: 340–55).

The politics of airport expansion is increasingly represented within and through these sorts of climate change narratives. Indeed, there is a growing sense among both scientific experts concerned about climate change and campaigners opposed to expansion that it is an 'emblematic problem' of contemporary environmental politics (Hajer, 1995: 19–20). Our study has also demonstrated that the problem of airport expansion has, during the first decade of the twenty-first century, become increasingly polarised between two dominant discourse coalitions, which compete to impose their rival demands upon government. What is more, the inability of either coalition to score a decisive victory has resulted in a policy stalemate, which has characterised both the Labour and Conservative-Liberal Democratic administrations. These competing coalitions each draw upon the popular myths of climate change, whether they are the horrific fanta-sies of catastrophic decline or the beatific fantasies of technological fixes and market solutions. Each calls upon government to take the lead, albeit in the direction of different policy outcomes.

Typically, then, two emergent discourses have elaborated competing visions about the future of aviation in the UK and across the world: either technological developments in air travel enable the maintenance of its continued expansion, or environmental constraints and the limits of peak oil combine to ensure its decline (see Bowen, 2010: 269–70; Urry, 2009: 36). We take the discourse of sustainable aviation to be a variant of high-modernism or techno-managerialism, though it also shares important family resemblances with ecological modernisation, and we see the discourse of demand management in relation to the role of state regulation and wider cultural change. In concluding this section, we examine each of these emergent discourses in more detail. We then go on to assess the challenges currently facing the UK govern-ment and authorities in endeavouring to resolve the problem, before setting out our alternative interim vision. Here, our proposal calls upon the government to construct a clear line in aviation – a defensible balance between economic growth and environmental protection – with which it can lead and educate the public.

*1. High-modernism or techno-managerialism: the discourse of
sustainable aviation*

What we have named the discourse of high-modernism or techno-managerialism, which is propounded by the pro-expansion coalition, embodies the 'self-confident' belief in scientific and technical progress, and thus the domination of human beings over nature (Scott, 1998: 4). Proponents of this discourse argue that technological fixes and human ingenuity can resolve any of the actual or potential contradictions between environmental protection, ecological destruction and airport expansion. High-modernist visions are often combined with the images and rhetoric of ecological modernisation in which the promises of green technology ensure a positive-sum game of economic growth *and* environmental protection. In this paradigm, collaborative networks exude a capacity for technological leadership, so that the aviation industry works with wider stakeholders and government departments to bring about change (see Hajer, 1995; Mol, 2000; Walker, 2011; Weale, 1992). With the right financial incentives in place to drive forward change within the industry, the challenges of climate change for aviation are thereby constructed as a set of manageable risks to be mitigated by technical innovation and human ingenuity.

Importantly, high-modernist discourses continue to buy into and reproduce sedimented narratives of aviation as an 'economic booster', thus attributing to aviation a pivotal role in future economic modernisation. A singularly high modernist like John Kasarda (2011) goes further, when he envisages the construction of 'aerotropolises' – airport production nodes – around which cluster time-sensitive and 'smart growth' economic activities, which will form pivotal elements in the global economy of the future. Of course, while articulating such claims of economic modernisation, enunciators of this discourse dispute the extent of the technical challenge facing aviation, with many high modernists repeatedly contrasting estimates of aviation's 2–3 per cent contribution to all global carbon emissions with what they point out are higher contributions from other industries, such as power generation and land use. The Aviation Foundation in its overview of aviation and the environment thus privileges comparative assessments of the contribution of aviation to carbon emissions, highlighting, for example, the fact that the grounding of all UK flights 'would reduce global carbon dioxide emissions by 0.1 per cent'.[6]

In policy terms, high modernists demand government support for the technological transformation of the industry, and they call for more airport capacity to protect the UK's economic competitiveness. They also defend aviation against any form of regulation that might hamper its economic competitiveness, while supporting global emissions trading schemes, for example, rather than regional schemes that might advantage global competitors. On the other hand, they oppose the imposition of unilateral national taxes on aviation (see for example the Fair Tax on Flying campaign which lobbied against rises in air passenger duty). In their view, more fuel-efficient aircraft and greater numbers of larger (1,000-seat) aircraft, as well as new open rotor or propfan rotor engines, alongside air management efficiencies, such as continuous descent, and the introduction of new biofuels, all offer potential technological fixes (Bowen, 2010: 270–81). In fact, these developments are deemed to be already under way, evident in initiatives such as the Airbus A380, the Boeing Dreamliner and recent experimentation with biofuels.[7]

Typically, the Sustainable Aviation network has committed its membership to reduce aviation emissions to 2000 levels by 2050, while predicting a three-fold growth in air travel (Sustainable Aviation, 2008: 1). In its *Manifesto for Copenhagen*, which was released before the 2009 international climate change summit, the industry network came out in support of global CO_2 targets, emissions trading and incentives for low-carbon aviation fuels (Sustainable Aviation, 2011: 11). Its 2011 progress report brought forward ongoing collaborative technological improvements for public approval, such as the air management operational improvements of the 'perfect flight', the benefits of continuous-climb departures and continuous-descent approaches, as well as work on sustainable aviation fuels and technological developments in aircraft design (Sustainable Aviation, 2011).

We have already noted the difficulties with the form and function of the pro-aviation discourse. By promising a neat solution to a seemingly intractable problem, the discourse of sustainable aviation takes the form of a fantasmatic narrative, which is deployed to cover over the ambiguities and contingencies of its more concrete policies and proposals. These difficulties are also evident in the content of the discourse, which both underplays the obstacles in the path of a genuinely sustainable approach to airport expansion, while overemphasising the ability of governments and the aviation industry to keep to their environmental targets and promises. There are serious doubts about delivering adequate supplies of biofuels and there are questions about the role of emissions trading schemes in reducing carbon emissions nationally and globally. Finally, there are powerful limits on new aviation technologies and more efficient operating systems. Indeed, in our view, it is because of these difficulties that the government and industry have increasingly resorted to fantasmatic narratives and ideological appeals.

2. State regulation and cultural change: the discourse of demand management

The discourse of demand management, by contrast, which is articulated by the anti-expansion forces, calls for government to intervene by imposing top-down regulations on the aviation industry and air passengers. In their discourse, rising emissions cannot be addressed without the concerted actions of local and national governments, as well as supranational bodies.[8] Appeals to demand management tap into fears about the rising carbon emissions generated by aviation, while articulating demands for government to tackle the social injustices and fiscal concessions associated with the current logics of aviation expansion. These demands are reproduced in tandem with calls to end government indecision, as well as concerns about the politics of producer capture and the inadequate regulation of the aviation industry (see McManners, 2012: 165–7). In part, this discourse coalition rearticulates elements of 'post-mobility' discourses, which foresee the inevitable end of mass aviation following the imminent arrival of peak oil and aviation's energy-intensive use of kerosene, while drawing upon horrific narratives of the impacts of climate change on humanity (Urry, 2011). It is striking that some proponents of demand management draw deliberate parallels between the aviation and tobacco industries. Aviation is thus portrayed as the 'new' tobacco industry, as it is enmeshed in irresponsible corporate profit-seeking; is seen to 'capture' key government departments (evident, for example, in the absence of tax on aviation fuel); and imposes harmful impacts on individuals and communities, especially those who do not fly, but who nevertheless suffer from the severe impacts of climate change on their local environments.

Proponents of demand management contest the effectiveness of market instruments and technological fixes, as well as the capacity of individual actions in meeting the challenge of reducing aviation emissions. Typically, its supporters attack emissions trading as an 'incomplete' policy instrument, which permits the continued growth of aviation through offsetting emissions and buying additional permits from other industries which cut their emissions.[9] Similarly, they cast doubt on future technological efficiencies and operational improvements in air travel, and challenge the potential for biofuels to substitute for kerosene (AirportWatch, 2011: 21–3). Key to their approach is a plea for the immediate end to all plans for airport expansion, as well as limits on short-haul and domestic flights, until the aviation industry can demonstrate that it has lowered its carbon emissions. Finally, they call on government, industry and citizens to develop alternative modes of transport and 'slower' practices of mobility (see for example Gilbert and Perl, 2010).

In the interim vision presented within demand management discourse, government must end the 'special status' accorded to aviation by bringing taxation policies on the industry into line with those on other industries, and by fully integrating air travel into broader climate change policies and emission targets (McManners, 2012). In order to achieve these goals, its proponents set out a policy agenda that advances: the inclusion of all international flights in emission targets; the bringing forward of 'robust' monitoring and reviewing mechanisms of airlines performance against emissions targets (in such a way as to update targets in light of the emerging scientific evidence on the non-CO_2 impacts of air travel); the imposition of regular increases to air passenger duty and aviation taxation so as to manage demand and move aviation 'to fiscal equality with motoring'; and support for rail substitution for short-haul flights, domestic 'staycation' holidays, as well as increasing use of virtual meetings and new information technologies to overcome demands for travel (AirportWatch, 2011: 30–4; WWF-UK, 2008).

Our critique of demand management discourse has noted its correlation with the majority scientific view about the linkages between aviation and carbon emissions, as well as its attentiveness to the contingency of things. As against the short-termism of the pro-aviation lobby, whose demands resonate with the desire for rapid economic growth today, the discourse of demand management is more in tune with the long-term view about environmental sustainability. Yet its current call for government to manage and regulate passenger demand in the UK runs the risk of being too narrow and too negative. It is too narrow because its protagonists must provide a wider vision of aviation's place in a sustainable transport policy (both in the UK and globally) and too negative because its supporters need to move from a 'strategy of opposition' to a 'strategy of constructing a new order' (Laclau and Mouffe, 1985: 189). More precisely, for the sup-porters of the demand management discourse to achieve their interim vision, their demands cannot be limited to the setting of targets for passenger numbers and constraints on airport expansion, but must also bring about and institutionalise a gestalt switch in thinking about aviation. The cultural resignification of aviation needs the production of a new common sense about the role and limits of air transport and its attendant infrastructural requirements. But this will require the anti-expansion groups to connect with other anti-airport groups in different national contexts, and with other environmental move-ments in the UK and elsewhere, to form a wider hegemonic project, which can transform our attitudes towards flying and transport more generally. Of course, in our view, this will require a different role for government, to which we now turn.

The challenges facing government

Our reflections upon, and evaluations of, these emergent discourses need to be seen in relation to our genealogical narrative of airport politics, which has plotted the role of competing political projects and the construction of multiple lines of conflict and interaction between rival discourse coalitions. More precisely, at the end of a ten-year policy cycle surrounding airport expansion, which began with the Labour government's consultation exercise at the start of the new century, opposition to expansion at Heathrow has not subsided, while the coalition government has wavered in its opposition to a third runway in the face of an intensive campaign by the aviation industry to expand the international hub. At the global level, both China and the US have come out against the EU ETS (*Guardian*, 6 June 2011).[10] Indeed, Giovanni Bisignani, who was director general and chief executive of the International Air Transport Association (IATA) from 2002 to 2011, repeatedly questioned the EU scheme. In early June 2011, for example, he called for it to be abandoned, thus challenging governments not to 'kill the goose [aviation] that lays golden eggs'.[11] Environmental organisations have not been slow to challenge such claims, offering evidence to the European Court of Justice against the case of the US Air Transport Association and in support of six EU member states which defend the regime: the UK, France, Spain, Sweden, Poland and Denmark.[12] Endemic conflicts and competing demands like these present particular challenges for governments, which in modern times have become a privileged site for constructing policy 'problems' out of competing social demands and claims across policy sectors. Our story of the failure of New Labour to engineer a settlement in aviation, and the current stalemate faced by the coalition, thus require us to think carefully about the role of government. How is government to deal with the rival demands that are articulated by different actors and groups? How is it to avoid losing legitimacy by excluding particular demands or privileging some over others?

The UK government under Labour sought to legitimise its practices and discourse by engaging in a range of consultative activities designed to win over the hearts and minds of the British public to the idea of 'sustainable aviation'. But real questions were raised about these processes of consultation and democratic deliberation. Are these practices merely smokescreens and window-dressing exercises, which are designed to co-opt protestors or buy them off, thus neutralising legitimate demands and democratic protest? Some affected groups and organisations certainly believe this to be the case. And their case is strengthened when even these seemingly token forms of public engagement are threatened by policy reversals and further expansion. In short, the perceived vacillation of government in dealing decisively with the issue has led many local protesters and environmental campaigners to question the very logic of traditional democratic engagement, and they have turned instead to other forms of political activity, such as civil disobedience, mass demonstrations and direct action (though these strategies have also prompted pro-aviation groups to become more vocal in pursuing their objectives). Equally, supporters of expansion have grown increasingly frustrated with government indecision, and so have renewed the campaigns for airport expansion in the south-east and articulated grievances over the unfair treatment of aviation, poor planning procedures and incremental decision-making.

The narrative of 'broken promises', which has been repeatedly expressed by local residents and protest groups, reflects the crisis of governance and collective decision-making and is prompted by the twists and turns of government. Talk of 'broken promises' places immense pressure on government to maintain public trust if it is to engineer an enduring settlement. However, our stress on the primacy of political practices and processes, which underpins our post-structuralist theory of policy-making, also challenges those forces and approaches that are tempted by the ideal of a rational consensus as the desired outcome of policy formulation, implementation and evaluation. In part, we do so by rendering obsolete the belief in the potential eradication of antagonism and disagreement through negotiation and dialogue. In fact, as this study clearly demonstrates, there is currently no ideological response or form of ideological cover left open to government. In short, the failure of New Labour and its endeavours to put in place a policy of sustainable aviation, which balances competing demands in aviation, has bankrupted the appeal of such policy responses.

Interim visions and positive problematics

Now, as Connolly rightly insists, because every interpretation in political analysis is an 'ontopolitical interpretation', it not only pre-supposes a specific and contestable ontological perspective, but it also involves the projection of certain *ideals* into our objects of investigation, so as to characterise, explain and criticise problematised practices, policies and regimes (Connolly, 1995). Our interpretation of the battle over airport expansion in the UK is thus rooted in a particular normative and critical understanding of government and its role in democratic societies, what Connolly has called a 'positive problematic' (Connolly, 2008: 215). More precisely, we argue that, in the current policy context, and under certain conditions, government can and ought to be an active *agent*, one which can bring about a certain degree of social and political change. Its functions thus include the provision of proper democratic procedures, practices of persuasion, the manufacturing of alliances and compromises between forces, the education of the public, the exercise of leadership, as well as the transformation of subjective preferences, interests and even identities. Indeed, in this view, an important task of government is to crystallise 'partial equilibria' from a whole range of pressures, griev-ances and claims, before it should then seek to persuade the public of the merits of its case. In short, governments are entrusted to reach just and mutually acceptable balances between multiple demands and objectives, such as economic growth, environmental protection, levels of taxation, the safeguarding of local communities, and concerns for non-human forms of life, although in our view these agreements should remain contestable and revisable. In this sense, governments and the state can to some extent transcend the particularities of con-tending forces and assume a more universal stance.

Importantly, in the current policy context, what we deem to be progressive governments should work on forging connections between different struggles, preferences and interests that aim to bring about more sustainable forms of aviation and mobility. As our study has shown, the policy process almost inevitably leads to the drawing of boundaries between different social groups and their demands, while the formation of policy regimes, understood as 'sites' for political contestation, is more often than not predicated upon patterns of exclusion, as conflicting groups seek to universalise their narrow sectional interests and values (Howarth, 2006).

How, then, can progressive alliances be constructed in a democratic fashion? And what is the role of government? In the first place, government should endeavour to include all relevant and affected policy actors and discourse coalitions on an issue like aviation by designing public spaces and arenas that are transparent, responsive and fair. It should also strive to provide a capacious definition of the issue under consideration so as to ensure that all voices are heard in a democratic fashion (Dryzek, 1996; Held, 1995: 236; Sørensen, 2005: 354). From our point of view, and especially with respect to the problem of airport capacity, rhetoric, affect and passion should not be sacrificed on a too narrow conception of public reason (Norval, 2007; Young, 2000.) In order to mitigate the adverse effects of structural power and exclusion, which we documented, for example, in our analysis of the 2000–03 consultation, governments should also experiment with alternative forms of democratic consultation and will-formation, including the convening of citizens' juries, the use of deliberative polling or the construction of other sorts of mini-public (Smith, 2009; Ward *et al.*, 2003).

Going further, governments can even strive to engineer democratically constituted governance networks, comprising a range of public and private agencies, while ensuring that the deliberations and decisions that are taken in these networks are fair and reasonable. But in certain circumstances government may also have to intervene more directly in order to build or support progressive coalitions, which can connect popular demands and interests in ways that are more inclusive and legitimate than traditional forms of interest representation and mediation. Of course, the bringing together of broader coalitions will not necessarily resolve conflicts that traverse a given policy arena. On the contrary, it may well harden the boundaries that exist between opposing stakeholders, or it may generate a false consensus in which antagonisms are wrongly displaced or concealed, leaving groups unrepresented and excluded from a particular policy domain, and unable to challenge the terms of their exclusion (Griggs and Howarth, 2007b). As we have demonstrated in our empirical case study this can, and often does, pose further problems for government.

Our response to this dilemma is twofold. To begin with, as Chantal Mouffe, Aletta Norval and others argue, antagonistic relations do not necessarily have to take the form of an absolute division between 'us' and 'them', or distinctions between 'friends' and 'enemies', where the existence of the 'other' necessarily threatens the identity of the 'we' (Mouffe, 2005: 20–1).[13] Nor do we believe, along with agonistic theories of democracy, that governments and public authorities can and ought to eliminate antagonisms altogether. Instead, with the right kind of ethos, backed up by suitably designed democratic institutions and practices, antagonists may be encouraged to recognise the legitimacy of each other's demands and strive to produce more satisfactory agreements. It is here, therefore, that we argue that governments can work to construct agonistic 'we/they' relations between competing coalitions in which adversaries acknowledge the rights and interests of their opponents, so that 'while in conflict, they see themselves as belonging to the same political association, as sharing a common symbolic space within which the conflict takes place' (Mouffe, 2005: 20).

At the same time, as we have noted, on an issue like aviation, governments of a progressive hue should also strive to construct a clear policy line – a relatively clear and defensible balance between economic growth and environmental protection, mobility and the well-being of local communities – and then seek to lead and educate the public. This is not easy. Governments have first to understand and construct the problem; their problematisations must yield an understanding and knowledge of the problems they must tackle, though these understandings are liable to disclose the 'messiness' and 'complications' of problems rather than purely rational, tractable and easily consensual policy solutions. Moreover, as in many policy arenas – taxation, public spending, security, health and so forth – governments confront an objective dilemma: the public, and even individual subjects, are profoundly split in many contemporary liberal democracies. For example, most citizens say that they want action on the environment and measures to protect their 'quality of life'; yet at the same time they also baulk at the idea of higher aviation costs, the imposition of fuel taxes and various moves to limit private consumption and mobility. The logics of electoral competition exacerbate the difficulties confronting governments, further constraining the art of the possible.

But governments with the right will and nerve can in our view strike appropriate settlements. And they still have some room for manoeuvre to cajole, manage and negotiate between a range of opposed interests and identities, which means that they do have the power to frame politics and wicked policy issues in imaginative ways. They can, in short, present what Connolly calls 'positive futures' or social imaginaries that are better. And they are, of course, assisted by movements and groups in society who articulate and disseminate more progressive visions of an 'eco-egalitarian capitalism' (Connolly, 2008). Abandoning the ideal of a rational consensus does not, therefore, mean the impossibility of a reasonable and workable compromise.

What, finally, is to be done? In the case of UK aviation, governments should place an immediate moratorium on the expansion of airports across the UK (not simply in the south-east) and tax aviation fuel at the same rate as road fuel. They should also look to strengthen the caps imposed through emissions trading for airplanes to encourage the use of cleaner technology, while promoting high-speed rail routes to reduce short-haul aviation.[14] Broadly speaking, such policies would rest upon a shift towards what Thomas Princen has called a 'logic of sufficiency', and which Anders Hayden has employed in the field of aviation policy (Princen, 2003; Hayden, 2011). Rather than seeking ever more productive or efficient uses of resources, the principles and politics of sufficiency draw upon the 'sense that, as one does more and more of an activity, there can be enough and there can be too much' (Princen, 2003: 43). Sufficiency principles privilege restraint, coupling the precautionary principle and adherence to 'polluter pays' regulations with the pre-emptive principles of zero impacts and 'reverse onus' principle, which both oblige producers to prove the environmental sustainability of development programmes before embarking upon any such initiatives (Princen, 2003: 8, 47–8; 86, 357). Indeed, as Hayden (2011) suggests, the decision by the coalition to reverse government approval for the construction of the third runway is one example of the principle of sufficiency in practice. But only time will tell if a politics of sufficiency can maintain its precarious hold over aviation and airport policy in the UK, or whether the logics of efficiency, growth and competition will reassert their hegemony.

Notes

1 Daily Politics Election Debates, 26 April 2010, www.bbc.co.uk/programmes/b00s781d (accessed 23 April 2012).

2 In November 2010, for example, Simon Buck, chief executive of the British Air Transport Association (BATA), criticised the coalition's failure to 'develop any tangible aviation policy', characterising aviation as 'the Cinderella of the Coalition's Transport Strategy'. BATA press release, 1 November 2010, p. 1, www.bata.uk.com/category/media-centre/media-releases (accessed 3 July 2011).

3 One source of this idea is the work of Deleuze and Guattari, who make a useful distinction between macropolitics and micropolitics – what they term the molecular and molar levels of analysis respectively – and then seek to connect the two levels in a dynamic understanding of social and political processes. For example, in their compelling, if controversial account of the emergence of fascism, Deleuze and Guattari argue that 'the concept of the totalitarian state applies only at the macropolitical level', whereas 'fascism is inseparable from a proliferation of molecular forces in interaction, which skip from point to point, before beginning to resonate together in the National Socialist State. Rural fascism and city or neighbourhood fascism, youth fascism and war veteran's fascism, fascism of the Left and fascism of the Right, fascism of the couple, family, school, and office: every fascism is defined by a micro-black hole that stands on its own and communicates with the others, before resonating in a great central black hole' (Deleuze and Guattari, 1987: 236). The interaction of multiple ideological resonances and discursive affinities among disparate elements is thus important in efforts to account for the construction and success of wider assemblages and coalitions.

4 Hence the concept of ideological cover captures both a logic of 'covering over', in which discourses conceal radical contingency, and a logic of providing room for manoeuvre, where contingency may not be completely concealed and denied, but tarried with.

5 BBC News, 22 June 2003, news.bbc.co.uk/1/hi/england/essex/3009912.stm (accessed 19 April 2012).

6 See Aviation Foundation, Fast Facts: Impact on the Environment, www.aviation-foundation.org/Fast-Facts (accessed 18 July 2012). Equally, the Enviro-Aero group, which is funded by the global Air Transport Action Group and commercial aviation, undertakes such tactics in its efforts to 'provide clear information on the many industry measures underway to limit the impact of aviation on the environment' – www.enviro.areo/Enviroaeroabout.aspx (accessed 5 August 2011).

7 Virgin Atlantic has undertaken test flights from London to Amsterdam using blended fuels (20 per cent biofuels and 80 per cent kerosene) in one of four engines on a Boeing 747 – see www.virgin-atlantic.com/en/us/allaboutus/environment/biofuel.jsp (accessed 30 March 2012).

8 Such demands resonate with the appeals for the development of an 'ensuring state' (Giddens, 2009: 8, see also 69–72). They equally echo the agenda for green conservatism (Gray, 1993: 126).

9 See Daley and Preston (2009: 358), AirportWatch (2011: 31) and Aviation Environment Federation press release, www.aef.org.uk/?p=1067 (accessed 12 May 2010).

10 The American Air Transport Association and three US airlines (United, Continental and American) launched in early July 2011 a legal challenge to emissions trading in the European Court of Justice. In July 2011, the US House of Representatives proposed measures to stop US airlines from participating in the EU scheme – see Air Transport Association press release, 20 July 2011, www.airlines.org (accessed 4 August 2011); *Aviation Week*, 10 June 2011, www.aviationweek.com (accessed 17 June 2011).

11 Aviation Brief, 7 June 2011, www.aviationbrief.com/?p=1991 (accessed 25 June 2011).

12 The five environmental organisations were the Aviation Environment Federation, the World Wide Fund for Nature, the European Federation for Transport and Environment, and the US organisations Environmental Defense Fund and Earthjustice – WWF-UK press release, 5 July 2011, www.wwf.org.uk (accessed 15 July 2011); AirportWatch press release, www.airportwatch.org.uk/news/detail.php?art_id=3126 (accessed 15 July 2011).

13 See also Connolly (1991), Mouffe (2000), Norval (2007), Owen (1994, 2012), Tully (1999, 2008). For our reflections on the limits of network governance and the possibilities of more democratic and agonistic engagements, see Griggs and Howarth (2007b).

14 See, for example, Juniper (2007: 141–51).

Epilogue

This is a very difficult debate, but the reality is that since the 1960s Britain has failed to keep pace with our international competitors in addressing long term aviation capacity and connectivity needs. Germany, France and the Netherlands have all grown their capacity more extensively than the UK over the years, and so are better equipped, now and in the future, to connect with the fast growing markets of emerging economies. The consequences are clear. Our largest airport and our only hub airport – Heathrow – is already operating at capacity. Gatwick, the world's busiest single runway airport, will be full early in the next decade, while spare capacity at Stansted airport is forecast to run out in the early 2030s. (Patrick McLoughlin, Secretary of State for Transport, 7 September 2012)[1]

A fresh and independent view, at arm's length from politics, may well be able to make progress. A body without any vested interests or preconceived views, which is able to review the evidence dispassionately, to engage widely, to exercise its judgement and make well-considered and integrated recommendations, provides the best chance of enabling broad agreement to be reached and lasting decisions taken. (Sir Howard Davies; Airports Commission, 2013: 5)

In the immediate aftermath of the 2010 general election, the Conservative–Liberal Democratic coalition was steadfast in its commitment to impose a moratorium on new runways at Heathrow, Gatwick and Stansted. It set up the South East Airports Task Force in June 2010, which was charged with examining ways to 'make our airports better not bigger' (DfT, 2011b: 5), and then launched a broad consultation exercise in March 2011, publishing its scoping paper on a sustainable framework for aviation. Its scoping document unveiled a stinging critique of Labour's expansionist plans, in which the Secretary of State for Transport, Philip Hammond, dismissed the 2003 air transport white paper (ATWP) because it failed to pay proper attention to the problem of climate change. The Labour government, he alleged, had 'got the balance [between environmental protection and expansion] wrong' (DfT, 2011b: 4). In contrast, the coalition government promised to develop a 'genuinely sustainable framework' for aviation, one which subordinated airport expansion to the demands of tackling climate change (DfT, 2011b: 4, 5, 27). Yet the coalition still felt it necessary to mollify its new demands on the aviation industry by declaring that 'we are not anti-aviation. We are anti-carbon' (DfT, 2011b: 4). This maxim was repeated in its public response to the Committee on Climate Change in August 2011, when it put further responsibility on the aviation industry to produce 'headroom' for expansion, by reducing its carbon emissions as well as its contribution to noise and air pollution (DfT, 2011c: 4).

As if to further confirm its intentions to transform aviation policy, Prime Minister David Cameron appointed Justine Greening as Secretary of State for Transport in the October 2011 ministerial reshuffle. Greening, who was the MP for Putney, which is directly under Heathrow's flight path, had taken on a highly public role in the campaign against the third runway, in which she had been strongly critical of the Department for Transport (DfT), especially castigating its allegedly closed practices of policy-making. With her appointment, it was widely believed that the anti-expansion lobby had effectively captured the transport ministry. Indeed, Greening joined Theresa Villiers at the DfT, who herself had been a key actor in shifting the Conservative Party towards rail and away from aviation, and who had been appointed Minister of State for Transport in May 2010. In Greening's first conference keynote speech as Secretary of State, to the Airport Operators Association (AOA) in late October of the same year, she sent a bold message to the assembled delegates: 'the political reality is that the runway decision [at Heathrow] has been made. It's done.' She called upon the aviation industry to 'turn the page and write a new chapter in the story of aviation'. This new chapter, she added, 'has to be far broader-based than just the capacity question'.[2]

The backlash

Yet, as the consultation began to unfold, the coalition encountered a resolute pro-expansion public campaign from the aviation industry and its supporters. In March 2011, twenty-five airlines, airports and other industry groups launched a campaign entitled 'Fair Tax on Flying', which attacked the economic impact of rises in air passenger duty (APD) on UK aviation, while dismissing the green (environmental) credentials of these rises, saying they were no more than a 'revenue raising exercise' (Fair Tax on Flying press release, 3 March 2011). Alongside such developments, Boris Johnson, the London mayor and an opponent of Heathrow expansion, continued to lobby vociferously for a new international airport in the Thames estuary, which could expand capacity on routes to developing markets in Asia.

While not met with widespread support from the aviation industry, Johnson's interventions kept the issue of airport capacity constraints high on the policy agenda. They were not lost on Colin Matthews, the chief executive of the British Airports Authority (BAA), who, while rejecting plans for an estuary airport, declared himself 'pleased there was an acknowledgement that there was a need' for additional airport capacity, especially given the persistence of economic recession and slow growth (*Guardian*, 12 January 2012). In fact, in September 2011 BAA published a newly commissioned report on the role of Heathrow (as the UK's international hub) in leading the economic recovery. The study was accompanied by the development of a new website, which was organised around the question: 'How can the UK connect to growth?'[3] In his foreword to the report, Matthews reiterated the still powerful horrific narrative of 'lost' economic opportunities from the failure to expand Heathrow, which stemmed from 'the lack of direct flights to Emerging Markets [and which] may already be costing the economy £1.2bn a year as trade goes to better-connected competitors' (Frontier Economics, 2011: 5). These messages were repeated in a new report commissioned by the British Chambers of Commerce (BCC) – *Flying in the Face of Jobs and Growth* – which, in support of the economic contribution of aviation, called for government to take 'bold decisions' on new infrastructure, including 'strategic decisions both on where airports can be expanded and how flights to and from them should be regulated' (BCC, 2011: 8).

The growing backlash tested the political and ideological resolution of the coalition. Its stance against expansion appeared to waver, at least in its public rearticulation of the balance between the economy and the environment, as well as its acknowledgement of the importance of the economic contribution of aviation to recovery. In his 2011 autumn forecast statement to Parliament, the Chancellor,

George Osborne, thus raised concerns about 'burden[ing]' industry 'with endless social and environmental goals'. He announced that the government would consider 'all options for maintaining the UK's aviation hub status', although he did maintain that the expansion of Heathrow was not one of these options (HM Treasury, 2011). In early January 2012, Cameron announced that the consultation exercise would indeed consider the feasibility of a new international airport in the London estuary (*Telegraph*, 17 January 2012). In a speech on national infrastructure in the middle of March 2012, he went on to declare that he was 'not blind to the need to increase airport capacity, particularly in the south-east', arguing that 'we need to retain our status as a key global hub for air travel'.[4] By spring 2012, rumours abounded in the press that the coalition was preparing for a policy reversal on Heathrow (see *Observer*, 25 March 2012; *Independent on Sunday*, 25 March 2012).

In the midst of this speculation, Tim Yeo, a Conservative grandee and former chair of the Environmental Audit Committee (EAC), and then chair of the Energy and Climate Change Select Committee, appeared on BBC Radio 4's *Today* programme in late March to claim that the economic case for airport expansion was 'now overwhelming'. He argued that the new constraints of the European Union emissions trading scheme (EU ETS), which had taken effect since January 2012, had completely changed the policy context for air transport. Because caps were now imposed on total aviation emissions – and therefore the construction of a third runway would not add to overall emissions from air travel – new airport capacity in the south-east should not be ruled out. In the words of this former EAC chair, the coalition government should thus 'make a decision this year to go ahead with the third runway [at Heathrow] and start to catch up the ground we are losing to all sorts of other countries'.[5] Earlier, it had been announced by the government that the launch of the formal consultation document, which had been initially planned for the end of March 2012, was to be delayed until the summer, thus raising further doubts about the desire or will of the coalition to publish a new aviation white paper in March 2013, as it had initially planned.

In fact, the late spring and early summer of 2012 brought forth a concerted public campaign for airport expansion. The demands were persistently couched in terms of threats to UK hub capacity, the declining market position of Heathrow and the pressing need to increase the number of flights to 'emerging markets' (see Business

Leader, *Observer*, 24 June 2012). Notably, at the end of June, British Airways (BA), Virgin Atlantic, BAA and the Manchester Airports Group launched a new pro-expansion aviation lobby, which they named the Aviation Foundation. Supported by the BCC, the Trades Union Congress (TUC), AOA and the British Air Transport Association (BATA), it followed in the footsteps of Freedom to Fly and Flying Matters in its efforts to promote the 'vital economic and social impact of aviation to the UK'. One of its first initiatives was to begin an online pledge in support of the industry as it dedicated itself to 'actively seek[ing] parliamentary and public support to recognise the fact that aviation is a UK success story'.[6] Indeed, appeals to the 'success story' of UK aviation drew succour from the deeply embedded narratives about airlines and airports, which extolled the virtues of the industry's vital contribution to the UK economy. Such narratives had been persistently articulated throughout the campaign for the third runway at Heathrow and during the debates and discussions leading up to the 2003 white paper.

In a similar vein, at its inaugural press conference, the Aviation Foundation repeated its long-standing demands for government to take the lead in aviation policy, arguing that any consultation should ensure 'a clear policy conclusion that can be progressed without delay', and which 'lasts beyond the term of one Parliament and ensures the policy will be implemented'.[7] At the beginning of July 2012, this 'clear policy conclusion' was interpreted by Conservative MPs in the Free Enterprise Group as being at least one new runway by 2020 at Gatwick, Heathrow or Stansted, with the implicit preference for Heathrow, given its analysis of the falling competitive advantage of the airport as an international hub (Free Enterprise Group, 2012).

Nonetheless, the demand for increased hub capacity (at Heathrow) was still met with some opposition from within the aviation industry, not least from the chief executives of Gatwick and Birmingham airports, who privileged respectively the continued importance of 'point-to-point' journeys and the advantages of a 'balanced national' strategy over that of hub expansion (*Guardian*, 26 June 2012). Earlier, Boris Johnson had also rebuffed plans for expansion at Heathrow, although he called for additional runway capacity at Stansted as a short-term measure before the building of a new international hub in the London estuary (*London Evening Standard*, 18 June 2012). Importantly, and despite such tensions in the ranks of those supporting expansion, the coalition government continued to send uncertain public signals about the strength of its opposition to expansion at Heathrow. When asked in the House of Commons by Zac Goldsmith – the MP for Richmond Park and North Kingston and a campaigner against a third runway – to rule out expansion at Heathrow, Cameron confirmed that the coalition's position on Heathrow had not changed. Yet he added a significant proviso to this commitment by saying that 'clearly we [the government] must not be blind to two important considerations: how we expand airport capacity overall, and how we ensure that Heathrow operates better'.[8] Cameron's recognition of capacity constraints at UK airports was once again interpreted as evidence of a looming policy reversal on the third runway at Heathrow, with the *Financial Times* reporting that political insiders were suggesting that Cameron had an 'open mind' on Heathrow expansion.[9] Indeed, the intervention of the pro-expansion Free Enterprise Group in the campaign for greater airport capacity was portrayed as the work of supporters of George Osborne – a further signal of the shifting position of the Chancellor in favour of airport expansion in the south-east (*Guardian*, 9 July 2012).

The draft aviation framework and the Davies Commission

In mid-July 2012, amid this turbulent and shifting political context, the coalition released its draft aviation framework. Opening a further round of consultation, Greening, still in charge at the DfT, reinforced the priority that the coalition accorded to a transparent and collaborative working relationship with all affected stakeholders, and she criticised what she saw as the lack of ambition of previous governments in developing a long-term strategy, as well as their failure to build a wide consensus on the issue (DfT, 2012: 5). In her foreword to the draft framework, Greening recognised runway capacity as the 'main issue of contention', and while she confirmed the cancellation of the third runway at Heathrow, she reiterated her commitment to the November 2011 National Infrastructure Plan, which pledged to maintain the position of the UK as an aviation hub (HM Treasury and Infrastructure UK, 2011: 43). Yet, in another attack on New Labour, she still argued that 'any solution will have to be genuinely sustainable' (DfT, 2012: 5).

Such rhetorical jousting went hand in hand with argumentative strategies to defuse or rebuff demands for short-term agreement over additional capacity at specific airports. The draft framework firmly anchored questions of additional capacity in the long term, reaffirming the position that even if the coalition agreed to provide it, no new operational capacity could become available before 2020. Making better use of existing capacity was still the best feasible short-term option. Greening thus made reference to the 'incompatible' positions and antagonisms structuring the field of aviation policy and she declared that 'without sufficient support, particularly at a political level, it would not be possible for any government to deliver new capacity, however hard some shout for it' (DfT, 2012: 4).

Pursuing this line of thinking, the draft framework prioritised a sustained analysis of alternatives and generation of evidence to inform any decisions over expansion (p. 33). The DfT thus announced a call for evidence in late 2012 (pp. 34–5), with Greening making clear her desire to 'focus on the "big picture" before putting forward any proposals for new capacity' (p. 5). The authors of the draft framework thus reprimanded those stakeholders who, in response to the 2011 scoping document, had put forward specific airport expansion plans, when they declared that 'it was not the purpose of the scoping document' to consider such proposals. (It was also asserted that such proposals had not in any case been supported by sufficient evidence on environmental impacts and the business case for expansion.)

In the medium to long term, the government maintained its commitment to high-speed rail as an alternative to domestic and short-haul European flights by suggesting that, once in place, an extended high-speed rail network could substitute for up to 4.5 million trips that otherwise would have been made by plane (p. 33). Although this might lower capacity pressures on airports, the DfT nonetheless forecast capacity constraints after 2020, particularly in the south-east of England. However, the draft strategy proposed no specific plans to address such constraints. In keeping with the attempts to defuse demands for expansion, the domain of the draft framework was repeatedly defined as that of 'high-level policies' (p. 5) or of 'high-level strategy that sets out … overall objectives for aviation and the policies … to achieve those objectives' (p. 7).

Yet, during the summer of 2012, rumours began to circulate that senior Conservatives were putting pressure on Cameron to remove Greening from the DfT, while at the end of August the Parliamentary Aviation Group demanded that the government either expand Heathrow or build a new hub airport (*Independent*, 29 August 2012; *Telegraph*, 23 August 2012). With such rumours circulating in the press, it seemed that Greening's days at the DfT were numbered. In the September 2012 reshuffle, amid press reports that Greening was prepared to quit if the government shifted its policy on Heathrow, and in what was seen as a move to open the way for airport expansion, Greening was shifted from the DfT to the Department for International Development, while Villiers found herself at the Northern Ireland Office (*Telegraph*, 4 September 2012). The arrival of Patrick McLoughlin, Greening's successor at the DfT and a former aviation minister under Margaret Thatcher and John Major, was met with 'positive' approval from aviation insiders, while HACAN ClearSkies lamented the fact that 'the aviation industry will be popping open the champagne as two independent-minded ministers have gone. There will be fury in west London and beyond at the moving of Justine Greening' (*Financial Times*, 4 September 2012).

Just three days after Greening was moved from the DfT, the coalition announced the formation of an independent commission into airport capacity. The commission was to deliver its final conclusions only in 2015, after the general election, with interim conclusions on changes to the use of existing capacity presented at the end of 2013. It was headed by Sir Howard Davies, former head of the Financial Services Authority.[10] Significantly, its terms of reference, which were announced in early November 2012, were to 'examine the scale and timing of any additional capacity to maintain the UK's position *as Europe's most important aviation hub*' (our emphasis). In setting out these terms of reference, the new Secretary of State for Transport declared that 'aviation is vital to the UK economy and we need to have a long term aviation policy which meets the challenges of the future'. In the words of Davies, 'the experience of recent years shows we need a robust evidence base which has the support of a broad consensus of opinion. We aim to put the next government into a position in which rapid and implementable decisions can be soundly made.'[11]

Explaining a (further) policy reversal: the power of discourse

It seems therefore that we are witnessing the beginnings of a further policy reversal, in which the demands of the economy will once again trump those of the environment and the concerns of local citizens. Indeed, in the eyes of many observers, putting the possibility of a third runway at Heathrow back onto the policy agenda and announcing the Davies Commission signals a double reversal. In the first place, it represents a reassertion of the economic arguments for airport expansion. But secondly, following the failure of New Labour to forge a broad societal consensus about the future of aviation in the early part of the century, it suggests a return to a top-down form of technocratic politics led by an expert commission to resolve a wicked issue.

What has brought about this apparent reversal? There is no doubt that the recession placed increased pressure on the coalition to kick-start the failing UK economy. One of its responses has been to promise public infrastructure projects and to commit to building more houses, while relaxing planning procedures. But such proposals have been derided as 'too little too late'. It is here that the third runway at Heathrow appears to offer a trump card: an infrastructure programme led by the private sector that would, its supporters suggest, generate some £30 billion a year for the national economy, thus increasing UK competitiveness not least through additional routes to developing markets in Asia. Whatever the disputed benefits of such investments, there are strong grounds to believe that such appeals resonate effectively during a period of economic downturn.

At the same time, there has been a shift in the balance of power within the Conservative Party. The free-market wing, and some would say the more climate-sceptical faction of the party, has become more vocal. Cameron may have sought to 'detoxify' the Conservatives by embracing the environment, in part by committing his party to stop the building of a third runway – the latter functioned as an emblematic sign of change within the party – but the political pendulum appears to have swung back towards the Tory right, or at least to the more instrumental wing of the party.

But there have also been significant changes beyond the ranks of the Conservative Party. There has been a coordinated and well funded campaign by the aviation industry to get Heathrow back onto the policy agenda. Strategically, this campaign has sought to reframe the public debate about airport capacity so that it is less about the negative environmental effects of aviation and more about its economic benefits. Attention has thus been shifted back to the spectre of international competition in the form of rival airports in Europe and the need for the UK to maintain its international hub. For many, this aggressive media campaign has successfully coupled the interests of BA and BAA – and the aviation industry more generally – with those of 'UK plc'. Indeed, the Competition Commission's ruling that BAA relax its grip on south-east airports by selling off Gatwick and Stansted amplified the financial significance of the third runway to BAA's Spanish owners, Ferrovial. In October 2012, resigned to the sale of Stansted, BAA renamed itself Heathrow Airport Holdings.

Of course, this campaign also benefited in part from the 'Boris island' proposal, which has functioned to keep the issue of aviation capacity on the political agenda. Johnson's public opposition to further expansion at Heathrow contributed much to turning public attention back towards the politics of site location and to questions about where – rather than whether – to build. At the same time, the inclusion of aviation in the EU ETS has been used as an argument to endorse the third runway. As we noted, Tim Yeo, among others, suggested that the emissions cap on aviation means that any additional airport capacity in the UK will not alter the total level of carbon emissions from aviation, thereby making expansion at Heathrow a 'carbon neutral' measure. All in all, then, this campaign has opened the coalition up to charges of dithering, as well as taunts of 'man or mouse' political leadership and accusations of 'do nothing' politics, thus inviting negative comparisons with Victorian politicians, who, by contrast, acted decisively and in the long term.

Faced with a powerful and orchestrated campaign, the opponents of Heathrow expansion suddenly found themselves on the back foot. Most commentators accept that the broad coalition that came together to stop the third runway in 2008 decisively won the argument, thus reversing the victory of the pro-expansion Freedom to Fly lobby in 2003. The campaign against a third runway had successfully linked the expansion of Heathrow to the growth of the aviation industry and its increasing impacts on climate change; it had also negated economic arguments in favour of expansion. But with the new messages on climate change in the 2011 aviation policy scoping document, and with Greening and Villiers installed at the DfT, the campaign became less vocal in its critiques of government. It looked instead to support the work of Greening rather than holding the coalition to account. Arguably the campaigners ceded too much ground to the pro-expansion lobby, although in reality they could simply not match the financial and organisational resources mobilised by the aviation industry.

But the very success of their campaign at Heathrow was also part of their own undoing. That campaign had brought together a broad coalition which tied aviation to climate change, thus shifting the terrain of arguments: any expansion threatened the UK's international commitments to lower its carbon emissions. Paradoxically, however, the strong focus on Heathrow inadvertently made it possible for the pro-expansion forces to reframe the debate not in terms of aviation and climate change, but in terms of the UK's overriding need for an international hub – Heathrow – and the added global competitiveness it brings. When you add the falling public concern over climate change, and the possibility of a new airport in the Thames estuary, which could easily divide opposition forces, it is not difficult to see how the strong position of the anti-expansion began to unravel in the summer of 2012.

The to-ings and fro-ings of the contemporary political scene are thus finely balanced. But these conjunctural tussles have to be located within the wider set of social structures and political practices that we have presented in this book. There is little question that the actions and campaigns of the pro-aviation forces resonate more strongly with the dominant discourses and narratives that have elevated the aviation industry into its powerful position in British society and the UK state. As we have shown, since the Second World War the logic of aviation expansion has been systematically constructed as an essential component of capital accumulation, whether state-led or market-driven, while the dominant myths of British aviation have been etched into key institutions of the UK state. What is more, the aviation industry is often portrayed within what we have termed a dominant fantasmatic narrative that promises economic triumph if aviation is set free and properly provided for, but augurs catastrophic failure if expansion is blocked.

All this suggests a powerful aviation industry, backed by the UK state and integral to the dominant economic logics. Yet this is not to say that these wider structures and discourses determine once and for all aviation's continued supremacy. On the contrary, expansionist plans have consistently met with strong resistance and counter-hegemonic struggles. The delays in choosing London's third airport, the battles at Manchester and Stansted, as well as the blocking of plans to build a third runway at Heathrow, are testimony to the power and organisation of these forces. The future is thus far from certain.

The itinerary

What, then, does this all mean for the Davies Commission and the future trajectories of UK aviation? The jury is still out on the commitment of Cameron and the coalition government to expand aviation

(Rootes and Carter, 2010). Is the Commission simply a short-term measure to manage the political difficulties of the coalition by kicking the issue of airport expansion into the sidelines? Or does it signal a policy reversal and a dropping of its commitments against expansion? Time will tell. The Davies Commission has declared its intention to work in 'comprehensive, rigorous, open and inclusive' ways in order to achieve the 'greatest degree of consensus' (Airports Commission, 2013: 7). But it faces a divided public opinion and antagonistic coalitions. As a YouGov poll revealed in September 2012, public opinion is neatly split, with 34 per cent opposing expansion and 34 per cent supporting it (*Guardian*, 13 September 2012). Across the aviation policy sector, the key stakeholders in aviation politics hold increasingly antagonistic positions. The two rival coalitions that were forged during the consultations for the 2003 white paper, and in particular during the campaign for the third runway, are likely to resurface and join battle even more intensely than before. Direct action protest is likely to accompany these new struggles.

For Cameron, these splits pose even more immediate political difficulties, for they cut right across the coalition. While supporters of the Conservative Party tend to privilege the economic benefits of the third runway over its negative environmental impacts, the opposite is true of Liberal Democrat supporters, who generally give far more significance to the environmental costs of airport expansion (*Guardian*, 13 September 2012). In his 2012 conference speech, Nick Clegg made much of Liberal Democrat influence in holding Conservative ministers to their environmental commitments, telling assembled party members that to 'turn blue green, you need yellow'. To make matters worse, one of Cameron's chief rivals within the Conservative leadership, Boris Johnson, has repeatedly come out against the third runway, supporting the development of an international airport in the Thames estuary.

Against this background, the Davies Commission could well be interpreted as yet another attempt to kick the issue of airports into the long grass, at least until after the next election. Its ability to engineer any sort of compromise will no doubt be hampered by the lukewarm support given to the Commission by the Labour Party. In this regard, we should not forget that, as Secretary of State for Energy and Climate Change, Labour leader Ed Miliband had fought in the Cabinet against the third runway, and that the opposition has yet to declare publicly that any future Labour administration will necessarily abide by any decision of the Commission.[12] Labour will not, however, escape the political divisions generated by airport expansion: its 2009 support for the third runway split the party, its backbench MPs and its supporters, particularly the trade unions.

More importantly, following the Climate Change Act, the Davies Commission will operate under different institutional constraints and legal obligations. It will have to put forward its plans for expansion at a time when there are still doubts about the need for additional capacity and the longevity of the hub model, while facing intense public scrutiny. In fact, it is quite likely that the Commission will provide a focal point for those opposing expansion to reinvigorate their campaigns, even though they face the divisive element of 'Boris island'. And finally, let us not forget the fate of the Roskill Commission into the third airport at London in the late 1960s and early 1970s. Its findings were ignored by government in favour of a new airport at Maplin, only for government to abandon construction at Maplin as the 1973 oil crisis hit the aviation industry and backbenchers threatened to rebel. This time around it may well be fears about peak oil and the destruction of the planet that play on the minds of politicians, as well as the electoral politics of Tory marginals under Heathrow or 'Boris island' flight paths. Zac Goldsmith has already made clear his intentions to force a by-election should the coalition reverse its opposition to Heathrow expansion.

But perhaps our peculiar fascination with aviation, airports and global mobility, and its intimate links with key industries like aerospace and tourism, will not go away that easily. After all, for many citizens and consumers across the country air travel has become part of everyday life, vital for holidays in the sun and quick getaways, as well as the food we see on display in supermarkets and the documentaries and dramas we watch on television. Air travel in the UK is still set to increase between 1 and 3 per cent a year over the next forty years, and while this represents a decline from its average of 5 per cent growth a year over the last forty years, it still amounts to an increase in passenger numbers at UK airports from 219 million in 2011 to 315 million in 2030 and 445 million in 2050 (DfT, 2013: 1). The undoubted grip of aviation on our collective consciousness has perhaps weakened, but it has certainly not disappeared. It will take new forms of political leadership and social change, accompanied by alternative visions of leisure, business and mobility, to shake it off.

5 February 2013

Notes

1 'Independent Airports Commission – increasing the international competitiveness of UK airlines and airports', written statement, 7 September 2012, www.gov.uk/government/speeches/increasing-international-competitiveness-of-uk-airlines-and-airports (accessed 23 January 2013).

2 Justine Greening, speech to AOA conference, 31 October 2011; for a full transcript see www.dft.gov.uk/news/speeches/greening-20111031 (accessed 2 April 2012).

3 See hub.heathrowairport.com (accessed 2 April 2012).

4 Speech to the Institute of Civil Engineers, 19 March 2012; full transcript available at www.number10.gov.uk/news/pm-speech-on-infrastructure (accessed 22 March 2012).

5 BBC Radio 4, *Today*, 26 March 2012; full transcript available at news.bbc.co.uk/today/hi/today/newsid_9708000/9708889.stm (accessed 27 March 2012).

6 See www.aviation-foundation.org/About-Us (accessed 18 July 2012).

7 Aviation Foundation, launch press conference, see www.aviation-foundation.org/PressconferenceJune2012/index.asp (accessed 18 July 2012).

8 Prime Minister's questions, 13 June 2012, see www.parliament.uk/business/news/2012/june/prime-ministers-questions-13-june-2012 (accessed 22 July 2012).

9 G. Parker and A. Parker, 'Cameron clears way for Heathrow U-turn', *Financial Times*, 13 June 2012, see www.ft.com/cms/s/0/5a0b7cd0-b578-11e1-b8d0-00144feabdc0.html#axzz21YozMjnB (accessed 21 July 2012).

10 Davies was joined by: Geoff Muirhead, former chief executive of Manchester Airport Group; Professor Dame Julia King, vice-chancellor of Aston University and member of the Committee on Climate Change, with a background in aerospace; Sir John Armitt, former chief executive of Network Rail and chair of the Olympic Delivery Authority; Professor Ricky Burdett, Professor of Urban Studies at the London School of Economics; and Vivienne Cox, former chief executive and executive vice-president of BP Alternative Energy.

11 'Airports Commission membership', http://pressreleases.dft.gov.uk/Press-Releases/Airports-Commission-membership-68298.aspx (accessed 23 January 2013).

12 Interestingly, John Armitt, a member of the Davies Commission, was appointed as an adviser to the Labour leadership in the autumn of 2012 (*Economist*, 2 November 2012).

References

Primary sources

AEF (Aviation Environment Federation) and FoE (Friends of the Earth) (1999) *Plane Crazy: Airport Growth in the UK* (London: AEF and FoE).

Airport Operators Association (2002) *Building a Sustainable Aviation Policy* (London: Airport Operators Association).

Airports Commission (2013) *Guidance Document 01: Submitting Evidence and Proposals to the Airports Commission* (London: Airports Commission).

AirportWatch (2002a) *Flying Into Trouble. 2002: The Threat of Airport Growth* (London: AEF).

AirportWatch (2002b) 'You're Flying Into Trouble', Press Release, 19 July.

AirportWatch (2009a) *Copenhagen and Aviation*, 20 November, www.aef.org.uk/downloads/AW_Copenhagen_aviation_briefing_November2009.pdf (accessed 27 December 2012).

AirportWatch [R. Bridger] (2009b) *Air Freight: The Impacts* (London: AirportWatch).

AirportWatch [P. Lockley] (2011) *Aviation and Climate Change Policy in the United Kingdom: A Report for AirportWatch* (London: AirportWatch).

Aviation Economics Group (2008) *Flaws Galore: A Critique of the Economic Case for Heathrow Expansion* (London: AirportWatch).

BAA (British Airports Authority) (1967) *Report and Accounts 1966–67*, House of Commons Paper No. 583 (London: HMSO).

BAA (2005) *Heathrow Airport Interim Master Plan: Draft for Consultation* (Hayes: BAA Heathrow).

BAA (2008) *Making the Case for Responsible Growth: BAA's Response to the Government Consultation 'Adding Capacity at Heathrow Airport'* (London: BAA).

BCC (British Chambers of Commerce) (2009) *Economic Impacts of Hub Airports* (London: BCC).

BCC (2011) *Flying in the Face of Jobs and Growth: How Aviation Policy Needs to Change to Support UK Business* (London: BCC).

Blair, T. (2004) 'PM Speech on Climate Change', 14 September, http://groups. yahoo.com/group/nhnenews/message/7885 (accessed 5 January 2013).

Buchanan, C. (1971) 'Note of Dissent', in Roskill Commission, *Report of the Commission on the Third London Airport* (London: HSMO), pp. 149–60.

CAA (Civil Aviation Authority) (1993) *Passengers at London Airports in 1991*, CAP 610 (London: CAA).

CAA (1998) *The Single European Aviation Market: The First Five Years*, CAP 685 (London: CAA).

CAA (2005) *UK Regional Air Services: A Study by the CAA*, CAP 754 (London: CAA).

CAA (2006) *No-Frills Carriers: Revolution or Evolution*, CAP 770 (London: CAA).

CAA (2008) *Recent Trends in Growth of UK Air Passenger Demand* (London: CAA).

Cabinet Office (1952) *Gatwick Airport: Memorandum by the Minister of Civil Aviation*, C(52) 220, 22 July, National Archives, Catalogue Reference: CAB/129/53, www.nationalarchives.gov.uk (accessed 20 June 2009).

Cabinet Office (1967) *The Third London Airport Draft White Paper: Note by the President of the Board of Trade and the Minister of Housing and Local Government*, C(67)50, 12 April, National Archives, Catalogue Reference: CAB/129/128, www.nationalarchives.gov.uk (accessed 29 June 2009).

Cabinet Office (1978) *White Paper on Airports Policy: Memorandum by the Secretary of State for Trade*, CP(78)4, 16 January, National Archives, Catalogue Reference: CAB/129/199/4, www.nationalarchives.gov.uk (accessed 29 June 2009).

Cabinet Office (1979) *Conclusions of a Meeting of the Cabinet held at 10 Downing Street on Thursday 30 August*, National Archives, Catalogue Reference: CAB/128/66/14, www.nationalarchives.gov.uk (accessed 1 January 2013).

Cameron, D. (2006) 'The Planet First, Politics Second', *Independent on Sunday*, 3 September.

Campaign to Protect Rural England (2003) *Flying to Distraction: Future Growth in Air Travel Threatens to Shatter the Tranquillity of the Countryside*, June (London: CPRE).

CC (Competition Commission) (2008) *BAA Airports Market Investigation: Provisional Findings Report* (London: Competition Commission).

CCC (Committee on Climate Change) (2008) *Building a Low-Carbon Economy: The UK's Contribution to Tackling Climate Change* (London: TSO).

CCC (2009a) *Meeting the UK Aviation Targets: Options for Reducing Emissions to 2050* (London: TSO).

CCC (2009b) *Meeting the UK Aviation Targets: Options for Reducing Emissions to 2050. Executive Summary* (London: TSO).

CCC (2009c) 'Committee on Climate Change Sets Out Options to Meet the

UK's Aviation Emissions Target', Press Release No. 18, www.theccc.org. uk/reports/aviation-report (accessed 5 January 2010).

CE [B.H. Boon and R.C.N. Wit] (2005) *The Contribution of Aviation to the Economy: Assessment of Arguments Put Forward* (Delft: CE).

CE Delft [B.H. Boon, M. Davidson, J. Faber, D. Nelissen and C. van de Vreede] (2008) *The Economics of Heathrow Expansion. Final Report* (Delft: CE Delft).

Conservative Party (2007a) *Greener Skies: A Consultation on the Environmental Taxation of Aviation* (London: Conservative Party).

Conservative Party (2007b) *Power to the People: The Decentralised Energy Revolution* (London: Conservative Party).

Conservative Party (2009) *The Low Carbon Economy: Security, Stability and Green Growth*, Protecting Security Policy Green Paper No. 8 (London: Conservative Party).

Conservative Party (2010) *Invitation to Join the Government of Britain: The Conservative Manifesto 2010* (London: Conservative Party).

Conservative Political Centre [L. Robinson and B. Waters] (1973) *London's Flight East*, No. 526 (London: Conservative Political Centre).

Cox, D. (2002) 'Letter to the "Future Development of Air Transport"', 29 November.

DEFRA (Department for Environment, Food and Rural Affairs) (2005) *Securing Our Future: Delivering the UK Sustainable Development Strategy*, Cm 6467 (Norwich: TSO).

DEFRA (2006) *Climate Change: The UK Programme 2006*, Cm 6764 (Norwich: TSO).

Department of Trade (1975) *Airport Strategy for Great Britain Part 1: The London Area* (London: HMSO).

Department of Trade (1976a) *Airport Strategy for Great Britain Part 2: The Regional Airports* (London: HMSO).

Department of Trade (1976b) *Future Civil Aviation Policy*, Cm 6400 (London: HMSO), National Archives, Catalogue Reference: CAB/129/187/13, www.nationalarchives.gov.uk (accessed 1 January 2013).

Department of Transport (1985) *Airports Policy White Paper*, Cm 9542 (London: Stationery Office).

Department of Transport (1987) *Guidelines on Airport Consultative Committees*, December, www.ukaccs.info/oldguidelines.pdf (accessed 21 July 2012).

DETR (Department of the Environment, Transport and the Regions) (1997) *Developing an Integrated Transport Policy: Consultation Document* (London: TSO).

DETR (1998) *A New Deal for Transport: Better for Everyone – The Government's White Paper on the Future of Transport*, Cm 3950 (London: TSO).

DETR (2000a) *The Future of Aviation: Consultation on Air Transport Policy* (London: DETR).

DETR (2000b) *South East and East of England Regional Air Service Study: Terms of Reference* (DETR: London).

DfT (Department for Transport) (2002a) *The Future Development of Air Transport in the UK: Regional Air Services Co-ordination Study* (London: DfT).

DfT (2002b) *The Future Development of Air Transport in the UK: South East* (London: DfT).

DfT (2003a) *The Future of Air Transport*, Cm 6046 (London: DfT).

DfT (2003b) *The Future Development of Air Transport in the UK: South East* (London: DfT, 2nd edn).

DfT [Avia Solutions] (2003c) *The Future Development of Air Transport in the UK: A National Consultation. A Report on the Responses to the Government's Consultation: UK Wide Report* (London: DfT).

DfT (2003d) *The Future of Air Transport. Summary* (London: DfT).

DfT (2006a) *The Future of Air Transport Progress Report*, Cm 6977 (London: DfT).

DfT (2006b) *Civil Aviation Act 2006* (London: TSO).

DfT (2007a) *Executive Summary: Project for the Sustainable Development of Heathrow*, www.dft.gov.uk (accessed 9 March 2009).

DfT (2007b) *Adding Capacity at Heathrow Airport: Consultation Document* (London: DfT).

DfT (2007c) *Improving the Air Passenger Experience: An Analysis of End-to-End Journeys With a Focus on Heathrow* (London: DfT).

DfT (2007d) *Attitudes to Noise from Aviation Sources in England (ANASE): Final Report* (London: DfT).

DfT (2007e) *Towards a Sustainable Transport System: Supporting Economic Growth in a Low Carbon World*, Cm 7226 (London: DfT).

DfT (2009) *Transport Trends 2009* (London: DfT, 2nd edn).

DfT (2011a) *Transport Statistics Great Britain: 2011* (London: DfT).

DfT (2011b) *Developing a Sustainable Framework for UK Aviation: Scoping Document* (London: DfT).

DfT (2011c) *South East Airports Taskforce: Report* (London: DfT).

DfT (2011d) *Government Response to the Committee on Climate Change Report on Reducing CO_2 Emissions from UK Aviation to 2050* (London: DfT).

DfT (2012) *Draft Aviation Framework* (London: DfT).

DfT (2013) *UK Aviation Forecasts* (DfT: London).

DTI (Department of Trade and Industry) (2003) *Energy White Paper. Our Energy, Our Future – Creating a Low Carbon Economy*, Cm 5761 (Norwich: TSO).

DTLR (Department for Transport, Local Government and the Regions) (2001) *The Future of Aviation: Consultation on Air Transport Policy (Response)* (London: DTLR).

EAC (Environmental Audit Committee) (2003) *Energy White Paper: Empowering Change?*, HC618 (London: TSO).

EAC (2004a) *Pre-Budget Report 2003: Aviation Follow-Up, Volume 1*, HC233-1 (London: TSO).

EAC (2004b) *Aviation: Sustainability and the Government Response*, HC623 (London: TSO).

EAC (2004c) *Aviation: Sustainability and the Government's Second Response*, HC1063 (London: TSO).

EAC (2004d) *The Sustainable Development Strategy: Illusion or Reality? Volume 1*, HC624-1 (London: TSO).

EAC (2006) *Reducing Carbon Emissions from Transport: Volume 1*, HC981-1 (London: TSO).

Edwards Committee (1969) *British Air Transport in the Seventies: Report of the Committee of Inquiry into Civil Air Transport*, Cmnd 4018 (London: HSMO).

Environmental Change Institute (2006) *Predict and Decide: Aviation, Climate Change and UK Policy* (Oxford: University of Oxford).

Eyre, G., W. Woodruff and P. Maynard (1985) *The Airport Inquiries: Expansion at Stansted Airport, Fifth Terminal at Heathrow, Case for the Regions and Their Airports, Maplin, Severnside, Yardely Chase and Other Considerations: Report of the Public Inquiries, 29 September 1981–5 July 1983* (London: Department of Environment/Department of Transport).

FoE (Friends of the Earth) [R. Higman] (1997) *Developing an Integrated Transport Policy: Response from Friends of the Earth* (London: FoE).

FoE (2003) *Submission to the Government's Aviation Consultation*, www.foe. co.uk/resource/consultation_responses/air_transport_foe.pdf (accessed 25 April 2012).

FoE (2004) *Briefing: Airport Master Plans* (London: FoE).

FoE (2006) *Pie in the Sky: Why the Costs of Airport Expansion Outweigh the Benefits*, Briefing, September (London: FoE).

Franklin, D.A. (2002) *Aviation Policy in the United Kingdom, With Particular Reference to Heathrow* (London: HACAN ClearSkies).

Freedom to Fly (2002) *Flying Responsibly Into the Future* (London: Freedom to Fly Coalition).

Free Enterprise Group [K. Kwarteng] (2012) *The Case for Aviation* (London: Free Enterprise Group).

Frontier Economics (2011) *Connecting for Growth: The Role of Britain's Hub Airport in Economic Recovery* (London: Frontier Economics).

Future Heathrow (2008) *Response to the Government's Consultation 'Adding Capacity at Heathrow Airport'*, www.priorityheathrow.com/press-release. php?id=125 (accessed 16 February 2012).

Gill, M. and J. Humphreys (2007) *Aviation and Climate Change: Public Opinion and the Scope for Action* (London: Woodnewton Associates).

Glidewell, I.D.L. (1979) *Fourth Terminal, Heathrow and Associated Road Access: Report of the Public Inquiry 31 May–15 December 1978* (London: HMSO).

Grimley, P.M. (2002) *The Effectiveness of Airports' Consultation as Required by the UK Civil Aviation Act 1982*, Abbreviated Project Summary, Annual Meeting of the Liaison Group of UK Airport Consultative Committees, www.ukaccs.info/02almfiles/02studypaper.PDF (accessed 22 July 2012).

HACAN (Heathrow Association for the Control of Aircraft Noise) (1995) *Opening Statement to the Public Inquiry into a Fifth Terminal at Heathrow by the Chairman of HACAN, Dermot Cox*, 16 May, www.hacan.org.uk/resources/consultation_responses/hacan.5th_terminal.opening.pdf (accessed 11 January 2012).

HACAN (1999) *Final Submission to the Public Inquiry into a Fifth Terminal at Heathrow by the Chairman of HACAN, Dermot Cox*, 2 February, www.hacan.org.uk/resources/consultation_responses/hacan.5th_terminal.final.pdf (accessed 11 January 2012).

HACAN ClearSkies (2003a) *It's the Economy, Stupid* (London: HACAN).

HACAN ClearSkies (2003b) *A Poor Deal* (London: HACAN).

HACAN ClearSkies (2006) *Short-Haul Flights: Clogging Up Heathrow's Runways* (London: HACAN).

HACAN ClearSkies (2007a) *Aviation and the Economy* (London: HACAN).

HACAN ClearSkies (2007b) *The Economic Benefits of Heathrow Expansion – An Assessment* (London: HACAN).

HACAN ClearSkies (2008) *Turning Heathrow into London's Premium Airport* (London: HACAN).

HM Government (2010) *The Coalition: Our Programme for Government* (London: Cabinet Office).

HM Treasury (2005) *Britain Meeting the Global Challenge: Enterprise, Fairness and Responsibility. Pre-Budget Report 2005*, Cm 6701 (London: HM Treasury).

HM Treasury (2006) *Investing in Britain's Potential: Building Our Long-Term Future. Pre-Budget Report 2006*, Cm 6984 (London: HM Treasury).

HM Treasury (2011) *Autumn Forecast Statement by the Chancellor of the Exchequer, Rt. Hon. George Osborne MP*, 29 November, www.hm-treasury.gov.uk/press_136_11.htm (accessed 23 April 2012).

HM Treasury and DfT (Department for Transport) (2003) *Aviation and the Environment: Using Economic Instruments* (London: DfT).

HM Treasury and DfT (2006) *The Eddington Transport Study: The Case for Action, Sir Rod Eddington's Advice to Government* (London: TSO).

HM Treasury and Infrastructure UK (2011) *National Infrastructure Plan 2011*, November (London: HMT).

House of Commons Library [E. Ares, C. Barclay, L. Butcher and A. Mellows-Facer] (2009) *Expansion of Heathrow Airport*, Research Paper 09/11, www.parliament.uk/documents/commons/lib/research/rp2009/rp09-011.pdf (accessed 2 January 2013).

House of Commons Library [L. Butcher] (2010) *Aviation: European Liberalisation, 1986–2002*, Standard Note: SN/BT/182, 13 May, House of Commons Library, www.parliament.uk/briefing-papers/SN00182.pdf (accessed 23 December 2011).

House of Commons Library [T. Rutherford] (2011a) *Air Transport Statistics*, Standard Note: SN/SG/3760, www.parliament.uk/briefing-papers/SN037 60 (accessed 7 August 2011).

House of Commons Library [L. Butcher] (2011b) *Aviation: London Heathrow Airport*, Standard Note: SN1136, www.parliament.uk/briefing-papers/ SN1136 (accessed 23 December 2011).

House of Commons Library [L. Butcher] (2011c) *Aviation: Airport Regulation*, Standard Note: SN5333, www.parliament.uk/briefing-papers/SN 05333 (accessed 23 December 2011).

House of Commons Library [L. Butcher] (2011d) *Aviation: Regional Airports*, Standard Note: SN323, www.parliament.uk/briefing-papers/SN00 323 (accessed 23 December 2011).

House of Commons Trade and Industry Committee (2005) *The UK Aerospace Industry: Fifteenth Report of Session 2004–05*, HC 151-I (London: TSO).

House of Commons Transport Select Committee (2007) *Passengers' Experience of Air Travel*, HC 435-1 (London: TSO).

House of Commons Transport Select Committee (2008) *The Future of BAA*, HC 119 (London: TSO).

House of Commons Transport Select Committee (2009) *The Future of Aviation*, HC 251-1 (London: TSO).

IATA (International Air Transport Association) (2011a) *Fact Sheet: Industry Statistics*, www.iata.org/pressroom/facts_figures/fact_sheets/Pages/index. aspx (accessed 18 November 2011).

IATA (2011b) *Fact Sheet: Economic and Social Benefits of Air Transport*, www.iata.org/pressroom/facts_figures/fact_sheets/Pages/index.aspx (accessed 18 November 2011).

Institute for Public Policy Research [S. Bishop and T. Grayling] (2003) *The Sky's the Limit: Policies for Sustainable Aviation* (London: IPPR).

IPCC (Intergovernmental Panel on Climate Change) [J.E. Penner, D.H. Lister, D.J. Griggs, D.J. Dokken and M. McFarland (eds)] (1999) *Aviation and the Global Atmosphere* (Cambridge: Cambridge University Press).

IPCC [S. Solomon, D. Qin, M. Manning, Z. Chen, M. Marquis, K.B.M. Tignor and H.L. Miller (eds)] (2007) *Climate Change 2007: The Physical Science Basis. Contribution of Working Group I to the Fourth Assessment Report of the Intergovernmental Panel on Climate Change* (Cambridge: Cambridge University Press).

IPSOS-MORI (2006) *Climate Change and Taxing Air Travel: Research Conducted for the Airfields Environment Trust* (London: IPSOS-MORI).

IPSOS-MORI (2007) *Attitudes to Aviation and Climate Change: Research Conducted for the Commission for Integrated Transport* (London: IPSOS-MORI).

Liberal Democrats (2010) *Liberal Democrat Manifesto 2010* (London: Liberal Democrats).

London First (2008) *Imagine a World Class Heathrow* (London: London First).

Mayor of London (2008) *Adding Capacity at Heathrow. Mayor of London's Response to the Consultation* (London: Greater London Authority).

Ministry of Civil Aviation (1953) *London's Airports White Paper*, Cmd 8902 (London: HMSO).

NEF (New Economics Foundation) [H. Kersely and E. Lawlor] (2010) *Grounded: A New Approach to Evaluating Runway 3* (London: NEF).

Newey, J. (1981) *Second Terminal, Gatwick and Other Works: Report of the Public Inquiry, 29 January–11 July 1980* (London: HMSO).

OEF (Oxford Economic Forecasting) (1999) *The Contribution of the Aviation Industry to the UK Economy* (Oxford: OEF).

OEF (2006) *The Economic Contribution of the Aviation Industry in the UK* (Oxford: OEF).

Office for National Statistics (2011) *Public Attitudes to Climate Change and the Impact of Transport: Opinions (Omnibus) Survey* (Newport: ONS).

Oxera (2009) *What Is the Contribution of Aviation to the UK Economy? Final Report Prepared for the Airport Operators Association* (Oxford: Oxera).

PASC (Public Administration Select Committee) (2009) *Lobbying: Access and Influence in Whitehall, Volume 1*, HC 36-1 (London: TSO).

Quality of Life Policy Group (2007) *Blueprint for a Green Economy. Submission to the Shadow Cabinet* (London: Conservative Party).

RCEP (Royal Commission on Environmental Pollution) (2002) *The Environmental Effects of Civil Aircraft in Flight: Special Report* (London: RCEP).

RMT (2008) *Who Says There Is No Alternative? An Assessment of the Potential of Rail to Cut Air Travel (With Particular Reference to Heathrow)* (London: RMT).

Roskill Commission (1971) *Report of the Commission on the Third London Airport* (London: HSMO).

SASIG (Strategic Aviation Special Interest Group) (2000) *Does Aviation Matter? The Economic Implications of Managing and Meeting Demand* (Kingston upon Thames: SASIG).

SDC (Sustainable Development Commission) (2002) *Air Transport and Sustainable Development: A Submission from the SDC* (London: SDC).

SDC (2004) *Missed Opportunity: Summary Critique of the Air Transport White Paper* (London: SDC).

Sewill, B. (2003) *The Hidden Cost of Flying* (London: AEF).

Sewill, B. (2005) *Fly Now, Grieve Later: How to Reduce the Impact of Air Travel on Climate Change* (London: AEF).

Sewill, B. (2007) *Alexander's Ragtime Band: A Critique of the Department for*

Transport's Reliance on Economic Research Sponsored by the Aviation Industry (London: AirportWatch).

SSE (Stop Stansted Expansion) (2003a) *Submission to House of Commons Transport Committee*, 27 January, www.stopstanstedexpansion.com/documents/TC_Submission_by_SSE.doc (accessed 27 November 2009).

SSE (2003b) *Stansted: The Case Against Irresponsible Growth. Response to the Second Edition of the Department for Transport's Consultation Document: The Future Development of Air Transport in the United Kingdom: South East, Summary*, www.stopstanstedexpansion.com/documents/SSE_Summary2.doc (accessed 24 November 2009).

Stern, N. (2006a) *The Economics of Climate Change: The Stern Review* (London: Cabinet Office/HM Treasury).

Stern, N. (2006b) *The Economics of Climate Change: The Stern Review, Executive Summary (Full)* (London: Cabinet Office/HM Treasury).

Stewart, J. (2010) *Victory Against All The Odds: The Story of How the Campaign to Stop a Third Runway at Heathrow Was Won* (London: HACAN).

Sustainable Aviation (2005) *A Strategy Towards Sustainable Development of UK Aviation* (London: Sustainable Aviation).

Sustainable Aviation (2008) *Sustainable Aviation CO_2 Roadmap* (London: Sustainable Aviation).

Sustainable Aviation (2011) *Sustainable Aviation Progress Report 2011* (London: Sustainable Aviation).

Tyndall Centre for Climate Change Research (2005a) *Decarbonising the UK. Energy for a Climate Conscious Future* (Manchester: Tyndall Centre).

Tyndall Centre for Climate Change Research (2005b) *Growth Scenarios for EU and UK Aviation: Contradictions with Climate Policy. A Report for the Friends of the Earth Trust* (London: FoE).

Vandermeer, R. (2001a) *Heathrow Terminal Five and Associated Public Inquiries. Report by Roy Vandermeer QC to the Secretary of State for the Environment, Transport and the Regions, Main Report: Chapters 1–20* (London: DTLR).

Vandermeer, R. (2001b) *Heathrow Terminal Five and Associated Public Inquiries. Report by Roy Vandermeer QC to the Secretary of State for the Environment, Transport and the Regions, Main Report: Chapters 21–25* (London: DTLR).

World Commission on Environment and Development (1987) *Our Common Future* (Oxford: Oxford University Press).

WWF-UK (2008) *Travelling Light: Why the UK's Companies Are Seeking Alternatives to Flying* (Godalming: WWF-UK).

Secondary sources

Ames, C. (2008) 'Labour "Dithering" over Third Runway', *New Statesman*, 4 December.

Appleyard, D. (1983) 'Case Studies of Citizen Action and Citizen Participation in Brussels, Convent Garden, Delft and Camden', in L. Susskind and M. Elliot (eds), *Paternalism, Conflict and Coproduction: Learning from Citizen Action and Citizen Participation in Western Europe* (New York: Plenum Press), pp. 69–118.

Apter, D.E. (1987) *Rethinking Development: Modernisation, Dependency and Postmodern Politics* (London: Sage).

Apter, D.E. and N. Sawa (1984) *Against the State: Politics and Protest in Japan* (Cambridge, MA: Harvard University Press).

Bacchi, C. (2009) *Analysing Policy: What's the Problem Represented To Be?* (French Forest, NSW: Pearson Education Australia).

Bacchi, C. (2010) *Foucault, Policy and Rule: Challenging the Problem-Solving Paradigm*, FREIA Working Paper Series, 74, Aalborg University, http://freia.ihis.aau.dk (accessed 3 January 2013).

Bachrach, P. and M.S. Baratz (1962) 'Two Faces of Power', *American Political Science Review*, 56:4, 947–52.

Bachrach, P. and M.S. Baratz (1963) 'Decisions and Nondecision: An Analytical Framework', *American Political Science Review*, 57:3, 632–42.

Bachrach, P. and M.S. Baratz (1970) *Poverty and Power: Theory and Practice* (Oxford: Oxford University Press).

Bagwell, P.S. (1988) *The Transport Revolution, 1770–1985* (London: Routledge).

Bale, T. (2010) *The Conservative Party: From Thatcher to Cameron* (Cambridge: Polity Press).

Balfour, H.H. (1973) *Wings Over Westminster* (London: Hutchinson).

Ball, S.J. (1994) *Education Reform: A Critical and Post-Structural Approach* (Buckingham: Open University Press).

Barnes, C. (1983) 'Local Government and a National Airports Policy', *Local Government Studies*, 9:1, 53–64.

Barnett, C. (1995) *The Lost Victory: British Dreams, British Realities, 1945–1950* (London: Macmillan).

Barrett, R.H. and I.A. Waitz (2010) 'Aviation and the Environment: Which Way Forward?', *AeroAstro, Environment and Energy*, December, 15–19.

Baumgartner, F.R. and B.D. Jones (1993) *Agendas and Instability in American Politics* (Chicago, IL: University of Chicago Press).

Beaverstock, J.V., B. Derudder, J. Faulconbridge and F. Witlox (2010) 'International Business Travel and the Global Economy: Setting the Context', in J.V. Beaverstock, B. Derudder, J. Faulconbridge and F. Witlox (eds), *International Business Travel in the Global Economy* (Farnham: Ashgate), pp. 1–11.

Beecroft, M. (2002) *From DETR to Dft via DTLR: What Are the Potential*

Implications for Transport Planning of These Changes in Departmental Organisation?, Transport Planning Society Paper, www.tps.org.uk/files/Main/Library/2002/0102beecroft.pdf (accessed 15 June 2012).

Berlin, I. (1969) *Four Essays on Liberty* (Oxford: Oxford University Press).

Bevir, M. and R.A.W. Rhodes (2003) *Interpreting British Governance* (London: Routledge).

Bovens, M. and P. 't Hart (1998) *Understanding Policy Fiascoes* (New Brunswick, NJ: Transaction Publishers).

Bowen, J.T. (2010) *The Economic Geography of Air Transportation: Space, Time and the Freedom of the Sky* (London: Routledge).

Bridge, G. and P. McManus (2000) 'Sticks and Stones: Environmental Narratives and Discursive Regulation in the Forestry and Mining Sectors', *Antipode*, 31:4, 10–47.

Bromhead, P. (1973) *The Great White Elephant of Maplin Sands: The Neglect of Comprehensive Transport Planning in Government Decision-Making* (London: Elek).

Brooks, P.W. (1961) *The Modern Airliner: Its Origins and Development* (London: Putnam).

Buchanan, C. (1981) *No Way to the Airport* (London: Longman).

Budd, L.C.S. (2011) 'On Being Aeromobile: Airline Passengers and the Affective Experience of Flight', *Journal of Transport Geography*, 19:5, 1010–16.

Budd, L.C.S. and B. Graham (2009) 'Unintended Trajectories: Liberalization and the Geographies of Private Business Flight', *Journal of Transport Geography*, 17:4, 285–92.

Budd, L.C.S., S. Griggs, D. Howarth and S.G. Ison (2011) 'A Fiasco of Volcanic Proportions? Eyjafjallajökull and the Close of European Airspace', *Mobilities*, 6:1, 31–40.

Byrne, P. (1997) *Social Movements in Britain: Theory and Practice in British Politics* (London: Routledge).

Calder, S. (2006) *No Frills: The Truth Behind the Low-Cost Revolution in the Skies* (London: Virgin Books).

Campbell, D. (1998) *National Deconstruction* (Minneapolis, MN: University of Minnesota Press).

Carpenter, C. (2001) 'Businesses, Green Groups and the Media: The Role of Non-Governmental Organisations in the Climate Change Debate', *International Affairs*, 77:7, 313–28.

Castells, M. (1996) *The Information Age: Economy, Society and Culture. Volume 1: The Rise of the Network Society* (Oxford: Blackwell).

Caves, R.E. and G.D. Gosling (1997) *Strategic Airport Planning* (Oxford: Pergamon).

Chong, D. (1991) *Collective Action and the Civil Rights Movement* (Chicago, IL: Chicago University Press).

Chouliaraki, L. and N. Fairclough (1999) *Discourse in Late Modernity* (Edinburgh: Edinburgh University Press).

Clark, A. (2002) 'Battle Looms Over Airport Expansion', *Guardian*, 22 July.

Connelly, J. (2009) 'Voting Blue, Going Green? David Cameron and the Environment', in S. Lee and M. Beech (eds), *The Conservatives Under David Cameron: Built to Last?* (Basingstoke: Palgrave Macmillan), pp. 134–50.

Connelly, J. (2011) 'Vote Blue, Go Green, What's a Bit of Yellow in Between?', in S. Lee and M. Beech (eds), *The Cameron–Clegg Government: Coalition Politics in an Age of Austerity* (Basingstoke: Palgrave Macmillan), pp. 118–33.

Connolly, W.E. (1991) *Identity/Difference: Democratic Negotiations of Political Paradox* (Ithaca, NY: Cornell University Press).

Connolly, W.E. (1995) *The Ethos of Pluralization* (Minneapolis, MN: University of Minnesota).

Connolly, W.E. (2008) *Capitalism and Christianity, American Style* (Durham, NC: Duke University Press).

Cook, O. (1967) *The Stansted Affair: A Case For The People* (London: Pan Books).

Coopey, R. and P. Lyth, (2009) 'Back to the Future: The Aircraft and IT Industries in Britain Since 1945', in R. Coopey and P. Lyth (eds), *Business in Britain in the Twentieth Century: Decline and Renaissance?* (Oxford: Oxford University Press), pp. 225–51.

Corbett, D. (1965) *Politics and the Airlines* (London: George Allen and Unwin).

Creaton, S. (2005) *Ryanair: How a Small Irish Airline Conquered Europe* (London: Aurum, rev. edn).

Critchley, S. (2004) 'Is there a Normative Deficit in the Theory of Hegemony?', in S. Critchley and O. Marchart (eds), *Laclau: A Critical Reader* (London: Palgrave), pp. 113–22.

Culler, J. (1997) *Literary Theory* (Oxford: Oxford University Press).

Cwerner, S. (2009) 'Introducing Aeromobilities', in S. Cwerner, S. Kesselring and J. Urry (eds), *Aeromobilities* (London: Routledge), pp. 1–22.

Daley, B. and H. Preston (2009) 'Aviation and Climate Change: Assessment of Policy Options', in S. Gössling and P. Upham (eds), *Climate Change and Aviation: Issues, Challenges and Solutions* (London: Earthscan), pp. 347–72.

Deleuze, G. and F. Guattari (1987) *A Thousand Plateaus*, trans. B. Massumi (Minneapolis, MN: University of Minneapolis Press).

Derrida, J. (1978) *Writing and Difference*, trans. A. Bass (London: Routledge).

Derrida, J. (1981) *Positions* (Chicago, IL: University of Chicago Press).

Derrida, J. (1982) *Margins of Philosophy* (Brighton: Harvester Press).

Derudder, B., J.V. Beaverstock, J.R. Faulconbridge, T. Storme and F. Witlox (2011) 'You Are the Way You Fly: On the Association Between Business Travel and Business Class Travel', *Journal of Transport Geography*, 19:4, 997–1000.

Dery, D. (2000) 'Agenda Setting and Problem Definition', *Policy Studies*, 21:1, 37–48.

Devons, E. (1958) 'The Aircraft Industry', in D. Burn (ed.), *The Structure of British Industry* (Cambridge: Cambridge University Press), pp. 42–92.

Dienel, H-L. and P.J. Lyth (1998) 'Introduction', in H-L. Dienel and P.J. Lyth (eds), *Flying the Flag: European Commercial Air Transport Since 1945* (Basingstoke: Macmillan), pp. 1–17.

Dobson, A. (1991) *Peaceful Air Warfare: United States, Britain and the Politics of International Aviation* (Oxford: Clarendon).

Dobson, A. (1995) *Flying in the Face of Competition: The Policies and Diplomacy of Airline Regulatory Reform in Britain, the USA, and the European Community, 1968–94* (Aldershot: Avebury).

Dobson, A. (2007) *Globalisation and Regional Integration: The Origins, Development and Impact of the Single European Market* (London: Routledge).

Docherty, I. and J. Shaw (2008) 'New Deal or No New Deal? A Decade of "Sustainable" Transport in the UK', in I. Docherty and J. Shaw (eds), *Traffic Jam: Ten Years of 'Sustainable' Transport in the UK* (Bristol: Policy Press), pp. 3–28.

Doganis, R. (1973) 'Air Transport – A Case Study in International Regulation', *Journal of Transport Economics and Policy*, 11:2, 109–33.

Doganis, R. (2006) *The Airline Business* (London: Routledge, 2nd edn).

Doherty, B. (1999) 'Paving the Way: The Rise of Direct Action Against Road-Building and the Changing Character of British Environmentalism', *Political Studies*, 47:2, 275–91.

Dryzek, J. S. (1996) *Democracy in Capitalist Times: Ideals, Limits and Struggles* (Oxford: Oxford University Press).

Dryzek, J. (1997) *The Politics of the Earth: Environmental Discourses* (Oxford: Oxford University Press).

Dudley, G. (2004) '"Predict and Provide" Dominates New Air Transport White Paper', *Local Transport Today*, 382, 14–15.

Dudley, G. and J. Richardson (2000) *Why Does Policy Change? Lessons from British Transport Policy 1945–99* (London: Routledge).

Egan, J.L. (1990) 'Planning Airports for the Future', *The Handley Page Lecture*, Royal Aeronautical Society, London, 23 April.

Engel, J.A. (2005) 'The Surly Bonds: American Cold War Constraints on British Aviation', *Enterprise and Society*, 6:1, 1–44.

Engel, J.A. (2007) *Cold War at 30,000 Feet: The Anglo-American Fight for Aviation Supremacy* (Cambridge, MA: Harvard University Press).

Fairclough, I. and N. Fairclough (2012) *Political Discourse Analysis* (London: Routledge).

Fairclough, N. (2001) 'Critical Discourse Analysis as a Method in Social Science Research', in R. Wodak and M. Meyer (eds), *Methods of Critical Discourse Analysis* (London: Sage), pp. 121–38.

Fairclough, N. (2003) *Analysing Discourse: Textual Analysis for Social Research* (London: Routledge).

Fairclough, N. and R. Wodak (1997) 'Critical Discourse Analysis', in T. van Dijk (ed.), *Discourse as Social Interaction* (London: Sage), pp. 258–84.

Faulconbridge, J.R. and J.V. Beaverstock (2008) 'Geographies of International Business Travel in the Professional Service Economy', in D. Hislop (ed.), *Mobility and Technology in the Workplace* (London: Routledge), pp. 87–102.

Feldman, E.J. (1985) *Concorde and Dissent: Explaining High Technology Failures in Great Britain and France* (Cambridge: Cambridge University Press).

Feldman, E.J. and J. Milch (1982) *Technocracy Versus Democracy: The Comparative Politics of International Airports* (Boston, MA: Auburn House Publishing).

Finlayson, A. (2007) 'From Beliefs to Arguments: Interpretive Methodology and Rhetorical Political Analysis', *British Journal of Politics and International Relations*, 9:4, 545–63.

Fischer, F. (1995) *Evaluating Public Policy* (Florence, KY: Wadsworth).

Fischer, F. (2000) *Citizens, Experts and the Environment: The Politics of Local Knowledge* (Durham, NC: Duke University Press).

Fischer, F. (2003) *Reframing Public Policy: Discursive Politics and Deliberative Practices* (Oxford: Oxford University Press).

Fischer, F. (2009) *Democracy and Expertise: Reorienting Policy Inquiry* (Oxford: Oxford University Press).

Flynn, T.R. (2005) *Sartre, Foucault and Historical Reason. Volume 2: A Poststructuralist Mapping of History* (Chicago, IL: Chicago University Press).

Flyvbjerg, B. (2001) *Making Social Science Matter: Why Social Inquiry Fails and How It Can Succeed Again* (Cambridge: Cambridge University Press).

Flyvbjerg, B. (2005) *Policy and Planning for Large Infrastructure Projects: Problems, Causes, Cures*, World Bank Policy Research Working Paper 3781 (Washington, DC: World Bank).

Flyvbjerg, B. (2009) 'Survival of the Unfittest: Why the Worst Infrastructure Gets Built – And What We Can Do About It', *Oxford Review of Economic Policy*, 25:3, 344–67.

Flyvbjerg, B., N. Bruzelius and W. Rottengatter (2003) *Megaprojects and Risk: An Anatomy of Ambition* (Cambridge: Cambridge University Press).

Flyvbjerg, B., M. Garbuio and D. Lovallo (2009) 'Delusion and Deception in Large Infrastructure Projects: Two Models for Explaining and Preventing Executive Disaster', *California Management Review*, 51:2, 170–93.

Flyvbjerg, B., T. Landman and S.F. Schram (eds) (2012) *Real Social Science: Applied Phronesis* (Cambridge: Cambridge University Press).

Fordham, R.C. (1970) 'Airport Planning in the Context of the Third London Airport', *Economic Journal*, June, 80:318, 307–22.

Foucault, M. (1972) *The Archaeology of Knowledge* (London: Tavistock).

Foucault, M. (1977) *Discipline and Punish* (Harmondsworth: Penguin Books).

Foucault, M. (1981) 'The Order of Discourse', in R. Young (ed.), *Untying the Text* (London: Routledge), pp. 48–79.

Foucault, M. (1984a) 'Nietzsche, Genealogy, History', in P. Rabinow (ed.), *The Foucault Reader* (Harmondsworth: Penguin Books), pp. 76–100.

Foucault, M. (1984b) 'What Is Enlightenment?', in P. Rabinow (ed.), *The Foucault Reader* (Harmondsworth: Penguin Books), pp. 32–50.

Foucault, M. (1985) *The Use of Pleasure* (New York: Pantheon).

Foucault, M. (1988) *The Care of the Self* (Harmondsworth: Penguin Books).

Foucault, M. (1997) *Ethics* (New York: New Press).

Foucault, M. (2008) *Birth of Biopolitics* (London: Palgrave Macmillan).

Franke, M. and J. Florian (2011) 'What Comes After Recession? Airline Industry Scenarios and Potential End Games', *Journal of Air Transport Management*, 17:1, 19–26.

Giddens, A. (1979) *Central Problems in Social Theory: Action, Structure and Contradiction in Social Analysis* (London: Macmillan).

Giddens, A. (1984) *The Constitution of Society: Outline of the Theory of Structuration* (Oxford: Polity Press).

Giddens, A. (1991) *The Consequences of Modernity* (Stanford, CA: Stanford University Press).

Giddens, A. (2009) *The Politics of Climate Change* (Cambridge: Polity Press).

Gilbert, R. and A. Perl (2010) *Transport Revolutions: Moving People and Freight* (Washington, DC: Earthscan, rev. edn).

Glaister, S., J. Burnham, H. Stevens and T. Travers (2006) *Transport Policy in Britain* (Basingstoke: Palgrave Macmillan).

Glynos, J. (2001) 'The Grip of Ideology', *Journal of Political Ideologies*, 6:2, 191–214.

Glynos, J. (2008a) 'Self-Transgressive Enjoyment as a Freedom Fetter', *Political Studies*, 56:3, 679–704.

Glynos, J. (2008b) 'Ideological Fantasy at Work', *Journal of Political Ideologies*, 13:3, 275–96.

Glynos, J. and D. Howarth (2007) *Logics of Critical Explanation in Social and Political Theory* (London: Routledge).

Glynos, J. and D. Howarth (2008a) 'Critical Explanation in Social Science: A Logics Approach', *Swiss Journal of Sociology*, 34:1, 5–35.

Glynos, J. and D. Howarth (2008b) 'Logics of Critical Explanation: Beyond Contextualized Self-interpretations and Causal Mechanisms?', Paper Presented to the APSA Annual Meeting, 28–31 August, Boston, MA, USA.

Glynos, J., D. Howarth, A. Norval and E. Speed (2009) *Discourse Analysis: Varieties and Methods*, ESRC National Centre for Research Methods Review Paper NCRM 014 (Southampton: ESRC National Centre for Research Methods).

Goodall, C. (2011a) 'Peak Travel', www.carboncommentary.com/2011/02/06/1789 (accessed 29 March 2012).

Goodall, C. (2011b) '"Peak Stuff": Did the UK Reach a Maximum Use of

Material Resources in the Early Part of the Last Decade?', Carbon Commentary website, www.carboncommentary.com/wpcontent/uploads/2011/10/Peak_Stuff_17.10.11.pdf (accessed 29 March 2012).

Goodall, C. (2012) *Sustainability: All That Matters* (London: Hodder).

Gordon, A. (2008) *Naked Airport: A Cultural History of the World's Most Revolutionary Structure* (Chicago, IL: Chicago University Press).

Gössling, S. and P. Upham (eds) (2009) *Climate Change and Aviation: Issues, Challenges and Solutions* (London: Earthscan).

Gottweis, H. (2003) 'Theoretical Strategies of Poststructuralist Policy Analysis: Towards an Analytics of Government', in M. Hajer and H. Wagenaar (eds), *Deliberative Policy Analysis: Understanding Governance in the Network Society* (Cambridge: Cambridge University Press), pp. 247–65.

Gottweis, H. (2006) 'Rhetoric in Policy Making: Between Logos, Ethos, and Pathos', in F. Fischer, G. J. Miller and M.S. Sidney (eds), *Handbook of Public Policy* (London: Taylor and Francis), pp. 237–50.

Graham, A. (2008a) *Managing Airports: An International Perspective* (Oxford: Butterworth Heinemann, 3rd edn).

Graham, A. (2008b) 'Airport Planning and Regulation in the United Kingdom', in C. Winston and G. de Rus (eds), *Aviation Infrastructure Performance: A Study in Comparative Political Economy* (Washington, DC: Brookings Institute Press), pp. 100–36.

Graham, B. (2008) 'UK Air Travel: Taking Off for Growth', in I. Docherty and J. Shaw (eds), *Traffic Jam: Ten Years of 'Sustainable' Transport in the UK* (Bristol: Policy Press), pp. 139–60.

Graham, B. (2010) 'Foreword: Business Travel in the Global Economy', in J.V. Beaverstock, B. Derudder, J. Faulconbridge and F. Witlox (eds), *International Business Travel in the Global Economy* (Farnham: Ashgate), pp. xvii–xxv.

Gramsci, A. (1971) *Selections from Prison Notebooks* (London: Lawrence and Wishart).

Gray, J. (1993) *Beyond the New Right: Markets, Government and the Common Environment* (London: Routledge).

Griggs, S. and D. Howarth (2000) 'New Environmental Movements and Direct Action Protest: The Campaign Against Manchester Airport's Second Runway', in D. Howarth, A.J. Norval and Y. Stavrakakis (eds), *Discourse Theory and Political Analysis: Identities, Hegemonies and Social Change* (Manchester: Manchester University Press), pp. 52–69.

Griggs, S. and D. Howarth (2002) 'An Alliance of Interest and Identity? Explaining the Campaign Against Manchester Airport's Second Runway', *Mobilization*, 7:1, 43–58.

Griggs, S. and D. Howarth (2004) 'A Transformative Political Campaign? The New Rhetoric of Protest Against Airport Expansion in the UK', *Journal of Political Ideologies*, 9:2, 167–87.

Griggs, S. and D. Howarth (2007a) 'Protest Movements, Environmental Activism and Environmentalism in the UK', in J. Pretty, A. Ball, T. Benton, J. Guivant, D.R. Lee, D. Orr, M. Pfeffer and H. Ward (eds), *Handbook of Environment and Society* (London: Sage), pp. 314–24.

Griggs, S. and D. Howarth (2007b) 'Airport Governance, Politics and Protest Networks', in M. Marcussen and J. Torfing (eds), *Democratic Network Governance in Europe* (Basingstoke: Palgrave Macmillan), pp. 66–88.

Griggs, S. and D. Howarth (2008) 'Populism, Localism and Environmental Politics: The Logic and Rhetoric of the Stop Stansted Expansion Campaign', *Planning Theory*, 7:2, 123–44.

Griggs, S. and D. Howarth (2012) 'Phronesis, Logics, and Critical Policy Analysis: Heathrow's "Third Runway" and the Politics of Sustainable Aviation in the UK', in B. Flyvbjerg, T. Landman and S. Schram (eds), *Real Social Science: Applied Phronesis* (Cambridge: Cambridge University Press), pp. 167–203.

Griggs, S., D. Howarth and B. Jacobs (1998) 'The Second Runway at Manchester', *Parliamentary Affairs*, 51:3, 358–69.

Habermas, J. (1987) *The Philosophical Discourse of Modernity* (Cambridge: Polity Press).

Hajer, M. (1989) *City Politics: Hegemony and Discourse* (Aldershot: Avebury).

Hajer, M. (1995) *The Politics of Environmental Discourse: Ecological Modernization and the Policy Process* (Oxford: Clarendon Press).

Hajer, M. (2005) 'Coalitions, Practices and Meaning in Environmental Politics: From Acid Rain to BSE', in D. Howarth and J. Torfing (eds), *Discourse Theory in European Politics. Identity, Policy and Governance* (Basingstoke: Palgrave Macmillan), pp. 297–315.

Hajer, M. (2009) *Authoritative Governance: Policy-Making in the Age of Mediatization* (Oxford: Oxford University Press).

Hall, P. (1982) *Great Planning Disasters* (Berkeley, CA: University of California Press).

Hall, S. (1988) *The Hard Road to Renewal: Thatcherism and the Crisis of the Left* (London: Verso).

Hamilton-Paterson, J. (2010) *Empire of the Clouds: When Britain's Aircraft Ruled the World* (London: Faber and Faber).

Hanlon, P. (2000) *Global Airlines: Competition in a Transnational Industry* (Oxford: Butterworth-Heinemann, 2nd edn).

Hanson, N.R. (1961) *Patterns of Discovery* (Cambridge: Cambridge University Press).

Harvey, D. (1989) *The Condition of Postmodernity: An Enquiry into the Origins of Cultural Change* (Oxford: Blackwell).

Hayden, A. (2011) 'The UK's Decision to Stop Heathrow Airport Expansion: Sufficiency, Ecological Modernization and Core Political Imperatives', Unpublished Paper, www.cpsa-acsp.ca/papers-2011/Hayden.pdf (accessed 27 December 2012).

Hayward, K. (1983) *Government and British Civil Aerospace: A Case Study in Post-War Technology Policy* (Manchester: Manchester University Press).

Hayward, K. (1989) *The British Aircraft Industry* (Manchester: Manchester University Press).

Held, D. (1995) *Democracy and the Global Order: From the Modern State to Cosmopolitan Governance* (Cambridge: Polity Press).

Holdsworth, M. (1980) 'Airport Consultative Committees and Their Work in Great Britain', *Planning and Administration*, 8:1, 42–54.

Hood, C. (1998) *The Art of the State: Culture, Rhetoric, and Public Management* (Oxford: Oxford University Press).

Hoppe, R. (2010) *The Governance of Problems: Puzzling, Powering, Participation* (Bristol: Policy Press).

Howarth, D. (1997) 'Complexities of Identity/Difference', *Journal of Political Ideologies*, 2:1, 51–78.

Howarth, D. (2000) *Discourse* (Buckingham: Open University Press).

Howarth, D. (2004) 'Towards a Heideggerian Social Science: Heidegger, Kisiel and Wiener on the Limits of Anthropological Discourse', *Anthropological Theory*, 4:2, 229–47.

Howarth, D. (2005) 'Applying Discourse Theory', in D. Howarth and J. Torfing (eds), *Discourse Theory and European Politics* (Basingstoke: Palgrave Macmillan), pp. 316–49.

Howarth, D. (2006) 'Space, Subjectivity and the Political', *Alternatives*, 31:2, 105–34.

Howarth, D. (2008) 'Ethos, Agonism and Populism: William Connolly and the Case for Radical Democracy', *British Journal of Politics and International Relations*, 10(2): 171–93.

Howarth, D. (2009) 'Discourse, Power, and Policy: Articulating a Hegemony Approach to Critical Policy Studies', *Critical Policy Studies*, 3:3/4, 309–35.

Howarth, D. (2010) 'Pluralizing Methods: Contingency, Ethics and Critical Explanation', in A. Finlayson (ed.), *Democracy and Pluralism: The Political Thought of William E. Connolly* (London: Routledge), pp. 20–45.

Howarth, D. (2013) *Poststructuralism and After* (London: Palgrave).

Howarth, D. and S. Griggs (2006) 'Metaphor, Catachresis and Equivalence: The Rhetoric of Freedom to Fly in the Struggle Over Aviation Policy in the UK', *Policy and Society*, 25:2, 23–46.

Howarth, D. and S. Griggs (2012) 'Poststructuralist Policy Analysis: Discourse, Hegemony and Critical Explanation', in F. Fischer and H. Gottweis (eds), *The Argumentative Turn Revisited: Public Policy as Communicative Practice* (Durham, NC: Duke University Press), pp. 305–43.

Howarth, D. and Y. Stavrakakis (2000) 'Introducing Discourse Theory and Political Analysis', in D. Howarth, A.J. Norval and Y. Stavrakakis (eds), *Discourse Theory and Political Analysis* (Manchester: Manchester University Press), pp. 1–23.

Hudson, K. and J. Pettifer (1979) *Diamonds in the Sky: A Social History of Air Travel* (London: Bodley Head).

Hulme, M. (2009) *Why We Disagree About Climate Change: Understanding Controversy, Inaction and Opportunity* (Cambridge: Cambridge University Press).

Humphreys, I. (2003) 'Organisational and Growth Trends in Air Transport', in P. Upham, J. Maughan, D. Raper and C. Thomas (eds), *Towards Sustainable Aviation* (London: Earthscan), pp. 19–35.

Humphreys, I., S. Ison and G. Francis (2007) 'UK Airport Policy: Does the Government Have Any Influence?', *Public Money and Management*, 27:5, 339–43.

Ish-Shalom, P. (2008) 'The Rhetorical Capital of Theories: The Democratic Peace and the Road to the Roadmap', *International Political Science Review*, 29:3, 281–301.

Jackson, T. (2011) '"Peak Stuff" Message is Cold Comfort – We Need to Embrace Green Technology', *Guardian*, 1 November.

Jay, D. (1980) *Change and Fortune: A Political Record* (London: Hutchinson).

Jessop, B. (1982) *The Capitalist State: Marxist Theories and Methods* (Oxford: Martin Robertson).

Jessop, B. (2002a) *The Future of the Capitalist State* (Cambridge: Polity Press).

Jessop, B. (2002b) 'Revisiting Thatcherism and Its Political Economy: Hegemonic Projects, Accumulation Strategies and the Question of Internationalization', in A. Bakkan and E. MacDonald (eds), *Critical Political Studies* (Montreal: McGill University Press), pp. 41–56.

Juniper, T. (2007) *Saving Planet Earth: What Is Destroying the Earth and What You Can Do To Help* (London: Collins).

Kasarda, J.D. (2011) 'The Aerotropolis and Global Competitiveness', *Diplomatic Courier*, 26 December, pp. 16–19.

Kasarda, J.D. and G. Lindsay (2011) *Aerotropolis: The Way We'll Live Next* (New York: Farrar, Straw and Giroux).

Kassim, H. and H. Stevens (2009) *Air Transport and the European Union: Europeanization and Its Limits* (Basingstoke: Palgrave Macmillan).

King, P. (2011) *The New Politics: Liberal Conservatism or Same Old Tories?* (Bristol: Policy Press).

Kingdon, J.W. (1984) *Agendas, Alternatives and Public Policy* (Boston, MA: Little Brown).

Kirby, A. (1982) *The Politics of Location: An Introduction* (London: Methuen).

Lacan, J. (2006) *Écrits* (New York: W.W. Norton).

Laclau, E. (1990) *New Reflections on the Revolution of Our Time* (London: Verso).

Laclau, E. (1995) 'Why Do Empty Signifiers Matter to Politics?', in J. Weeks (ed.), *The Greater Evil and the Lesser Good* (London: Rivers Oram), pp. 168–77.

Laclau, E. (1996) *Emancipation(s)* (London: Verso).

Laclau, E. (2000) 'Identity and Hegemony', in J. Butler, E. Laclau and S. Žižek (eds), *Contingency, Hegemony and Universality: New Discussions on the Left* (London: Verso), p. 44–88.

Laclau, E. (2005) *On Populist Reason* (London: Verso).

Laclau, E. and C. Mouffe (1985) *Hegemony and Socialist Strategy: Towards a Radical Democratic Politics* (London: Verso).

Laclau, E. and C. Mouffe (1987) 'Post-Marxism Without Apologies', *New Left Review*, 166: 79–106.

Layard, R. and S. Glaister (eds) (1994) *Cost–Benefit Analysis* (Cambridge: Cambridge University Press, 2nd edn).

Lee, D.S. (2009) 'Aviation and Climate Change: The Science', in S. Gössling and P. Upham (eds), *Climate Change and Aviation: Issues, Challenges and Solutions* (London: Earthscan), pp. 27–68.

Levin, P.H. (1979) 'Highway Inquiries: A Study in Governmental Responsiveness', *Public Administration*, 57:1, 21–49.

Lichfield, N. (1971) 'Cost–Benefit Analysis in Planning: A Critique of the Roskill Commission', *Regional Studies*, 5:3, 157–83.

Lyth, P.J. (1995) 'The Changing Role of Government in British Civil Air Transport, 1919–49', in R. Millward and J. Singleton (eds), *The Political Economy of Nationalisation in Britain, 1920–50* (Cambridge: Cambridge University Press), pp. 65–87.

Lyth, P.J. (1998) 'Chosen Instruments: The Evolution of British Airways', in H-L. Dienel and P.J. Lyth (eds), *Flying the Flag: European Commercial Air Transport Since 1945* (Basingstoke: Macmillan), pp. 50–86.

Lyth, P.J. (2003) 'American Aerospace Dominance and the British Challenge in Jet Engines', in H. Trischler and S. Zeilinger (eds), *Tackling Transport, Volume 3* (London: NMSI), pp. 81–98.

MacCallum, G.C. (1967) 'Negative and Positive Freedom', *Philosophical Review*, 76: 312–34.

Mander, S. and S. Randles (2009) 'Aviation Coalitions: Drivers of Growth and Implications for Carbon Dioxide Emissions Reductions', in S. Gössling and P. Upham (eds), *Climate Change and Aviation: Issues, Challenges and Solutions* (London: Earthscan), pp. 273–92.

March, J.G. and J.P. Olsen (1989) *Rediscovering Institutions: The Organizational Basis of Politics* (New York: Free Press).

Marx, K. (1973) *Grundrisse* (London: Allen Lane).

McFlynn, A. and Gordon-Farleigh, J. (2011) 'The Aviation Justice Tour', *STIR*, winter, http://stirtoaction.com/?p=699 (accessed 5 January 2013).

McKie, D. (1973) *A Sadly Mismanaged Affair: Politics of the Third London Airport* (London: Croom Helm).

McLean, I. (2001) *Rational Choice and British Politics: An Analysis of Rhetoric and Manipulation from Peel to Blair* (Oxford: Oxford University Press).

McManners, P. (2012) *Fly and Be Damned. What Now for Aviation and Climate Change?* (London: Zed Books).

Miliband, R. (1969) *The State in Capitalist Society* (New York: Basic Books).

Millard-Ball, A. and L. Schipper (2011) 'Are We Reaching Peak Travel? Trends in Passenger Transport in Eight Industrialized Countries', *Transport Reviews*, 31:3, 357–78.

Miller, D. (ed.) (1991) *Liberty* (Oxford: Oxford University Press).

Miller, H.T. (2002) *Postmodern Public Policy* (Albany, NY: State University of New York Press).

Miller, H.T. (2012) *Governing Narratives: Symbolic Politics and Policy Change* (Tuscaloosa, AL: University of Alabama Press).

Miller, H.T. and C.J. Fox (2007) *Postmodern Public Administration* (New York: M.E. Sharpe, rev. edn).

Mitchell, T. (2011) *Carbon Democracy: Political Power in the Age of Oil* (London: Verso).

Mol, A. (2008) *The Logic of Care: Health and the Problem of Patient Choice* (London: Routledge).

Mol, A.P.J. (2000) 'Ecological Modernization: Industrial Transformations and Environmental Reforms', in M. Redclift and G. Woodgate (eds), *The International Handbook of Environmental Sociology* (Cheltenham: Edward Elgar), pp. 138–49.

Mol, A.P.J. (2001) *Globalization and Environmental Reform: The Ecological Modernization of the Global Economy* (Cambridge, MA: MIT Press).

Mol, A.P.J. and D.A. Sonnenfeld (eds) (2000) *Ecological Modernisation around the World: Perspectives and Critical Debates* (London: Frank Cass/Routledge).

Mol, A.P.J., D.A. Sonnenfeld and G. Spaargaren (eds) (2009) *The Ecological Modernisation Reader: Environmental Reform in Theory and Practice* (London: Routledge).

Morris, P.W.G. (1997) *The Management of Projects* (London: Thomas Telford).

Mouffe, C. (2000) *The Democratic Paradox* (London: Verso).

Mouffe, C. (2005) *On the Political* (London: Routledge).

Mulhall, S. (1996) *Heidegger and Being and Time* (London: Routledge).

Mullin, C. (2010) *A View from the Foothills: The Diaries of Chris Mullin* (London: Profile Books).

Nelkin, D. and H. Pollak (1977) 'The Politics of Participation and the Nuclear Debate in Sweden, the Netherlands and Austria', *Public Policy*, 25:3, 334–57.

Ney, S. (2009) *Resolving Messy Policy Problems* (London: Earthscan).

Nietzsche, F. (1994) *On the Genealogy of Morality* (Cambridge: Cambridge University Press).

Neitzsche, F. (2006) 'The Essay on Truth and Lies in a Nonmoral Sense', in K.A. Pearson and D. Large (eds), *The Neitzsche Reader* (Oxford: Blackwell), pp. 114–23.

Norval, A.J. (1994) 'Hegemony After Deconstruction: The Consequences of Undecidability', *Journal of Political Ideologies*, 9:2, 139–57.

Norval, A.J. (1996) *Deconstructing Apartheid Discourse* (London: Verso).

Norval, A.J. (2007) *Aversive Democracy: Inheritance and Originality in the Democratic Tradition* (Cambridge: Cambridge University Press).

Owen, D. (1994) *Maturity and Modernity* (London: Routledge).

Owen, D. (2012) 'Foucault, Tully, and Agonistic Struggles Over Recognition', in M. Bankovsky and A. Le Goff (eds), *Recognition Theory and Contemporary French Moral and Political Philosophy* (Manchester: Manchester University Press), pp. 133–65.

Parker, P. (1990) 'Metaphor and Catachresis', in J. Bender and D.E. Wellbery (eds), *The Ends of Rhetoric: History, Theory, Practice* (Stanford, CA: Stanford University Press), pp. 60–76.

Paterson, M. (2007) *Automobile Politics: Ecology and Cultural Political Economy* (Cambridge: Cambridge University Press).

Paterson, M. and J. Stripple (2010) 'My Space: Governing Individuals' Carbon Emissions', *Environment and Planning D: Society and Space*, 28:2, 341–62.

Peirce, C.S. (1957) *Essays in the Philosophy of Science* (New York: Liberal Arts Press).

Pepper, D. (1980) 'Environmentalism, the "Lifeboat Ethic" and Anti-airport Protest', *Area*, 12:3, 177–82.

Perman, D. (1973) *Cublington: A Blueprint for Resistance* (London: Bodley Head).

Priemus, H. (2008) 'How to Improve the Early Stages of Decision-Making on Mega-Projects', in H. Priemus, B. Flyvbjerg and B. van Wee (eds), *Decision-Making on Mega-Projects: Cost–Benefit Analysis, Planning and Innovation* (Cheltenham: Edward Elgar), pp. 105–19.

Priemus, H. (2010) 'Mega-Projects: Dealing with Pitfalls', *European Planning Studies*, 18:7, 1023–39.

Princen, T. (2003) 'Principles for Sustainability: From Cooperation and Efficiency to Sufficiency', *Global Environmental Politics*, 3:1, 33–50.

Princen, T. (2005) *The Logic of Sufficiency* (Cambridge, MA: Massachusetts Institute of Technology).

Pulford, C. (2008) *Air Madness: Road's Mistakes Repeated* (Ituri: Woodford Hale, 3rd edn).

Randles, S. and S. Mander (2009) 'Practices(s) and Ratchet(s): A Sociological Examination of Frequent Flying', in S. Gössling and P. Upham (eds), *Climate Change and Aviation: Issues, Challenges and Solutions* (London: Earthscan), pp. 245–72.

Rein, M. and D. Schön (1993) 'Reframing Policy Discourse', in F. Fischer and J. Forester (eds), *The Argumentative Turn in Policy Analysis and Planning* (Durham, NC: Duke University Press), pp. 145–66.

Rein, M. and D. Schön (1996) 'Frame-Critical Policy Analysis and Frame-Reflective Policy Practice', *Knowledge, Technology and Policy*, 9:1, 85–104.

Reisigl, M. (2008) 'Analyzing Political Rhetoric', in R. Wodak and M. Krzyżanowski (eds), *Qualitative Discourse Analysis in the Social Sciences* (Basingstoke: Palgrave Macmillan), pp. 96–120.

Riker, W.H. (1986) *The Art of Political Manipulation* (New Haven, CT: Yale University Press).

Riker, W.H. (1996) *The Strategy of Rhetoric: Campaigning for the American Constitution* (New Haven, CT: Yale University Press).

Rittel, H.W.J. and M.M. Webber (1973) 'Dilemmas in a General Theory of Planning', *Policy Sciences*, 4, 155–69.

Rochefort, D.A. and R.W. Cobb (eds) (1994) *The Politics of Problem Definition* (Lawrence, KS: University Press of Kansas).

Roffey, L. (2013) 'Privileged Actors in Environmental Policymaking: The Historical Development of the Aviation Industry in the UK', Unpublished Doctoral Thesis, University of East Anglia.

Rogers, R. (ed.) (2004) *An Introduction to Critical Discourse Analysis in Education* (New York: Routledge, 2nd edn).

Rootes, C. (2012) 'The Environmental Movement and Aviation', Paper Presented to the ESRC Seminar 'The Politics of UK Sustainable Aviation', 3 February, Centre for Theoretical Studies, University of Essex.

Rootes, C. and N. Carter (2010) 'Take Blue, Add Yellow, Get Green? The Environment in the UK General Election of 6 May 2010', *Environmental Politics*, 19:6, 992–9.

Rorty, R. (1989) *Contingency, Irony and Solidarity* (Cambridge: Cambridge University Press).

Rose, N. (1999) *Powers of Freedom* (Cambridge: Cambridge University Press).

Sabatier, P.A. (1988) 'An Advocacy Coalition Framework of Policy Change and the Role of Policy-Oriented Learning Therein', *Policy Sciences*, 21:2, 129–68.

Sabatier, P.A. (1991) 'Towards Better Theories of the Policy Process', *PS: Political Science and Politics*, 24:2, 147–56.

Sampson, A. (1984) *Empires of the Sky* (London: Hodder and Stroughton).

Saussure, F. de (1983) *Course in General Linguistics* (London: Duckworth).

Sayer, D. (1983) *Marx's Method* (Brighton: Harvester).

Schattschneider, E.E. (1960) *The Semisovereign People: A Realist's View of Democracy in America* (Austin, TX: Holt, Rinehart and Winston).

Schön, D.A. (1993) 'Generative Metaphor: A Perspective on Problem-Setting in Social Policy', in A. Ortony (ed.), *Metaphor and Thought* (Cambridge: Cambridge University Press, 2nd edn), pp. 137–63.

Schön, D.A. and M. Rein (1994) *Frame Reflection: Toward the Resolution of Intractable Policy Controversies* (New York: Basic Books).

Scott, J.C. (1998) *Seeing Like A State: How Certain Schemes to Improve the Human Condition Have Failed* (New Haven, CT: Yale University Press).

Sewill, B. (2012) *Tangled Wings: Gatwick Seen Through Green Tinted Glasses* (London: AEF).

Sharman, F.A. (1971) 'The Third London Airport as a Project Assessment Problem', *Regional Studies*, 5:3, 135–43.

Sharman, F.A. (1975) 'A United Kingdom View', in OECD (ed.), *Airports and the Environment* (Paris: OECD), pp. 43–50.

Sheller, M. and J. Urry (2006) 'The New Mobilities Paradigm', *Environment and Planning A*, 38:2, 207–26.

Shepsle, K.A. (2003) 'Losers in Politics (and How They Sometimes Become Winners): William Riker's Heresthetic', *Perspectives on Politics*, 1:2, 307–15.

Sherwood, T. (2009) *Heathrow: 2000 Years of History* (Stroud: History Press, 2nd edn).

Skinner, Q. (1999) 'Rhetoric and Conceptual Change', in K. Palonen (ed.), *Finnish Yearbook of Political Thought 1999: Conceptual Change and Contingency* (Helsinki: Sophi), pp. 60–73.

Skinner, Q. (2002) *Visions of Politics: Volume 1* (Cambridge: Cambridge University Press).

Smith, G. (2009) *Democratic Innovations* (Cambridge: Cambridge University Press).

Smith, S. (2007) 'UK: Environmental Policymaking in a Centralised, Market-Driven System', in A. Breton, G. Brosio, S. Dalmazzone and G. Garrone (eds), *Environmental Governance and Decentralisation* (Cheltenham: Edward Elgar), pp. 584–617.

Sørensen, E. (2005) 'The Democratic Problems and Potentials of Network Governance', *European Political Science*, 4, 348–57.

Starkie, D. (2004) 'Testing the Regulatory Model: The Expansion of Stansted Airport', *Fiscal Studies*, 25:4, 389–413.

Staten, H. (1984) *Wittgenstein and Derrida* (Lincoln, NE: University of Nebraska Press).

Stavrakakis, Y. (1999) *Lacan and the Political* (London: Routledge).

Stavrakakis, Y. (2007) *The Lacanian Left* (Edinburgh: Edinburgh University Press).

Stone, D.A. (2001) *Policy Paradox: The Art of Political Decision Making* (London: W.W. Norton, 3rd edn).

Stroud, J. (1962) *Annals of British and Commonwealth Air Transport, 1919–1960* (London: Putnam).

Taylor, C. (1985a) *Philosophical Papers: Human Agency and Language* (Cambridge: Cambridge University Press).

Taylor, C. (1985b) *Philosophical Papers: Philosophy and the Human Sciences* (Cambridge: Cambridge University Press).

Taylor, C. (1985c) 'Connolly, Foucault, and Truth', *Political Theory*, 3, 377–85.

Taylor, C. (1989) *The Sources of the Self* (Cambridge: Cambridge University Press).

Thompson, F.P. (1972) 'Statistics and the Environment – The Third London Airport Study', *Journal of the Royal Statistical Society. Series D (The Statistician)*, 21:1, 19–30.

Torfing, J. (1998) *Politics, Regulation and the Modern Welfare State* (Basingstoke: Palgrave Macmillan).

Torfing, J. (1999) *New Theories of Discourse: Laclau, Mouffe and Žižek* (Oxford: Blackwell).

Torfing, J. (2005) 'Discourse Theory: Achievements, Arguments, and Challenges', in D. Howarth and J. Torfing (eds), *Discourse Theory in European Politics* (Basingstoke: Palgrave Macmillan), pp. 1–32.

Torfing, J., B.G. Peters, J. Pierre and E. Sørensen (2012) *Interactive Governance: Advancing the Paradigm* (Oxford: Oxford University Press).

Torgerson, D. (1999) *The Promise of Green Politics: Environmentalism and the Public Sphere* (Durham, NC: Duke University Press).

Townshend, J. (2003) 'Discourse Theory and Political Analysis: A New Paradigm from the Essex School', *British Journal of Political Science*, 5:1, 129–42.

Tully, J. (1999) 'The Agonic Freedom of Citizens', *Economy and Society*, 28, 161–82.

Tully, J. (2008) *Public Philosophy in a New Key, Volume I: Democracy and Civic Freedom* (Cambridge: Cambridge University Press).

Urry, J. (2000) *Sociology Beyond Societies: Mobilities for the Twenty-First Century* (London: Routledge).

Urry, J. (2009) 'Aeromobilities and the Global', in S. Cwerner, S. Kesselring and J. Urry (eds), *Aeromobilities* (London: Routledge), pp. 25–38.

Urry, J. (2011) 'Does Mobility Have a Future?', in M. Grieco and J. Urry (eds), *Mobilities: New Perspectives on Transport and Society* (Farnham: Ashgate), pp. 3–20.

Verweij, M. and M. Thompson (eds) (2006) *Clumsy Solutions for a Complex World* (Basingstoke: Palgrave Macmillan).

Verweij, M., M. Douglas, R. Ellis, C. Engel, F. Hendriks, S. Lohman, S. Ney, S. Rayner and M. Thompson (2006) 'The Case for Clumsiness', in M. Verweij and M. Thompson (eds), *Clumsy Solutions for a Complex World* (Basingstoke: Palgrave Macmillan), pp. 1–30.

Vidal, J. (2009) '"Heathrow Is a Monster: It Must Be Fed"', *Guardian*, 10 January.

Wagenaar, H. (2011) *Meaning in Action: Interpretation and Dialogue in Policy Analysis* (Armonk, NY: M.E. Sharpe).

Waitz, I.A., S.P. Lukachko and J.J. Lee (2005) 'Military Aviation and the Environment: Historical Trends and Comparison to Civil Aviation', *AIAA Journal of Aircraft*, 42:2, 329–339.

Walker, G. (2011) 'Harder, Better, Faster, Stronger: Energy Policy and the Logic of Modernisation in the Neo-Liberal Hegemonic Project', Paper Presented to the 6th International Conference in Interpretative Policy Analysis, 'Discursive Spaces, Politics, Practices and Power', 23–25 June, University of Cardiff.

Ward, H., A. Norval, T. Landman, and J. Pretty (2003) 'Open Citizens' Juries and the Politics of Sustainability', *Political Studies*, 51:2, 282–99.

Weale, A. (1992) *The New Politics of Pollution* (Manchester: Manchester University Press).

Wheatcroft, S. (1964) *Air Transport Policy* (London: Michael Joseph).

Whitelegg, J. (2003) 'The Case for "No Growth"', in P. Upham, J. Maugham, D. Raper and C. Thomas (eds), *Towards Sustainable Aviation* (London: Earthscan), pp. 234–8.

Wynne, B. (2010) *Rationality and Ritual: Participation and Exclusion in Nuclear Decision-Making* (London: Routledge, 2nd edn).

Yanow, D. (1996) *How Does a Policy Mean? Interpreting Policy and Organizational Actions* (Washington, DC: Georgetown University Press).

Yanow, D. (2000) *Conducting Interpretive Policy Analysis* (London: Sage).

Young, I. M. (2000) *Inclusion and Democracy* (Oxford: Oxford University Press).

Žižek, S. (1989) *The Sublime Object of Ideology* (London: Verso).

Žižek, S. (1997) *Plague of Fantasies* (London: Verso).

Žižek, S. (1998) 'The Seven Veils of Fantasy', in D. Nobus (ed.), *Key Concepts of Lacanian Psychoanalysis* (London: Rebus Press), pp. 190–218.

Index